SCHAUM'S OUTLINE OF

THEORY AND PROBLEMS

of

FUNDAMENTALS
OF COMPUTING
WITH C++

•

JOHN R. HUBBARD, Ph.D.

Professor of Mathematics and Computer Science
University of Richmond

D1534479

SCHAUM'S OUTLINE SERIES

McGRAW-HILL

New York   San Francisco   Washington, D.C.   Auckland   Bogotá   Caracas   Lisbon
London   Madrid   Mexico City   Milan   Montreal   New Dehli
San Juan   Singapore   Sydney   Tokyo   Toronto

JOHN R. HUBBARD is Professor of Mathematics and Computer Science at the University of Richmond. He received his Ph.D. from The University of Michigan (1973) and has been a member of the Richmond faculty since 1983. His primary interests are in numerical algorithms and database systems. Dr. Hubbard is the author of several other books, including *Schaum's Outline of Programming with C++*.

Schaum's Outline of Theory and Problems of

PROGRAMMING WITH C++

2 3 4 5 6 7 8 9 10 11 12 13 14 15 16 17 18 19 20   PRS PRS 9 0 1 0 9 8

ISBN 0-07-030868-3

Sponsoring Editor: Barbara Gilson
Production Supervisor: Sherri Souffrance
Editing Supervisor: Maureen Walker

Library of Congress Cataloging-in-Publication Data

Hubbard, J. R. (John R.), date
    Schaum's outline of theory and problems of fundamentals of
  computing with C++ / John R. Hubbard.
        p. cm. -- (Schaum's outline series)
  Includes bibliographical references and index.
    ISBN 0-07-030868-3 (pbk.)
    1. C++ (Computer program language) 2. Computer science.
I. Title   II. Series
QA76.73.C153H82   1998
005.13'3--dc21
                             98-16860
                             CIP

McGraw-Hill

A Division of The McGraw-Hill Companies

Preface

Like all Schaum's Outline Series books, this is intended to be used primarily for self study, preferably in conjunction with a regular course in the fundamentals of computer science using the new ANSI/ISO Standard C++. The book covers topics from the following fundamental units of the 1991 A.C.M. Computing Curricula:

AL1: Basic Data Structures
AL2: Abstract Data Types
AL3: Recursive Algorithms
AL4: Complexity Analysis
AL5: Complexity Classes
AL6: Searching and Sorting

The book includes over 500 examples and solved problems. The author firmly believes that computing is learned best by practice, following a well-constructed collection of examples with complete explanations. This book is designed to provide that support.

Source code for the examples and solved problems in this book may be downloaded from the author's World Wide Web home page:

`http://www.richmond.edu/~hubbard/`

This site will also contain any corrections and addenda for the book.

I wish to thank all my friends, colleagues, students, and the McGraw-Hill staff who have helped me with the critical review of this manuscript. Special thanks to Anita Hubbard, Jim Simons, and Maureen Walker. Their debugging skills are gratefully appreciated.

JOHN R. HUBBARD
Richmond, Virginia

Dedicated to my 1997 computer science students:

Miriam Albin, Allison Bannon, Carolyn Bennett, Ben Brown,
Jon-Eric Burgess, Andre Chambers, Kenric Chu, Danielle Clement,
Jim Copenhafer, Mark DeSantis, John M. Ewing, John R. Ewing,
Jeff Frick, Shannon Greening, Russ Haskin, Kevin Hawkins,
Hunt Heffner, John Hettler, William Hooker, Sara Hoopengardner,
Tim Hospodar, Michelle Hucher, Rob Hunt, Rob James,
Tony Kirilusha, Brian Magliaro, Joel Mascardo, Marc Meulener,
Cavan Miller, Nick Gardiakos, Brock Parker, Jeremy Perella,
Betsy Plunket, Kathleen Ribeiro, Christian Schwarzkopf, Chris Severino,
Randy Shehady, Jim Simons, Mike Smith, Heather Smucker,
Ted Solley, Sarah Spence, Seef Syed, David Vermette,
John Vitale, John Wells, Brian Williams, and Josh Young

Contents

Chapter 1

Introduction to Computing

1.1 A BRIEF HISTORY OF COMPUTING

Computing is a human process. It involves recognizing and clarifying a problem, devising a method for solving the problem, executing the solution, and then correcting and revising the solution. A computer is a mechanical device that facilitates the last two stages of this process. These days computers are electronic devices that can perform tasks millions to billions times faster than humans. But they are still just mechanical devices designed and built by humans.

Usually the most difficult part of computing is the second stage of the process: devising a method for solving the problem. The resulting method is called an *algorithm*, which is a step-by-step procedure that can be carried out automatically by a computer. Here is a simple example of an algorithm, discovered by the ancient Babylonians over 4000 years ago:

Algorithm 1.1 The Babylonian Algorithm for Computing the Square Root of 2

This is the algorithm that the ancient Babylonians used to compute the square root of two ($\sqrt{2}$):

1. Set $y = 1.0$.
2. Replace y with the average of y and $2/y$.
3. Repeat Step 2 until its effect upon y is insignificant.
4. Return y.

EXAMPLE 1.1 The Babylonian Algorithm

The Babylonians and the Egyptians apparently used this algorithm to lay square foundations for their buildings. It remains to this day the best way to compute the square root of 2. Here are the resulting calculations using a 12-digit calculator:

y	$2/y$	$(y + 2/y)/2$
1.0	2.0	1.5
1.5	1.33333333333	1.41666666667
1.4166666667	1.41176470588	1.41421568628
1.41421568628	1.41421143847	1.41421356238
1.41421356238	1.41421356237	1.41421356237
1.41421356237	1.41421356237	1.41421356237

Square the answer to see that it is correct: $(1.41421356237)^2 = 1.99999999999 = 2.0000000000$.

The history of computing is even older than the Babylonian Algorithm. Indeed it is fair to say that computing began with simple counting. The first computing devices were the fingers on a hand. We still use the word "digit" (meaning "finger") to describe the symbols "4", "9", *etc.* that we use for numbers. The simple task of counting is a common task performed by modern computers perform.

Another prehistoric computing device that is still in use today is the *abacus*. This Oriental device allows rapid addition and subtraction by sliding beads along parallel wires held in a frame. Experienced users of the abacus can often outperform western shoppers using a modern calculator.

1

The first mechanical calculator was designed and built by the German mathematician Wilhelm Schickard (1592–1635) in 1623. It was capable of addition, subtraction, multiplication, and division. But in 1624 his only working copy was destroyed in a fire. Schickard and his entire family perished in the plagues brought on by the Thirty Years War. His design was not discovered until 1957 when his complete description with sketches were found in a letter to Kepler.

Because Schickard's achievement went unnoticed by historians, the French mathematician Blaise Pascal (1623–1662) is usually credited with inventing the first calculator. Capable of only addition and subtraction, this device was inferior to Schickard's calculator. But Pascal was actually successful in marketing his device, and several of them exist to this day.

The great German mathematician Gottfried Wilhelm Leibniz (1646–1716) expanded upon Pascal's idea, building a calculator in 1673 known as the *Leibniz wheel*. It completely automated all the four basic arithmetic operations: addition, subtraction, multiplication, and division. Leibniz had one copy of his machine built for Peter the Great to send to the Emperor of China.

The first modern computer was designed by the English mathematician Charles Babbage (1791–1871). He actually designed two computing devices: his *Difference Engine* in 1823 and his *Analytical Engine* in 1833. The Difference Engine was designed to tabulate tables of functions using the *method of finite differences*. There was a genuine need in England for such a machine: British navigational tables of the time, upon which British shipping depended, were rife with human errors. Babbage recognized that completely accurate tables could be constructed automatically "by steam." But before the construction of his Difference Engine could be completed, Babbage abandoned it in favor of a much better machine: his Analytical Engine. This would be the first truly general purpose programmable computer with its own processor, memory, secondary storage, input device, and output device. The programs would be stored on a belt of punched paste cards, the same way that Joseph Marie Jacquard's loom stored programs for patterns to be weaved into fabrics.

The idea of using punched cards was taken up by the American engineer Herman Hollerith (1860–1929). In 1889 he contracted with the U.S. Census Bureau to process the 1890 census data automatically. He invented an electronic tabulating machine which was a great success. In 1896 Hollerith established the Tabulating Machine Company, which later evolved into the International Business Machine company (IBM).

The next major achievement in the history of computing occurred in 1939 at Harvard University when Howard H. Aiken persuaded IBM to support a project to build a modernized version of Babbage's Analytical Engine. Building upon the already-successful punch-card business machines marketed by IBM, Aiken wanted to build a computer that would do for science what IBM's machines were doing for business. When completed in 1944, the Mark I electromechanical computer was able to perform automatically scientific computations with far greater speed and accuracy than had been possible previously. It stored its programs on punched tape, similar to Jacquard's belts of punched paste cards.

Near end of the Second World War, John W. Mauchly and J. Presper Eckert, Jr. designed and built the Electronic Numerical Integrator and Computer (ENIAC). This huge machine was the first electronic digital computer. It was built to tabulate firing tables for the U.S. Army. After the war, Mauchly and Eckert formed a private company which built and marketed the Universal Automatic Computer (UNIVAC), the first commercial computer designed for both business and scientific applications. The first one was bought by the U.S. Census Bureau in 1951.

Charles Babbage had borrowed Jacquard's idea of storing programs on external punch cards. But it was the great Hungarian-American mathematician John von Neumann who thought of storing programs in the computer's memory itself, the same way that data is stored. He suggested this idea in 1945 and incorporated it into the design of the IAS (Institute for Advanced Study) computer which became the basis for the design of all modern computers.

Computers in the 1940s used vacuum tubes to store data. These were unreliable, took up a lot of space, and consumed a lot of electricity. In the 1950s, vacuum tubes were replaced by *magnetic core* memory. This consisted of tiny magnetic rings threaded on wire mesh racks. The transition made computer memory faster, cheaper, and more compact.

In 1948 at Bell Labs, William Shockley and associates invented the *transistor*, a tiny electrical device that transfers electrical signals across a resistor. These were found to be effective devices for storing and processing data electronically, and by 1959 were replacing magnetic core memory.

Around 1965, fabrication plants in Santa Clara, California were successful in replacing individual transistors with integrated circuits impressed on a silicon chip. This region, now called *Silicon Valley*, has became a world center of microcomputer technology. Progress in the VLSI (very large scale integration) of integrated circuits on silicon microchips has been continuous and dramatic.

In 1974, the Intel Corporation released its 8080 microprocessor. This inexpensive CPU (*central processing unit*) made the microcomputer possible. Progress in microcomputer technology can be measured by the successors to the *i*8080: the *i*8086 in 1977, the *i*80286 in 1984, the *i*80386 in 1986, the *i*80486 in 1989, the Pentium (also called the *i*80586) in 1993, and the Pentium II in 1996.

In the 1960s the U.S. Defense Department developed a nationwide computer network called ARPANet (Advanced Research Projects Agency Network) to facilitate communication among its researchers. This network later expanded and combined with other networks, and evolved into today's Internet. In 1990 Tim Berners-Lee, working at the CERN laboratory in Switzerland developed software that made it easy to link to distant computers on the Internet and to send email (electronic mail). His work marks the beginning of the World Wide Web.

The unprecedented growth in the computer industry in the past 50 years is difficult to overstate. A new generation of technology appears about every three years which makes computing much faster, easier, and cheaper. In less than 50 years, the computer industry has become the third largest sector of the world economy (after energy and illegal drugs). It has been observed that if the automobile industry had developed as fast, we would now be able to purchase a car for under a dollar that could take us to the moon and back in a few minutes.

1.2 COMPUTER HARDWARE

A computer is usually defined as a machine that has five essential parts: a central processor, memory, secondary storage, an input device, and an output device.

The CPU controls nearly all the activities the computer performs. In modern computers the CPU resides on a single computer chip, called a *microprocessor*. The Intel Pentium II processor is a popular example. Microprocessors are usually rated according to how fast their internal clock runs. A computer's *clock speed* is usually measured in *megahertz*, abbreviated MHz. A 300-MHz processor has a clock that "ticks" 300,000,000 times per second. This means that in the best of circum-

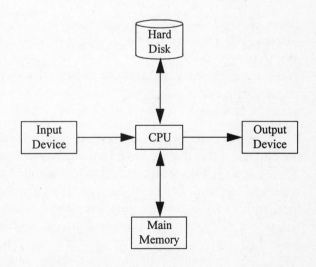

stances, the processor can execute 300,000,000 machine instructions per second, which suggests that each instruction takes only about 3.3 nanoseconds to execute. (A *nanosecond* is one billionth of a second: 10^{-9} seconds.) In practice, that speed is rarely attained because the processor often has to wait for other components to catch up to it. Even to read one byte from its memory may take more than 1,000 nanoseconds, and to read a byte from the hard disk may take 100 times longer. In general, a 300-MHz processor will run faster than a 150-MHz processor, but not twice as fast.

Some computers have more than one microprocessor. Such multiprocessor computers are able to do some things much faster than single processor computers. But the advantage of running several processors simultaneously is mostly dependent upon the software that the processors run. Some algorithms are amenable to parallel processing, and in those cases the greater expense of many processors is justified. For example, the U.S. Weather Bureau uses several large multiprocessor computers to run its weather simulation programs, which are becoming increasingly effective at predicting severe weather. Some multiprocessor computers have as many as 65,536 processors, all capable of running simultaneously.

The *main memory* of a computer is the storage place for the data that is directly accessed by the CPU. It typically consists of a set of single in-line memory modules (SIMMs) mounted on the computer's motherboard close to the CPU. These SIMMs are available in various sizes, from 1 MB to 128 MB. ("MB" stands for "megabyte." 1 MB = 2^{20} bytes = 1,048,576 bytes.)

Conceptually, it is best to imagine main memory as consisting of a very long list of individual bytes, each byte having its own address. For example, a 32 MB PC would have 33,554,432 (= 2^{25}) individual bytes, numbered from 0 to 33,554,431. (Computer scientists typically begin counting locations with 0 instead of 1.)

The picture at right shows the first block of 256 bytes in memory. The numbers on the left are the addresses. For example, the third byte has address `00000010` (= 2_{10}) and contains the data byte `00111100`. A 32-MB RAM would be 8,388,608 times as long as this, with the last binary address being `00000001111111111111111111111111` (= 33,554,431$_{10}$).

00000000	01110011
00000001	01001001
00000010	00111100
00000011	01111111
00000100	00000000
00000101	00000000
00000110	00000000
00000111	00001011
00001000	01001011
⋮	⋮
11111011	00000000
11111100	01100110
11111101	11111011
11111110	00001011
11111111	01101010

EXAMPLE 1.2 Memory size

In a PC with 64 MB of RAM, how many actual bytes would memory hold and what would be the last address?

The actual memory would hold 67,108,864 bytes because 64 MB = $64 \cdot 1$ MB = $64 \cdot 1024$ KB = $64 \cdot 1024 \cdot 1024$ B = $2^6 \cdot 2^{10} \cdot 2^{10}$ = 2^{26} = 67,108,864 bytes of memory. The addresses would run from 0 to `00000011111111111111111111111111` (= 67,108,863$_{10}$).

1.3 BINARY NUMERALS

Primitive cultures learned to count using decimal (base 10) numerals, a natural consequence of the biological fact that we have 10 digits on our hands. We use the 10 *Hindu-Arabic symbols* 0, 1, 2, 3, 4, 5, 6, 7, 8, 9 to form our decimal numerals. These "digits" are used to represent powers of 10 in a decimal numeral. For example, the `8` in the numeral `380745` represents not eight, but eight ten-thousands ($8 \cdot 10^4$). Similarly, the 3 represents three hundred-thousands ($3 \cdot 10^5$), and the 5 represents five ones ($5 \cdot 10^0$). If we number the digits of a decimal numeral from right to left starting with 0, then each digit represents that many powers of 10 where the power is the digit number. The `8` in `38102945` represents $8 \cdot 10^6$ because it is digit number 6.

Most people use decimal numerals quite well without ever thinking about the actual digit numbers as powers of 10. But that understanding is important for students of computer science because computers don't use base 10. They use binary numerals (base 2) instead. Binary numerals use only the first two Hindu-Arabic symbols: 0 and 1. These are called *bits*, for "binary digit". A *binary numeral* is any string of bits, such as 10001101. The meaning of the bits in a binary numeral is completely analogous to the meaning of the digits in a decimal numeral. Just as the left-most digit 3 in the decimal numeral 38102945 represents $3 \cdot 10^7 = 30,000,000$, the left-most bit 1 in the binary numeral 10001101 represents $1 \cdot 2^7 = 128$.

Algorithm 1.2 Conversion from Binary to Decimal

To convert the stored bit string $b_k \cdots b_2 b_1 b_0$ to a positive integer:

   1. Set $x = 0$.

   2. For each $b_j = 1$, add 2^j to x. (Note that j is the number of bits to the right of b_j).

   3. Return x.

EXAMPLE 1.3 Translating a Binary Numeral into its Decimal Equivalent

To find the decimal equivalent of the binary numeral $y = 10001101$:

$$10000000_2 = 2^7 = 128_{10}$$
$$1000_2 = 2^3 = 8_{10}$$
$$100_2 = 2^2 = 4_{10}$$
$$1_2 = 2^0 = 1_{10}$$

The answer is $128 + 8 + 4 + 1 = 141$. The subscripts 2 and 10 are used to designate "binary" and "decimal". So this correspondence can be written $10001101_2 = 141_{10}$.

Translating decimal numerals into binary is not as straightforward as the reverse process. One way to do it is to reverse the algorithm described in Example 1.3: instead of adding powers of 2 to get the decimal numeral, subtract powers of 2 from the given decimal numeral.

The next algorithm has the same effect as Algorithm 1.2, but it uses *Horner's Method* for greater efficiency. This method factors the sum to replace exponentiation with multiplication. For example, it would perform the operation $128 + 8 + 4 + 1 = 141$ as

$$(((((((0 + \underline{1}) \cdot 2 + \underline{0}) \cdot 2 + \underline{0}) \cdot 2 + \underline{0}) \cdot 2 + \underline{1}) \cdot 2 + \underline{1}) \cdot 2 + \underline{0}) \cdot 2 + \underline{1} = 141$$

Note that the (underlined) bits from original bit string 10001101 appear in order in this expression. Although it looks more complicated, this algorithm is easier to implement and is more efficient.

Algorithm 1.3 Conversion from Binary to Decimal by Horner's Method

This uses Horner's Method to convert the stored bit string $b_k \cdots b_2 b_1 b_0$ to a positive integer:

   1. Set $x = 0$.

   2. Set $j = k + 1$ (the actual number of bits in the string $b_k \cdots b_2 b_1 b_0$).

   3. Subtract 1 from j.

   4. Multiply x by 2.

   5. Add b_j to x.

   6. If $j > 0$, repeat steps 3–6.

   7. Return x.

EXAMPLE 1.4 Binary to Decimal by Horner's Method

Convert the bit string 10110000_2 to decimal:

j	b_j	$x = 2x + b_j$
8		0
7	1	$2 \cdot 0 + 1 =$ 1
6	0	$2 \cdot 1 + 0 =$ 2
5	1	$2 \cdot 2 + 1 =$ 5
4	1	$2 \cdot 5 + 1 =$ 11
3	0	$2 \cdot 11 + 0 =$ 22
2	0	$2 \cdot 22 + 0 =$ 44
1	0	$2 \cdot 44 + 0 =$ 88
0	0	$2 \cdot 88 + 0 =$ 176

Thus $10110000_2 = b_7 b_6 b_5 b_4 b_3 b_2 b_1 b_0 = 176_{10}$.

The next algorithm reverses Algorithm 1.2, converting a decimal numeral back into binary.

Algorithm 1.4 Conversion from Decimal to Binary

To convert the integer x into its equivalent binary numeral:

1. Assert $x > 0$.
2. Set $k = 0$.
3. If x is odd, set $b_k = 1$; otherwise set $b_k = 0$.
4. Subtract b_k from x.
5. Divide x by 2.
6. Add 1 to k.
7. If $x > 0$, repeat steps 3–6.
8. Return $b_k \cdots b_2 b_1 b_0$.

EXAMPLE 1.5 Decimal Integer to Binary

To convert the integer 176 into its equivalent binary numeral:

k	x	b_k
0	176	
1	88	0
2	44	0
3	22	0
4	11	0
5	5	1
6	2	1
7	1	0
8	0	1

Thus $176_{10} = b_7 b_6 b_5 b_4 b_3 b_2 b_1 b_0 = 10110000_2$.

1.4 COMPUTER STORAGE

Every byte of memory always contains some string of 8 zeros and ones. If those 8 bits are set by some program, then we say that the byte has been *initialized*. Otherwise the byte remains *uninitialized*, which usually means that the zeros and ones in the byte are unpredictable.

A byte of memory that has been initialized by a program contains data that can be interpreted meaningfully by other programs. The way that it is interpreted is determined by the *data type* that has been assigned to the byte. It could be text, numeric, sound, graphics, or some other binary type. It could be the machine language for some program, part of a compressed file, or an encrypted message.

EXAMPLE 1.6 Interpreting Four Bytes

Suppose that the four bytes with address 10000011–10000111 are as shown at right.

These 32 bits can be interpreted to have different meanings depending upon the data type assigned to them.

10000011	01000010
10000100	01111001
10000101	01100101
10000110	00000000

Suppose that a C++ program has assigned the character data type char to these four bytes. Then since each char occupies one byte, these four bytes represent the three letters 'B', 'y', 'e', and the null character NUL. These characters are obtained from the ASCII code. Each byte is interpreted as an integer and then translated into the character that has that code value. For example, the byte 01000010 is read as a binary numeral whose decimal equivalent is 66. The ASCII code for the letter B is 66.

If the program instructs the computer to print these four characters, it prints Bye. When the null character is "printed," it does not appear. When used this way its purpose is to mark the end of the character string.

10000011	01000010	$01000010_2 = 66_{10} = \text{'B'}$
10000100	01111001	$01111001_2 = 121_{10} = \text{'y'}$
10000101	01100101	$01100101_2 = 101_{10} = \text{'e'}$
10000110	00000000	$00000000_2 = 0_{10} = \text{NUL}$

Suppose that the C++ program has assigned the integer data type short to these four bytes. This type uses two bytes (16 bits) for each integer, so these four bytes will be interpreted as two integers.

As decimal numerals, these two integers are 17,017 and 25,856. Note that 16-bit (signed) integers will be in the range −32,768 to 32,767.

10000011	01000010	
10000100	01111001	$0100001001111001_2 = 17017_{10}$
10000101	01100101	
10000110	00000000	$0110010100000000_2 = 25856_{10}$

Now suppose that these same four bytes are interpreted with the Standard C++ data type wchar_t. This type uses two bytes (16 bits) for each character, so these four bytes will be interpreted as two Unicode characters. The first of these two 16-bit characters (Unicode 17,017) is a Chinese glyph.

Another possible interpretation of the same four bytes is as a single 32-bit integer of type int. These four bytes represent the single (decimal) integer 1,115,251,968. Note that, in general, 32-bit (signed) integers range from −2,147,483,648 to 2,147,483,647.

10000011	01000010	
10000100	01111001	
10000101	01100101	
10000110	00000000	$01000010011110010110010100000000_2 = 1,115,251,968_{10}$

If these four bytes are assigned the C++ floating-point type float, they evaluate to the decimal number 62.34863. The algorithm used for this conversion is complicated. It divides the 32 bits into three parts: the left-most bit is called the *sign bit*, the next 8 bits form the *exponent*, and the right-most 23 bits form the *fraction*. For the 32-bit string   01000010011110010110010100000000, the sign bit is   0, the exponent is 10000100, and the fraction is 11110010110010100000000. These three components determine that the number is positive, it has an exponent value of $10000100_2 - 127 = 132 - 127 = 5$, and a fraction value of 1.111100101100101_2. That forms the number $+1.111100101100101_2 \times 2^5 = 111110.0101100101_2 = 2^5 + 2^4 + 2^3 + 2^2 + 2^1 + 2^{-2} + 2^{-4} + 2^{-5} + 2^{-8} + 2^{-10} = 62.34863$. Note that 127 is subtracted from the stored 8-bit exponent and 1 is added to the 23-bit fraction. This algorithm is known as the *excess-127 floating-point representation*.

This example shows that the same four bytes can represent the text "Bye", the four integers {66, 121, 101, 0}, the two integers 17,017 and 25,856, two Unicode characters, the single integer 1,115,251,968, or the single real number 62.34863, depending upon whether the data type is `char`, `unsigned char`, `short`, `wchar_t`, `int`, or `float`. There are several other data types available in C++ that would yield other different values for these same 32 bits.

The correspondences between memory bits and the characters that they represent are called *character code*s. Standard C++ uses the 8-bit ASCII code and the 16-bit Unicode. ASCII (pronounced "as-key") is an acronym for the American Standard Code for Information Interchange. Unicode is a newer international code that includes all the standard European and Asian characters and many special symbols, such as mathematics and music symbols.

1.5 OPERATING SYSTEMS

There is a special program that is always running when the computer is turned on; it is called its *operating system*, because it "operates" the computer, controlling all its hardware and software functions. When you turn on your computer, as soon as it finishes running its diagnostic tests, it copies its operating system from its hard disk into its memory and starts it running. This is called *booting the system* because the computer is getting itself running, like pulling itself up by its bootstraps.

Different computers use different operating systems. The most popular are Windows 95, MacOS, MS-DOS, Windows NT, OS/2, and various dialects of UNIX such as LINUX, Solaris, FreeBSD, AIX, XENIX, HP-UX, IRIX, and NEXTSTEP. Most PCs use Windows 95, most Macintoshes use MacOS, and most workstations use some dialect of UNIX. Since all programs that run on your computer must be controlled by its operating system, any new software that you install has to be compatible with that system. So most popular software like the Netscape web browser have different versions for the most popular operating systems.

The computer's OS (operating system) controls all the computer's hardware. This is done through the CPU. When you run a program like Netscape, the OS starts the program and remains ready to respond to every request that the program and its client programs make. For example, if you want to read your email you click on a button that requests access to your new mail. That request goes to the OS which looks up where your mail is stored and then returns information (*e.g.*, how many messages there are) to your mail program which then displays it for you.

The most common activity performed by the CPU is simple arithmetic. This is handled by the *arithmetic and logic unit* (the ALU) which is an internal part of the most modern CPUs. To illustrate how this is done, consider the problem of adding the integers 37 ($= 00100101_2$) and 84 ($= 01010100_2$). First the CPU fetches these two numbers from memory and loads them into registers which are storage places within the CPU. Then it carries out the addition, placing the sum into another register. Then it stores that answer back into memory. These operations themselves are translated into binary numerals, called *opcodes*, and stored with the data in memory. The opcodes are appended to the memory addresses of the data, called *operands*, upon which they operate. For example, if the opcode for the LOAD operation is 16 ($= 00010000_2$) and its operand (*i.e.*, the memory address of the number to be loaded) is 97 (= 01100001_2), then the first machine language instruction would be 0001000000000100, which means "load the number stored at byte number 4 into the accumulator (the register in the CPU where arithmetic is performed).

Suppose that the machine language uses the following opcodes:

```
LOAD            00010000
STORE           00010001
ADD             00100011
MULTIPLY        00100100
```

Then our complete machine language program would be

0001000001100001	LOAD the number stored at byte #97
0010001101100010	ADD to it the number stored at byte #98
0001000101100011	STORE the result at byte #99

When executed, this program would have the effect shown here:

Of course the 48-bit program will be stored somewhere else in memory. The OS reads each 16-bit instruction one-at-a-time. Each time, the OS "fetches" (*i.e.,*

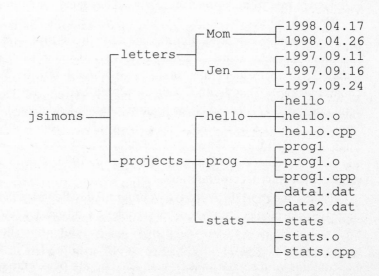

copies) the instruction into one of its registers, and then executes it. That two-step process is called the *fetch-execute cycle*. A 120-MHz CPU can do that 120,000,000 times per second. So it would take that CPU about 25 nanoseconds (3 × 1/120,000,000 seconds) to perform the addition 37 + 84 = 121.

The 3-line machine language program above would be written in *assembly language* as

```
LOAD A
ADD B
STORE C
```

where A and B are symbolic names for the addresses where 37 and 84 are stored, and C is a symbolic name for the address where the sum is to be stored.

1.6 FILE SYSTEMS

Nearly everything stored in a computer is organized into individual units, called *files*. These units are organized into a hierarchical structure called a *file system*. Each operating system has its own file system, but most work the same way these days. There are several kinds of files, but most files are classified as either *plain files* or *directory files*. A plain file may be a text file like a letter to your mother, a data file, a source code file for a program, or an executable file. A directory file is a file that is used to navigate around the file system. The diagram above shows a very simple file system. The file names at the right all represent plain files, while the other file names represent directory files. The left-most directory file is called the *root directory*. In this example, the root directory is named `jsimons`, which is the *user name* of the person who "owns" this account. This directory has two *subdirectories*: `letters` and `projects`. Each of them has subdirectories, and each of them contains plain files. Analogous to a family tree, a directory immediately to the left of a file is called its parent directory. So in the example above, `letters` is the parent directory of `Mom`.

Whenever you are running your computer, one of your directories will be your *current directory* (also called the *working directory*). On most systems, when you log in your own root directory will be your current directory. The operating system that runs your computer will have commands for listing all the files in your current directory; in DOS the command is `DIR`; in UNIX it is `ls`. It will also have commands for "navigating" about your directory tree. For example, in UNIX you can "move down" into a subdirectory named `projects` by executing the command `cd projects`, and you can "move up" to your parent directory with the command `cd ..` . Here the double dot (`..`) always refers to the parent directory.

Every file in your directory tree has a *path* which locates it relative to the root of the tree. In the example above, the path to the file named `1997.09.15` is `~/letters/Jennifer/`, and the path to the directory `stats` is `~/projects/`. The tilde symbol "`~`" represents your home directory. The *absolute file name* of a file is the file's name preceded by its path. So the absolute file name for the file named `1997.09.15` is `~/letters/Jennifer/1997.09.15`.

1.7 SOFTWARE DEVELOPMENT

A *programming language* is an artificial language invented to allow humans to instruct computers on how to execute algorithms. The process of writing those instructions is called *software development*, or more simply *programming*.

The first programmer is often purported to be Countess Augusta Ada Byron Lovelace (1815–1852) because in an annotation to a lecture by Charles Babbage she suggested the possibility that his Analytical Engine would have the capacity to do repetition automatically. But computer programs were not created until the 1940s, and no simple means of programming was devised until 1954 when the first high-level programming language was created by John Backus and a team at IBM. Named FORTRAN for "formula translator," it was designed for solving problems in scientific and engineering. Since then hundreds of programming languages have been invented.

The second major programming language that is still widely used today was named COBOL for "common business oriented language." It was created in 1959 at the U.S. Department of Defense by a team led by Grace Hopper, the first female admiral in the U.S. Navy. In the 1965, John Kemeny and Thomas Kurtz at Dartmouth College invented BASIC (for beginners' all-purpose symbolic instruction code). In 1971 the Swiss computer scientist Niklaus Wirth created another successful teaching language, named Pascal after Blaise Pascal (1623–1662). In 1972 Dennis Ritchie developed the C language at Bell Labs. Ten years later, the Danish computer scientist Bjarne Stroustrup expanded C into C++ for object-oriented programming. In 1995, a team at Sun Microsystems created the Java language for Internet programming.

Usually the most difficult part of program development is the invention of the algorithm: *i.e.*, the language-independent outline of the problem solution. Once that has been completed and tested by hand, one is ready to sit down in front of the computer to write the program. This next stage involves several steps using several different software systems. The first step is to use an editor to create a file that contains your source code text. In the diagram below the source code file is named `prog.cc`.

The next step is to translate your C++ program into machine language. This is done by a *compiler*, which is an independent program. If the compiler is unable to complete its compilation of your program, it will list the compile-time errors that it found. In this case, you will have to go back to the editor to correct these mistakes and then re-compile your revised source code. This edit-compile-edit loop may have to be repeated several times before the compiler is able to compile your program. If you separate the compile step from the linking step, then when it is successful, the compiler will produce an *object module* containing the machine language translation of your source code. In the diagram below, this is the file named `prog.o`.

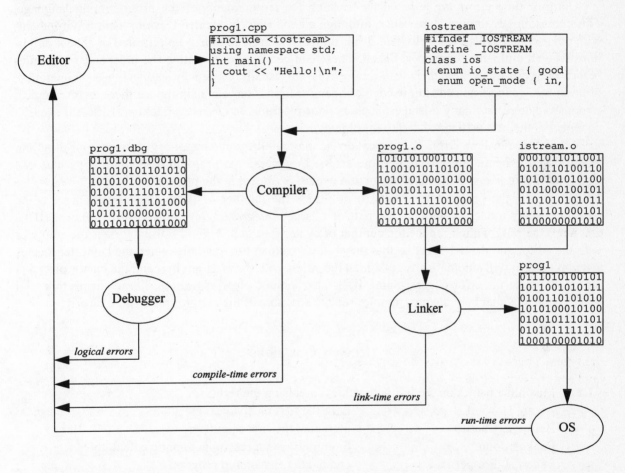

The compiler includes a separate program that can link your object module(s) to the other machine language code needed to produce an executable program. For example, in C++, the instructions on how the input stream `cin` and the output stream `cout` work are located in the system library file `iostream.h`, so that information has to be linked to any program that uses `cin` or `cout`. If you forget to `#include` some necessary header file, the linker will issue an error message, and you will have to go back to the editor to fix the problem. If there are no such problems, then the linker will create a new file (named `prog` in the diagram below) and load it into memory.

The next step is to run your program. But the operating system may encounter instructions in your program that it cannot carry out with its current data. For example, if your have the expression `y/x` in your program and the current value of `x` is 0, then the OS will not be able to do the division and will stop the execution of your program at that step. Such run-time errors are often called "crashes." When your program crashes, you will have to go back to the editor to fix it.

Finally, once your program is running, the last step is to test it with various input sets. If it does not run correctly, you will have to return again to the editor to fix your *logical errors*. These are the most troublesome errors because none of the development systems (the compile, the linker/loader, the OS) is able to find them for you. It's up to you do a logical re-analysis of your algorithm to find the problem. With large programs, this task can be very difficult. Fortunately, most compilers come equipped with a *debugger* that can help you with this task. A debugger allows you to trace through your program step-by-step so you can see its logic. It also allows you to check the values of your variables at each step so you can see the details of the execution.

Compile-time errors are reduced by learning the requirements of the programming language. This comes mostly through experience, although a good IDE (Integrated Development Environment) with color-coded syntax can help here. Link-time errors are due mostly to repeated or absent definitions when a multi-file program is linked. These can be reduced by testing the independent modules before they are linked together. Run-time errors are usually caused by careless use of operators. Programming experience and knowledge of operator limitations can help reduce these errors. Logical errors are caused my many mistakes, such as poor planning and careless hacking. Efficient use of a debugger is the best way to solve those problems.

Correcting run-time errors and logical errors may require some major revisions to your program, which might generate more compile-time errors. In general, the program development process can lead to retracing many of the inner correction cycles, as shown in the picture.

Obviously, the programmer wants to minimize the number of times these cycles have to be repeated. Many modern compilers are part of a larger *Integrated Development Environment* (IDE) that helps the programmer reduce the number of cycles repeated. A good IDE integrates the compiler with the editor and the debugger so that they work together. For example, when the compiler locates a syntax error it will automatically re-launch the editor with the program in it and the cursor placed at the point where the error occurs. Some IDEs also include class inspectors, library inspectors, and other visual aids that help the programmer see the structure of his/her programs more clearly.

Review Questions

1.1   Match the names on the left with achievements on the right:

Aiken, Howard H.	built the first mechanical calculator
Babbage, Charles	marketed the first calculator
Backus, John	built the first successful automatic calculator
Eckert, J. Presper	created the first stored program
Hollerith, Herman	designed the first programmable computer
Jacquard, Joseph Marie	built the first commercially successful data processor
Leibniz, Gottfried Wilhelm	built the first successful electromechanical computer
Mauchly, John W.	jointly built the first electronic digital computer
Pascal, Blaise	jointly built the first electronic digital computer
Schickard, Wilhelm	designed the prototype of the modern computer
Stroustrup, Bjarne	created FORTRAN, the first programming language
von Neumann, John	created the C++ programming language

1.2   Match the acronyms on the left with the descriptions on the right:

ASCII	the modern computer design created by John von Neumann in 1945
CD	a small computer usually owned by a single person independently
COBOL	secondary storage that cannot be changed

CPU	memory or disk space for 2^{10} bytes; about 1,000 bytes
ENIAC	the main memory in a computer
FORTRAN	a small optical disk used for secondary storage
GB	the first company to sell computers, founded by Eckert and Mauchly in 1949
IAS	a removable memory module; typical sizes: 1 MB, 4 MB, 16 MB, 64 MB
IDE	the original programming language designed for business applications
KB	units of speed for a computer clock: 1,000,000 cycles/second
MB	a software systems that integrates an editor, a compiler, and a debugger
MHz	the "brain" of a computer
OS	memory or disk space for 2^{20} bytes; about 1,000,000 bytes
PC	memory or disk space for 2^{30} bytes; about 1,000,000,000 bytes
RAM	memory or disk space for 2^{40} bytes; about 1,000,000,000,000 bytes
ROM	the program that controls all operations of a computer
SIMM	the first high-level programming language, used mostly by scientists
TB	the huge computer built by Eckert and Mauchly in 1945
UNIVAC	the code used by most computer systems to translate characters into integers

1.3 Describe the basic components of a computer.

1.4 What various kinds of memory units are found in modern computers?

1.5 How is memory organized in a computer?

1.6 What happens when you "boot" a computer?

1.7 What is an operating system?

1.8 What is a file system?

1.9 What is a file path name?

1.10 What is a computer program?

1.11 How is a computer program executed?

1.12 What kinds of errors typically occur in the programming process?

1.13 What is the fundamental distinction between integers and real numbers in a computer?

Problems

1.14 In a PC with 16 MB of RAM, how many actual bytes would memory hold and what would be the last address?

1.15 In a PC with 1 GB of RAM, how many actual bytes would memory hold and what would be the last address?

1.16 Charles Babbage (see page 2) won the first government research grant in history when in 1823 he persuaded the British government to finance the construction of his Difference Engine. In his proposal to the government he used $y = x^2 + x + 41$ as an example of a mathematical function that the computer would tabulate by means of the *Method of Finite Differences*. Construct a difference table for this function and explain how it facilitates its evaluation.

1.17 Use the method of Finite Differences to tabulate the function $x^2 - 3x + 5$.

1.18 Use the method of Finite Differences to tabulate the function $x^3 - 3x + 5$.

1.19 Explain why the Babylonian Algorithm (Algorithm 1.1) works.

1.20 The Babylonain Algorithm (Algorithm 1.1) can be modified easily to compute the square root of any positive number: just change the 2 in Step 2 to the number whose square root you want. For example, to compute the square root of six ($\sqrt{6}$), do this for Step 2:

2. Replace x with the average of x and $6/x$.

a. Use a modified Babylonian Algorithm to compute $\sqrt{6}$.
b. Use a modified Babylonian Algorithm to compute $\sqrt{666}$.
c. Use a modified Babylonian Algorithm to compute $\sqrt{0.0066}$.

Be sure to check your answers by squaring them.

1.21 Determine empirically how many iterations are needed for the Babylonian Algorithm to compute $\sqrt{25}$ to:

a. 3 decimal place accuracy;
b. 6 decimal place accuracy;
c. 9 decimal place accuracy;
d. 12 decimal place accuracy.

1.22 Determine what 4 one-byte integers are stored in these 4 bytes:

1.23 Determine what 2 two-byte integers are stored in the 4 bytes shown in Problem 1.22.

1.24 Determine what four-byte integer is stored in the 4 bytes of memory shown in Problem 1.22.

⋮
00100010
01100001
00010001
00000000
⋮

1.25 Convert 11011100_2 to decimal. (Use Algorithm 1.2 on page 5.)

1.26 Convert each of the following binary numerals to decimal:

a. 11011110
b. 10101010
c. 11111111
d. 1000000000000000000000000000000 (31 zeros)

1.27 Convert 555_{10} to binary.

1.28 Convert each of the following decimal numerals to binary:

a. 888
b. 4444
c. 1025
d. 255

1.29 A *hexadecimal* numeral uses base 16. This requires the use of 16 symbols ("digits"). We use the 10 ordinary digits plus the first 6 letters of the alphabet. For example, the hexadecimal numeral 9ca2f represents $9 \cdot 16^4 + 12 \cdot 16^3 + 10 \cdot 16^2 + 2 \cdot 16^1 + 15 \cdot 16^0 = 641,583_{10}$. Devise an algorithm similar to that in Algorithm 1.4 to convert decimal to hexadecimal, and then apply it to find the hexadecimal representation for $100,000_{10}$.

1.30 Convert each of the decimal numbers in Problem 1.28 to hexadecimal (see Problem 1.29):

1.31 Convert the hexadecimal 2d7b into decimal.

1.32 Create an algorithm that uses Horner's Method to convert hexadecimal to decimal, reversing Algorithm 1.4 on page 6. The algorithm should be similar to Algorithm 1.2 on page 5. Use it to convert each of the following hexadecimal numerals (see Problem 1.29) to decimal:

a. f4d9
b. 543ab
c. 100000
d. ffffff

1.33 Create an algorithm to convert binary to hexadecimal, and then apply it to find the hexadecimal representation for each of the numerals in Problem 1.26.

1.34 Horner's Method (page 5) is more efficient than the usual method for evaluating a polynomial. For example, the polynomial $p(x) = 2x^5 - 7x^4 + 6x^3 + 9x^2 + 8x - 5$ can be written as

$$p(x) = ((((2x - 7)x + 6)x + 9)x + 8)x - 5$$

Then a value such as $p(4.1)$ can be computed as

$$p(4.1) = ((((2 \cdot 4.1 - 7) \cdot 4.1 + 6) \cdot 4.1 + 9) \cdot 4.1 + 8)4.1 - 5$$
$$= (((1.2 \cdot 4.1 + 6) \cdot 4.1 + 9) \cdot 4.1 + 8)4.1 - 5$$
$$= ((10.92 \cdot 4.1 + 9) \cdot 4.1 + 8)4.1 - 5$$
$$= (53.772 \cdot 4.1 + 8) \cdot 4.1 - 5$$
$$= 228.4652 \cdot 4.1 - 5$$
$$= 931.70732$$

The advantage of Horner's Method is that it eliminates exponentiation.

Use Horner's Method to evaluate $p(3.4)$ for this polynomial.

1.35   Use Horner's Method to evaluate $p(3.4)$ for $p(x) = 3x^5 - 5x^4 + 2x^3 + x^2 - 8x - 6$.

1.36   Use Horner's Method to evaluate $p(3.4)$ for $p(x) = 3x^8 - 2x^5 + 4x^3 - 5x$.

1.37   Consider the general nth degree polyomial $p(x) = a_0x^n + a_1x^{n-1} + \cdots + a_{n-2}x^2 + a_{n-1}x + a_n$. Compare the number of multiplications that it takes to evaluate this directly (using exponentiation) with the number of multiplications required by Horner's Method.

Solutions

1.1   Howard H. Aiken built the first successful electromechanical computer;
Charles Babbage designed the first programmable computer;
John Backus created FORTRAN, the first programming language;
J. Presper Eckert jointly built the first electronic digital computer with J. W. Mauchly;
Herman Hollerith built the first commercially successful data processor;
Joseph Marie Jacquard created the first stored program;
Gottfried Wilhelm Leibniz built the first successful automatic calculator;
John W. Mauchly jointly built the first electronic digital computer with J. P. Eckert;
Blaise Pascal marketed the first calculator;
Wilhelm Schickard built the first mechanical calculator;
Bjarne Stroustrup created the C++ programming language;
John von Neumann designed the prototype of the modern computer.

1.2   ASCII: the code used by most computer systems to translate characters into integers;
CD: a small magnetic disk used for secondary storage;
COBOL: the original programming language designed for business applications;
CPU: the "brain" of a computer;
ENIAC: the huge computer built by Eckert and Mauchly in 1945;
FORTRAN: the first high-level programming language, used mostly by scientists;
GB: memory or disk space for 2^{30} bytes; about 1,000,000,000 bytes;
IAS: the modern computer design created by John von Neumann in 1945;
IDE: a software systems that integrates an editor, a compiler, and a debugger;
KB: memory or disk space for 2^{10} bytes; about 1,000 bytes;
MB: memory or disk space for 2^{20} bytes; about 1,000,000 bytes;
MHz: units of speed for a computer clock: 1,000,000 cycles/second;
OS: the program that controls all operations of a computer;
PC: a small computer usually owned by a single person independently;
RAM: the main memory in a computer;
ROM: secondary storage that cannot be changed;
SIMM: a removable memory module; typical sizes: 1 MB, 4 MB, 16 MB, 64 MB;
TB: memory or disk space for 2^{40} bytes; about 1,000,000,000,000 bytes;
UNIVAC: the first company to sell computers, founded by Eckert and Mauchly in 1949;

1.3   The five basic components are its processor (CPU), its main memory (RAM), its secondary memory (disks), its input devices (keyboard, mouse, *etc.*), and its output devices (monitor, printer, *etc.*).

1.4   The main memory unit of a computer is called its RAM (random access memory), typically ranging from 8 MB to 128 MB in modern PCs (personal computers). Other internal memory units include EPROM (erasable programmable memory) chips, cache memory (typically 128 KB to 512 KB), and video memory (VRAM) used by the computer's windowing system. The secondary memory unit in a computer is usually its hard disk, typically 1 GB to 9 GB. This is supplemented by removable floppy disks (1.44 MB), removable optical disks (100 MB to 1 GB), CD ROM (compact disk, read-only memory) drives, tape drives, and other external hard disks.

1.5   All computer data is stored in bits (binary digits). Bits are grouped into bytes. Each byte has a unique address. Quantities of memory are measured in kilobytes (KB), megabytes (MB), gigabytes (GB), and terabytes (TB). One kilobyte is 1024 bytes, one megabyte is 1024 kilobytes, one gigabyte is 1024 megabytes, and one terabyte is 1024 gigabytes.

1.6   When you turn on the computer or restart it, a small program stored in the computer's EPROM loads the computer's operating system from disk into memory and then starts it. This runs brief diagnostics on the computer's components, reports any problems, and then starts its windowing system. When finished, the windowing system usually offers a user login prompt. The process is called "booting" because it is a "boot-strap" process starting itself.

1.7   The computer's operating system (*e.g.*, Windows 95, UNIX) is its main program that controls the computer. It runs continuously while the computer is on.

1.8   Data stored on secondary storage devices (disks, tape, *etc.*) is organized into files. Each file has a name, an owner, a size, a location, *etc.* This information is maintained by the file system. It organizes the files into a tree hierarchy where every file (except the "root") has a parent file, called its directory.

1.9   A file's path name is a symbolic description of the file's ancestry, listing the file's parent, its parent, *etc.*, up to the root of the hierarchy. In UNIX, a file path name looks like this:

```
/Users/jsmith/cs101/projects/Hello.cc
```

Each directory is denoted by the directory's name ending with the slash character `'/'`.

1.10 A computer program is a file containing instructions for the computer to carry out an algorithm. When the program is run, the computer carries out (executes) its instructions.

1.11 Most computer programs are written in high level programming languages such as C++ or Java. The file containing this source code is then compiled into the equivalent machine language program stored in a separate file. In UNIX, the program is then run by using the name of its executable file as a command.

1.12 The three main kinds of errors are compile-time errors, run-time errors, and logical errors. Compile-time errors are detected and reported by the compiler when the programmer attempts to compile the program. Run-time errors can be detected and reported by the operating system when the programmer attempts to run the program. Logical errors must be detected by the programmer by means of testing the program on various input sets.

1.13 Integers are exact; real numbers are only approximate.

1.14 16 MB = 16 × (1024 KB) = 16,384 KB = 16,384 × (1024 B) = 16,777,216 B. This is 16 × 1024 × 1024 = $2^4 \times 2^{10} \times 2^{10} = 2^{24}$, so the last memory address would be `111111111111111111111111`.

1.15 1 GB = 2^{10} MB = $2^{10} \times (2^{10}$ KB$) = 2^{20}$ KB = $2^{20} \times (2^{10}$ B$) = 2^{30}$ B = 1,073,741,824 B, so the last memory address would be `111111111111111111111111111111` (30 1s).

1.16 The difference table at the right shows the values for $y = x^2 + x + 41$, Δy and $\Delta^2 y$ computed for x from 0 to 20. Each number in the column labeled y is equal to $x^2 + x + 41$ where x is the number on its left. For example, $83 = 6^2 + 6 + 41$. Each number in the column labeled Δy is equal to the number on its left minus the number above it. For example, $12 = 83 - 71$. Similarly, each number in the column labeled $\Delta^2 y$ is equal to the number on its left minus the number above it. For example, $2 = 12 - 10$. After the first few rows have been completed it is easy to see that every number in the $\Delta^2 y$ column will be 2. (This is due to the fact that the highest exponent in the function $x^2 + x + 41$ is 2.) So each number in the Δy column is equal to the number above it + 2. For example, $14 = 12 + 2$. Similarly, each number in the y column is equal to the number above it plus the number on its right. For example, $97 = 83 + 14$. So all the y values from row 7 down can be calculated using only simple addition. This is the Method of Finite Differences that Babbage planned to have his Difference Engine use to tabulate functions. He used the example of $x^2 + x + 41$ because this function has the peculiar property that its first 21 values are all prime numbers.

x	y	Δy	$\Delta^2 y$
0	41		
1	43	2	
2	47	4	2
3	53	6	2
4	61	8	2
5	71	10	2
6	83	12	2
7	97	14	2
8	113	16	2
9	131	18	2
10	151	20	2
11	173	22	2
12	197	24	2
13	223	26	2
14	251	28	2
15	281	30	2
16	313	32	2
17	347	34	2
18	383	36	2
19	421	38	2
20	461	40	2

1.17 Tabulating the function $x^2 - 3x + 5$ using only subtraction and addition:

x	y	Δy	$\Delta^2 y$
0	5		
1	3	−2	
2	3	0	2
3	5	2	2
4	9	4	2
5	15	6	2
6	23	8	2

1.18 Tabulating the function $x^3 - 3x + 5$ using only subtraction and addition:

1.19 If x is close to $\sqrt{2}$, then $2/x$ will also be close because: $x \approx \sqrt{2} \Rightarrow x^2 \approx 2 \Rightarrow x \approx 2/x \Rightarrow 2/x \approx x \approx \sqrt{2}$. Also, $\sqrt{2}$ will be between x and $2/x$ because as long as $x > 0$, $x < \sqrt{2} = 2/\sqrt{2} \Leftrightarrow \sqrt{2}\,x < 2 \Leftrightarrow \sqrt{2} < 2/x$. Thus the average of x and $2/x$ will be closer to $\sqrt{2}$ than either x or $2/x$, so each repetition brings x closer to $\sqrt{2}$.

1.20 *a.* The square root of 6 is computed from
```
1.0
3.5
2.607142857
2.454256360
2.449494372
2.449489743
```
Check: $(2.449489743)^2 = 6.000000001 = 6.00000000 = 6$.

x	y	Δy	$\Delta^2 y$	$\Delta^3 y$
0	5			
1	3	−2		
2	7	4	6	
3	23	16	12	6
4	57	34	18	6
5	115	58	24	6
6	203	88	30	6
7	327	124	36	6
8	493	166	42	6
9	707	214	48	6

b. The square root of 666 is computed from

```
1.0
333.5
167.7485007
85.85936499
46.80811789
30.51820954
26.17062301
25.80950228
25.80697592
25.80697580
```

Check: $(25.80697580)^2 = 665.9999999 = 666.000000 = 666$

c. The square root of 0.0066 is computed from

```
1.0
0.5033
0.258206726
0.141883820
0.094200376
0.082131895
0.081245223
0.081240384
```

Check: $(0.081240384)^2 = 0.006599999 = 0.006600000 = 0.0066.$

1.21   *a.* It takes 5 iterations to obtain 3 decimal place accuracy for $\sqrt{25}$.

      b. It takes 6 iterations to obtain 6 decimal place accuracy for $\sqrt{25}$.

      c. It takes 6 iterations to obtain 9 decimal place accuracy for $\sqrt{25}$.

      d. It takes 7 iterations to obtain 12 decimal place accuracy for $\sqrt{25}$.

1.22 $00100010_2 = 2^5 + 2^1 = 32 + 2 = 34.$

      $01100001_2 = 2^6 + 2^5 + 2^0 = 64 + 32 + 1 = 97.$

      $00010001_2 = 2^4 + 2^0 = 16 + 1 = 17.$

      $00000000_2 = 0.$

1.23 $0110000100100010_2 = 2^{14} + 2^{13} + 2^8 + 2^5 + 2^1 = 16,384 + 8192 + 256 + 32 + 2 = 24,866.$ Note that this result can also be computed from the answers to Problem 1.16: $97{\cdot}2^8 + 34 = 97{\cdot}256 + 17 = 24,866.$ $0000000000010001_2 = 2^4 + 2^0 = 16 + 1 = 17.$

1.24 $00000000000100010110000100100010_2 = 2^{20} + 2^{16} + 2^{14} + 2^{13} + 2^8 + 2^5 + 2^1 = 1,048,576 + 65,536 + 16,384 + 8192 + 256 + 32 + 2 = 1,138,978.$ Note that this result can also be computed from the answers to Problem 1.23: $24,866{\cdot}2^{16} + 17 = 24,866{\cdot}655,36 + 17 = 1,138,978.$

1.25 $11011100_2 = 2^7 + 2^6 + 2^4 + 2^3 + 2^2 = 128 + 64 + 16 + 8 + 4 = 220_{10}$

1.26   Using Algorithm 1.2 on page 5:

a. Converting 11011110 to decimal:

j	b_j	$x = 2x + b_j$	
8			0
7	1	$2{\cdot}0$	$+1 = \quad 1$
6	1	$2{\cdot}1$	$+1 = \quad 3$
5	0	$2{\cdot}3$	$+0 = \quad 6$
4	1	$2{\cdot}6$	$+1 = \quad 13$
3	1	$2{\cdot}13$	$+1 = \quad 27$
2	1	$2{\cdot}27$	$+1 = \quad 55$
1	1	$2{\cdot}55$	$+1 = 111$
0	0	$2{\cdot}111$	$+0 = 222$

b. Converting `10101010` to decimal:

j	b_j	$x = 2x + b_j$	
8			0
7	1	$2 \cdot 0 \ + 1 =$	1
6	0	$2 \cdot 1 \ + 0 =$	2
5	1	$2 \cdot 2 \ + 1 =$	5
4	0	$2 \cdot 5 \ + 0 =$	10
3	1	$2 \cdot 10 + 1 =$	21
2	0	$2 \cdot 21 + 0 =$	42
1	1	$2 \cdot 42 + 1 =$	85
0	0	$2 \cdot 85 + 0 =$	170

c. Converting `11111111` to decimal:

j	b_j	$x = 2x + b_j$	
8			0
7	1	$2 \cdot 0 \ + 1 =$	1
6	1	$2 \cdot 1 \ + 1 =$	3
5	1	$2 \cdot 3 \ + 1 =$	7
4	1	$2 \cdot 6 \ + 1 =$	15
3	1	$2 \cdot 13 + 1 =$	31
2	1	$2 \cdot 27 + 1 =$	63
1	1	$2 \cdot 55 + 1 =$	127
0	1	$2 \cdot 111 + 1 =$	255

Note here that each partial sum is 1 less than the next power of two (*e.g.*, $63 = 2^6 - 1$).

d. $10000000000000000000000000000000 = 2^{31} = 2{,}147{,}483{,}648$.

1.27   Converting 555 to binary:

k	x	b_k
0	555	1
1	277	1
2	138	0
3	69	1
4	34	0
5	17	1
6	8	0
7	4	0
8	2	0
9	1	1
10	0	

So $555_{10} = b_7b_6b_5b_4b_3b_2b_1b_0 = 1000101011_2$.

1.28   Using Algorithm 1.4 on page 6:

a.   Converting 888 to binary:

k	x	b_k
	888	
0	444	0
1	222	0
2	111	0
3	55	1
4	27	1
5	13	1
6	6	1
7	3	0
8	1	1
9	0	1

So $888_{10} = 1101111000_2$.

b. Converting 4444 to binary:

k	x	b_k
	4444	
0	2222	0
1	1111	0
2	555	1
3	277	1
4	138	1
5	69	0
6	34	1
7	17	0
8	8	1
9	4	0
10	2	0
11	1	0
12	0	1

So $4444_{10} = 1000101011100_2$.

c. Converting 1025 to binary is easy because $1025 = 1024 + 1 = 2^{10} + 2^0 = 10000000001_2$.

d. Converting 255 to binary is easy because $255 = 256 - 1 = 2^8 - 1 = 11111111_2$. Imagine a binary odometer on a car: the next mile after 011111111 would be 100000000.

1.29   The algorithm is the same except that the repeated division is by 16 instead of 2:

Algorithm 1.5 Decimal Integer to Hexadecimal

To convert the integer x into its equivalent hexadecimal numeral:

1. Assert $x > 0$.

2. Set $k = 0$.

3. Divide x by 16, setting x equal to the (integer) quotient.

4. Set h_k equal to the remainder from the previous division. Use one of the 16 *hexadecimal digits* 0, 1, 2, 3, 4, 5, 6, 7, 8, 9, a, b, c, d, e, f, representing the numbers 0, 1, 2, 3, 4, 5, 6, 7, 8, 9, 10, 11, 12, 13, 14, 15, for h_k.

5. Add 1 to k.

6. If $x > 0$, repeat steps 3–6.

7. Return $h_k \cdots h_2 h_1 h_0$ (*i.e.*, the hexadecimal numeral whose jth hex symbol is h_j)

Applying Algorithm 1.4 to 100,000 yields $100000_{10} = h_4 h_3 h_2 h_1 h_0 = 186a0_{16}$:

k	x	h_k
0	100000	
1	6250	0
2	390	a
3	24	6
4	1	8
8	0	1

1.30 Use Algorithm 1.4 on page 6:

    a.   `Converting 888 to hexadecimal:`

k	x	h_k
	888	
0	55	8
1	3	7
2	0	3

So $888_{10} = 378_{16}$.

    b. Converting `4444` to hexadecimal:

k	x	h_k
	4444	
0	277	c
1	17	5
2	1	1
3	0	1

So $4444_{10} = 115c_{16}$.

    c. Converting `1025` to hexadecimal:

k	x	h_k
	1025	
0	64	1
1	4	0
2	0	4

So $1025_{10} = 401_{16}$.

    d. Converting `255` to hexadecimal:

k	x	h_k
	255	
0	15	f
1	0	f

Thus $255_{10} = ff_{16}$. Note that $ff_{16} + 1 = 100_{16} = 16^2{}_{10} = 256_{10}$.

1.31 Conversion of 0x2d7b into decimal:

$$2d7b_{16} = 2 \cdot 16^3 + 13 \cdot 16^2 + 7 \cdot 16^1 + 11 \cdot 16^0 = 8192 + 3328 + 112 + 11 = 11,643_{10}.$$

1.32 This algorithm is similar to Algorithm 1.2 on page 5:

Algorithm 1.6 Converting Hexadecimal to Decimal by Horner's Method

To convert the hexadecimal integer $h_k \cdots h_2 h_1 h_0$ into its equivalent decimal numeral:

1. Set $x = 0$.
2. Set $j = k + 1$ (the actual number of bits in the hexadecimal string).
3. Subtract 1 from j.
4. Multiply x by 16.
5. Add h_j to x.
6. If $j > 0$, repeat steps 3–6.
7. Return x.

a.   Converting `f4d9` to decimal:

j	h_j	$x = 2x + h_j$	
4			0
3	f	$16 \cdot 0 + f =$	15
2	4	$16 \cdot 15 + 4 =$	244
1	d	$16 \cdot 244 + 13 =$	3917
0	9	$16 \cdot 3917 + 9 =$	62,681

So $\text{f4d9}_{16} = 62{,}681_{10}$.

b. Converting `543ab` to decimal:

j	h_j	$x = 2x + h_j$	
5			0
4	5	$16 \cdot 0 + 5 =$	5
3	4	$16 \cdot 5 + 4 =$	84
2	3	$16 \cdot 84 + 3 =$	1347
1	a	$16 \cdot 1347 + a =$	21,562
0	b	$16 \cdot 21{,}562 + b =$	345,003

So $543\text{ab}_{16} = 345{,}003_{10}$.

c. Converting `100000` to decimal: $1000000_{16} = 16^5{}_{10} = 1{,}048{,}576_{10}$.

d. Converting `ffffff` to decimal: note that $\text{ffffff}_{16} + 1 = 1000000_{16} = 16^6{}_{16} = 16{,}777{,}216_{10}$, so $\text{ffffff}_{16} = 16{,}777{,}216_{10} - 1 = 16{,}777{,}215_{10}$.

1.33   This algorithm is based upon the following one-to-one correspondence between 4-bits strings (called *nibbles*) and the hexadecimal digits:

Binary	Hex	Binary	Hex
0000	0	1000	8
0001	1	1001	9
0010	2	1010	a
0011	3	1011	b
0100	4	1100	c
0101	5	1101	d
0110	6	1110	e
0111	7	1111	f

Algorithm 1.7 Converting Binary to Hexadecimal

To convert the binary integer $b_k \cdots b_2 b_1 b_0$ into its equivalent hexadecimal numeral:

1. Use the table above to convert the nibble $b_3 b_2 b_1 b_0$ to the hexadecimal digit h_0.
2. Use the table above to convert the nibble $b_7 b_6 b_5 b_4$ to the hexadecimal digit h_1.
3. Repeat using the table to convert the nibble $b_{j+3} b_{j+2} b_{j+1} b_j$ to the hexadecimal digit h_j for $j = 2, 3, \ldots$.

    a. Converting 11011110 to hexadecimal:
      $h_0 = b_3b_2b_1b_0 = 1110_2 =$ e and $h_1 = b_7b_6b_5b_4 = 1101_2 =$ d, so $11011110_2 =$ de.
    b. Converting 10101010 to hexadecimal:
      $h_0 = b_3b_2b_1b_0 = 1010_2 =$ a and $h_1 = b_7b_6b_5b_4 = 1010_2 =$ a, so $10101010_2 =$ aa.
    c. Converting 11111111 to hexadecimal:
      $h_0 = b_3b_2b_1b_0 = 1111_2 =$ f and $h_1 = b_7b_6b_5b_4 = 1111_2 =$ f, so $11111111_2 =$ ff.
    d. Converting $10000000000000000000000000000000$ to hexadecimal:
      $h_0 = b_3b_2b_1b_0 = 0000_2 = 0$;
      similarly, $h_1 = h_2 = h_3 = h_4 = h_5 = h_6 = 0000_2 = 0$, and $h_7 = b_{31}b_{30}b_{29}b_{28} = 1000_2 = 8$,
      so $10000000000000000000000000000000_2 = h_7h_6h_5h_4h_3h_2h_1h_0 = 80000000_{16}$.

1.34 $p(3.4) = (((((2{\cdot}3.4 - 7){\cdot}3.4 + 6){\cdot}3.4 + 9){\cdot}3.4 + 8){\cdot}3.4 - 5 = ((((-0.2){\cdot}3.4 + 6){\cdot}3.4 + 9){\cdot}3.4 + 8)3.4 - 5$
     $= ((5.32{\cdot}3.4 + 9){\cdot}3.4 + 8){\cdot}3.4 - 5 = (27.088{\cdot}3.4 + 8){\cdot}3.4 - 5 = 100.0992{\cdot}3.4 - 5 = 335.33728.$

1.35 $p(x) = 3x^5 - 5x^4 + 2x^3 + x^2 - 8x - 6 = (((((3x - 5)x + 2)x + 1)x - 8)x - 6$, so

$$p(3.4) = ((((3 \cdot 3.4 - 5) \cdot 3.4 + 2) \cdot 3.4 + 1) \cdot 3.4 - 8) \cdot 3.4 - 6$$

$$= (((5.2 \cdot 3.4 + 2) \cdot 3.4 + 1) \cdot 3.4 - 8) \cdot 3.4 - 6$$

$$= ((19.68 \cdot 3.4 + 1) \cdot 3.4 - 8) \cdot 3.4 - 6$$

$$= (67.912 \cdot 3.4 - 8) \cdot 3.4 - 6$$

$$= 222.9008 \cdot 3.4 - 6$$

$$= 751.86272$$

1.36 $p(x) = 3x^8 - 2x^5 + 4x^3 - 5x = (((((((3x)x)x - 2)x)x + 4)x)x - 5)x = (((3x^3 - 2)x^2 + 4)x^2 - 5)x$, so

$$p(3.4) = (((3 \cdot 3.4^3 - 2) \cdot 3.4^2 + 4) \cdot 3.4^2 - 5) \cdot 3.4$$

$$= ((115.912 \cdot 3.4^2 + 4) \cdot 3.4^2 - 5) \cdot 3.4$$

$$= (1343.943 \cdot 3.4^2 - 5) \cdot 3.4$$

$$= 15,530.978 \cdot 3.4$$

$$= 52,805.325$$

1.37 If the general nth degree polyomial $p(x) = a_0x^n + a_1x^{n-1} + \cdots + a_{n-2}x^2 + a_{n-1}x + a_n$ is evaluated directly, it requires $n(n + 1)/2$ multiplications, where the exponentiation x^k is counted as $k - 1$ multiplications. However, by Horner's Method, the evaluation $p(x) = ((\cdots(a_0x + a_1)x + \cdots + a_{n-2})x + a_{n-1})x + a_n$ requires only n multiplications.

Chapter 2

C++ Fundamentals

2.1 THE "Hello World" PROGRAM

Every C++ program must include the following code:
```
int main()
{
}
```
This is called the `main()` function. The program statements that are to be executed are placed between the braces. That section is called the *body* of the `main()` function. This simplest version has no statements, so it would do nothing. But it would compile and run.

Warning: Some pre-Standard C++ compilers require the statement
```
return 0;
```
within the body of the `main()` function.

EXAMPLE 2.1 The "Hello World" Program
Here is a simple program that prints a message:
```
#include <iostream>
using namespace std;
int main()
{ cout << "Hello, World!\n";
}
```
The first line directs the precompiler to copy all the source code from the file `iostream` into this program, replacing the `#include` statement. This file is part of the ISO Standard C++ Library, so the precompiler knows where to find it. It defines various objects and functions, including the stream object `std::cout` that is used on the fourth line. This precompiler directive is required in every program that has input or output; *i.e.*, in every useful program. The second line is needed to access commonly used names like `cout` that are defined in the `std` namespace.

The fourth line tells the system to print the message "`Hello, World!`". The complete string of characters ends with the non-printing character `'\n'`, which simply directs the printer (or monitor) to move the cursor down to the beginning of the next line after printing the exclamation point (!). This non-printing character, which is formed from the two characters "\" and "n", is called the *newline* character. The two-character symbol "<<" is called the *insertion operator*. It is used to indicate that the string should be "inserted" into the output stream `cout`. This output stream acts as a conduit to the computer's output device: either the printer or the monitor. So inserting a string into that stream causes it to be printed (or displayed).

EXAMPLE 2.2 The Pre-Standard Version of the "Hello World" Program
If you are using an older C++ compiler that does not conform to the 1998 ISO Standard, then the program in Example 2.1 should be written like this:
```
#include <iostream.h>
int main()
{ cout << "Hello, World!\n";
}
```
The two differences are (1) write `<iostream.h>` instead of `<iostream>`, and (2) omit the second line: `using namespace std;`.

Henceforth, we will omit the two required lines

```
#include <iostream>
using namespace std;
```

from the programs in this book. If you are using a Standard C++ compiler, you should insert them at the beginning of your programs. If you are using a pre-Standard compiler, insert the single line

```
#include <iostream.h>
```

instead. Note that the `#include` line is a *precompiler directive* and therefore contains no semicolon, but the `using` line is a Standard C++ statement so it ends with a semicolon.

2.2 VARIABLES AND DECLARATIONS

Here is a simple program that uses a variable named `n`:

EXAMPLE 2.3 Using a Variable

```
int main()
{ int n;
  n = 44;
  cout << "The value of n is " << n << '\n';
}
```

The variable `n` is declared in the second line. The keyword `int` means that `n` represents an integer. On the third line, `n` is assigned the value 44. Then when it is used on the fourth line, its value is printed, like this:

```
The value of n is 44
```

Note in the output statement the difference between the character `n` in the string literal, the variable `n`, and the character `'\n'`. In a string literal, `n` is printed as the letter `n`; as a variable, the value 44 is printed for `n`; and when `'\n'` is printed, it simply advances the cursor to the beginning of the next line.

All names in a C++ program must be declared. A variable like `n` in Example 2.3 is declared by specifying its name after its type, like this:

```
int n;
```

The type of a variable specifies how the variable can be used and how its value is stored in memory. Here is a picture of the object `n`:

The box represents the variable itself, its name `n` is on its left, and its type `int` is below it.

After the value 44 is assigned to `n`, we can visualize it like this:

The value of the variable is stored inside it, like putting a hat in a hat box.

The statement

```
n = 44;
```

is called an *assignment statement*, and the equal sign `=` is called the *assignment operator*. Note that the action of an assignment is right-to-left: the *value* being assigned is on the right side of the assignment operator, and the name of the object to which it is assigned is on the left side. When used this way, a name is called an *lvalue*.

2.3 KEYWORDS AND IDENTIFIERS

A computer source code program consists of a sequence of *tokens* (predefined symbols, literals, keywords, and user-defined names) and *whitespace* (blanks, tabs, and newlines). The source code in Example 2.3 contains 14 tokens: the seven tokens `(`, `)`, `{`, `;`, `=`, `<<`, and `}` are predefined symbols; the three tokens `44`, `"The value of n is "`, and `"\n"` are literals; the token `int` is a keyword, and the three tokens `main`, `n`, and `cout` are user-defined names.

A *name* (also called an *identifier*) is a string of characters that identifies something. In C++ the only characters that can be used in a name are the 26 capital letters, the 26 lowercase letters, the underscore character ( ), and the 10 digits. The first character in a name cannot be a digit.

EXAMPLE 2.4 Declarations

```
int sum;        // ok
int Sum;        // ok
int sum;        // ILLEGAL: "sum" is already declared
int _sum;       // ok
int r2d2;       // ok
int C3PO;       // ok
int 3PO;        // ILLEGAL: names must begin with a letter
int maxSize;    // ok
int max_size;   // ok
int max size;   // ILLEGAL: names may not includes blanks
int class;      // ILLEGAL: reserved word
int O00ol111;   // ok, but not good
```

Every programming language has a special set of reserved words that have special meaning and cannot be used as names. These reserved words together with the language's predefined names are called *keywords*. ISO Standard C++ defines 63 keywords:

asm	do	if	return	typedef
auto	double	inline	short	typeid
bool	dynamic_cast	int	signed	typename
break	else	long	sizeof	union
case	enum	mutable	static	unsigned
catch	explicit	namespace	static_cast	using
char	export	new	struct	virtual
class	extern	operator	switch	void
const	false	private	template	volatile
const_cast	float	protected	this	wchar_t
continue	for	public	throw	while
default	friend	register	true	
delete	goto	reinterpret_cast	try	

The compiler knows these words and interprets each according to the definition of the language. For example, class and if are reserved words, bool and int are names of predefined types, and delete and new are names of predefined operators.

2.4 INPUT AND OUTPUT

The simplest way to produce output in a C++ program is through the standard output stream object named cout. A stream object can be visualized as a conduit between the program and the outside. For example, the results of the program in Example 2.3 can be viewed las shown in the picture below. The output flows from the program through cout to the output device (*e.g.*, the monitor).

Similarly, C++ defines an *input stream* named cin through which data flows from an input device (*e.g.*, the keyboard). Like cout, the input stream object cin is also defined in the <iostream> file.

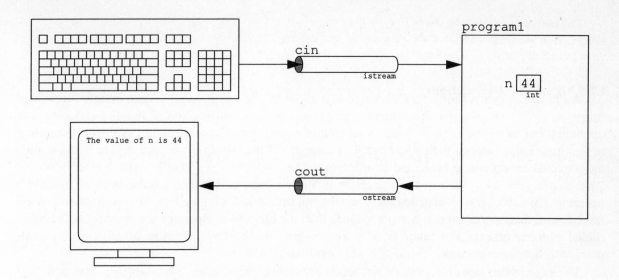

EXAMPLE 2.5 Using the `cin` Object

```
int main()
{ int n;
  cin >> n;
  cout << "The value of n is " << n << "\n";
}
```

When this program runs, the system will wait until the user types in an integer and presses **<Enter>**. If she inputs 44, then the output will be the same as in Example 2.3, as indicated in the picture above.

The symbol `>>` is called the *extraction operator*, or simply the *input operator*. It is used to extract input from the `cin` input stream, similarly to how the insertion operator `<<` is used to insert output into the `cout` output stream.

2.5 EXPRESSIONS AND OPERATORS

The insertion operator `>>` and the extraction operator `<<` are two of a set of over 60 operators defined in C++. These operators are categorized according to the types of objects upon which they operate.

The *arithmetic operators* are `+`, `-`, `*`, `/`, and `%`. All but the last of these are the familiar arithmetic operations that operate on integer and real numbers. The `%` operator, called the *modulus* operator, operates only on integers. The expression `m%n` evaluates to the remainder from the division of `m` by `n`. If `q == m/n` and `r == m%n`, then `q*n + r == m`.

EXAMPLE 2.6 Using the Modulus Operator

```
int main()
{ int m = 33;
  int n = 7;
  int q = m/n;  // the quotient of m by n
  int r = m%n;  // the remainder of m by n
  cout << m << "/" << n << " = " << q << endl;
  cout << m << "%" << n << " = " << r << endl;
  cout << q << "*" << n << " + " << r << " = " << q*n + r << endl;
}
```

The output from this program is

```
33/7 = 4
33%7 = 5
4*7 + 5 = 33
```

A *literal* is a symbol for a specific value of a variable. For example, 33 is an integer literal, and "Hello, World!\n" is a string literal. An *expression* is a combination of literals, variables, and operators. For example, 2*m - n%3 is an integer expression. Expressions are evaluated according to the precedence rules of their operators. For example, if the values of m and n are 8 and 4, then the previous expression is evaluated in order: (1) 2*m == 2*8 == 16; (2) n%3 == 4%3 == 1; 2*m - n%3 == 16 - 1 == 15. The multiplication is done before the modulus because those two operators have the same precedence level and the multiplication is on the left. The subtraction is done last because that operator has lower precedence than the other two. Operator precedence can be over-ridden with parentheses. For example, if m and n are 7 and 5, the expression 2*(m - n)%3 evaluates to 1, but the expression 2*(m - n%3) evaluates to 10.

The expressions that an operator operates on are called its *operands*. For example, 2*m and n%3 are the operands for the - operator in the expression 2*m - n%3. A *binary operator* is an operator that takes two operands. All the operators described above are binary operators. Besides binary operators, C++ also has several *unary operators* (operating on a single operand) and one *ternary operator* (operating on three operands). For example, the minus symbol - is used for both the binary operation of subtraction and the unary operation of negation.

The most widely used operator is the assignment operator = introduced in Section 2.2. In C++, the assignment operator can be combined with many other operators to produce combination assignment operators. For most binary operators op whose operands have the same type, the combination operator op= can be used as

```
                    variable op= expression
```

to perform the combined operations

```
                    variable = variable op expression;
```

EXAMPLE 2.7 Using Combination Assignment Operators

```
    int main()
    { int n = 33;
      n += 5;       // same as n = n + 5; makes n == 33 + 5 == 38
      n %= 8;       // same as n = n%8;   makes n == 38%8 == 6
      n *= n;       // same as n = n*n;   makes n == 6*6 == 36
    }
```

The double symbol ++ defines two unary operators in C++, called the *prefix increment* operator and the *postfix increment* operator, or, more simply, the *pre increment* and *post increment* operators. When applied to an integer variable, each of these increases its value by 1. If the variable being incre-mented is part of a larger expression, then the pre-increment operator will increment the variable before using its value in the expression, whereas the post-increment operator will use the value before incrementing the variable.

EXAMPLE 2.8 Using the Pre-Increment and the Post-Increment Operators

```
    int main()
    { int n = 44;
      cout << n++ << endl;  // prints 44 and then increments n to 45
      cout << ++n << endl;  // increments n to 46 and then prints 46
    }
```

Two decrement operators are similar. The pre-decrement operator `--n` reduces the value of `n` by 1 first and then uses that reduced value, whereas the post-decrement operator `n--` uses the current value of `n` and then decreases it by 1.

When Bjarne Stroustrup chose the name C++ for his enhancement of the C language in 1983, he obviously had in mind the effect of the post-increment operator.

2.6 INITIALIZATIONS AND CONSTANTS

Ordinary variables defined in functions like `main()` are <u>not</u> automatically given initial values.

EXAMPLE 2.9 Local Variables are Not Initialized by Default

```
int main()
{ int n;
  cout << n << endl;  // unpredictable output!
}
```

The output from this program when run on a UNIX workstation was

```
302025904
```

This is an example of what is technically known as *garbage*. It is the result of the system trying to interpret a string of 32 random bits as an integer.

Fortunately, it is easy to initialize variables. This is done with an *initializer*, which is an expression of the form `= constant` appended to the declaration of the variable. Note that, in an initializer, the `=` symbol is not the assignment operator; an initialization is not the same as an assignment.

EXAMPLE 2.10 Initializing a Variable

```
int main()
{ int n = 44;          // n is initialized with the value 44
  cout << n << endl;  // predictable output
}
```

The output from this program is, of course

```
44
```

A *constant* is an object whose value cannot be changed. An object is designated to be constant when it declared by preceding its type with the keyword `const`. All constants must be initialized.

EXAMPLE 2.11 Declaring a constant

```
int main()
{ const int n = 44;    // n is a constant integer with value 44
  cout << n << endl;  // predictable output
}
```

Using constants wherever appropriate is considered good "defensive programming" because it gives the compiler more opportunities to find your mistakes for you. It also makes your programs easier to maintain.

2.7 STANDARD C++ DATA TYPES

Data types in Standard C++ are classified as shown in the diagram below. This includes the new Boolean type `bool` whose values are either `false` or `true`, and the new character type `wchar_t`, which usually represents the international 16-bit Unicode character set.

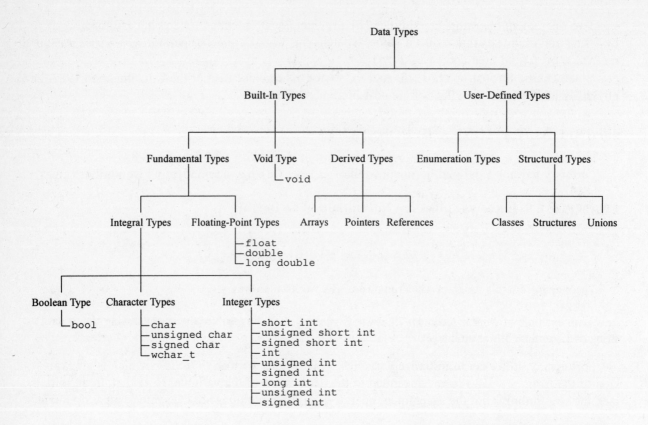

The 17 *fundamental types* and the `void` type have keyword names such as `signed long int`. The multi-word names for the integer types can be abbreviated by omitting the word `int`. For example, `unsigned short` means `unsigned short int`. The only difference between the `short`, `int`, and `long` types is the number of bytes (and therefore the range of values) used to store the objects. Typically (although not necessarily), `short` uses 2 bytes and `long` uses 4 bytes. Similarly, `float` usually uses 4 bytes and `double` uses 8. The `unsigned` types are used for bit strings.

Normally the `bool` values `false` and `true` are printed as 0 or 1. However, that can be overridden with the `boolalpha` flag that is defined in the `<iomanip>` file.

EXAMPLE 2.12 Printing `bool` Values

Here is a complete Standard C++ program:

```
#include <iomanip>              // use <iomanip.h> in pre-Standard C++
#include <iostream>             // use <iostream.h> in pre-Standard C++
using namespace std;                // omit in pre-Standard C++
int main()
{ cout << false << " " << true << " "
     << boolalpha << false << " " << true << endl;
}
```

Its output is

```
0 1 false true
```

The character types store integers (determined by their character codes) but print characters. In addition, the `char` type reads characters and can be assigned character literals delimited by apostrophes.

EXAMPLE 2.13 Using `char` Type

```
int main()
{ char ch = 'A';          // ch is stored in one byte as the integer 65
  cout << ch << " " << int(ch) << endl;
```

The output is

```
A 65
```

Here, the `int` type was used to cast the value of `ch` from `char` to `int`.

The `void` type is used only with functions and pointers. (See Chapters 4 and 8.)

Derived types are constructed from other types using the special symbols `[]`, `*`, and `&`.

EXAMPLE 2.14 Derived Types

```
float x = 666.66;
float y[8] = {0}; // y is an array of 8 floats, all initialized to 0
float* p = &x;      // p is a pointer to the float x
float& r = x;       // y is a reference to the float x
```

Here, `x` has the fundamental type `float`, and `y`, `p`, and `r` have types derived from `float` type.

An *array* is a sequence of elements, all of the same type, that can be accessed with the same name using an integer subscript. Arrays are described in Chapter 6. A *pointer* is a memory address that can be used to access an object stored at that address. A *reference* is a synonym for an existing object. Pointers and references are described in Chapter 9. The fundamental types, the `void` type, and the derived types are called *built-in types* because they can be used without any special definitions.

2.8 ENUMERATION TYPES

An *enumeration type* is one that is defined by the user simply by listing its set of possible values.

EXAMPLE 2.15 An Enumeration Type

```
enum Direction {NORTH, EAST, SOUTH, WEST};
```

This defines the type `Direction` and the four constants `NORTH`, `EAST`, `SOUTH`, and `WEST` as its possible values. Then objects can be defined and assigned in the normal way:

```
Direction current = EAST;
current = SOUTH;
```

Like character values, enumeration values are stored as integers. Normally the defined constant values are assigned the integers in order beginning with 0. Thus in Example 2.15, the assignment of the value `SOUTH` to `current` actually stores the integer 2 in that variable.

EXAMPLE 2.16 Specifying Enumeration Constant Values

```
enum Roman {I=1, V=5, X=10, L=50, C=100, D=500, M=1000};
enum Rank {DEUCE=2, TREY, FOUR, FIVE, SIX, SEVEN, EIGHT, NINE, TEN,
           JACK, QUEEN, KING, ACE};
enum Color {WHITE, BLUE=0xff, GREEN=0xff00, RED=0xff0000};
enum {SIZE=100};  // an anonymous enumeration type
```

The definition of type `Rank` initializes the constants `DEUCE` to 2, `TREY` to 3, ..., `KING` to 13, and `ACE` to 14. The definition of the type `Color` uses the standard (hexadecimal) integer values for the basic colors. The anonymous enumeration type illustrates an alternative way to define integer constants. This is equivalent to

```
const int SIZE = 100;
```

2.9 THE STANDARD LIBRARY

The C++ language includes a set of files which is called the *Standard C++ Library*. These files define various extensions to the language. They included by means of the `#include` precompiler directive. For example, in Example 2.12 we included the `<iomanip>` file in order to use the `boolalpha` flag, and we included the `<iostream>` file in order to use the `cout` stream object and the `endl` inserter.

EXAMPLE 2.17 Using the `<iomanip>` File

This complete C++ program illustrates the `<iomanip>` file (`<iomanip.h>` in pre-Standard C++):

```
#include <iomanip>                 // use <iomanip.h> in pre-Standard C++
#include <iostream>                // use <iostream.h> in pre-Standard C++
using namespace std;                    // omit in pre-Standard C++
int main()
{ int n = 75;
  cout << '\t' << oct << n << '\t' << hex << n
       << '\t' << dec << n << endl;
  cout << '\t' << setw(16) << n << endl;
  cout << '\t' << setfill('.') << setw(16) << n << endl;
  cout << '\t' << setfill('*') << setw(16) << n << endl;
  cout.setf(ios::left, ios::adjustfield);  // left justify output
  cout << '\t' << setfill('<') << setw(16) << n << endl;
  cout << setfill('.') << setw(40) << "Chapter 13";
  cout.setf(ios::right, ios::adjustfield);
  cout << setw(30) << "415" << endl;
  const double PI = 3.14159265358979323846;
  cout << PI << endl;
  cout << setprecision(10) << PI << endl;
  cout << setprecision(12) << PI << endl;
  cout << setprecision(14) << PI << endl;
  cout << setprecision(16) << PI << endl;
  cout << setprecision(18) << PI << endl;
}
```

Here is the output:

```
        113     4b        75
                     75
        ..............75
        *************75
        75<<<<<<<<<<<<<<
Chapter 13.................................................415
3.14159
3.141592654
3.14159265359
3.1415926535898
3.141592653589793
3.14159265358979312
```

The first `cout` statement prints `n` in octal, hexadecimal, and decimal on the same line. The next four lines of output print `n` (in decimal) in a 16-column field using various fill characters. The first three of these use the default right-justification within the field; the last uses left-justification. The next three lines of code print a 70-character line using the dot `'.'` as a fill character as you would in a table of contents. The last six lines of output show how to obtain a number of significant digits of precision when printing a floating-point number. Note that the number is rounded to the specified number of digits. Also note that 16 is the maximum number of accurate digits obtainable for a `double` on this computer.

EXAMPLE 2.18 Using the `<cmath>` File

Here is a complete C++ program that illustrates some of the useful functions defined in the `<cmath>` file (`<math.h>` in pre-Standard C++):

```
#include <cmath>                        // use <math.h> in pre-Standard C++
#include <iostream>                     // use <iostream.h> in pre-Standard C++
using namespace std;                         // omit in pre-Standard C++
int main()
{ double x = 2.718281828459045;
  cout << "ceil(x)     = " << ceil(x) << endl;
  cout << "floor(x)    = " << floor(x) << endl;
  cout << "sqrt(x)     = " << sqrt(x) << endl;
  cout << "pow(x, 0.5) = " << pow(x, 0.5) << endl;
  cout << "log(x)      = " << log(x) << endl;
  cout << "log10(x)    = " << log10(x) << endl;
  cout << "exp(x)      = " << exp(x) << endl;
  cout << "sin(x)      = " << sin(x) << endl;
}
```

Here is its output:

```
ceil(x)     = 3
floor(x)    = 2
sqrt(x)     = 1.64872
pow(x, 0.5) = 1.64872
log(x)      = 1
log10(x)    = 0.434294
exp(x)      = 15.1543
sin(x)      = 0.410781
```

The `ceil(x)` (for "ceiling") and `floor(x)` functions return the integers that bracket x. The `sqrt(x)` function returns the square root of x. The `pow(x, y)` function returns the value of x raised to the power y; *i.e.*, x^y. The `log(x)` function returns the natural logarithm (base e) of x. The `log10(x)` function returns the common logarithm (base 10) of x. The `exp(x)` function returns the exponential (base e) of x; *i.e.*, e^x. And `sin(x)` is the trigonometric sine function.

2.10 ERRORS

The art of defensive programming is based upon a faith in *Murphy's Law*: "If something can go wrong, it will." A good programmer tries to anticipate what could go wrong in order to prevent it. This skill requires an understanding of the kinds of errors that can occur.

The simplest kind of computer programming errors are *syntax errors*. (See the diagram on page 11.) These are usually easy to discover and fix because the compiler usually tells you exactly where they are.

EXAMPLE 2.19 Syntax Errors

Here's an incorrect version of the program in Example 2.1:

```
int main()
{ cout << "Hello, World!\n;
}
```

When compiled, the compiler printed the following diagnostic error messages:

```
ex0219.cc:8: unterminated string or character constant
ex0219.cc:8: possible real start of unterminated constant
```

The first line refers to line 8 of the source code file named `ex0219.cc`. That is the line

```
{ cout << "Hello, World!\n;
```

The phrase "unterminated string" simply means that it is missing its right quotation mark. The second error message means that the beginning of this "unterminated string" is also on line 8.

The compiler will also locate other kinds of errors; *e.g.*, names that have not been declared.

EXAMPLE 2.20 Other Compile-Time Errors

Here's another incorrect version of the program in Example 2.1:

```
int main()
{ count << "Hello, World!\n";
}
```

When compiled, the compiler printed the following diagnostic error messages:

```
ex0220.cc: In function `int main()':
ex0220.cc:8: 'count' undeclared (first use this function)
ex0220.cc:8: (Each undeclared identifier is reported only once
ex0220.cc:8: for each function it appears in.)
```

All this is simply reporting that the name count is undeclared. The programmer obviously meant to write cout instead of count.

After the compiler compiles your source code, it links it with other source code needed from the Standard Library. If you neglect to include the necessary files, the linkage will fail.

EXAMPLE 2.21 Link-Time Errors

Here is the correct version of the program in Example 2.1 but without the necessary #include <iostream> precompiler directive:

```
int main()
{ cout << "Hello, World!\n";
}
```

After compiling, the compiler printed the following diagnostic error messages:

```
eex0221.cc: In function `int main()':
ex0221.cc:7: 'cout' undeclared (first use this function)
ex0221.cc:7: (Each undeclared identifier is reported only once
ex0221.cc:7: for each function it appears in.)
```

Although this looks like the same kind of error as in Example 2.20, it is not a compile-time error. There is nothing wrong with this source code. It is simply incomplete. Just add the missing two lines shown in Example 2.1 (or for pre-Standard C++ compilers, the equivalent one line shown in Example 2.2).

Programs can fail even after they have been compiled and linked successfully. There are many situations where the operating system may be unable to execute the program's instructions. These are called *run-time errors*.

EXAMPLE 2.22 A Run-Time Error

Here is a complete C++ program that compiles, links, and runs:

```
#include <iostream>
#include <math>
using namespace std;
int main()
{ int n = 2000;
  cout << n << endl;
  n *= n;
  cout << n << endl;
  n *= n;
  cout << n << endl;
}
```

But the output is
```
2000
4000000
1246822400
```
The second number is correct: 2000*2000 = 4,000,000. But the third number should then be 4,000,000*4,000,000 = 16,000,000,000,000. That number is too large for an `int` type. This error is called *integer overflow*.

A program will give incorrect answers if its numeric values exceed the bounds of their types. This is called *overflow*. That can happen with integer types and with floating-point types. Other kinds of numeric run-time errors include *floating-point underflow* (values are too small), *roundoff errors*, attempted division by zero, and function arguments that are out of range.

EXAMPLE 2.23 Round-Off Error

This program implements the quadratic formula for solving the quadratic equation $ax^2 + bx + c = 0$:
```
#include <iostream>
#include <cmath>
int main()
{ float a = 1e0;        // == 1.0
  float b = -1e10;      // == -10,000,000,000.0
  float c = 1e0;        // == 1.0
  float d = b*b - 4.0*a*c;
  float x1 = (-b + sqrt(d))/(2.0*a);
  float x2 = (-b - sqrt(d))/(2.0*a);
  cout << x1 << '\t' << x2 << endl;
}
```
for the case where $a = 1$, $b = -10^{-10}$, and $c = 1$. The output is
```
1e+10    -50.1022
```
These two solutions are incorrect: $ax_1^2 + bx_1 + c = (1)(10^{10})^2 + (-10^{10})(10^{10}) + (1) = 1 \neq 0$, and $ax_2^2 + bx_2 + c = (1)(-50.1022)^2 + (-10^{10})(-50.1022) + (1) = 501,022,002,511.230445 \neq 0$. The first solution is close, considering the size of the numbers. But the second solution is way off. This is the result of roundoff error.

Run-time errors are more difficult to repair than compile-time errors because the operating system may not be able to pinpoint the problem. It can tell you why your program failed, but it may not be able to tell you where the failure occurred in your program.

Usually the worst kind of errors programmers have to handle are logical errors because there may be no easy way to detect their existence. A *logical error* is an error in the algorithm itself. The computer compiles and executes the program without signalling any problems. The problem is that the programmer gave the wrong instructions to the computer.

EXAMPLE 2.24 A Logical Error

Here is an implementation of the quadratic formula to solve the equation $3x^2 - 3x - 6 = 0$:
```
#include <iostream>
#include <cmath>
int main()
{ float a = 3.0;
  float b = -3.0;
  float c = -6.0;
  float d = b*b - 4.0*a*c;
  float x1 = (-b + sqrt(d))/2.0*a;
  float x2 = (-b - sqrt(d))/2.0*a;
  cout << x1 << '\t' << x2 << endl;
}
```

The output is

```
18        -9
```

But these solutions are wrong: $ax_1^2 + bx_1 + c = 3(18)^2 - 3(18) - 6 = 912 \neq 0$; $ax_2^2 + bx_2 + c = 3(-9)^2 - 3(-9) - 6 = 264 \neq 0$. And there is no hint from the computer about where the problem is.

The logical errors here are at the ends of the lines that assign values to `x1` and `x2`. The quadratic formula requires the expression $2a$ to be in the denominator. But `num/2.0*a` means `(num/2.0)*a` in C++.

Most C++ compilers come with a *debugger*, which is a separate program that allows you to step through your program one instruction at a time, checking the values of the variables at each step. This is often the best way to debug your programs.

Review Questions

2.1   What is the purpose of the two lines:
```
#include <iostream>
using namespace std;
```

2.2   If your C++ compiler does not conform to the new C++ Standard, how should your precompiler directives differ from those illustrated in this book?

2.3   Which of the following declarations are illegal:
```
int the_cat's_pyjamas;
int the_second_largest_numer_in_the_list_of_minimum_values;
int union;
int 44;
int last?;
int NextNumber;
int round-up;
```

2.4   Why isn't `main` a keyword in C++?

2.5   What is a literal?

2.6   What is an operator?

2.7   What is wrong with the following code fragment?
```
cout >> "Enter x :";
cin << x;
```

2.8   How do the following two statements differ?
```
char ch = 'A';
char ch = 65;
```

2.9   What code could you execute to find the character whose ASCII code is 100?

2.10 What is wrong with the following code fragment?
```
enum Season { SPRING, SUMMER, FALL, WINTER };
enum Semester { FALL, SPRING, SUMMER };
```

Programming Problems

2.11 Write a complete C++ program that prints your name and address.

2.12 Write a complete C++ program that inputs two integers and then prints the sum, difference, product, quotient, and remainder of the two integers.

2.13 Each of the following programs has an error. Locate the error, classify it as either a syntax error, a (non-syntax) compile-time error, a link-time error, a run-time error, or a logical error, and then correct it.:

a.
```
#include <iostream>
using namespace std
int main()
{ int n = 22;
  cout << n << endl;
}
```

b.
```
int main()
{ float x = 100.0;
}
```

c.
```
#include <iostream>
using namespace std;
int main()
{ int n += 22;
  cout << n << endl;
}
```

d.
```
#include <iostream>
using namespace std;
int main()
{ int n = 0;
  n /= n;
  cout << n << endl;
}
```

e.
```
#include <iostream>
using namespace std;
int main()
{ float x = 1e20;
  x *= x;
  cout << x << endl;
}
```

f.
```
#include <iostream>
using namespace std;
int main()
{ float x = sqrt(1.01);
  cout << x << endl;
}
```

g.
```
#include <iostream>
#include <math>
using namespace std;
int main()
{ float x = sqrt(-1.01);
  cout << x << endl;
}
```

h.
```
#include <iostream>
#include <math>
using namespace std;
int main()
{ float x = 100.0;
  cout << pow(x, -x) << endl;
}
```

2.14 The number h of different 7-card hands that can be dealt from an ordinary deck of 52 playing cards is $(52 \cdot 51 \cdot 50 \cdot 49 \cdot 48 \cdot 47 \cdot 46)/(7 \cdot 6 \cdot 5 \cdot 4 \cdot 3 \cdot 2 \cdot 1)$.

   a. Run a program that performs this calculation directly, using only 4-byte integers.

   b. Rewrite the formula so that your program, still using only 4-byte integers, gives the correct value (133,784,560) for the integer h.

2.15 Rewrite and then rerun the program in Example 2.23 on page 35 to minimize the effects of round-off error. Use the following algebraic identity to reformulate the assignment to x2:

$$\frac{-b - \sqrt{b^2 - 4ac}}{2a} = \frac{2c}{-b + \sqrt{b^2 - 4ac}}$$

   Then explain why the output from this version is so much more accurate.

2.16 Write and run a program that causes floating-point overflow.

2.17 Write and run a program that causes floating-point underflow.

2.18 Write a program that converts a given number of inches to centimeters. (1 inch = 2.54 cm.)

2.19 Write a program that returns the Celsius value for a given temperature measured in Fahrenheit. For example, the input 68 would output 20. Use the conversion formula $5(F - 32) = 9C$.

2.20 Write a program that returns the Fahrenheit value for a given temperature measured in Celsius. For example, the input 20 would output 68. This is the inverse of the function in Problem 2.19.

2.21 Write a program that inputs a number of hours and outputs the equivalent number of weeks, days, and hours. For example, an input of 4000 would output 23 weeks, 5 days, and 16 hours.

2.22 Write a program that inputs a number of cents (from 0 to 99) and outputs the minimal number of pennies, nickels, dimes, and quarters with the same value. For example, 94 cents is the same as 3 quarters, 1 dime, 1 nickel, and 4 pennies.

2.23 Write a program that inputs a 6-digit positive integer (*i.e.*, in the range 100,000–999,999) and then constructs and outputs the integer whose digits are the reverse of the input. For example, if 289405 is input, then the integer 504982 is constructed and printed.

2.24 Write a program that rounds a real number to a given number of digits.

Solutions

2.1 The directive #include <iostream> tells the precompiler to insert the contents of the Standard C++ library file iostream which contains the definitions necessary for doing stream input and output. The directive using namespace std; tells the compiler that it should look in the *namespace* std (defined in iostream) for the definitions of cin and cout (and any other unresolved references).

2.2 If you are using a nonstandard C++ compiler, you should use

```
#include <iostream.h>
```

instead of

```
#include <iostream>
using namespace std;
```

You will also have to write your own bool, string, and vector classes unless your compiler provides its own version of these standard classes.

2.3   The following declarations are illegal for the reasons indicated in the comments:

```
int the_cat's_pyjamas; // identifiers cannot contain apostrophes
int union;                      // union is a keyword in C++
int 44;              // identifiers cannot begin with a digit
int last?;         // identifiers cannot contain question marks
int round-up;              // identifiers cannot contain hyphens
```

2.4   The word `main` is not a keyword because it is a name. It is the name of a function that is defined in the program.

2.5   A literal is a specific anonymous constant value. For example, `88` is an integer literal, `3.14159` is a floating-point literal, `'G'` is a character literal, `"Hello, World!n"` is a string literal.

2.6   An operator is a function that has a special symbol for a name. For example, `+` is the addition operator.

2.7   In this code, the input and output operators are reversed. The output stream object `cout` uses the output operator `<<`, and the input stream object `cin` uses the input operator `>>`. If you imagine the input and output objects as being external conduits that lie to the left of the program, then it is easier to remember that output flows out to the left and input flows in from the left. (See the figure on page 27.)

2.8   Both statements have the same effect: declare `ch` to be a `char` and initialize it with the value 65. Since this is the ASCII code for `'A'`, that character constant can also be used to initialize ch to 65.

2.9   One way to print the character whose ASCII code is 100 would be to create the correct `char` object and then print it:

```
char ch=100;
cout << ch << endl;
```

A simpler (but equivalent) way would be to cast the integer 100 as a character and then print that:

```
cout << char(100) << endl;
```

2.10   The identifiers listed for the values of an enumeration type are constants and therefore must be unique within the same program scope. For example, the identifier `FALL` cannot be used in two different enumeration types.

2.11
```
#include <iostream>
using namespace std;
int main()
{ cout << "\tSara Somers\n";
  cout << "\t2401 Wadebridge Road\n";
  cout << "\tMidlothian, VA 23113-3841\n";
}
```

2.12
```
#include <iostream>
using namespace std;
int main()
{ int m, n;
  cout << "Enter two integers: ";
  cin >> m >> n;
  cout << '\t' << m << " + " << n << " = " << m + n << endl;
  cout << '\t' << m << " - " << n << " = " << m - n << endl;
  cout << '\t' << m << " * " << n << " = " << m * n << endl;
  cout << '\t' << m << " / " << n << " = " << m / n << endl;
  cout << '\t' << m << " % " << n << " = " << m % n << endl;
}
```

2.13   *a.* Syntax error: the required semicolon at the end of the `using namespace` line is missing.
   b. Logical error; this program has no output, so it is useless.
   c. Compile-time error: the assignment operator `+=` cannot be used in an initialization.
   d. Run-time error: since `n` is initialized to be 0, the assignment `n /= n` would divide n by 0;
   e. Run-time error: since `x` is initialized to be 10^{20}, the assignment `x *= x` will overflow.
   f. Link-time error: the `sqrt()` function is defined in `<math>`, so that file must be `#included`.
   g. Run-time error: the call `sqrt(-1.01)` will fail because `-1.01` is negative.
   h. Run-time error: since `x` is initialized to be 100, the call `pow(x, -x)` will underflow.

2.14 **a.** `int main()`
```
{ cout << (52*51*50*49*48*47*46)/(7*6*5*4*3*2*1) << endl;
}
```

b. `int main()`
```
{ int h = 1;
  int c = 52;
  int n = 1;
  h *= c;
  h /= n;
  cout << c-- << '\t' << n++ << '\t' << h << endl;
  h *= c;
  h /= n;
  cout << c-- << '\t' << n++ << '\t' << h << endl;
  h *= c;
  h /= n;
  cout << c-- << '\t' << n++ << '\t' << h << endl;
  h *= c;
  h /= n;
  cout << c-- << '\t' << n++ << '\t' << h << endl;
  h *= c;
  h /= n;
  cout << c-- << '\t' << n++ << '\t' << h << endl;
  h *= c;
  h /= n;
  cout << c-- << '\t' << n++ << '\t' << h << endl;
  h *= c;
  h /= n;
  cout << c-- << '\t' << n++ << '\t' << h << endl;
}
```

2.15
```
#include <iostream>
#include <cmath>
int main()
{ float a = 1e0;
  float b = -1e10;
  float c = 1e0;
  float d = b*b - 4*a*c;
  float x1 = (-b + sqrt(d))/(2*a);
  float x2 = (2*c)/(-b + sqrt(d));
  cout << x1 << '\t' << x2 << endl;
}
```

The output from this version of the program is
```
1e+10    1e-10
```

The first solution is 10^{10} which is the same as in Example 2.23 on page 35. But the second solution ($10^{-10} = 0.0000000001$) is now very close to satisfying the equation: $ax^2 + bx + c = x^2 - 10^{10}x + 1 = (10^{-10})^2 - 10^{10}(10^{-10}) + 1 = 10^{-20} - 1 + 1 = 10^{-20} \approx 0$. This dramatic improvement is a result avoiding the near cancellation that occurred in the expression $-b - \sqrt{d}$. Since $4ac$ is very much less than b^2, $d = b^2 - 4ac \approx b^2$, making $\sqrt{d} \approx b = 10^{10}$. The worst kind of round-off error occurs when one very large number is subtracted from another nearly equal number.

2.16 This program crashes due to floating-point overflow:
```
int main()
{ float x = 1.0;
  cout << x << endl;
  x *= 1e10;
  cout << x << endl;
  x *= 1e10;
  cout << x << endl;
  x *= 1e10;
  cout << x << endl;
  x *= 1e10;
  cout << x << endl;
}
```

2.17 This program crashes due to floating-point underflow:
```
int main()
{ float x = 1.0;
  cout << x << endl;
  x /= 1e10;
  cout << x << endl;
  x /= 1e10;
  cout << x << endl;
  x /= 1e10;
  cout << x << endl;
  x /= 1e10;
  cout << x << endl;
  x /= 1e10;
  cout << x << endl;
}
```

2.18
```
int main()
{ float inches, cm;
  cout << "Input inches: ";
  cin >> inches;
  cm = 2.54*inches;
  cout << inches << " inches = " << cm << " centimeters\n";
}
```

2.19
```
int main()
{ float far, cel;
  cout << "Input temperature in degrees Farenheit: ";
  cin >> far;
  cel = 5.0*(far - 32.0)/9.0;
  cout << far << " degrees Farenheit = "
       << cel << " degrees Celsius\n";
}
```

2.20
```
int main()
{ float cel, far;
  cout << "Input temperature in degrees Celsius: ";
  cin >> cel;
  far = 1.8*cel + 32.0;
  cout << cel << " degrees Celsius = "
       << far << " degrees Farenheit\n";
}
```

2.21
```
int main()
  { int hours, days, weeks;
    cout << "Enter number of hours: ";
    cin >> hours;
    cout << hours << " hours = ";
    days = hours/24;
    hours %= 24;
    weeks = days/7;
    days %= 7;
    cout << weeks << " weeks, " << days << " days, and "
         << hours << " hours.\n";
  }
```

2.22
```
int main()
  { int pennies, nickels, dimes, quarters;
    cout << "Enter number of cents: ";
    cin >> pennies;
    cout << pennies << " cents = ";
    quarters = pennies/25;
    pennies %= 25;
    dimes = pennies/10;
    pennies %= 10;
    nickels = pennies/5;
    pennies %= 5;
    cout << quarters << " quarters, " << dimes << " dimes, "
         << nickels << " nickels, and " << pennies << " pen-
nies.\n";
  }
```

2.23
```
int main()
  { int n, d0, d1, d2, d3, d4, d5;
    cout << "Enter a 6-digit positive integer: ";
    cin >> n;
    d0 = n%10;
    n /= 10;
    d1 = n%10;
    n /= 10;
    d2 = n%10;
    n /= 10;
    d3 = n%10;
    n /= 10;
    d4 = n%10;
    n /= 10;
    d5 = n%10;
    n = ((((d0*10 + d1)*10 + d2)*10 + d3)*10 + d4)*10 + d5;
    cout << n << endl;
  }
```

2.24
```
int main()
  { double x = 3.1415926535897932;
    cout << setprecision(16) << x << endl;
    int n;
    cout << "Enter number of digits: ";
    cin >> n;
    x *= pow(10,n);
    int round = int(x + 0.5);
    x = double(round)/pow(10,n);
    cout << x << endl;
  }
```

Chapter 3

Control Structures

3.1 BLOCKS AND SCOPE

A *block* is a sequence of statements enclosed in braces. It can be used wherever a single statement can be used. When used in place of a single statement it is also called a *compound statement*.

EXAMPLE 3.1 A Statement Block

Enclosing the statements within braces forms a statement block:

```
{ int n;
  cin >> n;
  cout << 2*n << endl;
}
```

The *scope* of an object is that part of the program where the object may be used. If it is declared within a block, its scope extends from the point where it is declared to the end of the innermost block that contains it. In this case we say it is *local* to the block that defines its scope. If an object's declaration is outside all blocks, then its scope extends from its point of declaration to the end of the file in which it is declared. In this case the object is called a *global* object.

No two objects may have the same name within the same block. However, two objects may have the same name within separate blocks. If one block is nested inside another, any object declared in the inner block masks any object with the same name that is declared in the outer block. So the scope of the object declared outside of a block may have holes in it.

EXAMPLE 3.2 Nested Blocks

Here is a complete C++ program that contains three blocks, one which serves as the body of the `main()` function, and the other two nested inside the first.

```
    int main()
    { int x = 22;
      { int x = 44;
        cout << x << endl;      // prints 44
      }
      cout << x << endl;        // prints 22
      { int x = 66;
        cout << x << endl;      // prints 66
      }
      cout << x << endl;        // prints 22
    }
```

Note that this program contains three different objects, all named `x`. Their scopes are determined by the blocks within which they are defined. The first `x` has scope that extends throughout the `main()` block except where it is overridden by more local objects with the same name. The second `x` is local to the inner block where it is declared, and within that scope it masks the scope of the first `x`. So any reference to `x` within that limited scope will be interpreted as referring to the second `x`. Similarly, the scope of the third `x` within its inner block also masks the scope of the first `x`.

43

Recall that, for brevity, we have omitted from the examples the two lines

```
#include <iostream>
using namespace std;
```

for Standard C++ programs, or the equivalent single line

```
#include <iostream.h>
```

for pre-Standard C++ programs. These are required for any program that uses `cin` or `cout`.

3.2 NAMESPACES

A *namespace* is a named block that is used to express a logical grouping of statements within a program. ISO Standard C++ allows namespaces. The block name is simply an identifier declared with the `namespace` keyword at the head of the block:

$$\texttt{namespace}\ \textit{block-name block}$$

It is then used outside the block to allow external reference to the names declared inside the block:

$$\textit{block-name}\texttt{::}\textit{name}$$

The double colon `::` is called the *scope resolution operator*.

EXAMPLE 3.3 Using Namespaces to Access Names from Outside Their Scopes

```
int main()
{ namespace Block1
  { int x = 44;
    cout << x << endl;          // prints 44
  }
  namespace Block2
  { int x = 66;
    cout << x << endl;          // prints 66
  }
  cout << Block1::x << endl;   // prints 44
  cout << Block2::x << endl;   // prints 66
}
```

Note the required `namespace` keyword preceding each block name.

In addition to allowing out-of-scope access to names defined within namespaces, the scope resolution operator `::` can also be used without a block name to refer to global variables.

EXAMPLE 3.4 Using the Scope Resolution Operator to Access Global Names

```
int x = 33;               // x is a global variable
int main()
{ int x = 66;
  cout << x << endl;      // prints 66
  cout << ::x << endl;    // prints 33
  return 0;
}
```

If there is no conflict in names, scope resolution prefixes can be avoided by means of `using` declarations and directives. Indeed, that is the purpose of the statement

```
using namespace std;
```

that we have been assuming in all of our examples. This simply alerts the compiler to that fact that the names `cin` and `cout` (and others) are defined in the `std` namespace that is declared in the `<iostream>` file. Without that statement, every reference to `cin` would have to be `std::cin`, and every reference to `cout` would have to be `std::cout`.

EXAMPLE 3.5 Resolving Scope with a `using` Directive

```
namespace X
{ int x = 22;
}
namespace Y
{ int y = 33;
  namespace Z
  { int z = 44;
  }
}
int main()
{ int x = 55;
  cout << X::x << " " << Y::Z::z << " " << x << endl;
  using namespace Y;                    // after this, Y:: can be omitted
  cout << y << "" << Z::z << endl;
}
```

The output is

```
22 44 55
33 44
```

Note that it would be risky to include the directive

```
using namespace X;
```

within `main()` because then any reference to `x` would be ambiguous.

3.3 THE `if` AND `if...else` STATEMENTS

The `if` statement is used for conditional execution. Its syntax is

```
if (condition) statement;
```

The `statement` will be executed only if the `condition` is true.

The parentheses around the `condition` are required.

EXAMPLE 3.6 Using an `if` Statement

```
int n;
cin >> n;
if (n > 2) cout << "ok. Thanks. ";
cout << "Goodbye.\n";
```

If the user inputs an integer that is greater than 2, then the output will be

```
ok. Thanks. Good-bye.
```

Otherwise, the output will be only

```
Good-bye.
```

Note that only the statement that immediately follows the condition is part of the `if` statement. The statement that follows it is independent of the condition and executes regardless of whether `n` > 2.

Also note that the condition `n > 2` must be enclosed within parentheses:

```
if n == 4 cout << "ok. Thanks. ";   //  ERROR: missing parentheses
```

EXAMPLE 3.7 Using a Block in an `if` Statement

```
if (n > 20)
{ cout << "That is too big!  Enter a smaller n: ";
  cin >> n;
}
cout << "Thank you\n";
```

This executes both statements between the braces if `n` is greater than 20.

The `if...else` statement is the same as the `if` statement with an appended `else` clause:

```
if (condition) statement1;
else statement2;
```

If the `condition` is `true`, only `statement1` is executed; otherwise only `statement2` is.
The semicolon that precedes the `else` is required.

EXAMPLE 3.8 Using an `if...else` Statement

```
if (n%2 == 0) cout << "n is even\n";
else cout "n is odd\n";
```

The value of the expression `n%2` is the remainder from dividing `n` by 2; that will be 0 if `n` is even, or 1 if `n` is odd. So this `if...else` statement will print `n is even` only if n is even, and it will print `n is odd` only if n is odd.

Like blocks, `if` statements and `if...else` statements can be used anywhere that single statements can be used. This allows nested conditionals:

EXAMPLE 3.9 Nested Conditionals

```
if (n > 5)
  if (n > 8) cout << "n > 8" << endl;
  else cout << "5 < n <= 8" << endl;
else
  if (n > 2) cout << "2 < n <= 5" << endl;
  else cout << n <= 2" << endl;
```

This will execute exactly one of the four output statements, depending upon which conditions are true.

It is usually better to avoid nested conditionals like the one in Example 3.9 because the logic can be confusing. An alternative is to use compound conditions:

EXAMPLE 3.10 Using Compound Conditions

```
if (n > 8)            cout << "8 < n"        << endl;
if (n > 5 && n <= 8) cout << "5 < n <= 8" << endl;
if (n > 2 && n <= 5) cout << "2 < n <= 5" << endl;
if (n <= 2)          cout <<      "n <= 2" << endl;
```

This makes the logic much easier to follow, and consequently less prone to error.

A third alternative is a series of nested `if...else` statements in a specialized form, called `else if` forms:

EXAMPLE 3.11 Using Sequential `else if` Forms

```
if (n > 8)       cout << "8 < n"        << endl;
else if (n > 5) cout << "5 < n <= 8" << endl;
else if (n > 2) cout << "2 < n <= 5" << endl;
else             cout <<      "n <= 2" << endl;
```

This looks very similar to the code in Example 3.10, and the logic is just as easy to follow. But it is actually simpler.

Note that, to be consistent with general nested conditionals, it could have been indented like this:

```
if (n > 8) cout << "8 < n" << endl;
else
  if (n > 5) cout << "5 < n <= 8" << endl;
  else
    if (n > 2) cout << "2 < n <= 5" << endl;
    else cout << "n <= 2" << endl;
```

But the first format is more succinct, just as clear, and more widely used.

3.4 THE CONDITIONAL EXPRESSION OPERATOR

Among its many operators, C++ provides one ternary operator, called the *conditional expression operator*. It is simply an abbreviated alternative to a special case of the `if...else` statement. The syntax for the conditional expression operator is

```
condition ? expression1 : expression2
```

The resulting value of this expression is either `expression1` or `expression2` according to whether the `condition` is `true` or `false`.

EXAMPLE 3.12 Using the Conditional Expression Operator in an Assignment

The statement

```
abs = (x >= 0 ? x : -x);
```

has the same effect as the statement

```
if (x >= 0) abs = x;
else abs = -x;
```

It assigns `x` to abs if `x >= 0`; otherwise it assigns `-x` to `abs`.

The conditional expression operator is useful whenever one of two alternative values is needed.

EXAMPLE 3.13 Using the Conditional Expression Operator in an Output Statement

```
cout << "You " << (x >= 60 ? "passed" : "failed") << " the test.\n";
```

If $x \geq 60$, this prints `You passed the test`. Otherwise it prints `You failed the test`.

3.5 OPERATORS

An *operator* is a built-in function that is called by means of a special symbol that replaces the usual function notation. The *arithmetic operators* are familiar examples:

```
x = z - y;
y = x*z;
z = x/y;
```

Like most operators, these are *binary operators*, combining two *operands*. ISO Standard C++ defines 68 different built-in operators, and the Standard Library defines many more. These are categorized according to how they are used.

The five binary *arithmetic operators* are: `+`, `-`, `*`, `/`, and `%`, pronounced "plus," "minus," "times," "divided by," and "modulo." There are also six *unary* arithmetic operators, that are used like this:

```
y = +x;     // same as y = x;
y = -x;     // same as y = -1*x;
m = ++n;    // same as m = n = n + 1;
m = --n;    // same as m = n = n - 1;
m = n++;    // same as m = n; n = n + 1;
m = n--;    // same as m = n; n = n - 1;
```

Note that the unary plus operator is really useless since it does not change the value of its operand.

The six *assignment operators* `=`, `+=`, `-=`, `*=`, `/=`, and `%=` were described on page 28.

The six *relational operators* are `==`, `!=`, `<`, `<=`, `>`, and `>=`. These are used in conditions (boolean expressions) such as

```
if (x >= y) y = x;
```

Conditional statements also use the *logical operators* (also called *boolean operators*) `&&`, `||`, and `!`, pronounced "and", "or", and "not."

EXAMPLE 3.14 Using Logical Operators

```
if (x > 2 && x < 6) cout << "x is between 2 and 6" << endl;
if (x == 2 || x > 6) cout << "x is 2 or greater than 6" << endl;
if (!(x > 6)) cout << "x is not greater than 6" << endl;
```

The three logical operators are defined by the following *truth tables*:

p	q	p && q		p	q	p || q		p	!p
true	true	true		true	true	true		true	false
true	false	false		true	false	true		false	true
false	true	false		false	true	true			
false	false	false		false	false	false			

Each of these tables is read from left to right. For example, the second table shows that if p is true and q is false, then p || q is true.

Each of the two binary logical operators (&& and ||) will evaluate the first operand and then use that value to determine whether to evaluate the second operand. If p is false, then p && q will return false without even evaluating q. Similarly, if p is true, then p || q will return true without even evaluating q. This is called *short-circuiting*. It is quite useful in certain circumstances.

EXAMPLE 3.15 Depending upon Short Circuiting

```
if (d >= 0 && sqrt(d) < y) cout << (-b + sqrt(d))/(2*a);
```

The call sqrt(d) will crash if d < 0. But because of short circuiting, the condition sqrt(d) < y will not even be evaluated unless the condition d >= 0 is true.

In a complex expression involving several operators, such as

```
m = 2*n - m%n/3 + 5*sqrt(X::x*Y::y);
```

the order in which the operators are evaluated is affected by their *order of precedence*. Among those operators already considered, that order is:

Operator Category	Operators
scope	::
function, post increment, post decrement	(), ++, --
pre increment, pre decrement, not, unary minus	++, --, !, -
multiply, divide, modulo	*, /, %
add, subtract	+, -
input, output	>>, <<
less than, greater than	<, <=, >, >=
equal, not equal	==, !=
assignment	=, +=, -=, *=, /=, %=
conditional expression	? :

Grouping by parentheses overrides these rules. For example in the expression a*(b + c), the sum is evaluated before the product. Except for the assignment operator, all of these operators are *left associative*; this means that an expression like x/y*z is evaluated from left to right: (x/y)*z.

The assignment operators are exceptions to this rule. When they are chained, as in

```
z += y = x *= 2;
```

the evaluation is done from right to left: z += (y = (x *= 2)); So if the values of z, y, and x are initially 10, 7, and 3, then this statement will change the value of x to 6, then change the value of y to 6, then change the value of z to 16.

3.6 THE while STATEMENT

The `while` statement repeats the execution of a statement while its control condition is true. Its syntax is

```
while (condition) statement;
```

The system will repeatedly evaluate the `condition` and execute the `statement` until the `condition` is false. Of course the `statement` may be a block, or any other kind of statement, including another while statement. Note that if the `statement` is a block, the `condition` is evaluated only at the beginning of each iteration, before the statements in the block are executed. So on each iteration, all the statements within the block are executed regardless of whether the `condition` becomes false during their execution.

EXAMPLE 3.16 Using a while Statement to Add the First 100 Squares

This code adds $1*1 + 2*2 + 3*3 + \cdots + 100*100$ and then prints the sum:

```
int n = 1;
int sum = 0;
while (n <= 100)
{ sum += n*n;
  ++n;
}
cout << sum << endl;  // prints 338350
```

The loop iterates 100 times, once for each value of `n` from 1 to 100. After accumulating 100*100 into `sum`, it increments `n` to 101. Then the control condition `(n <= 100)` is `false`, which stops the loop. After that, the statement that follows the loop executes, printing the sum 338,350.

The following is equivalent to the above code:

```
int n = 0;
int sum = 0;
while (++n <= 100)
  sum += n*n;
cout << sum << endl;  // prints 338350
```

By initializing `n` at 0 instead of 1, we can use the pre-increment operator `++n` inside the control condition instead of in the loop's block.

Note that the control condition of a `while` loop is evaluated only once for each iteration, at the beginning of the iteration before any of the statements in the loop's block are executed.

EXAMPLE 3.17 Controlling a Loop Interactively with the End-of-File Signal

```
float x;
float sum = 0.0;
while (cin >> x)
  sum += x;
cout << "The sum is " << sum << endl;
```

This loop will continue to iterate as long as values are input for `x`. The loop stops when the system detects the *end-of-file* signal. On a UNIX or Windows system, that signal is transmitted by pressing <Ctrl-D>.

Here is a sample run:

```
5.5 8.8 1.1 4.4
<Ctrl-D>
The sum is 19.8
```

(Note that <Ctrl-D> is entered by holding down the **Ctrl** key and pressing the **D** key.)

This works because an input expression such as `cin >> x` returns the `bool` value `true` if and only if the input is successful. When the end-of-file signal is received, the input fails and the expression evaluates to `false`, which stops the loop.

Note that since any type of input failure will stop the loop, the same result could be obtained from the input
```
5.5 8.8 1.1 4.4 STOP!
```
Here, the S would stop the loop because only numbers are legal input for the numeric variable x.

EXAMPLE 3.18 Controlling a Loop Interactively with a Sentinel
```
char c = ' ';
while (c != '\n')
{ cin.get(c);
  if (c >= 'a' && c <= 'z') c = char(c - 'a' + 'A');
  cout.put(c);
}
```
This will read individual characters from the keyboard until **<Return>** key is pressed. Within the loop, the character that are lowercase letters are capitalized, and every character is echoed to the output stream cout.

After the loop terminates, the contents of the cout buffer are sent to the screen.

Here is a sample run:
```
We hold these Truths to be self-evident
WE HOLD THESE TRUTHS TO BE SELF-EVIDENT
```
The first line (in **boldface**) was the input.

A special input value like '\n' that is used to terminate an input loop is called a *sentinel*.

3.7 THE do...while STATEMENT

In some cases, it is preferable to execute a loop's statement once before its control condition is evaluated. That can be done with a do...while loop. Its syntax is
```
do statement while (condition);
```
It works the same way as a while loop except that the condition is evaluated after the statement (or statement block) is executed instead of before.

EXAMPLE 3.19 A do Loop for User-Friendly Input
```
bool cont;
char ans;
do
{ cout << "Continue? (y/n): ";
  cin >> ans;
  if (ans == 'y' || ans == 'Y') cont = true;
  else if (ans == 'n' || ans == 'N') cont = false;
  else cout << "Please answer either y or n.\n";
} while (ans != 'y' && ans != 'Y' && ans != 'n' && ans != 'N');
```
This loop will repeatedly ask for an answer until one of the four letters y, Y, n, or N is input.

EXAMPLE 3.20 An Interesting Number Sequence
Here is a complete C++ program that produces number sequences whose lengths are rather unpredictable:
```
#include <iomanip>                       // defines setw() and int
#include <iostream>
using namespace std;
main()
{ int n;
  cout << "Enter a positive integer: ";
  cin >> n;
  int count = 0;
```

```
   do
   { if (n%2 == 0) n /= 2;
     else n = 3*n + 1;
     cout << setw(6) << n;        // use a field of 6 columns per number
     ++count;
     if (count%10 == 0) cout << endl;    // prints 10 numbers per line
   } while (n > 1);
   cout << "\nThat sequence has " << count << " terms.\n";
}
```

Here are some sample runs. (The dollar sign is the UNIX prompt.)

```
$ ex0317
Enter a positive integer: 3
    10     5    16     8     4     2     1
That sequence has 7 terms.
$ ex0317
Enter a positive integer: 13
    40    20    10     5    16     8     4     2     1
That sequence has 9 terms.
$ ex0317
Enter a positive integer: 23
    70    35   106    53   160    80    40    20    10     5
    16     8     4     2     1
That sequence has 15 terms.
$ ex0317
Enter a positive integer: 31
    94    47   142    71   214   107   322   161   484   242
   121   364   182    91   274   137   412   206   103   310
   155   466   233   700   350   175   526   263   790   395
  1186   593  1780   890   445  1336   668   334   167   502
   251   754   377  1132   566   283   850   425  1276   638
   319   958   479  1438   719  2158  1079  3238  1619  4858
  2429  7288  3644  1822   911  2734  1367  4102  2051  6154
  3077  9232  4616  2308  1154   577  1732   866   433  1300
   650   325   976   488   244   122    61   184    92    46
    23    70    35   106    53   160    80    40    20    10
     5    16     8     4     2     1
That sequence has 106 terms.
```

3.8 THE for STATEMENT

The for statement is the third kind of loop provided by C++. Its syntax is

   for (*initializer; condition; expression***)** *statement;*

The   initializer   executes first (and only then). Then the loop repeatedly evaluates the condition and, if it is true, executes the statement and then the expression.

EXAMPLE 3.21 Using a for Loop to Add the First 100 Squares

This code does the same as that in Example 3.16

```
int sum = 0;
for (int n=1; n <= 100; n++)
   sum += n*n;
cout << sum << endl;  // prints 338350
```

The `for` loop is more succinct than the `while` loop and the `do...while` loop; its three-part control mechanism includes the initialization, the continuation condition, and the update expression that have to be done separately in the other two loop forms.

Note that a variable may be declared within the `initializer` of a `for` loop. If so, ISO Standard C++ restricts the scope of the variable to the `statement` of the loop. The variable cannot be used outside of the loop:

```
for (int x=0; x<20; x++)
  cout << x*x + x + 41 << endl;
cout << x << endl;                   // ILLEGAL: x is out of scope!
```

Note that in many pre-Standard C++ compilers, this restriction is not observed.

3.9 THE `break` AND `continue` STATEMENTS

All three standard loop forms, the `while` loop, the `do...while` loop, and the `for` loop, evaluate their continuation condition only at the beginning or end of each iteration. If the body of the loop is a block of statements, the loop will execute them all before evaluating its control condition again. This inflexibility can be overridden with the `continue` and the `break` statements.

The `continue` statement terminates the current iteration without executing the rest of the statements in the loop block; control goes back immediately to the control condition to determine whether to terminate the loop itself or continue with the next iteration.

EXAMPLE 3.22 Using the `continue` Statement

```
int n =7;
for (int k=50; k<75; k++)
{ if (k%n == 0) continue;
  cout << k << " ";
}
cout << endl;
```

Here is the output from this code:

```
50 51 52 53 54 55 57 58 59 60 61 62 64 65 66 67 68 69 71 72 73 74
```

Note that the multiples of 7 (56, 73, and 7) are missing from the output. That is because when `k%7 == 0`, the `continue` statement skips over the remaining output statement in the body of the loop.

The `break` statement has the same effect as the continue statement inside a loop's block except that it not only skips the remainder of the current iteration but it also immediately terminates the loop itself, going immediately to the next statement that follows the loop.

EXAMPLE 3.23 Using the `break` Statement

```
int n =7;
for (int k=50; k<75; k++)
{ if (k%n == 0) break;
  cout << k << " ";
}
cout << endl;
```

Here is the output from this code:

```
50 51 52 53 54 55
```

This is the same as Example 3.22 except that the `break` statement immediately terminates the loop the first time that the condition `(k%7 == 0)` is true.

In some cases, it is easier to control loops entirely with `break` statements. In these cases, the built-in control condition is set to `true`, or simply omitted in `for` loops.

EXAMPLE 3.24 Controlling an Infinite `while` Loop

```
int n =4;
while (true)
{ cout << 1.0/n << '\t';
  if (n == 9) break;
  ++n;
}
cout << '\n' << n << endl;
```

The output is:

```
0.25     0.2      0.166667        0.142857       0.125    0.111111
9
```

On the sixth iteration, when `n` is 9, the loop prints `0.111111` and then terminates before incrementing `n` again. The control condition is `true`, so without the break statement the loop would iterate forever.

EXAMPLE 3.25 Controlling a "`forever`" Loop

```
int product=1, factor, count=0;
cout << "Enter factors. Terminate with 0: ";
for (;;)
{ cin >> factor;
  if (factor == 0) break;
  product *= factor;
  ++count;
}
cout << "The product of the " << count << " factors is "
     << product << endl;
```

Here is a sample run:

```
Enter factors. Terminate with 0: 3 5 7 9 0
The product of the 4 factors is 945
```

The `for(;;)` construct sets up an infinite loop, just like the `while (true)` form. In this example, the input value 0 is used as a sentinel. But since the inputs are used as multipliers, the 0 value should not be used after it is input. The `break` statement prevents the sentinel from being factored in or counted.

Bjarne Stroustrup suggests that the form `for(;;)` be pronounced "forever."

3.10 LOOP INVARIANTS

Loops are an essential part of any software system. They are also a major source of logical errors. Loop invariants are an effective strategy against these errors.

A *loop invariant* is an assertion about the variables in a loop that is intended to be true at the beginning of each iteration of the loop and after the loop has terminated.

EXAMPLE 3.26 Using a Loop Invariant

Here is some code that computes the power $y = x^n$:

```
double y = 1.0;
for (int i=0; i<n; i++)
    // INVARIANT: y == x*x*...*x (i times)
    y *= x;
```

The loop invariant is expressed as a comment at the beginning of the loop. It asserts that $y = x \cdot x \cdots x$ (*i* times). If that assertion is true at the end of the loop, then the code is correct: it does compute $y = x^n$. So to verify that the code really is correct, we need only check it against the loop invariant.

When the first iteration begins, y = 1 and $i = 0$, so the invariant $y = x \cdot x \cdots x$ (*i* times) is true. Next, if we assume that the invariant was true at the beginning of some (unspecified) iteration *i*, then we can deduce that it is also true at the beginning of the next iteration from the fact that during that iteration *y* was multiplied by *x* one more time. It follows then, by the *Principle of Mathematical Induction*, that the loop invariant is indeed true at the beginning of every iteration. This proves conclusively that the code is correct.

EXAMPLE 3.27 Multiplying in $O(\lg n)$ Time

The power function in Example 3.26 is implemented with the standard algorithm: to raise x to the power n, simply multiply x by itself n times. The following is a more efficient (but less obvious) method for computing the power function:

```
double y = 1.0, z = x;
int i = n;
while (i > 0)
  // INVARIANT: y*pow(z,i) == pow(x,n)
  if (i%2 == 0)   // i is even
  { z *= z;       // square z
    i /= 2;       // halve i
  }
  else            // i is odd
  { y *= z;
    --i;
  }
```

Here is a trace of the execution of this code in computing $y = 3^{10}$:

z	y	i	z^i	$y \cdot z^i$
3	1	10	59,049	59,049
9	1	5	59,049	59,049
9	9	4	6,561	59,049
81	9	2	6,561	59,049
6,561	9	1	6,561	59,049
6,561	59,049	0	1	59,049

When the loop ends, y = 59,049 = 2187 = 3^{10}.

The loop invariant is $y \cdot z^i = x^n$. This is discovered from the trace: $y \cdot z^i$ is always 59,049. We can use this to prove that the code is correct. If the invariant is true after the loop terminates, then $y = y \cdot 1 = y \cdot z^0 = y \cdot z^i = x^n$, since $i = 0$ at that time. When the loop begins, the invariant is true because $y = 1$, $z = x$, and $i = n$. To show that the invariant is true at the beginning of every iteration of the loop, we use mathematical induction again. Suppose that $y \cdot z^i = x^n$ at the beginning of some iteration. If i is even, then z will be squared and i will be halved on that iteration, so the equation $y \cdot z^i = x^n$ will still balance when that iteration has finished (because the value of $y \cdot z^i$ remains *invariant*). Similarly, if i is odd, then y will be multiplied once by x and i will be decremented once, so again $y \cdot z^i$ is invariant and the equation balances at the end of the iteration.

The symbol $O(\lg n)$ ("order $\lg n$") is used to describe this implementation of the power function because it has the property that its running time is proportional to the logarithm of the power n. Here, lg is the *binary logarithm* (base 2), which is the logarithm usually used in computer science. It is proportional to other logarithms.

3.11 NESTED LOOPS

A `for` statement (or a `while` statement or a `do..while` statement) can be used anywhere that a simple statement can be used, including inside another loop. Such combinations are called *nested loops*.

EXAMPLE 3.28 Printing a Multiplication Table

This program uses two nested `for` loops to print a multiplication table:

```
#include <iomanip>
#include <iostream>
using namespace std;
int main()
{ setiosflags(ios::right);
  int n;
  cout << "How many columns? (1-16): ";
  cin >> n;
  for (int x=1; x <= n; x++)
  { for (int y=1; y <= n; y++)
      cout << setw(5) << x*y;
    cout << endl;
  }
}
```

Here is a sample run:

```
How many columns? (1-16): 12
    1    2    3    4    5    6    7    8    9   10   11   12
    2    4    6    8   10   12   14   16   18   20   22   24
    3    6    9   12   15   18   21   24   27   30   33   36
    4    8   12   16   20   24   28   32   36   40   44   48
    5   10   15   20   25   30   35   40   45   50   55   60
    6   12   18   24   30   36   42   48   54   60   66   72
    7   14   21   28   35   42   49   56   63   70   77   84
    8   16   24   32   40   48   56   64   72   80   88   96
    9   18   27   36   45   54   63   72   81   90   99  108
   10   20   30   40   50   60   70   80   90  100  110  120
   11   22   33   44   55   66   77   88   99  110  121  132
   12   24   36   48   60   72   84   96  108  120  132  144
```

Note the essential block inside the outer loop. It contains two independent statements: the inner loop and the last `cout` statement. Each iteration of the outer loop prints one line.

When a `break` or `continue` statement is used in a nested loop, it interrupts only its closest containing loop; the outer loop(s) are unaffected.

EXAMPLE 3.29 Using a `break` Statement in a Nested Loop

```
for (int i=1; i<5; i++)
  for (int j=1; j<5; j++)
    for (int k=1; k<5; k++)
      if (i + j + k > 5) break;
      else cout << '\t' << i << '\t' << j << '\t' << k << endl;
```

The output is

```
        1       1       1
        1       1       2
        1       1       3
        1       2       1
        1       2       2
        1       3       1
        2       1       1
        2       1       2
        2       2       1
        3       1       1
```

Each time the sum `i + j + k` exceeds 5, the inner loop (controlled by `k`) terminates and the middle loop (controlled by `j`) begins a new iteration.

Review Questions

3.1   What is a compound statement?

3.2   What is scope of a variable?

3.3   What is a namespace?

3.4   What does a `using` directive do?

Problems

3.5   List by line number the scope of each variable declared in the following program. Then give its output:

```
int x = 22;                                      //  1
int main()                                       //  2
{ int y = 33;                                    //  3
  cout << x << " " << y << endl;                 //  4
  namespace local1                               //  5
  { int x = 44;                                  //  6
    int z = 55;                                  //  7
    cout << x << " " << y << " " << z << endl;   //  8
  }                                              //  9
  int x = 66;                                    // 10
  namespace local2                               // 11
  { int y = 77;                                  // 12
    int z = 88;                                  // 13
    cout << x << " " << y << " " << z << endl;   // 14
  }                                              // 15
  cout << x << " " << y << endl;                 // 16
}                                                // 17
```

3.6   In the following program, replace the comments with statements that perform the task:

```
int n = 33;
int main()
( int n = 55;
  namespace block1
  { int n = 77;
  }
  namespace block2
  { int n = 99;
  }
  // print the n whose value is 33
  // print the n whose value is 55
  // print the n whose value is 77
  // print the n whose value is 99
}
```

3.7   Find the error in each of the following code fragments:

a.   `if n < 0 cout << "n is negative\n";`

b.   `if (n < 0) cout << "n is negative\n"`
       `else cout << "n is non-negative\n";`

c.   `if (n < 0) cout << "n is negative\n";`
       `cout << "Is that ok?\n";`
       `else cout << "n is non-negative\n";`

    d.
```
if (n < 0) cout << "n < 0";
if (n == 0) cout << "n == 0";
else cout << "n > 0";
```

3.8 How many numbers will be printed in each of the following if the value of n is 22:

    a.
```
if (n < 20) cout << n << " ";
cout << 2*n << endl;
```
    b.
```
if (n > 20) cout << n << " ";
cout << 2*n << endl;
```
    c.
```
if (n < 20) cout << n << " ";
else cout << 2*n << " ";
cout << 3*n << endl;
```
    d.
```
if (n > 20)
{ cout << n << " ";
  cout << 2*n << " ";
}
else
{ cout << 3*n << " ";
  cout << 4*n << " ";
}
cout << -n << endl;
```

3.9 Find the error in each of the following loops:

    a.
```
while (n < 20);
    cout << n++ << endl;
```
    b.
```
for (int i=1, i <= 8, i++)
    cout << 1.0/i << endl;
```
    c.
```
int n =10;
do
    cout << 1.0/n;
    ++n;
while (n < 20);
```
    d.
```
for (int i=10; i<20; i--)
    cout << i*i << endl;
```

Programming Problems

3.10 A year is a leap year if it is divisible by 4 but not by 100 unless it is also divisible by 400. So the years 1996 and 2000 are leap years, but the years 1999 and 1900 are not. Write a program that inputs a year and prints whether it is a leap year.

3.11 Implement the quadratic formula to solve the quadratic equation $ax^2 + bx + c = 0$:

$$x = \frac{-b \pm \sqrt{b^2 - 4ac}}{2a}$$

Be sure to handle the special cases: where $a = 0$, where the two roots are equal, and where the discriminant $b^2 - 4ac$ is negative.

3.12 Write a program that inputs a day number of the year and prints the month and day of the month. Assume that the year is not a leap year.

3.13 Use the conditional expression operator to translate the following code into a single assignment statement:
```
if (x >= 0) sqrtx = sqrt(x);
else sqrtx = sqrt(-x);
```

3.14 Use `if...else` statements to remove the conditional expression operators from

```
sgn = ( x >= 0 ? ( x > 0 ? 1 : 0 ) : -1 );
```

3.15 The (integral) *binary logarithm* of a positive number is the number of times it can be divided in two until the result is less than 2. That is, lg x is the largest power of 2 that is ≤ x. For example, lg 4 = 2, lg 7.9 = 2, and lg 8 = 3. Write a program that inputs a number and then uses a `while` loop to find and print its binary logarithm.

3.16 Rewrite the following `while` loop as a `for` loop:

```
int i = 4;
while (i < 20)
{ cout << 1.0/i << endl;
  ++i;
}
```

3.17 Rewrite the following `for` loop as a `while` loop:

```
for (int j = 22; j > 8; j--)
   sum += log(j*j);
```

3.18 The program in Problem 2.24 on page 38 is prone to integer overflow. For example, if $n = 9$, the initialization

```
int round = int(x + 0.5);
```

fails because $x + 0.5 = 3{,}141{,}592{,}634.089793$, so that `int(x + 0.5)` = 3,141,592,634. The largest value for 32-bit integers is 2,147,483,647. Re-write this program so that it works for values $0 \le n \le 15$.

3.19 The sum of the first n positive integers $(1 + 2 + 3 + \cdots + n)$ is given by the formula:

$$\sum_{i=1}^{n} i = \frac{n(n+1)}{2}$$

Write a complete program that checks this formula by inputting n and then computing and comparing the values of both sides of this equation.

3.20 The sum of the first n squares $(1 + 4 + 9 + \cdots + n^2)$ is given by the formula

$$\sum_{i=1}^{n} i^2 = \frac{n(n+1)(2n+1)}{6}$$

Write a complete program that checks this formula by inputting n and then computing and comparing the values of both sides of this equation.

3.21 The sum of the first n cubes $(1 + 8 + 27 + ... + n^3)$ is given by the formula

$$\sum_{i=1}^{n} i^3 = \frac{n^2(n+1)^2}{4}$$

Write a complete program that checks this formula by inputting n and then computing and comparing the values of both sides of this equation.

3.22 The *factorial function* is defined by the formula $n! = 1 \cdot 2 \cdot 3 \cdot \ldots \cdot n$; that is, "$n$ factorial" is the product of the first n positive integers. For example, $5! = 120$ because $120 = 1 \cdot 2 \cdot 3 \cdot 4 \cdot 5$. Write a complete program that inputs n and then computes and prints the value of $n!$.

3.23 The *permutation function* is defined by the formula $p(n,k) = n(n-1)\cdots(n-k+1)$; that is, $p(n,k)$ is the product of the k largest integers that are ≤ n. For example, $p(11,4) = 11 \cdot 10 \cdot 9 \cdot 8 = 7920$. Write a complete program that inputs n and k and then computes and prints the value of $p(11,4)$.

3.24 The *combination function* is defined by the formula $c(n,k) = (n/1)((n-1)/2)\cdots((n-k+1)/k)$; that is, $c(n,k)$ is the product of the k ratios j/i, where j ranges from n down to $n-k+1$ and i ranges from 1 up to k. For example, $c(11,4) = (11/1)(10/2)(9/3)(8/4) = 11\cdot5\cdot3\cdot2 = 330$. Write a complete program that inputs n and k and then computes and prints the value of $c(11,4)$. (Note that $c(n,k)$ is always a positive integer.)

3.25 Write a complete program that inputs a positive integer n and then prints a triangle of asterisks n lines high and $2n - 1$ columns wide. For example, if the input is 5 then the output should be

```
    *
   ***
  *****
 *******
*********
```

3.26 Write a complete program that inputs a positive integer n and then prints a rectangle of asterisks n lines high and $2n$ columns wide. For example, if the input is 5 then the output should be

```
**********
*        *
*        *
*        *
**********
```

3.27 Write a complete program that implements the following algorithm that computes the greatest common divisor of two given positive integers. For example, if 441 and 252 are input, then the program should print that 63 is their greatest common divisor:

Algorithm 3.1 The Euclidean Algorithm
To find the greatest common divisor gcd of two positive integers m and n:
1. Subtract m from n repeatedly until $n < m$.
2. Interchange the values of m and n.
3. Repeat steps 1–2 until $m = 0$.
4. Then n is the greatest common divisor of the two original numbers.
This is Proposition 2 in Book VII of Euclid's *Elements*, written around 300 B.C.

3.28 The *Fibonacci numbers* are those in the sequence 0, 1, 1, 2, 3, 5, 8, ... in which each successive number is obtained by adding its two predecessors. Write a complete program that inputs a positive integer n and then prints the $n + 1$ Fibonacci numbers $f_0, f_1, f_2, ..., f_n$. For example, if 6 is input, then it would print 0, 1, 1, 2, 3, 5, 8.

3.29 The *golden mean* is defined to be the constant $\varphi = (1 + \sqrt{5})/2 = 1.61803...$. It is the solution to the ancient Greek mathematical question about where to divide a segment so that the ratio of the larger piece to the smaller piece is the same as the ratio of the original segment to the larger piece. The constant plays an important role in geometry, computer science, and art history. For example, each intersection of each line in the mystic pentagram is at the golden mean. Some important Renaissance artists used the ratio of the golden mean to achieve aesthetic balance in 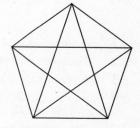 their paintings. The ratios of adjacent Fibonacci numbers converge to the golden mean. For example, $f_{10}/f_9 = 55/34 = 1.61765$, and $f_{14}/f_{13} = 377/233 = 1.61803$. Modify your solution to Problem 3.28 so that it also prints the ratios f_k/f_{k-1} for $k = 2, 3, ..., n$, and then print the decimal value of φ for comparison.

3.30 The *least squares method* discovered by Carl Friedrich Gauss (1777–1855) for interpolating data produces the following formulas for the *regression line* that best fits a given set of data points $\{(x_1, y_1), (x_2, y_2), (x_3, y_3), ..., (x_n, y_n)\}$:

$$s_x = \sum_{i=1}^{n} x_i$$

$$s_y = \sum_{i=1}^{n} y_i$$

$$s_{xx} = \sum_{i=1}^{n} x_i^2$$

$$s_{xy} = \sum_{i=1}^{n} x_i y_i$$

$$\bar{x} = \frac{s_x}{n}$$

$$\bar{y} = \frac{s_y}{n}$$

$$m = \frac{n \cdot s_{xy} - s_x \cdot s_y}{n \cdot s_{xx} - s_x \cdot s_y}$$

$$b = \bar{y} - m \cdot \bar{x}$$

Then the equation for the best fit regression line is $y = mx + b$. Write a complete program that inputs the number *n* of data point and then the *n* pairs of numbers x_i, y_i. It should then implement these formulas to obtain and print the regression line equation. Finally, it should ask the user to input other *x* values for which it will then use the equation to compute the corresponding predicted (interpolated) *y* values.

3.31 A loan is *amortized* by printing its schedule of periodic payments along with the remaining balance after each payment. Write a complete program that prints an amortization schedule for a given loan amount *a* at a given interest rate *r* and a given monthly payment *p*. Your program should input *a*, *n*, and *p*, and then print a series of lines, one for each monthly payment, showing the payment number and the remaining balance after that payment.

Solutions

3.1 A compound statement, also called a block, is a sequence of statements delimited by braces.

3.2 The scope of a variable is that part of the program where it may be used.

3.3 A namespace is a named block.

3.4 A using directive simply obviates the need for the scope resolution prefix in references to names outside of their scopes.

3.5 The scope of the x that is defined on line 1 is lines 1–5.
The scope of the y that is defined on line 3 is lines 3–11 and 16–17.
The scope of the x that is defined on line 6 is lines 6–9.
The scope of the z that is defined on line 7 is lines 7–9.
The scope of the x that is defined on line 10 is lines 10–17.
The scope of the y that is defined on line 12 is lines 12–15.
The scope of the z that is defined on line 13 is lines 13–15.

The output is
```
22 33
44 33 55
66 77 88
66 33
```

3.6
```
cout << ::n << endl;          // prints the n whose value is 33
cout << n << endl;            // prints the n whose value is 55
cout << block1::n << endl;    // prints the n whose value is 77
cout << block2::n << endl;    // prints the n whose value is 99
```

3.7 *a.* Syntax error: missing parentheses around the condition.

b. Syntax error: missing semicolon before the else.

c. Compile-time error: an independent statement cannot precede an else.

d. Logical error: the else is independent of the first condition, so the code will print both n > 0 and n < 0 if n is negative. Another else is needed, before the second if:
```
if (n < 0) cout << "n < 0";
else if (n == 0) cout << "n == 0";
else cout << "n > 0";
```

3.8 *a.* One: 44

b. Two: 22 44

c. Two: 44 66

d. Three: 22 44 -22

3.9 *a.* Logical error: the semicolon after the left parenthesis means that the loop statement is empty. That results in an *infinite loop* because the control variable n does not change.

b. Syntax error: the three parts of the for loop control must be separated by semicolons, not commas.

c. Compile-time error: only one statement or block is allowed between the do and the while.

d. Logical error: this is an infinite loop because i is decreasing and the control condition is i<20.

3.10
```
int main()
{ int n;
  cout << "Enter year: ";
  cin >> n;
  if (n % 400 == 0) cout << n << " is a leap year.\n";
  else if (n % 100 == 0) cout << n << " is a not leap year.\n";
  else if (n % 4 == 0) cout << n << " is a leap year.\n";
  else cout << n << " is a not leap year.\n";
}
```

3.11
```
int main()
{ double a, b, c;
  cout << "Enter the coefficients a, b, and c: ";
  cin >> a >> b >> c;
  if (a == 0)
    if (b == 0)
      if (c == 0) cout << "Every real number is a solution";
      else cout << "There are no solutions";
    else cout << "The unique solution is " << -c/b;
  else
  { double d = b*b - 4*a*c;
    if (d < 0) cout << "There are no real solutions";
    else if (d == 0) cout << "The unique solution is "<<-b/(2*a);
    else
    { double sqrtd = sqrt(d);
      double x1 = (-b + sqrtd)/(2*a);
      double x2 = (-b - sqrtd)/(2*a);
      cout << "The two solutions are " << x1 << " and " << x2;
    }
  }
  cout << endl;
}
```

3.12
```
        int main()
        { int day;
          cout << "Enter the day of the year (1-365): ";
          cin >> day;
          if (day < 32) cout << "January ";
          else
          { day -= 31;
            if (day < 29) cout << "February ";
            else
            { day -= 28;
              if (day < 32) cout << "March ";
              else
              { day -= 31;
                if (day < 31) cout << "April ";
                else
                { day -= 30;
                  if (day < 32) cout << "May ";
                  else
                  { day -= 31;
                    if (day < 31) cout << "June ";
                    else
                    { day -= 30;
                      if (day < 32) cout << "July ";
                      else
                      { day -= 31;
                        if (day < 32) cout << "August ";
                        else
                        { day -= 31;
                          if (day < 31) cout << "September ";
                          else
                          { day -= 30;
                            if (day < 32) cout << "October ";
                            else
                            { day -= 31;
                              if (day < 31) cout << "November ";
                              else
                              { day -= 30;
                                cout << "December ";
                              }
                            }
                          }
                        }
                      }
                    }
                  }
                }
              }
            }
          }
          cout << day << endl;
        }
```

3.13
```
        sqrt = ( x >= 0 ? sqrt(x) : sqrt(-x) );
```

3.14
```
        if (x > 0) sgn = 1;
        else if (x == 0) sgn = 0;
        else sgn = -1;
```

3.15
```
int main()
{ float x;
  int n=2;
  int lgx=0;
  cin >> x;
  while (n <= x)
  { n *= 2;
    ++lgx;
  }
  cout << "lg(" << x << ") = " << lgx << endl;
```

3.16
```
for(int i = 4; i < 20; i++)
  cout << 1.0/i << endl;
```

3.17
```
int j = 22;
while (j > 8)
{ sum += log(j*j);
  --j;
}
```

3.18
```
#include <iomanip>
#include <iostream>
#include <cmath>
using namespace std;
int main()
{ double x = 3.141592653589793;
  cout << setprecision(16) << x << endl;
  int n;
  cout << "Enter number of digits: ";
  cin >> n;
  if (n < 9)
  { x *= pow(10,n);
    int round = int(x + 0.5);
    x = double(round)/pow(10,n);
  }
  else                                  // e.g., n == 13
  { x *= pow(10,8);                      // x == 314,159,265.3589793
    int m = int(x);                      // m == 314,159,265
    double y = (x - m)*pow(10,n-8);      // y == 35897.93
    int round = int(y + 0.5);            // round = 35898
   y = double(m)*pow(10,n-8) + round;// y ==31,415,926,535,898.0
    x = y/pow(10,n);                     // x == 3.1415926535898
  }
  cout << x << endl;
}
```

3.19
```
int main()
{ int n, sum=0;
  cout << "Enter n: ";
  cin >> n;
  for (int i=1; i <= n; i++)
    sum += i;
  cout << "1 + 2 + 3 + ... + n = " << sum << endl;
  cout << "n*(n+1)/2          = " << n*(n+1)/2 << endl;
}
```

3.20
```
int main()
{ int n, sum=0;
  cout << "Enter n: ";
  cin >> n;
  for (int i=1; i <= n; i++)
    sum += i*i;
  cout << "1 + 4 + 9 + ... + n*n =  " << sum << endl;
  cout << "n*(n+1)*(2*n+1)/6     =  " <<n*(n+1)*(2*n+1)/6 <<endl;
}
```

3.21
```cpp
int main()
{ int n, sum=0;
  cout << "Enter n: ";
  cin >> n;
  for (int i=1; i <= n; i++)
    sum += i*i*i;
  cout << "1 + 8 + 27 + ... + n*n*n =  " << sum << endl;
  cout << "n*n*(n+1)*(n+1)/4      =  " <<n*n*(n+1)*(n+1)/4<<endl;
}
```

3.22
```cpp
int main()
{ int n, fact=1;
  cout << "Enter n: ";
  cin >> n;
  for (int i=2; i <= n; i++)
    fact *= i;
  cout << n << "! = 1*2*...*" << n << " = " << fact << endl;
```

3.23
```cpp
int main()
{ int n, k, perm=1;
  cout << "Enter n and k: ";
  cin >> n >> k;
  for (int i=1; i <= k; i++, n--)
    perm *= n;
  cout << "p(" << n+k << "," << k << ") = " << perm << endl;
}
```

3.24
```cpp
int main()
{ int n, k, comb=1;
  cout << "Enter n and k: ";
  cin >> n >> k;
  for (int i=1; i <= k; i++, n--)
    comb = comb*n/i;
  cout << "c(" << n+k << "," << k << ") = " << comb << endl;
}
```

3.25
```cpp
int main()
{ int n;
  cout << "How many lines? (1-40): ";
  cin >> n;
  for (int i=0; i<n; i++)            // i = number of lines printed
  { for (int j=1; j <= n + i; j++)    // j = current column number
      cout << (j < n - i ? ' ' : '*');   // print n - i - 1 blanks
    cout << endl;
  }
}
```

3.26
```cpp
int main()
{ int n;
  cout << "How many lines? (1-40): ";
  cin >> n;
  for (int i=0; i<n; i++)            // i = number of lines printed
  { for (int j=1; j <= 2*n; j++)     // j = current column number
      cout << (i > 0 && i < n-1 && j > 1 && j < 2*n ? ' ' : '*');
    cout << endl;
  }
}
```

3.27

```
int main()
{ int m, n, tmp, gcd;
  cout << "Enter two positive integers: ";
  cin >> m >> n;
  cout << "The greatest common divisor of " << m << " and " << n;
  do
  { while (m <= n)
      n -= m;
    tmp = m;
    m = n;
    n = tmp;
  } while (m > 0);
  cout << " is " << n << endl; }
```

3.28

```
int main()
{ int f0=0, f1=1, f2, n;
  cout << "How many Fibonacci numbers do you want? ";
  cin >> n;
  cout << "\tf1 = 1\n";
  for (int i=2; i <= n; i++)
  { f2 = f1 + f0;
    cout << "\tf" << i << " = " << f2 << endl;
    f0 = f1;
    f1 = f2;
  }
}
```

3.29

```
int main()
{ setiosflags(ios::right);
  cout.setf(ios::fixed, ios::floatfield);
  cout << setprecision(14);
  int f0=0, f1=1, f2, n;
  cout << "How many Fibonacci numbers do you want? ";
  cin >> n;
  cout << setw(8) << "f1 =" << setw(12) << "1\n";
  for (int i=2; i <= n; i++)
  { f2 = f1 + f0;
    cout << setw(5) << "f" << i << " ="
         << (i < 10 ? setw(11) : setw(10)) << f2
         << setw(9) << "f" << i << "/f" << i-1
                    << (i == 10 ? " " : "") << " = "
         << (i<10? setw(18): setw(16)) << double(f2)/f1 << endl;
    f0 = f1;
    f1 = f2;
  }
  double phi = (1 + sqrt(5))/2;
  cout << " The Golden Mean = (1 + sqrt(5))/2 = " << phi << endl;
}
```

3.30

```
int main()
{ double x, y, sumx=0.0, sumy=0.0, sumxx=0.0, sumxy=0.0;
  int n;
  cout << "How many data points do you have: ";
  cin >> n;
  cout << "Enter " << n << " pairs x and y:\n";
  setiosflags(ios::right);
  for (int i=1; i <= n; i++)
  { cout << setw(8) << i << ": ";
    cin >> x >> y;
    sumx += x;
    sumy += y;
    sumxx += x*x;
    sumxy += x*y;
  }
```

```
        double meanx = sumx/n;
        double meany = sumy/n;
        double m = (n*sumxy - sumx*sumy)/(n*sumxx - sumx*sumx);
        double b = meany - m*meanx;
        cout << "The equation of the Gaussian regression line is: y = "
            << m << "x + " << b << endl;
        char ans;
        cout << "Do you want to interpolate? (y/n): ";
        cin >> ans;
        if (ans == 'y' || ans == 'Y')
        { cout << "Enter x values, one per line.\n"
                << "Terminate input with <Ctrl-D>:\n";
          while (cin >> x)
            cout << "\ty = " << m*x +b << endl;
        }
    }
```

3.31
```
    int main()
    { float a;   // original amount of loan
      float r;   // interest rate; e.g., r = 0.06 for 6%
      float p;   // monthly payment
      int m=0;   // month number
      float x;   // remaining balance after m months
      cout << "Enter amount of loan (e.g., 10000.00): ";
      cin >> a;
      cout << "Enter annual interest rate (e.g., 0.06): ";
      cin >> r;
      r /= 12;  // convert r to a monthly rate
      cout << "Enter monthly payment (e.g., 350.00): ";
      cin >> p;
      x = a;
      while (x > 0.0)
      { cout << m << ".\t" << x << endl;
        x += r*x;  // add interest to remaining balance
        x -= p;    // subtract monthly payment
        ++m;
      }
    }
```

Chapter 4

Functions

A *function* is a subprogram that is executed by being *called* from within another function. Every C++ program must include a function named `main()`. That is where program execution begins.

A function is called by using its name as variables, as in

```
double y = sqrt(x);
```

or as an independent statement, as in

```
print(a, n);
```

Functions allows *program modularization* which is essential for good software development.

4.1 FUNCTION DECLARATIONS AND DEFINITIONS

Like a variable, a function must be declared before it is called. A *function declaration* has three parts: its return type, its name, and its parameter list. A function declaration should also include a comment that describes what the function does.

EXAMPLE 4.1 A Function Declaration

```
double power(double x, int n);
// PRECONDITION: x > 0
// Returns the value of x raised to the power n
```

Here, `double` is the return type, `power` is the name of the function, and `(double x, int n)` is its parameter list. This function has two parameters: `x` and `n`.

A function *parameter list* is a list of variable declarations enclosed in parentheses. The variables are called *parameters* (or *formal parameters*). The parameter list may be empty, but the enclosing parentheses are still required.

A function declaration is also called a *prototype*. It contains the minimal information that the compiler needs to compile code that uses the function. Consequently, the names of the parameters may be omitted, like this:

```
double power(double, int);
```

However, it is usually better to include the parameter names.

A *function definition* contains all the information needed to execute code that calls it: its header and its main block of executable statements.

EXAMPLE 4.2 A Function Definition

```
double power(double x, int n)
{ double y = 1.0;
  for (int i=0; i<n; i++)   // if n>0, return x*x*...*x (n times)
    y *= x;
  for (int i=0; i>n; i--)     // if n<0, return 1/(x*x*...*x) (n times)
    y /= x;
  return y;
}
```

Note that only one of the two loops will execute (or neither if n = 0).

If the function definition is given before it is called, then it does not need a separate declaration.

EXAMPLE 4.3 Declaring a Function with Its Definition

Here is a complete C++ program:

```
#include <iostream>
using namespace std;

double power(double x, int n)
{ double y = 1.0;
  for (int i=0; i<n; i++)  // if n > 0, return x*x*...*x (n times)
    y *= x;
  for (int i=0; i>n; i--)  //if n < 0, return 1/(x*x*...*x) (-n times)
    y /= x;
  return y;
}

int main()
{ cout << power(7.4, 3) << endl;
  cout << power(7.4, -3) << endl;
}
```

The output is

```
405.224
0.00246777
```

The alternative is to give only the function's declaration prior to the code from which it is called. In this case, the function definition is given elsewhere, either later in the file or in another file linked to the file that contains the code from which it is called.

EXAMPLE 4.4 Separating the Function Declaration from Its Definition

Here is another complete C++ program, equivalent to that in Example 4.3:

```
#include <iostream>
using namespace std;

double power(double x, int n);
// PRECONDITION: x > 0
// Returns the value of x raised to the power n

int main()
{ cout << power(7.4, 3) << endl;
  cout << power(7.4, -3) << endl;
}

double power(double x, int n)
{ double y = 1.0;
  for (int i=0; i<n; i++) // if n > 0, return x*x*...*x (n times)
    y *= x;
  for (int i=0; i>n; i--) // if n < 0, return 1/(x*x*...*x) (-n times)
    y /= x;
  return y;
}
```

The parameter names may be omitted from a function declaration (but not from its definition). For example, `double power(double, int);` is a valid declaration. The only purpose of the declaration is to provide the compiler with the information it needs to compile calls to the function.

The `return` statement in a function specifies the value to be returned to point where the function was called. In Example 4.4, the statement `return y;` terminates the execution of the function and returns the value of `y` (61043.7) to the `cout` statement in `main()` where the function was called.

Note that the `main()` function itself has a return statement. Its return type is `int`, so we usually simply return 0. The value returned can be used by the operating system after the program has terminated.

A function may have several `return` statements. Although it is usually best to place one at the end of the function definition, a `return` statement can be placed anywhere.

EXAMPLE 4.5 A Function with More than One `return` Statement

```
int factorial(int n)
// Returns n! = n*(n-1)*(n-1)*...*2*1
{ assert(n >= 0);
  if (n < 2) return 1;  // 0! = 1 and 1! = 1
  int f = 1;
  while (n > 1)
    f *= n--;
  return f;
}
```

The condition `(n < 2)` in the `if` statement will be true only if the value of `n` is 0 or 1, and in both of those two special cases the factorial function should return 1. The function would be correct without the `if` statement, because in those two special cases the `while` loop will be skipped and the return value of `f` is 1. But the separate `return` statement within the `if` statement makes the function more efficient, because in the two special (and not uncommon) cases it avoids the declaration of the local variable `f` and the evaluation of the condition `(n > 1)`.

4.2 `void` FUNCTIONS

A `void` function is a function whose return type is `void`. This means that it returns no value. It may have one or more `return` statements, but they must have the simpler form: `return;`

EXAMPLE 4.6 A `void` Function

This `void` function has no `return` statements:

```
void print_literal_digit(int n)
//   Prints the digit n in literal form.
//   EXAMPLE: print_literal_digit(7) would print "seven".
//   PRECONDITION: n >= 0 && n <= 9
{ assert(n >= 0 && n <= 9);
  if (n == 0) cout << "zero";
  else if (n == 1) cout << "one";
  else if (n == 2) cout << "two";
  else if (n == 3) cout << "three";
  else if (n == 4) cout << "four";
  else if (n == 5) cout << "five";
  else if (n == 6) cout << "six";
  else if (n == 7) cout << "seven";
  else if (n == 8) cout << "eight";
  else cout << "nine";
}
```

A `void` function is called by using its name as an executable statement. The function that is defined in Example 4.6 could be called like this:

```
int main()
{ print_literal_digit(7);
}
```

Since the function name is used like an independent C++ statement, it is usually helpful to use a verb phrase for the name of a `void` function.

4.3 TRACING A FUNCTION

It is wise to *trace* a function to ensure that it works properly. This means to track through the execution of calls to the function, executing its statements by hand (or with the aid of a calculator) to check the correctness of its logic. Each value of each variable should be shown.

EXAMPLE 4.7 Tracing a Function

Here is a trace of the call `power(4.0, 5)`:

x	n	i	y
4.0	5		1.0
		0	4.0
		1	16.0
		2	64.0
		3	256.0
		4	1024.0
		5	

The function returns 1024.0, which is the correct value for 4.0^5.

Here is a trace of the call `power(4.0, -3)`:

x	n	i	y
4.0	3		1.0
		0	0.25
		1	0.0625
		2	0.015625
		3	

The function returns 0.015625, which is the correct value for $4.0^{-3} = 1/64$.

Here is a trace of the call `power(4.0, 0)`:

x	n	i	y
4.0	3		1.0
		0	

The function returns 1.0, which is the correct value for any positive number raised to the power 0.

4.4 TEST DRIVERS

A *test driver* is a complete program whose sole purpose is to test a function. It should be short, simple, obvious, and easy to use.

EXAMPLE 4.8 A Test Driver for the `power()` FUNCTION

```
main()
{ double x;
  int n = 1;
  while (n != 0)
  { cin >> x >> n;
    cout << "power(" << x << "," << n << ")= " << power(x, n) << endl;
  }
  return 0;
}
```

Note how Spartan this program is. It has no documentation (comments) or user prompts. Those features are important in ordinary (long-lived) programs. But test drivers are only temporary programs. They are used only by the function's creator and only long enough to test the function.

A thorough testing with this driver might look like this:

```
4.0 5
power(4,5)= 1024
4.0 -3
power(4,-3)= 0.015625
10 100
power(10,100)= 1e+100
100 10
power(100,10)= 1e+20
100 -10
power(100,-10)= 1e-20
10 -100
power(10,-100)= 1e-100
1 100
power(1,100)= 1
1 -100
power(1,-100)= 1
100 1
power(100,1)= 100
100 -1
power(100,-1)= 0.01
12345 1
power(12345,1)= 12345
12345 0
power(12345,0)= 1
```

The best strategy is to choose input values whose output is predictable. For example, the call `power(13579.08642, 28)` is just as good as `power(100, 10)` for checking the function's logic; but it is a bad choice because its output is not predictable (even with a good calculator!).

It is also important to try to test all the different cases and "boundary conditions" of a function. For example, the three obvious cases `n > 0`, `n == 0`, and `n < 0` for the `power()` function should be tested. Also, the special case `x == 1` should be tested.

Testing a function is a difficult art. You can never prove that a (non-trivial) function is correct just by testing it. But extensive testing is usually the best way to discover logical errors before the function is used in software development.

4.5 USING THE `assert()` FUNCTION TO CHECK PRECONDITIONS

Most function do not work properly on all possible values of their parameters. Restrictions on these parameter values are called *preconditions*. These preconditions should be listed clearly in comments that accompany the function's declaration. But those comments won't help prevent improper values from being passed to the function.

One simple but effective method for handling illegal parameter values is to use the standard `assert()` function to check preconditions. This function is defined in the `<assert>` header file. The function is used by passing the precondition to it as a `bool` expression. When the function is called, it evaluates the expression. If it evaluates to `false`, then the function aborts the program and prints a message reporting that the assertion failed.

EXAMPLE 4.9 Using `assert()` to Check Preconditions

```
#include <assert>

double power(double x, int n)
{ assert(x > 0);
  double y = 1.0;
  for (int i=0; i<n; i++) // if n > 0, return x*x*...*x (n times)
    y *= x;
  for (int i=0; i>n; i--) // if n < 0, return 1/(x*x*...*x) (-n times)
    y /= x;
  return y;
}
```

Here is what happens on a UNIX system when the precondition is violated:

```
-4.0 5
ex0407.cc:10: failed assertion 'x > 0'
IOT trap
```

The value -4.0 was input for `x`. The first line of output reports that the assertion failed at line 10 in the program whose source code is in the file `ex0407.cc`. The second line simply classifies the abortion as an "IOT trap".

Technically, `assert` is a *parametrized macro*. Unlike a real function that gets compiled, a macro works more like an `include` directive. The compiler actually replaces the expression that uses its name with other code defined in the `<assert>` file, and then that code gets compiled. This replacement process is called *expanding* the macro.

4.6 PREDICATES

A *predicate* is a boolean function; *i.e.*, a function whose return type is `bool`. It is used to test some condition about its arguments.

EXAMPLE 4.10 The Predicate `is_prime()` Function

This function tests the condition that its argument is a prime number:

```
bool is_prime(int n)
// Returns true iff n has no divisors except 1 and itself
{ assert(n > 0);
  if (n == 1) return false;
  if (n == 2) return true;          // 2 is the first prime
  if (n % 2 == 0) return false;     // 2 is the only even prime
  for (int d=3; d<n; d += 2)        // look for an odd divisor
    if (n % d == 0) return false;
  return true;                      // no odd divisors were found
}
```

Here is a test driver for the `is_prime()` function:

```
int main()
{ int n = 2;
  while (n != 1)
  { cin >> n;
    if (is_prime(n)) cout << n << " is prime\n";
    else cout << n << " is not prime\n";
  }
  return 0;
}
```

The symbol "iff" stands for "if and only if." We use it to describe boolean functions. For example, here it means that the function returns `true` if n has no nontrivial divisors *and* it returns `false` if n *does* have some nontrivial divisor.

Comments are often essential for the understanding of a block of code. But the programmer should strive to make his or her code *self-documenting*. This means to choose programming structures that clarify the underlying logic and to choose names that describe what the things being named represent. In the case of function names, it is usually best to use only noun phrases for non-void functions, use only verb phrases for void functions, and use only predicate phrases for boolean functions:

```
double power(double x, int n);     // "power" is a noun
void print_literal_digit(int n);   // "print" is a verb
bool is_prime(int n);              // "is prime" is a predicate
```

4.7 DEFAULT ARGUMENTS

The expressions listed between the parentheses in a function call are called *arguments* (or *actual parameters*). For example, 4 and 5 are the arguments in the call `power(4, 5)`.

It is possible to define default values for some or all of the arguments simply by specifying those values as initializations in the function's parameter list. In computer science, the word *default* means a value that is used by the system when a specific value is not given. So a *default argument* is a value that is assigned to a parameter in place of a missing argument in a function call.

EXAMPLE 4.11 Specifying Default Arguments

```
double power(double x=1.0, int n=2)
{ assert(x > 0);
  double y = 1.0;
  for (int i=0; i<n; i++) // if n > 0, return x*x*...*x (n times)
    y *= x;
  for (int i=0; i>n; i--) // if n < 0, return 1/(x*x*...*x) (-n times)
    y /= x;
  return y;
}
```

Here, the parameter x is given the default argument 1.0, and the parameter n is given the default argument 2. Then the function could be called like this:

```
cout << power(7.4, 3) << endl;
cout << power(7.4) << endl;
cout << power() << endl;
```

The output from these three calls would be

```
405.224
54.76
1
```

These are the correct values for 7.4^3, 7.4^2, and 1.0^2.

Note that all, some, or none of the default arguments may be used in a function call. If fewer arguments than parameters are passed, then the system matches the given arguments with the parameters one-to-one, scanning left-to-right. When it runs out of arguments, it uses the default values for the remaining parameters.

A function may define default arguments for all, some, or none of its parameters. The only rule is that, to be consistent with the process described above, the parameters with default values must follow those without default values in the parameter list.

4.8 PASSING BY `const` VALUE, BY REFERENCE, AND `const` REFERENCE

There are four different ways that an argument can be passed to a parameter in a function call: by value, by `const` value, by reference, and by `const` reference. These distinct methods are determined by the function's parameter list, by preceding the parameters type with the `const` keyword and/or by preceding the parameter's name with the reference symbol `&`:

```
void f1(int x);         // x is a value parameter
void f2(const int x);   // x is a const value parameter
void f3(int& x);        // x is a reference parameter
void f4(const int& x);  // x is a const reference parameter
```

Passing an argument by value is the simplest and most common method. In this case, the parameter is a separate local variable that exists only during the execution of the function. The call `f1(u);` to the first function declared will copy the value of the argument `u` into the parameter `x`. Then, any changes made to `x` during the execution of the function will have no effect upon the variable `u`. Note that since this method only uses the value of the argument, it could be a constant or even a general expression. For example, `f1(44)` and `f1(2*u - 3*v)` would be valid calls.

Passing an argument by `const` value is the same as passing it by value except that the `const` keyword makes the parameter a constant, prohibiting the function from changing its value. This is the kind of restriction that good programmers often force upon themselves to prevent coding errors. If you don't want your function to change its parameter value, then make it a constant. That tells the compiler to "keep you honest." It will alert you if you accidentally code a change.

EXAMPLE 4.12 Passing by `const` Value

```
void f2(const int x)   // x is a const value parameter
{ cout << "The value of the const parameter x is " << x << endl;
}

int main()
{ f2(44);            // passing a constant
  int u = 55;
  f2(u);             // passing a variable
  int v = 33;
  f2(2*u - 3*v);     // passing an expression
  return 0;
}
```
The output is
```
The value of the const parameter x is 44
The value of the const parameter x is 55
The value of the const parameter x is 11
```

Passing an argument *by reference* allows the function to change the value of the argument. That is because the function's parameter is only a synonym (another name) for the existing argument.

EXAMPLE 4.13 Passing by Reference

```
void f3(int& x)  // x is a reference parameter
{ x *= 3;
}
```

The function triples the value of x. But x is just a synonym or "alias" for the argument passed to it, so the effect of the function is to triple the value of its argument.

```
int main()
{ int u = 33;
  f3(u);
  cout << u << endl;
  return 0;
}
```

The output from this program is

```
99
```

Here is a diagram to help explain the relationship between the argument u and the parameter x:

The parameter x   does not have its own storage area; it is just another name for the variable u. So when the statement x *= 3 executes, it triples the value of u.

Note that an argument that is passed by reference must be an actual variable. It is not possible to pass a constant or an expression by reference. That should seem reasonable because constants and expressions are read-only; values cannot be assigned to them. So only the second of the three calls made to f2() in Example 4.12 would be possible to f3().

Passing an argument *by constant reference* is the same as passing it by reference except that the function is prohibited from changing its value. This may seem like a contradiction since the purpose of passing an argument by reference is often to change its value. However, there are other situations when the purpose is simply to avoid duplicating the argument (which is what happens when it is passed by value). That is the situation when the argument is a large object.

EXAMPLE 4.14 Passing by `const` Reference

```
void f4(const int& x)  // x is a const reference parameter
{ cout << x << endl;
}
```

The reference here is not essential for the function to work properly.

When one system accesses a storage area of another system, there are three general modes of access: read-only, write-only, and read-write. The accessor is called the *client* and the provider is called the *server*. For example, if we think of the computer's processor as a client and its input-output devices as servers, then the keyboard is a read-only device, the hard disk is a read-write device, and the printer is a write-only device. We can also think of the main() function as a server and a

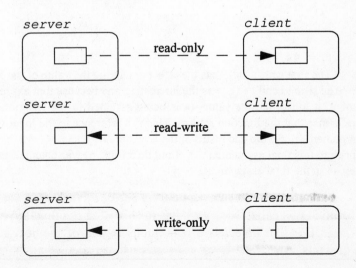

function that it calls as its client. In that context, we can see that a function's value parameters are read-only, its function return value is write-only, and its reference parameters are read-write. In other programming languages (namely, Ada), these are called *in parameters, out parameters,* and *in-out parameters.*

4.9 RETURNING BY REFERENCE

Non-`void` functions usually return by value. Like passing by value, this means that a copy of an existing variable or expression is returned. But like arguments, returns can also be made by reference. The advantage is the same: it avoids duplicating an object.

EXAMPLE 4.15 Returning a Reference

This function triples x and then returns it by reference:

```
int& f(int& x)
{ cout << "x = " << x << endl;
  x *= 3;
  cout << "x = " << x << endl;
  return x;
}
```

Note that the local variable x is a synonym for whatever argument is passed to the function.

Here is a test driver:

```
int main()
{ int m = 11;
  cout << "m = " << m << endl;
  int n = f(m);
  cout << "m = " << m << endl;
  cout << "n = " << n << endl;
  f(n) = 44;
  cout << "n = " << n << endl;
}
```

The output is

```
m = 11
x = 11
x = 33
m = 33
n = 33
x = 33
x = 99
n = 44
```

The first call f(m) has the effect of tripling the value of m from 11 to 33. That value is then assigned to n. The second call f(n) is the interesting one because that expression is placed on the <u>left</u> side of an assignment: it looks like the value 44 is being assigned to the function call. Actually, 44 is being assigned to the reference that the function returns. That is a reference to the local variable x, which itself is a reference to the argument n. So the end result of the assignment f(n) = 44 is to change the value of n to 44. Note that, prior to this final assignment, x (and therefore n) was changed from 33 to 99. But that value is then replaced by 44 in the final assignment f(n) = 44.

Note that if a function returns an object by reference, it must be an object that existed before the function was called because it has to exist after the function has returned.

In C++, an *object* is a contiguous region of memory. The simplest objects are variables and constants. An *lvalue* is an expression that refers to an object. The simplest lvalues are names of variables and constants. The expression $f(n)$ in Example 4.15 is an lvalue. It refers to the object named n. The term "lvalue" originally meant "anything that can be on the left side of an assignment." But that definition no longer applies because an lvalue can refer to a constant. An lvalue that can be on the left side of an assignment is now called a *modifiable lvalue*.

4.10 OVERLOADING A FUNCTION NAME

C++ allows different functions to have the same name. This is called *overloading*. The only requirement is that they have different parameter lists; *i.e.*, either a different number of parameters or different types in at least one parameter slot.

EXAMPLE 4.16 Overloading the `swap()` Function

Here are two different functions, both named `swap()`:

```
void swap(int& x, int& y)
{ int temp = x;
  x = y;
  y = temp;
}
void swap(float& x, float& y)
{ float temp = x;
  x = y;
  y = temp;
}
```

Here is a test driver:

```
int main()
{ int m=22, n=44;
  cout << "m = " << m << ", n = " << n << endl;
  swap(m, n);
  cout << "m = " << m << ", n = " << n << endl;
  float s=2.2, t=4.4;
  cout << "s = " << s << ", t = " << t << endl;
  swap(s, t);
  cout << "s = " << s << ", t = " << t << endl;
}
```

Here is the output:

```
m = 22, n = 44
m = 44, n = 22
s = 2.2, t = 4.4
s = 4.4, t = 2.2
```

The purpose of each function is simply to interchange the values of the two arguments passed (by reference). But the types of the arguments must match the types of the parameters, so being able both to swap integers and to swap floats requires two separate functions. Overloading simply allows us to use the same name `swap()` for both of them.

Note that the fact that these two functions perform the same operations is irrelevant to the issue of overloading, as are the facts that they are `void` functions and that they use reference parameters.

EXAMPLE 4.17 Overloading Different Functions

Here are three very different functions that overload the name `f()`:

```
void f(char c)
{ c = (c >= 'a' && c <= 'z' ? c - 'a' + 'A' : c);
  cout.put(c);
}
int f(int n)
{ return (n%2 == 0 ? n/2 : 3*n + 1);
}
float f(float x, float y, float z)
{ y = (y > x ? y : x);
  return (z > y ? z : y);
}
```

This overloading doesn't make much sense. It simply illustrates how different overloaded functions can be.

Review Questions

4.1 Does a function have to be declared before it is called?

4.2 What is the difference between a function declaration and a function definition?

4.3 What is a function prototype?

4.4 How many return statements can a function have?

4.5 Does a function have to return a value?

4.6 What is the difference between a value parameter and a reference parameter?

4.7 What is the difference between a `const` parameter and a non-`const` parameter?

4.8 What is the difference between returning by value and returning by reference?

4.9 What is wrong with the following version of the `swap()` function:

```
void swap(int x, int y)
{ int temp = x;
  x = y;
  y = temp;
}
```

4.10 What is wrong with the following version of the `swap()` function:

```
void swap(int& x, int& y)
{ x = y;
  y = x;
}
```

Problems

4.11 Trace the call `power(2, 5)` to the function defined in Example 4.2 on page 67.

4.12 Trace the call `factorial(5)` to the function defined in Example 4.5 on page 69.

4.13 Trace the call `is_prime(121)` to the function defined in Example 4.10 on page 72.

4.14 Trace the call `swap(m, n)` to the first function defined in Example 4.16 on page 77, assuming that the original values of `m` and `n` are 44 and 88, respectively.

Programming Problems

4.15   Implement the following function and test it with a test driver:
```
float mean(float x, float y, float z);
//   Returns the mean average of x, y, and z.
//   EXAMPLE: mean(4, 7, 4) returns 5.0;
```

4.16   Implement the following function and test it with a test driver:
```
float min(float x, float y, float z);
//   Returns the smallest of x, y, and z.
//   EXAMPLE: min(4, 7, 4) returns 4.0;
```

4.17   Implement the following function and test it with a test driver:
```
float median(float x, float y, float z);
//   Returns the middle number among x, y, and z.
//   EXAMPLE: median(4, 7, 4) returns 4.0;
```

4.18   Implement the Babylonian Algorithm (Algorithm 1.1 on page 1) as modified in Problem 1.20 on page 14:
```
double sqrt(double x);
//   Returns the square root of x.
//   PRECONDITION: x >= 0.
//   EXAMPLE: sqrt(49.0) returns 7.0;
```

4.19   Implement Algorithm 1.2 on page 5 to convert binary numerals to decimal:
```
int decimal(int b);
//   Returns the decimal numeral whose value equals that
//   represented in the binary form b.
//   PRECONDITION: each digit of b is a bit: 0 or 1
//   EXAMPLE: decimal(10001011) returns 139
```

4.20   Implement Algorithm 1.4 on page 6 to convert decimal numerals to binary:
```
int binary(int n);
//   Returns the binary numeral that represents n.
//   PRECONDITION: n >= 0
//   POSTCONDITION: each digit of the integer returned is a bit
//   EXAMPLE: binary(139) returns 10001011
```

4.21   Implement the following function which uses Horner's method (see Problem 1.34 on page 14) to evaluate the polynomial $2x^5 - 7x^4 + 6x^3 + 9x^2 + 8x - 5$:
```
double p(double x);
//   Returns 2x^5 - 7x^4 + 6x^3 + 9x^2 + 8x - 5.
//   EXAMPLE: p(4.1) returns 931.70732
```

4.22   Using only subtraction, implement the following function which returns the remainder from integer division:
```
int mod(int n, int d);
//   Returns n%d.
//   PRECONDITION: n >= d > 0
//   POSTCONDITION: (n/d)*d + r == n, where r is returned
//   EXAMPLE: mod(44, 7) returns 2
```

4.23   Implement the quadratic formula. (See Problem 3.11 on page 57):
```
int solutions(float& x1, float& x2, float a, float b, float c);
//   Modifies x1 and x2 so that they are the solutions to the
//   equation a*x*x + b*x + c == 0, and then returns either 0, 1,
//   2, or 3, according to whether the number of distinct
//   solutions is 0, 1, 2, or infinite.
//   POSTCONDITION: if 1 is returned, then x1 is the unique sol'n;
//      if 2 is returned, then x1 and x2 are the distinct sol'ns
//   EXAMPLE: solutions(x1, x2, 1, 6, 9) returns 1 with x1 == -3.0
```

4.24 Implement the solution to Problem 2.18 on page 38 as the function:

```
float centimeters(float x);
//   Returns the number of centimeters in x inches.
//   PRECONDITION: x > 0
//   POSTCONDITION: the returned value y == 2.54*x
//   EXAMPLE: centimeters(200) returns 508.0
```

4.25 Implement the solution to Problem 2.19 on page 38 as the function:

```
float celsius(float x);
//   Returns the temperature in Celsius degrees for a given
//   temperature in Farenheit degrees.
//   PRECONDITION: x >= -273.0
//   POSTCONDITION: the returned value y == 5*(x - 32)/9
//   EXAMPLE: celsius(68) returns 20.0
```

4.26 Implement the solution to Problem 2.21 on page 38 as the function:

```
void convert(int& weeks, int& days, int& hours, int x);
//   Modifies weeks, days, and hours so that they represent the
//   same time duration as x hours.
//   PRECONDITION: x >= 0
//   POSTCONDITION: (7*weeks + days)*24 + hours == x
//   EXAMPLE: convert(w, d, h, 4000) makes w = 23, d = 5, h = 16
```

4.27 Implement the solution to Problem 2.23 on page 38 as the function:

```
void reverse(int& n);
//   Reverses the digits of n.
//   PRECONDITION: 100,000 <= n <= 999,999
//   EXAMPLE: if n == 289405, reverse(n) makes n == 504982
```

4.28 Implement Example 3.20 on page 50 as the function:

```
void print(int n);
//   Prints the sequence of numbers n, n1, n2, ..., 1, where the
//   successor of each n > 1 is either n/2 or 3*n + 1 depending on
//   whether n is even or odd.
//   PRECONDITION: n > 0
//   EXAMPLE: print(3) prints 3, 10, 5, 16, 8, 4, 2, 1
```

4.29 Implement Example 3.27 on page 54 as the function:

```
double power(double x, int n);
//   Returns x^n; i.e., x raised to the nth power.
//   PRECONDITION: x > 0
//   EXAMPLE: power(2.01, 3) return 8.120601
```

4.30 Implement the solution to Problem 3.12 on page 57 as the function:

```
void print_date(int n);
//   Prints the month and day of the month for the year day n,
//   assuming that the year is not a leap year.
//   PRECONDITION: 1 <= n <= 365
//   EXAMPLE: print_date(65) prints: March 6
```

4.31 Implement the integer binary logarithm function. (See Problem 3.15 on page 58.):

```
int lg(int n);
//   Returns the number of times n can be divided by 2.
//   PRECONDITION: n > 0
//   POSTCONDITION: 2^p <= n < 2^(p+1), where p is returned
//   EXAMPLE: lg(100) returns 6
```

4.32 Implement the Euclidean Algorithm (Algorithm 3.1 on page 59) as the function:

```
int gcd(int m, int n);
//   Returns the greatest common divisor of m and n.
//   PRECONDITIONS: m > 0, n > 0
//   POSTCONDITIONS: g is a factor of both m and n, and no x > g
//      is a factor of both m and n
//   EXAMPLE: gcd(252, 441) returns 63
```

4.33   Implement the solution to Problem 3.19 on page 58 as the function:

```
int sum(int n);
//   Returns the sum of the first n positive integers.
//   PRECONDITION: n > 0
//   EXAMPLE: sum(10) returns 55
```

4.34   Implement the solution to Problem 3.20 on page 58 as the function:

```
int sum(int n);
//   Returns the sum of the first n squares.
//   PRECONDITION: n > 0
//   EXAMPLE: sum(10) returns 385
```

4.35   Implement the solution to Problem 3.20 on page 58 as the function:

```
int sum(int n);
//   Returns the sum of the first n cubes.
//   PRECONDITION: n > 0
//   EXAMPLE: sum(10) returns 3025
```

4.36   Implement the solution to Problem 3.20 on page 58 as the function:

```
int fact(int n);
//   Returns n factorial: n! = 1*2*3*...*n.
//   PRECONDITION: 0 <= n <= 12 (to avoid integer overflow)
//   EXAMPLE: fact(5) returns 120
```

4.37   Implement the solution to Problem 3.20 on page 58 as the function:

```
int perm(int n, int k);
//   Returns the number of permutations of size k from a set of
//   n elements.
//   PRECONDITION: 0 <= k <= n <= 12
//   EXAMPLE: perm(11, 4) returns 7920
```

4.38   Implement the solution to Problem 3.24 on page 59 as the function:

```
int comb(int n, int k);
//   Returns the number of combinations (subsets) of size k from
//   a set of n elements.
//   PRECONDITION: 0 <= k <= n <= 33
//   EXAMPLE: perm(11, 4) returns 330
```

4.39   Implement the Fibonacci function. (See Problem 3.28 on page 59.):

```
int fib(int n);
//   Returns the nth Fibonacci number.
//   PRECONDITION: 0 <= n <= 46
//   EXAMPLE: fib(10) returns 55
```

4.40   Implement the solution to Problem 3.31 on page 60 as the function:

```
void amortize(float a, float r, float p);
//   Prints the amortization schedule for a loan of an amount a,
//   with an interest rate r, and a monthly payment of p.
//   PRECONDITIONS: 0 < r < 1.0, 0.0 < p <= a
```

4.41   Implement the function:

```
bool is_prime_divisor(int d, int n);
//   Returns true iff d is a prime divisor of n.
//   PRECONDITION: 2 <= d <= n
//   EXAMPLE: is_prime_divisor(7, 350) returns true because 7 is a
//      prime number and a divisor of 350
```

Hint: use the `is_prime()` function from Example 4.10 on page 72.

4.42   Implement the function:

```
void print_dollars(float x);
//   Prints x in literal form as a dollar amount.
//   PRECONDITION: x >= 0.00 && x < 1000.00
//   EXAMPLE: print_dollars(123.45) would print
//      one hundred twenty-three dollars and 45 cents
```

Hint: use the `print_literal_digit()` function from Example 4.6 on page 69.

Solutions

4.1 Yes, a function must be declared before it is called. However, its complete definition also serves as its declaration, so if it is defined before it is called, then it does not need a separate declaration.

4.2 A function declaration consists of only its header: its return type, its name, and its parameter list. A function definition contains all the information about the function: its header and its body block of executable statement.

4.3 A function prototype is its declaration. It may omit the names of its parameters.

4.4 A non-`void` function must have at least one `return` statement and may have more. The required `main()` function (whose return type is `int`) is an exception: Standard C++ does not require it to have a `return` statement. A `void` function does not have to have a `return` statement, although it may have several.

4.5 Each `return` statement in a non-`void` function must return a value of the same type as the function's declared return type. Each `return` statement in a `void` function must not return a value.

4.6 A value parameter is a copy of the argument passed to it. A reference parameter is simply another name for the argument passed to it. So an argument passed to a reference parameter must be a named object, whereas an argument passed to a value parameter may be a literal or an expression.

4.7 A `const` parameter is constant: the function cannot change its value. It can change the value of a non-`const` parameter.

4.8 When a function returns by value (the most common method), it sends a copy of the expression returned to the point in the previous function where it was called. When a function returns by reference, the function call expression itself becomes a synonym for the object to which it refers. That object must exist after the function returns, so it cannot be local to the returning function.

4.9 The parameters `x` and `y` are passed by value, so the function will have no effect upon the arguments passed to it.

4.10 It takes three steps to interchange two values. This two-step version assigns the value of `y` to `x` without first saving the value of `x` first, so that the original `x`-value is lost.

4.11 Trace of the call `power(2, 5)`:

i	y
	1.0
0	2.0
1	4.0
2	8.0
3	16.0
4	32.0
5	

4.12 Trace of the call `factorial(5)`:

f	n
1	5
5	4
20	3
60	2
120	1

4.13 Trace of the call `is_prime(121)`:

d	n%d
3	1
5	14
7	2
960	4
11	0

4.14 Trace of the call `swap(m, n)`:

4.15
```
float mean(float x, float y, float z)
{ return (x + y + z)/3;
}
```

4.16
```
float min(float x, float y, float z)
{ if (x < y) y = x;
  if (y < z) z = y;
  return z;
}
```

4.17
```
float median(float x, float y, float z)
{ if (x <= y && y <= z || z <= y && y <= x) return y;
  if (x <= z && z <= y || y <= z && z <= x) return z;
  return x;
}
```

4.18
```
double sqrt(double x)
{ assert(x >= 0);
  double y = 1.0, z, r;
  do
  { z = x/y;
    y = (y + z)/2;
    r = (y - z)/y;          // signed relative error
    r = (r < 0 ? -r : r);   // unsigned relative error
  } while (r > 5e-13);       // for 12-digit precision
  return y;
}
```

4.19
```
int decimal(int b)
{ int b0 = b%10;  assert(b0 == 0 || b0 == 1);  b /= 10;
  int b1 = b%10;  assert(b1 == 0 || b1 == 1);  b /= 10;
  int b2 = b%10;  assert(b2 == 0 || b2 == 1);  b /= 10;
  int b3 = b%10;  assert(b3 == 0 || b3 == 1);  b /= 10;
  int b4 = b%10;  assert(b4 == 0 || b4 == 1);  b /= 10;
  int b5 = b%10;  assert(b5 == 0 || b5 == 1);  b /= 10;
  int b6 = b%10;  assert(b6 == 0 || b6 == 1);  b /= 10;
  int b7 = b%10;  assert(b7 == 0 || b7 == 1);  b /= 10;
  int b8 = b%10;  assert(b8 == 0 || b8 == 1);  b /= 10;
  int b9 = b%10;  assert(b9 == 0 || b9 == 1);  b /= 10;
  return ((((((((b9*2 + b8)*2 + b7)*2 + b6)*2 + b5)*2 + b4)*2
               + b3)*2 + b2)*2 + b1)*2 + b0;
}
```

4.20
```
int binary(int n)
{ // same as Problem 4.21 except use 10 for 2 and 2 for 10
}
```

4.21
```
double p(double x)
{ return ((((2*x - 7)*x + 6)*x + 9)*x + 8)*x -5;
}
```

4.22
```
int mod(int n, int d)
{ assert(n >= d && d > 0);
  while (n > d)
    n -= d;
  return n;
}
```

4.23
```
int solutions(float& x1, float& x2, float a, float b, float c)
{ if (a == 0)
  { if (b == 0)
      if (c == 0) return 3;
      else return 0;
    x1 =-c/b;
    return 1;
  }
  double d = b*b - 4*a*c;
  if (d < 0) return 0;
  if (d == 0)
  { x1 = -b/(2*a);
    return 1;
  }
  double sqrtd = sqrt(d);
  x1 = (-b + sqrtd)/(2*a);
  x2 = (-b - sqrtd)/(2*a);
  return 2;
}
```

4.24
```
float centimeters(float x)
{ assert(x > 0);
  return 2.54*x;
}
```

4.25
```
float celsius(float x)
{ assert(x >= -273.0);
  return 5.0*(x - 32.0)/9.0;
}
```

4.26
```
void convert(int& weeks, int& days, int& hours, int x)
{ assert(x >= 0);
  hours = x%24;
  x /= 24;
  days = x%7;
  weeks = x/7;
}
```

4.27
```
void reverse(int& n)
{ assert(n >= 100000 && n <= 999999);
  int temp = n;
  n = temp%10;
  temp /= 10;
  n = 10*n + temp%10;
  temp /= 10;
  n = 10*n + temp%10;
  temp /= 10;
  n = 10*n + temp%10;
  temp /= 10;
  n = 10*n + temp%10;
  temp /= 10;
  n = 10*n + temp;
}
```

4.28
```
void print(int n)
{ assert(n > 0);
```

```
          while (n > 1)
          { cout << n << ", ";
            if (n%2 == 0) n /= 2;
            else n = 3*n + 1;
          }
          cout << 1 << endl;
        }
```

4.29
```
        double power(double x, int n)
        { assert(x > 0);
          double y = 1.0;
          if (n < 0)
          { x = 1.0/x;
            n = -n;
          }
          while (n > 0)
            if (n%2 == 0)   // i is even
            { x *= x;        // square z
              n /= 2;        // halve n
            }
            else             // i is odd
            { y *= x;
              --n;
            }
          return y;
        }
```

4.30
```
        void print_date(int day)
        { // same as the solution to Problem 3.12 on page 57
        }
```

4.31
```
        int lg(int n)
        { assert(n > 0);
          int count = 0;
          while (n > 1)
          { n /= 2;
            ++count;
          }
          return count;
        }
```

4.32
```
        int gcd(int m, int n)
        { assert(m > 0  && n > 0);
          do
          { while (m <= n)
              n -= m;
            int tmp = m;
            m = n;
            n = tmp;
          } while (m > 0);
          return n;
        }
```

4.33
```
        int sum(int n)
        { assert(n > 0);
          int s = 0;
          for (int i=1; i <= n; i++)
            s += i;
          return s;
        }
```

4.34
```
        int sum(int n)
        { // same as the solution to Problem 4.33 except use s += i*i;
        }
```

4.35
```
        int sum(int n)
        { // same as the solution to Problem 4.33 except use s += i*i*i;
        }
```

4.36
```
int fact(int n)
{ assert(n >= 0 && n <= 12);
  int y = 1;
  for (int i=2; i <= n; i++)
    y *= i;
  return y;
}
```

4.37
```
int perm(int n)
{ assert(0 <= k && k <= n && n <= 12);
  int y = 1;
  for (int i=1; i <= k; i++, n--)
    y *= n;
  return y;
}
```

4.38
```
int comb(int n)
{ assert(0 <= k && k <= n && n <= 33);
  int y = 1;
  for (int i=1; i <= k; i++, n--)
    y = y*n/i;
  return y;
}
```

4.39
```
int fib(int n)
{ assert(n >= 0 && n <= 46);
  if (n == 0) return 0;
  int f0=0, f1=1, f2;
  for (int i=2; i <= n; i++)
  { f2 = f1 + f0;
    f0 = f1;
    f1 = f2;
  }
  return f1;
}
```

4.40
```
void amortize(float a, float r, float p)
{ assert(r > 0.0 && r < 1.0 && p > 0.0 && p <= a);
  setiosflags(ios::right);
  cout.setf(ios::fixed, ios::floatfield);
  cout << setprecision(2);
  int m=0;   // month number
  r /= 12;   // convert r to a monthly rate
  while (a > 0.0)
  { cout << setw(8) << m << "." << setw(12) << a << endl;
    a += r*a;  // add interest to remaining balance
    a -= p;    // subtract monthly payment
    ++m;
  }
}
```

4.41
```
bool is_prime_divisor(int d, int n)
{ assert(d >= 2 && d <= n);
  return is_prime(d) && bool(n%d == 0);
}
```

4.42
```
void print_literal_tens(int n)
{ assert(n >= 2 && n <= 9);
  if (n == 2) cout << "twenty";
  else if (n == 3) cout << "thirty";
  else if (n == 4) cout << "forty";
  else if (n == 5) cout << "fifty";
  else if (n == 6) cout << "sixty";
  else if (n == 7) cout << "seventy";
  else if (n == 8) cout << "eighty";
  else cout << "ninety";
}
```

```
      void print_literal_teens(int n)
    { assert(n >= 0 && n <= 9);
      if (n == 0) cout << "ten";
      else if (n == 1) cout << "eleven";
      else if (n == 2) cout << "twelve";
      else if (n == 3) cout << "thirteen";
      else if (n == 4) cout << "fourteen";
      else if (n == 5) cout << "fifteen";
      else if (n == 6) cout << "sixteen";
      else if (n == 7) cout << "seventeen";
      else if (n == 8) cout << "eighteen";
      else cout << "nineteen";
    }
      void print_dollars(float x)
    { assert(x >= 0.00 && x < 1000.00);
      int hundreds = int(x)/100;
      int tens = int(x)%100/10;
      int ones = int(x)%10;
      int cents = int(100*x)%100;
      if (hundreds >= 1)
      { print_literal_digit(hundreds);
        cout << " hundred ";
      }
      if (tens >= 2)
      { print_literal_tens(tens);
        if (ones >= 1)
        { cout << "-";
          print_literal_digit(ones);
        }
      }
      else if (tens == 1) print_literal_teens(ones);
      else if (ones >= 1) print_literal_digit(ones);
      if (x < 1.0) cout << "no";
      cout << " dollars and " << cents << " cents";
    }
```

Chapter 5

Arrays

5.1 DEFINING AND TRAVERSING ARRAYS

An *array* is a sequence of elements of the same type which are stored contiguously in memory and which can be accessed by means of an integer *subscript*. An array is declared by specifying its element type followed by its name followed by the number of elements enclosed in brackets [ ]. The elements are numbered consecutively, starting with 0. The elements of the array are accessed by specifying the array name followed by the element number enclosed in brackets.

EXAMPLE 5.1 An Array of `ints`
```
int a[5];   // defines a to be an array of 5 elements of type int
a[2] = 88;  // assigns 88 to element number 2
```
This array can be visualized as shown at right. Since array indexes always begin at 0, the array size will always be one more than the index number of the last element. For example, the last element in a 5-element array is element number 4.

	0	1	2	3	4
a			88		

Arrays are usually processed with `for` loops, where the loop control variable is used as a variable index to traverse the array.

EXAMPLE 5.2 Using a `for` Loop to Traverse an Array
```
const int SIZE = 8;
float x[SIZE];
for (int i=0; i<SIZE; i++)
    x[i] = sqrt[10.0*i];
for (int i=SIZE-1; i>=0; i--)
    cout << i << ": " << x[i] << endl;
```
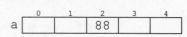

This array can be visualized like this:

x	0	1	2	3	4	5	6	7
	0.00000	3.16228	4.47214	5.47723	6.32456	7.07107	7.74597	8.36660

Note how naturally the loop control variable matches the array index. If increasing, the control variable is initialized at 0 (i=0) and the exit control should be i<SIZE. If decreasing, the control variable starts at SIZE-1 and is controlled by the condition i>=0.

The size of an array must be constant. It may be an actual constant, as in Example 5.1, or it may be a symbolic constant like SIZE in Example 5.2. But it cannot be a variable:
```
int size;
cin >> size;
float x[size];  // ILLEGAL: size must be constant
```
The reason for this restriction is that the compiler must be told how much space to allocate for the array when it compiles the code.

5.2 INITIALIZING AN ARRAY

An array can be initialized simply by listing its initial values.

EXAMPLE 5.3 Initializing an Array
```
int num[4] = {22, 88, 66, 44};
```
The initialized array can be visualized like this:

num │ 22 │ 88 │ 66 │ 44 │

The number of constants in the initializer list must be less than or equal to the size of the array. If it has fewer, then the remaining elements will be initialized to 0 automatically.

EXAMPLE 5.4 Using the Default Value 0
```
int list1[6] = {22, 88, 66, 44};
int list2[6] = {0};
```

Unlike the fundamental (atomic) types (`char`, `int`, `float`, `double`, *etc*.), arrays are composites, consisting of several values. Consequently, many of the operations used on fundamental types do not work as expected with arrays:

list1 │ 22 │ 88 │ 66 │ 44 │ 0 │ 0 │

list2 │ 0 │ 0 │ 0 │ 0 │ 0 │ 0 │

```
int list3[6] = list1;      // ILLEGAL initialization!
list2 = list1;             // DOES NOT WORK as expected
if (list1 == list2) ...    // DOES NOT WORK as expected
cin >> list1;              // ILLEGAL extraction!
list1 += 2;                // ILLEGAL arithmetic!
```
These operations must be performed on the individual elements of the arrays instead.

The statement
```
cout << list1;
```
is legal, but it does not print the contents of the array. It actually prints the memory address (in hexadecimal format) of the first element of the array.

5.3 DUPLICATING AN ARRAY

Arrays cannot be assigned:
```
list2 = list1;              // ILLEGAL!
list2 = {22, 88, 66, 44};   // ILLEGAL!
```
The reason that these statements are illegal is that an array name itself is actually a constant, and it is illegal for a constant to be on the left side of an assignment statement.

The best way to copy one array into another is with a traversing `for` loop:

EXAMPLE 5.5 Copying an Array
This uses the array `x` defined in Example 5.2:
```
float y[SIZE];
for (int i=0; i<SIZE; i++)
   y[i] = x[i];
```
The `for` loop makes `y` a duplicate of `x`.

5.4 CONSTANT ARRAYS

Like fundamental types, arrays may be declared to be constant. And like any other constant type, a constant array must be initialized.

EXAMPLE 5.6 Computing the Month for a Given Day of the Year

This code uses a constant array that keeps track of the number of days in each month (in non-leap years). It also uses a constant integer and twelve constants defined indirectly in the enumeration type:

```
const DAYS_IN_MONTH[13] =
    {0, 31, 28, 31, 30, 31, 30, 31, 31, 30, 31, 30, 31};
enum Month
    {JAN=1, FEB, MAR, APR, MAY, JUN, JUL, AUG, SEP, OCT, NOV, DEC};
const int DAYS_IN_YEAR = 365;

Month month(int day_of_year)
{ assert(day_of_year >= 1 && day_of_year <= DAYS_IN_YEAR);
  int days = 0;
  for (Month m=JAN; m<=DEC; m = Month(m+1))
  { if (days >= day_of_year) return Month(m-1);
    days += DAYS_IN_MONTH[m];
  }
  return DEC;
}

int main()
{ for (int d=1; d<=DAYS_IN_YEAR; d += 14)  // check each fortnight
    cout << "month(" << d << ") = " << month(d) << endl;
}
```

The function works by accumulating days one month at a time until the number exceeds the given number of days. Then the last `DAYS_IN_MONTH[m]` added should be the month after the current month, so it returns the preceding month.

Here is the output from this program:

```
month(1)  = 1
month(15) = 1
month(29) = 1
month(43) = 2
    :
month(323) = 11
month(337) = 12
month(351) = 12
month(365) = 12
```

There were 18 more lines (replaced here by the colon). This shows, for example, that the 43rd day of the year is in February and that the 323rd day of the year is in November.

5.5 ARRAY INDEX OUT OF RANGE

One of the problems with arrays in C++ is that the compiler will not check the values of an array index variable to ensure that it remains within range.

EXAMPLE 5.7 Array Index Out of Range

```
double list[6] = {101.01, 202.02, 303.03, 404.04, 505.05, 606.06};
for (int i=0; i<1000; i++)
    cout << list[i] << endl;
```

This code will compile without error, even though `list[6]`, `list[7]`, ..., `list[999]` are not defined! Of course, when it runs, it is likely to crash. But the compiler will be of no help in revealing this error.

Here is what happened when this code was run on a UNIX system:

```
101.01
202.02
303.03
404.04
505.05
606.06
7.82007e-320
2.15515e-314
    :
1.03302e-47
Segmentation fault
```

The system printed 110 lines of numbers, the first 8 and the last of which are shown here. Obviously 104 of these numbers are "garbage;" *i.e.*, the result of the system trying to interpret random bit strings as floating-point numbers. The output `Segmentation fault` is a message from the system that it reached the end of the process's memory segment. That is the block of computer memory reserved for that particular program.

In C++, it is the responsibility of the programmer to ensure that the index of an array stays within its bounds. Other programming languages (*e.g.*, Pascal and Java) force the compiler to do that checking for the programmer. That slows the compilation process. Bjarne Stroustrup, the inventor of C++, intentionally left that responsibility to the programmer to facilitate rapid software development.

Note that standard C++ does provide an equivalent `vector` class, described in Chapter 7, which gives the programmer the option of having the compiler do index bounds checking.

5.6 THE `sizeof` OPERATOR

C++ provides a special operator, named sizeof, that can be used to find the number of bytes that an object occupies. It is used like a function. For example,

```
cout << sizeof(int) << endl;
```

will print the number of bytes that any object of type `int` occupies in memory.

EXAMPLE 5.8 Getting the Sizes of the Fundamental Types

Here is a complete C++ program:

```
#include <iostream>
using namespace std;
int main()
{ cout << "sizeof(char)   = " << sizeof(char) << endl;
  cout << "sizeof(short)  = " << sizeof(short) << endl;
  cout << "sizeof(int)    = " << sizeof(int) << endl;
  cout << "sizeof(long)   = " << sizeof(long) << endl;
  cout << "sizeof(float)  = " << sizeof(float) << endl;
  cout << "sizeof(double) = " << sizeof(double) << endl;
}
```

Here is its output when run on a UNIX workstation:

```
sizeof(char)   = 1
sizeof(short)  = 2
sizeof(int)    = 4
sizeof(long)   = 4
sizeof(float)  = 4
sizeof(double) = 8
```

This shows, for example, that on this system an `int` uses 4 bytes.

The `sizeof` operator can also be used to find the total number of bytes that an array uses. Of course, that number is simply the product of the number of elements in the array with size of its element type:

sizeof(*array*) = (*number of elements*) × sizeof(*element type*)

EXAMPLE 5.9 Getting the Sizes of Arrays

```
int main()
{ char chars[10] = {0};
  short shorts[10] = {0};
  float floats[10] = {0.0};
  double doubles[10] = {0.0};
  cout << "sizeof(chars)   = " << sizeof(chars) << endl;
  cout << "sizeof(shorts)  = " << sizeof(shorts) << endl;
  cout << "sizeof(floats)  = " << sizeof(floats) << endl;
  cout << "sizeof(doubles) = " << sizeof(doubles) << endl;
}
```

Here is its output when run on the same UNIX workstation:

```
sizeof(chars)   = 10
sizeof(shorts)  = 20
sizeof(floats)  = 40
sizeof(doubles) = 80
```

This shows, for example, that an array of 10 elements of type `double` occupies 80 bytes.

5.7 PASSING AN ARRAY TO A FUNCTION

An array is passed to a function in the same way any other variable is passed, except that the array name must be followed by a pair of empty brackets to indicate that it is the name of an array.

EXAMPLE 5.10 A Function to Add the Elements of an Array

```
int sum(int a[], int n)
// Returns the sum of the first n elements in the array:
//    a[0] + a[1] + a[2] + ... + a[n-1];
// PRECONDITIONS: n >= 0, n <= number of elements in the array
{ int s=0;
  for (int i=0; i<n; i++)
    s += a[i];
  return s;
}
```

When an array is passed to a function, it is actually only the array name that is passed. This name is actually a constant which contains the memory address of the first element (`a[0]`) of the array. Since array names are constants, they are always passed by value. That does not prevent the function from changing the elements in the array. They remain accessible and changeable by the function.

Note that there is no way to determine from within the function what the size of the array is. The `sizeof` operator won't help because the function parameter `a` is not an array; it is actually only the address of the first element of the array (which is all the information about the array that the function needs in order to carry out its task). So the expression `sizeof(a)` will evaluate to whatever number of bytes the system uses to store a memory address, probably 4.

5.8 APPLICATIONS OF ARRAYS

A *counter* is an integer variable that is used to count objects.

EXAMPLE 5.11 Counting Primes

Here is a complete C++ program that uses the `is_prime()` from Example 4.10 on page 72:

```
#include <assert>
#include <iostream>
using namespace std;
bool is_prime(int n);
// Returns true iff n has no divisors except 1 and itself
int main()
{ int primes = 0;
  for (int n=1; n<1000; n++)
    if (is_prime(n)) ++primes;
  cout << "There are " << primes << " primes between 1 and 1000.\n";
}
```

The output is

```
There are 168 primes between 1 and 1000.
```

Here, the variable `primes` is a counter. It is initialized to be 0 and then it is incremented every time the `is_prime()` function returns true. That happened 168 times.

An array of counters is called a *frequency tally*. It is used to count elements in different categories so that their frequencies can be compared.

EXAMPLE 5.12 A Frequency Tally

Here is a list of test scores:

```
88  71  90  75  77  88  85  73  94  80
89  66  41  98  90  82  84  70  63  87
80  60  79  75  94  56  78  70  81  77
94  80  75  62  77  95  80  56  88  92
```

The following program reads all the scores and counts how many are in each of the following grade ranges: 90–100 for an A, 80–89 for a B, 70–79 for a C, 60–69 for a D, and 0–59 for an F. It keeps all five of these counts together in the `freq[]` array. Then it prints both the absolute and the relative frequencies of each grade.

```
enum {A, B, C, D, F};
int main()
{ int freq[5] = {0}, grade;
  cin >> grade;
  while (!cin.eof())
  { assert(grade >= 0 && grade <= 100);
    if (grade >= 90) ++freq[A];
    else if (grade >= 80) ++freq[B];
    else if (grade >= 70) ++freq[C];
    else if (grade >= 60) ++freq[D];
    else ++freq[F];
    cin >> grade;
  }
  float total = freq[A] + freq[B] + freq[C] + freq[D] + freq[F];
  cout << "total = " << total << endl;
  cout << "A: " << freq[A] << " = " << 100.0*freq[A]/total << "%\n";
  cout << "B: " << freq[B] << " = " << 100.0*freq[B]/total << "%\n";
  cout << "C: " << freq[C] << " = " << 100.0*freq[C]/total << "%\n";
  cout << "D: " << freq[D] << " = " << 100.0*freq[D]/total << "%\n";
  cout << "F: " << freq[F] << " = " << 100.0*freq[F]/total << "%\n";
}
```

The `while` loop continues as long as there is more input to be read through the `cin` input stream object. If the input is being input interactively on a UNIX system, then pressing **<Ctrl-D>** will send an end-of-file signal into the stream object which will then terminate the loop.

Notice the use of the anonymous enumeration type: `enum {A, B, C, D, F}`. This simply defines the five constants `A`, `B`, `C`, `D`, and `E` and gives them the default values 0, 1, 2, 3, and 4.

The next application is an implementation of an algorithm that is attributed to the ancient Greek astronomer Eratosthenes of Cyrene (*c.* 276–194 B.C.). He was the first person to have calculated an accurate estimate of the circumference of the Earth.

Algorithm 5.1 The Sieve of Eratosthenes

To obtain a list of all the prime numbers (2, 3, 5, 7, ···) that are less than a given bound `max`:

1. Initialize an array `prime[max]` of `bool`s to be all `true` except the first two.
2. Set `prime[2*j] = false` for all `j > 1` for which `2*j < max`.
3. Set `prime[3*j] = false` for all `j > 1` for which `3*j < max`.
4. Repeat setting `prime[p*j] = false` for all `j > 1` for which `p*j < max` for each prime number `p` (= 5, 7, 11, *etc.*). The next prime will be the next `i` for which `prime[i]` is `true`.
5. When Step 4 is finished, the values of `i` for which `prime[i]` is `true` are the primes.

EXAMPLE 5.13 The Sieve of Eratosthenes

```
int main()
{ const int MAX = 1000;
  bool prime[MAX];
  prime[0] = prime[1] = false;
  for (int i=2; i<MAX; i++)
    prime[i] = true;
  for (int j=2; 2*j < MAX; j++)        // even numbers > 2 are not prime
    prime[2*j] = false;
  int p = 3;
  while (p <= MAX/2)
  { for (int j=2; p*j < MAX; j++)      // multiples of p are not prime
      prime[p*j] = false;
    do ++p
    while (!prime[p]);                 // set p = next prime
  }
  for (i=2; i<MAX; i++)
  { if (prime[i]) cout << i << " ";    // print the primes
    if (i%80 == 0) cout << endl;       // avoid line wrap-around
  }
  cout << endl;
}
```

Note the effect of the `do` loop: it repeatedly increments `p` until `prime[p]` is true; *i.e.*, until `p` is a prime number again. Since `p` is already a prime when the loop begins, it must increment `p` before it evaluates `prime[p]`; so it must use the preincrement operator `++p`. The loop could also be written as

```
    do
    while (!prime[++p]);
```

or even more simply as

```
    while (!prime[++p]) ;
```

Both of those versions use the *empty statement* inside the loop.

Here is the output from the program:

```
2  3  5  7  11  13  17  19  23  29  31  37  41  43  47  53  59  61  67  71  73  79
83  89  97  101  103  107  109  113  127  131  137  139  149  151  157
163  167  173  179  181  191  193  197  199  211  223  227  229  233  239
241  251  257  263  269  271  277  281  283  293  307  311  313  317
331  337  347  349  353  359  367  373  379  383  389  397
401  409  419  421  431  433  439  443  449  457  461  463  467  479
487  491  499  503  509  521  523  541  547  557
563  569  571  577  587  593  599  601  607  613  617  619  631
641  643  647  653  659  661  673  677  683  691  701  709  719
727  733  739  743  751  757  761  769  773  787  797
809  811  821  823  827  829  839  853  857  859  863  877
881  883  887  907  911  919  929  937  941  947  953
967  971  977  983  991  997
```

Algorithm 5.2 The Bubble Sort

To sort a list of numbers into nondecreasing order:

1. Traverse the list, swapping adjacent pairs whenever they are out of order. The result will be that the largest element in the list is moved to the last position.
2. Repeat Step 1 except only on the sublist that omits the last element. The result will be that the largest element in the sublist is moved to the second-from-last position.
3. Repeat Step12 $n-3$ more times, each time on the sublist that omits the last element of the previous sublist and those after it. The result each time will be that the largest element in the sublist is moved to the end of that sublist.

EXAMPLE 5.14 The Bubble Sort for Arrays of int Type

```
void sort(int a[], int n)
{ for (int i=1; i < n; i++)
    for (int j=1; j <= n-i; j++)
      if (a[j-1] > a[j]) swap(a[j-1], a[j]);
    // INVARIANT: a[n-i], ..., a[n-1] are in their correct positions
}
```

Note that the array name is passed by value even though the function changes its elements. ·

i	j	a[0]	a[1]	a[2]	a[3]	a[4]	a[5]	a[6]	a[7]
		44	88	77	22	55	99	66	33
1	2		77	88					
	3			22	88				
	4				55	88			
	6						66	99	
	7							33	99
2	2		22	77					
	3			55	77				
	5					66	88		
	6						33	88	
3	1	22	44						
	4				66	77			
	5					33	77		
4	4				33	66			
5	3			33	55				
6	2		33	44					

Here is the `swap()` function that this algorithm uses:

```
void swap(int& x, int& y)
{ float t = x;
  x = y;
  y = t;
}
```

Note that the parameters `x` and `y` are passed by reference since the function must change them.

A trace of the call `sort(a, 8)` on the array `a[8] = {44,88,77,22,55,99,66,33}` is shown above. Note the correctness of the loop invariant: After the third iteration of the main loop (`i == 3`), the order of the elements is `{22,44,55,66,33,77,88,99}` so elements `a[5]`, `a[6]`, and `a[7]` (77, 88, and 99) are in their correct positions.

EXAMPLE 5.15 Reversing an Array

This function reverses the order of the first `n` elements in the array:

```
void reverse(float a[], int n)
{ for (int i=0; i < n/2; i++)
    swap(a[i], a[n-i-1]);
}
```

Here is the `swap()` function that this algorithm uses:

```
void swap(float& x, float& y)
{ float t = x;
  x = y;
  y = t;
}
```

Note that the only difference between this and the `swap()` function used in Example 5.14 is the type of its parameters: this swaps `float`s, the other swaps `int`s. This inefficiency of having two functions that do the same is remedied by means of a function template, described in Chapter 10.

5.9 TWO-DIMENSIONAL ARRAYS

A *two-dimensional array* is an array that has two independent subscripts. The syntax for its declaration is

```
<type> <name>[<num-rows>][<num-columns>];
```

Individual elements are accessed the same way as with one-dimensional arrays.

EXAMPLE 5.16 A Two-Dimensional Array

```
int m[3][6];    // m has 18 elements, arranged in 3 rows and 6 columns
m[0][4] = 88;   // assigns 88 to the element in row 0 and column 4
m[2][1] = 44;   // assigns 44 to the element in row 2 and column 1
```

The object `m` could be visualized as shown at right. Note that its rows are numbered 0–2 and its columns are numbered 0–5.

A two-dimensional array can be imagined as an array of (one-dimensional) arrays. That point of view helps to understand the way that a two-dimensional array is initialized. Its initialization list has to be a list of lists.

m

	0	1	2	3	4	5
0					88	
1						
2		44				

EXAMPLE 5.17 Initializing a Two-Dimensional Array

The code below initializes 9 of the 18 elements to non-zero values, as shown at right. Note that the initialization can be regarded as a list of rows.

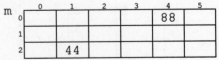

m

	0	1	2	3	4	5
0	77	55	11	33	88	0
1	99	0	0	0	0	0
2	66	44	22	0	0	0

```
int m[3][6] = { {77, 55, 11, 33, 88}, {99}, {66, 44, 22} };
```

EXAMPLE 5.18 Processing Test Scores

Here is a complete C++ program that processes student test scores:

```cpp
#include <iostream>
using namespace std;

const STUDENTS = 4;
const TESTS = 5;

typedef int Table[STUDENTS][TESTS];

void get(Table);
void print(const Table);
void print_test_averages(const Table);
void print_class_averages(const Table);

int main()
{ Table scores;
  get(scores);
  print(scores);
  print_test_averages(scores);
  print_class_averages(scores);
}
void get(Table x)
{ for (int s = 0; s < STUDENTS; s++)
    for (int t = 0; t < TESTS; t++)
      cin >> x[s][t];
}
void print(const Table scores)
{ cout << "Test scores:\n";
  for (int s = 0; s < STUDENTS; s++)
  { for (int t = 0; t < TESTS; t++)
      cout << scores[s][t] << "\t";
    cout << endl;
  }
}
void print_test_averages(const Table scores)
{ cout << "Test averages:\n";
  for (int s = 0; s < STUDENTS; s++)
  { float sum = 0.0;
    for (int t = 0; t < TESTS; t++)
      sum += scores[s][t];
    cout << "\tStudent " << s << ": " << sum/TESTS << endl;
  }
}
void print_class_averages(const Table scores)
{ cout << "Class averages:\n";
  for (int t = 0; t < TESTS; t++)
  { float sum = 0.0;
    for (int s = 0; s < STUDENTS; s++)
      sum += scores[s][t];
    cout << "\tTest " << t << ": " << sum/STUDENTS << endl;
  }
}
```

With this input
```
89 70 92 95 83
75 88 80 52 68
83 90 90 80 93
81 75 77 84 85
```
the output is
```
Test scores:
89        70        92        95        83
75        88        80        52        68
83        90        90        80        93
81        75        77        84        85
Test averages:
          Student 0: 85.8
          Student 1: 72.6
          Student 2: 87.2
          Student 3: 80.4
Class averages:
          Test 0: 82
          Test 1: 80.75
          Test 2: 84.75
          Test 3: 77.75
          Test 4: 82.25
```

5.10 MACHINE STORAGE OF ARRAYS

Machine storage is linear. Main memory can be regarded as a very long (one-dimensional) array of bytes. These bytes are accessed by their addresses, which are expressed in hexadecimal notation.

EXAMPLE 5.19 The Storage of an Array

Consider the array a defined as
```
short a[8] = {22, 33, 44, 55, 66, 77, 88, 99};
```
Here are two different ways to visualize the array:

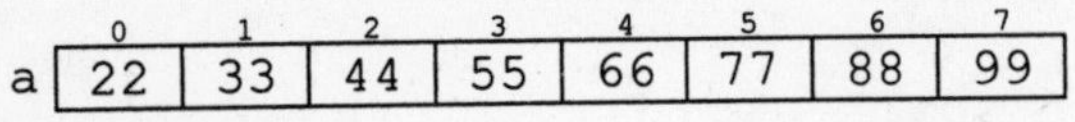

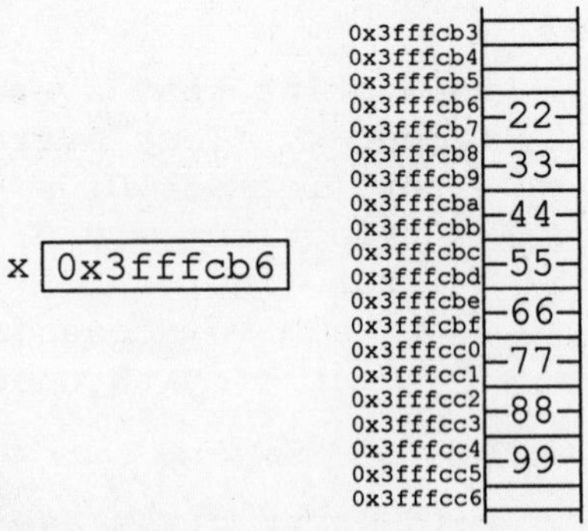

The drawing on the right shows a small segment of memory: 20 bytes, with addresses from 0x3fffcb3 to 0xfffcc6. The array contains 8 elements, each a 2-byte short integer, so the array occupies a total of 16 bytes. The picture shows it occupying bytes 0x3fffcb6–0x3fffcc5. The object a itself actually contains only a single memory address: the address 0x3fffcb6 where the array begins.

When an element of an array is accessed, the system computes the address of that element by adding an offset to the base address that is stored in the array name object. The *offset* of an element `a[p]` is simply the difference between the address of the element and the address of the first element `a[0]`. It is the number of bytes that the system adds to the starting byte to compute the address of the element `a[p]`. For a one-dimensional array, the formula is

$$offset = (p) \times (size\ of\ element)$$

EXAMPLE 5.20 Computing an Array Offset

Suppose the following statement executes for the array defined in Example 5.19:

```
a[5] = 11;
```

The offset for this element access is computed as

$$offset = (element\ subscript) \times (size\ of\ element) = (5) \times (2\ bytes) = 10\ bytes$$

Then the address of the element is computed by adding the offset to the base address stored in `a`:

$$address\ of\ \texttt{a[5]} = a + offset = \texttt{0x3fffcb6} + 10 = \texttt{0x3fffcc0}$$

This is the internal computation made by the system to locate `a[5]` in memory.

For a two-dimensional array, the offset has to include the number of bytes occupied by the preceding rows. For an array with `n` columns, the offset for the element `a[p][q]` is

$$offset = (n*p + q) \times (size\ of\ element)$$

This depends on the number of columns, but not on the number of rows in the array.

EXAMPLE 5.21 The Offset for a Two-Dimensional Array

Here is an array of 70 `doubles`, each element occupying 8 bytes:

```
double x[7][10] = {0};   // x has 7 rows and 10 columns
x[6][3] = 999.99;        // there are 5 full rows above x[6][3]
```

The offset for memory location of the element `x[6][3]` is computed by the system this way:

$$offset = (10*6 + 3) \times (8\ bytes) = (63) \times (8\ bytes) = 504\ bytes$$

So the actual location of element `x[6][3]` in memory is 504 bytes past the address stored in `x`.

Review Questions

5.1   Why are arrays usually processed with `for` loops?

5.2   Why doesn't the `sizeof` operator give the correct size of an array passed to a function?

Problems

5.3   Suppose that `x` is the array declared as

```
double x[8] = {0};
```

a. Compute the offset for the reference `x[5]`.

b. If `x` contains the address `0x3fffcb6`, what is the memory address of `x[5]`?

5.4   Suppose that `a` is the array declared as

```
int a[8][5] = {0};
```

a. Compute the offset for the reference `a[7][3]`.

b. If `a` contains the address `0x3fff000`, what is the memory address of `a[7][3]`?

Programming Problems

(handwritten notes in margin:) for [i=0; i < n; i++] { x[i] } y[i] - x[i] }

5.5 Implement the following `copy()` function:
```
void copy(float y[], float x[], int n);
// Copies the first n elements of the array x into the array y;
// PRECONDITION: x and y both have at least n elements.
// POSTCONDITION: x[i] == y[i] for 0 <= i < n.
```

(handwritten note:) if Boolequal == True for ?

5.6 Implement the following `are_equal()` function:
```
bool are_equal(float x[], float y[], int n);
// Returns true iff x[i] == y[i] for 0 <= i < n.
// PRECONDITION: x and y both have at least n elements.
```

5.7 Modify the program in Example 5.11 on page 93 so that you can input an integer `max` and then it will find the number of primes that are less than `max`. Then use it to find how many primes are less than 2000 and how many primes are less than 5000.

5.8 Implement the following `mean()` function:
```
float mean(float x[], int n);
// Returns mean average of the first n elements of the array x.
// PRECONDITION: x has at least n elements
// EXAMPLE: if x[] = {2.2, 8.8, 4.4, 6.6}, mean(x,4) returns 5.5
```

5.9 Implement the following `max()` function:
```
float max(float x[], int n);
// Returns the largest among the first n elements of array x.
// PRECONDITION: x has at least n elements
// EXAMPLE: if x[] = {2.2, 8.8, 4.4, 6.6}, max(x, 4) returns 8.8
```

5.10 Implement the following `float()` function:
```
void insert(float x[], int n, float t);
// Inserts t into the sorted array, maintaining its order.
// PRECONDITION: x[0] <= x[1] <= ... <= x[n-1]
// PROSTCONDITION: x[0] <= x[1] <= ... <= x[n-1] <= x[n]
// EXAMPLE: if x[] = {2.2, 4.4, 6.6, 8.8} then insert(x, 4, 5.5)
//     changes x to {2.2, 4.4, 5.5, 6.6, 8.8}
```

5.11 The *perfect shuffle* of an array interleaves its first half with its second half, like this:

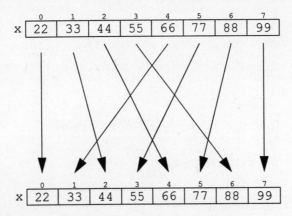

Implement the following `perfect shuffle()` function:
```
void shuffle(Array a);
// Performs a perfect shuffle of the first SIZE elements of a.
// PRECONDITION: a has at least SIZE elements
// POSTCONDITION: a[i] -> a[2*i] and a[SIZE/2+i] -> a[2*i+1]
//     for 0 <= i < SIZE/2
```

```
//    EXAMPLE: if a[] = {22, 33, 44, 55, 66, 77, 88, 99} then
//     shuffle(a, 8) changes a to {22, 55, 33, 66, 44, 77, 55, 88}
```
Use the definitions:
```
const int SIZE = 8;
typedef int Array[SIZE];
```

5.12 Write a program that determines empirically the minimum number of perfect shuffles required to restore an array to its original order. Use your `copy()` function from Problem 5.5, your `shuffle()` function from Problem 5.11, and your `are_equal()` from Problem 5.6.

5.13 Implement the following `rotate()` function:
```
void rotate(Array a, int k);
//    Shifts the left-most SIZE-k elements k places to the right
//    and wraps the right-most k elements around to the left.
//    PRECONDITION: 0 <= k < SIZE
//    POSTCONDITION: a[i] -> a[i+k] for 0 <= i < SIZE-k,
//       and a[i] -> a[i-SIZE+k] for SIZE-k <= i < SIZE
//    EXAMPLE: if a[] = {22, 33, 44, 55, 66, 77, 88, 99} then
//     shift(a, 3) changes a to {77, 55, 88, 22, 55, 33, 66, 44}
```

5.14 Write a program that reads characters and then prints the first most frequent character read. For example, if the input is

```
Master Pangloss taught the metaphysico-theologo-
cosmolonigology. He could prove to admiration that there is no
effect without a cause; and, that in this best of all possible
worlds, the Baron's castle was the most magnificent of all
castles, and My Lady the best of all possible baronesses.
```

Then the output should be
```
The first most frequent letter was t
It occurred 26 times.
```

5.15 Implement the following `std_dev()` function:
```
float std_dev(float x[], int n);
//    Returns the standard deviation of the first n elements of x.
//    PRECONDITION: x has at least n elements
```
The formula for the standard deviation of a sequence $\{x_0, x_1, x_2, \cdots, x_{n-1}\}$ of n numbers is

$$\sqrt{\frac{\sum_{i=0}^{n-1}(a_i - \mu)^2}{n-1}}$$

where μ is the mean average of the n numbers. For example, if $n = 3$, then the standard deviation of $\{x_0, x_1, x_2\}$ is

$$\sqrt{\frac{(x_0-\mu)^2 + (x_1-\mu)^2 + (x_2-\mu)^2}{2}}$$

Use your `mean()` function from Problem 5.8 for μ, and use the `<math>` header file for the `sqrt()` function.

5.16 Modify the Bubble Sort so that it is "smart" enough to stop when the array is sorted. Use a *flag* (*i.e.*, a `boolean` variable) named `sorted` that is set `true` at the start of each iteration of the outer loop and then gets reset `false` inside the inner loop whenever the `swap()` condition is `true`. Then use that flag to control the outer loop.

5.17 Implement the following `quintile()` function:

```
float quintile(float x[], int n, int q);
//   Returns the qth quintile of the first n elements of x.
//   PRECONDITION: x has at least n elements
//   POSTCONDITION: (20*q)% of the a[i] are <= the value returned
```

First sort the array. (Use your "smart" Bubble Sort from Problem 5.16.) Then compute the `stop` value, which the boundary for 20q percent of the numbers. Then use a loop which traverses the sorted array and `returns` when the values exceed your `stop` value.

5.18 The *trace* of a square matrix (*i.e.*, a two-dimensional array with the same number of rows as columns) is the sum of its diagonal elements. For example, the trace of the matrix

```
4.4   6.6   7.7   3.3   2.2
7.7   5.5   8.8   5.5   6.6
8.8   2.2   1.1   2.2   1.1
3.3   3.3   6.6   4.4   7.7
6.6   4.4   9.9   5.5   3.3
```

is $4.4 + 5.5 + 1.1 + 4.4 + 3.3 = 18.7$. Implement the following `trace()` function:

```
float trace(Matrix p);
//   Returns the sum of the diagonal elements:
//   p[0][0] + p[1][1] + ··· + p[SIZE-1][SIZE-1].
```

5.19 The *transpose* of a matrix (a two-dimensional array) is obtained by interchanging the elements that are are symmetrically opposite the diagonal. For example, the transpose of the matrix

```
4.4   6.6   7.7   3.3   2.2
7.7   5.5   8.8   5.5   6.6
8.8   2.2   1.1   2.2   1.1
3.3   3.3   6.6   4.4   7.7
```

is

```
4.4   7.7   8.8   3.3
6.6   5.5   2.2   3.3
7.7   8.8   1.1   6.6
3.3   5.5   2.2   4.4
2.2   6.6   1.1   7.7
```

Implement the following `transpose()` function:

```
void transpose(Matrix m);
//   Transposes the matrix by swapping the elements that are
//   symmetrically opposite the diagonal: m[i][j] <-> m[j][i].
```

5.20 In the theory of games and economic behavior, founded by John von Neumann, certain two-person games can be represented by a single two-dimensional array, called the *payoff matrix*. Players can obtain optimal strategies when the payoff matrix has a saddle point. A *saddle point* is an entry in the matrix that is both the minimax and the maximin. The *minimax* of a matrix is minimum of the column maxima, and the *maximin* is the maximum of the row minima. The optimal strategies are possible when these two values are equal. Write a program that prints the minimax and the maximin of a given matrix.

5.21 Pascal's Triangle looks like this:

```
1
1    1
1    2    1
1    3    3    1
1    4    6    4    1
1    5   10   10    5    1
1    6   15   20   15    6    1
```

Each interior number is the sum of the one above it and the one above and to its left. For example, $20 = 10 + 10$. Write a complete C++ program that computes Pascal's triangle down to row number 14, stores it in a 15×15 matrix, and then prints the non-zero part of it.

Solutions

5.1 A `for` loop easily traverses an array using its control variable for the array subscript. For example:
```
for (int i=0; i<n; i++)
    cout << a[i] << "\t";
```
This prints the first `n` element of the array `a`: `a[0]`, `a[1]`, ..., `a[n-1]`.

5.2 When an array is passed to a function, the only information about the array that the function receives is the array's element type and the memory address of its first element. So the function does not know how many elements the array has, and thus is unable to determine its size.

5.3 The array's element type is `double`, which occupies 8 bytes.
  a. The offset for the reference `x[5]` is $5 \cdot 8 = 40$.
  b. If `x` contains the address `0x3fffcb6`, then the memory address of `x[5]` is
  `0x3fffcb6 + 40 = 0x3fffcb6 + 0x28 = 0x3fffcde`

5.4 The array's element type is `int`, which we assume occupies 4 bytes.
  a. The offset for the reference `a[7][3]` is $(7 \cdot 5 + 3) \cdot 4 = 38 \cdot 4 = 152$
  b. If the array `a` contains the address `0x3fff000`, then the memory address of `a[7][3]` is
  `0x3fff000 + 152 = 0x3fff000 + 0x98 = 0x3fff098`

5.5
```
void copy(float b[], float a[], int n)
{ for (int i=0; i<n; i++)
      b[i] = a[i];
}
```

5.6
```
bool are_equal(float a[], float b[], int n)
{ for (int i=0; i<n; i++)
      if (a[i] != b[i]) return false;
    return true;
}
```

5.7
```
bool is_prime(int n)
// Returns true iff n has no divisors except 1 and itself
{ assert(n > 0);
  if (n == 1) return false;
  if (n == 2) return true;          // 2 is the first prime
  if (n % 2 == 0) return false;     // 2 is the only even prime
  for (int d=3; d<n; d += 2)        // look for an odd divisor
    if (n % d == 0) return false;
  return true;                      // no odd divisors were found
}

int main()
{ int max;
  cout << "Enter upper bound: ";
  cin >> max;
  int primes = 0;
  for (int n=1; n<max; n++)
    if (is_prime(n)) ++ primes;
  cout << "There are " << primes << " primes between 1 and "
      << max << endl;
}
```
There are 303 primes less than 2000, and there are 669 primes less than 5000.

5.8
```
float mean(float a[], int n)
{ float sum = 0.0;
  for (int i=0; i<n; i++)
    sum += a[i];
  return sum/n;
}
```

5.9
```
float max(float a[], int n)
{ int m = 0;
  for (int i=1; i<n; i++)
    if (a[i] > a[m]) m = i;
  return a[m];
}
```

5.10
```
void insert(float x[], int n, float t)
{ for (int i=n; i>0 && x[i-1] > t; i--)
    x[i] = x[i-1];  // shift larger elements up
  x[i] = t;
}
```

5.11
```
void shuffle(Array a)
{ int temp[SIZE];
  const half = SIZE/2;
  for (int i=0; i<half; i++)
  { temp[2*i] = a[i];
    temp[2*i+1] = a[half+i];
  }
  for (i=0; i<SIZE; i++)
    a[i] = temp[i];
}
```

5.12
```
const int SIZE = 6;
typedef int Array[SIZE];

void copy(Array y, Array x);
//  Copies the first SIZE elements the array x into array y;
//  PRECONDITION: x and y both have at least SIZE elements.
//  POSTCONDITION: x[i] == y[i] for 0 <= i < SIZE.

void shuffle(Array a);
//  Implements the perfect shuffle of first SIZE elements of a.
//  EXAMPLE: if a[] = {22, 33, 44, 55, 66, 77, 88, 99}, then
//  shuffle(a, 8) changes a to {22, 55, 33, 66, 44, 77, 55, 88}.
//  PRECONDITION: a has at least SIZE elements.
//  POSTCONDITION: a[i] -> a[2*i] and a[SIZE/2+i] -> a[2*i+1]
//     for 0 <= i < SIZE/2.

bool are_equal(Array a, Array b);
//  Returns true iff x[i] == y[i] for 0 <= i < SIZE.
//  PRECONDITION: x and y both have at least SIZE elements.

void print(Array a);
//  Prints the first SIZE elements of the array a.
//  PRECONDITION: a has at least SIZE element.
```

```
int main()
{ Array a = {22, 33, 44, 55, 66, 77};
  Array b;
  cout << "a =\t";
  print(a);
  copy(b, a);
  cout << "b =\t";
  print(b);
  int count = 0;
  do
  { shuffle(b);
    ++count;
    cout << count << ":\t";
    print(b);
  } while (!are_equal(a, b));
  cout << "It took " << count <<" shuffles to restore the "
       << SIZE << "-element array to its original state.\n";
}

void copy(Array b, Array a)
{ for (int i=0; i<SIZE; i++)
    b[i] = a[i];
}

void shuffle(Array a)
{ int temp[SIZE];
  const half = SIZE/2;
  for (int i=0; i<half; i++)
  { temp[2*i] = a[i];
    temp[2*i+1] = a[half+i];
  }
  for (i=0; i<SIZE; i++)
    a[i] = temp[i];
}

bool are_equal(Array a, Array b)
{ for (int i=0; i<SIZE; i++)
    if (a[i] != b[i]) return false;
  return true;
}

void print(Array a)
{ for (int i=0; i<SIZE; i++)
    cout << a[i] << "\t";
  cout << endl;
}
```

5.13
```
void rotate(Array a, int k)
{ Array temp;
  copy(temp, a);
  for (int i=0; i< SIZE-k; i++)
    a[i+k] = temp[i];
  for (i=SIZE-k; i<SIZE; i++)
    a[i-SIZE+k] = temp[i];
}
```

5.14
```cpp
int main()
{ const int SIZE = 128;
  int freq[SIZE] = {0};
  char c;
  cin >> c;
  while (!!cin)
  { if (c >= 'a' && c <= 'z')
      ++freq[c];
    cin >> c;
  }
  char m = 'a';
  for (c='b'; c <= 'z'; c++)
    if (freq[c] > freq[m]) m = c;
  cout << "The most frequent character was " << m << endl;
  cout << "It occurred " << freq[m] << " times.\n";
}
```

5.15
```cpp
float std_dev(float x[], int n)
{ assert(n > 1);
  float m = mean(x, n);
  float s = 0.0;
  for (int i=0; i<n; i++)
    s += (x[i] - m)*(x[i] - m);
  return sqrt(s/(n-1));
}
```

5.16
```cpp
void sort(float x[], int n)
{ bool sorted;
  for (int i=1; i < n; i++)
  { sorted = true;
    for (int j=1; j <= n-i; j++)
      if (x[j-1] > x[j])
      { swap(x[j-1], x[j]);
        sorted = false;
      }
  }
}
```

5.17
```cpp
float quintile(float x[], int n, int q)
{ sort(x, n);                 // after sorting, x[n-1] == max num
  float stop = x[n-1]*q/5;  // q/5 is proportion to be <= max
  for (int i=1; i<n; i++)
    if (x[i] > stop) return x[i-1];
  return x[n-1];
}
```

5.18
```cpp
float trace(Matrix p)
{ float sum = p[0][0];
  for (int i=1; i<SIZE; i++)
    sum += p[i][i];
  return sum;
}
```

5.19
```cpp
void transpose(Matrix m)
{ for (int i=1; i<SIZE; i++)
    for (int j=0; j<i; j++)
      swap(m[i][j], m[j][i]);
}
```

5.20

```
const int SIZE = 5;
typedef double Matrix[SIZE][SIZE];
typedef double Vector[SIZE];

void print(Matrix x);
//  Prints the matrix x.

float minimax(Matrix x);
//  Returns min{ max{x[i][j]: 0 <= i < SIZE}: 0 <= j < SIZE}.

float maximin(Matrix x);
//  Returns max{ min{x[i][j]: 0 <= j < SIZE}: 0 <= i < SIZE}.

int main()
{ Matrix x = { {44, 66, 77, 33, 22},
               {77, 55, 88, 55, 66},
               {88, 22, 11, 22, 11},
               {33, 33, 66, 44, 77},
               {66, 44, 99, 55, 44} };
  print(x);
  cout << "The minimax is " << minimax(x) << endl;
  cout << "The maximin is " << maximin(x) << endl;
}

void print(Matrix x)
{ for (int i=0; i<SIZE; i++)
  { for (int j=0; j<SIZE; j++)
      cout << x[i][j] << "\t";
    cout << endl;
  }
}

double col_max(Matrix x, int j)
{ double max = x[0][j];
  for (int i=1; i<SIZE; i++)
    if (x[i][j] > max) max = x[i][j];
  return max;
}

double row_min(Matrix x, int i)
{ double min = x[i][0];
  for (int j=1; j<SIZE; j++)
    if (x[i][j] < min) min = x[i][j];
  return min;
}

float minimax(Matrix x)
{ Vector max;
  for (int j=0; j<SIZE; j++)
    max[j] = col_max(x, j);
  double min = max[0];
  for (j=1; j<SIZE; j++)
    if (max[j] < min) min = max[j];
  return min;
}
float maximin(Matrix x)
```

```
                    { Vector min;
                        for (int i=0; i<SIZE; i++)
                            min[i] = row_min(x, i);
                        double max = min[0];
                        for (i=1; i<SIZE; i++)
                            if (min[i] > max) max = min[i];
                        return max;
                    }
```

5.21
```
            const int SIZE = 16;
            typedef int Matrix[SIZE][SIZE];

            void load_pascal(Matrix p);
            //  Loads the matrix so that p[i][j] = p[i-1][j-1] + p[i-1][j]

            void print(Matrix);
            //  Prints the lower triangle of the matrix x.

            int main()
            { Matrix p = {0};
                load_pascal(p);
                print(p);
            }

            void load_pascal(Matrix p)
            { for (int i=0; i<SIZE; i++)
                    p[i][0] = p[i][i] = 1;
                for (i=2; i<SIZE; i++)
                    for (int j=1; j<i; j++)
                        p[i][j] = p[i-1][j-1] + p[i-1][j];
            }

            void print(Matrix x)
            { setiosflags(ios::right);  // right justify each number printed
                for (int i=0; i<SIZE; i++)
                { for (int j=0; j <= i; j++)
                        cout << setw(5) << x[i][j];
                    cout << endl;
                }
            }
```

Chapter 6

Strings and Files

Data processed by computers (and humans) may be classified generally into three categories: numeric data, text data, and binary data. Numeric data consists of integer and floating-point values. Text data consists of character strings and arrays of characters. Binary data is used to store graphic images, sound files, compressed and encrypted files, *etc.* In C++, numeric data is processed using numeric types such as `int` and `float`, and text data is processed using C-strings and the Standard C++ `string` class.

6.1 C-STRINGS

A *C-string* is an array of `chars`. We call them "C-strings" because that is the standard type used for processing text in the C programming language (which is a subset of C++).

EXAMPLE 6.1 Using C-Strings
```
char s[20] = "ABCDEFG";   // s is a C-string
cout << s << endl;        // C-strings can be output like simple types
s[4] = '*';               // C-strings are arrays
cout << s << endl;
cin >> s;                 // C-strings can be input like simple types
cout << s << endl;
```
As a C-string, `s` can be input and output like a fundamental type (`int`, `char`, `float`, *etc.*) using the extraction and insertion operators `>>` and `<<`. And as an array, `s` can be manipulated using the subscript operator `[]`.

Here is a sample run of this code (with the input shown in **boldface**):
```
ABCDEFG
ABCD*FG
        Hi, Mom!
Hi,
```
Note that the extraction operator `>>` ignores whitespace (blanks, tabs, newlines, *etc.*) that precedes the input string, and it stops extracting characters as soon as it encounters a whitespace character. That's why only the three characters "Hi," were read into `s`. The rest of the input " Mom!" is still in the input buffer.

The declaration of `s` allocates 20 consecutive bytes in memory to the object named `s`. The initialization of s sets the first seven of those characters to the capital letters specified and then it sets the eighth character to 0 (called the *null character*). This can be viewed as

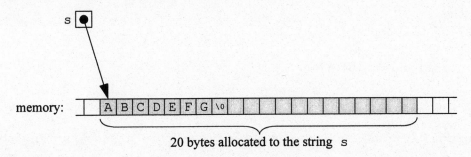

20 bytes allocated to the string s

109

When the assignment s[4] = '*'; executes, the system uses s to locate the starting byte (containing
'A') and then adds 4 to its memory address to find the byte represented by s[4] (which contains 'E').
Then it replaces the 'E' with the '*'.

Although it is important to remember that a C-string is really just a segment of memory,
it is usually easier to think of a C-string as a primitive object, as shown at right. Note that the
actual type for C-strings is char* which means "pointer to a char"; *i.e.*, a memory
address.

C-strings are like fundamental objects (ints, floats, *etc.*). We think of them as objects which
can be initialized and output as atomic units like ints and floats. But unlike fundamental objects,
C-strings have the following non-fundamental properties:

1. A C-string is an array of chars that are accessible using the subscript operator: s[i].
2. A C-string object has type char*.
3. The input operator >> can be used only if the string contains no whitespace.
4. C-strings cannot be assigned.

EXAMPLE 6.2 Passing a C-String to a Function

This function returns the number of capital letters that are in the C-string passed to it:

```
int caps(char* s)
{ int c=0;
  while (*s++)
    if (*s >= 'A' && *s <= 'Z') ++c;
  return c;
}
```

Note that the C-string type char* must be used in the parameter list.

The loop is controlled by the compact expression (*s++). The value of the expression *s is the actual
character that s points to in memory. Initially, that value is the first character of the string. The effect of the
postincrement operator is to advance the pointer to the next byte in memory. So on the second iteration, the
value of *s is the second character in the string. Remember that the char type is actually an integer type
which can act as a bool with zero meaning false and non-zero meaning true. So when a char is
used as a boolean condition, the value is true except when that char is the null character. Since every C-
string ends with the null character, the loop will continue iterating until it comes to the end of the string. This
construct while (*s++) is the standard method for traversing a C-string.

Inside the loop, the current character *s is compared to see if it lies in the range of capital letters. If it
does, the counter c is incremented.

Here is a test driver:

```
int main()
{ char s[] = "404 Oak Street, SW, Tulsa, OK, USA";
  cout << "caps(" << s << ") = " << caps(s) << endl;
}
```

The output is

```
caps(404 Oak Street, SW, Tulsa, OK, USA) = 10
```

6.2 THE <cstring> LIBRARY

C++ inherits from C a collection of special functions that work on C-strings. To use them,

```
#include <cstring>
```

in your program. (If you are using a pre-Standard C++ compiler, #include <string.h> instead.)

Here are the declarations of five of the more useful C-string functions:

strcat()	char* strcat(char* s1, const char* s2); Appends s2 to s1. Returns s1.
strchr()	char* strchr(const char* s, int c); Returns a pointer to the first occurrence of c in s. Returns NULL if c is not in s.
strcmp()	int strcmp(const char* s1, const char* s2); Compares s1 with substring s2. Returns a negative integer, zero, or a positive integer, according to whether s1 is lexicographically less than, equal to, or greater than s2.
strcpy()	char* strcpy(char* s1, const char* s2); Replaces s1 with s2. Returns s1.
strlen()	size_t strlen(const char* s); Returns the length of s, which is the number of characters beginning with s[0] that pre- cede the first occurrence of the NUL character.

EXAMPLE 6.3 Lexicographic Comparisons

Character strings are ordered alphabetically, as in a dictionary. This is called the *lexicographic ordering*. The strcmp() function is used to compare C-strings.

```
char* s1 = "pear";
char* s2 = "peach";
int cmp = strcmp(s1, s2);
cout << "cmp = " << cmp << endl;
if (cmp < 0) cout << s1 << " < " << s2 << endl;
else if (cmp == 0) cout << s1 << " == " << s2 << endl;
else cout << s1 << " > " << s2 << endl;
```

The word "pear" comes after the word "peach" in the dictionary because at the left-most letter where they differ (the fourth letter), "pear" has an "r" and "peach" has a "c". Therefore, the call strcmp(s1, s2) returns a positive integer:

```
cmp = 15
pear > peach
```

Note in these examples that a C-string can be defined using the char* type directly. The following three declarations are equivalent:

```
char* const s = "pear";
char s[] = "pear";
char s[5] = "pear";
```

Each declares s to be a constant pointer to a char, allocates 5 consecutive bytes in memory to s, copies the five characters 'p', 'e', 'a', 'r', and '\0' (the null character) to them, and then stores the address of the first byte into s. The declaration

```
char* s = "pear";
```

is also the same, except that this s is not constant; it can be incremented, as in the expression *s++.

EXAMPLE 6.4 Copying C-Strings with the strcpy() Function

C-strings cannot be assigned. Instead, the strcpy() function is used to copy one string to another.

```
int main()
{ char s1[] = "Beethoven";
  char s2[] = "Bartok";
  cout << "s1 = [" << s1 << "] , strlen(s1) = " << strlen(s1) << endl;
  cout << "s2 = [" << s2 << "] , strlen(s2) = " << strlen(s2) << endl;
  strcpy(s1, s2);
  cout << "s1 = [" << s1 << "] , strlen(s1) = " << strlen(s1) << endl;
  cout << "s2 = [" << s2 << "] , strlen(s2) = " << strlen(s2) << endl;
}
```

The output is
```
s1 = [Beethoven] , strlen(s1) = 9
s2 = [Bartok] , strlen(s2) = 6
s1 = [Bartok] , strlen(s1) = 6
s2 = [Bartok] , strlen(s2) = 6
```
Note that the call `strcpy(s1, s2)` copies the second string `s2` into the first string `s1`; like an assignment, the action is from right to left.

This example also illustrates the `strlen()` function which return the length of the string, not counting its null character.

6.3 FORMATTED INPUT

Recall the idea of a stream in C++ as a conduit through which data passes (page 27). Input passes through an `istream` object and output passes through an `ostream` object. The `istream` class defines the behavior of objects like `cin`. The most common behavior is the use of the *extraction operator* `>>` (also called the *input operator*). It has two operands: the istream object from which it is extracting characters, and the object to which it copies the corresponding value formed from those characters. This process of forming a typed value from raw input characters is called *formatting*.

EXAMPLE 6.5 The Extraction Operator `>>` Performs Formatted Input

Suppose the code
```
int n;
cin >> n;
```
executes on the input
```
    46
```
This input contains 7 characters: ' ', ' ', ' ', ' ', '4', '6', and '\n' (4 blanks, a 4, a 6, and the newline character). It could be viewed as coming

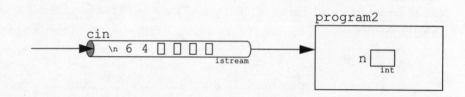

through the input stream. The stream object `cin` scans characters one at a time. If the first character it sees is a whitespace character (a blank, a tab, a newline, *etc.*) it extracts it and ignores it. It continues to extract and ignore the characters in the stream until it encounters a non-whitespace character. In this example, that would be the '4'. Since the second operand of the expression `cin >> n` has type `int`, the `cin` object is looking for digits to form an integer. So after "eating" any preceding whitespace, it expects to find one of the 12 characters '+', '-', '0', '1', '2', '3', '4', '5', '6', '7', '8', or '9'. If it encounters any of the other 244 characters, it will fail. In this case, it sees the '4'. So it extracts it and then continues, expecting more digits. As long as it encounters only digits, it continues to extract them. As soon as it sees a non-digit, it stops, leaving that non-digit in the stream. In this case, that means that `cin` will extract exactly 6 characters: the 4 blanks, the '4', and the '6'. It discards the 4 blanks and then combines the '4' and the '6' to form the integer value 46. Then it copies that value into the object `n`.

After that extraction has finished, the newline character is still in the input stream. If the next input statement is another formatted input, then like all whitespace characters that newline character will be ignored.

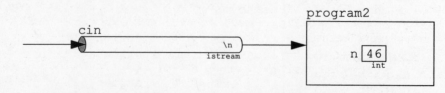

The extraction operator $>>$ *formats* the data that it receives through its input stream. This means that it extracts characters from the stream and uses them to form a value of the same type as its second operand. In the process it ignores all whitespace characters that precede the characters it uses. A direct consequence of this rule is that it is impossible to use the extraction operator to read whitespace characters. For that you must use an unformatted input function.

The operator expression

```
cin >> x
```

has a value that can be interpreted in a condition as boolean; *i.e.*, either `true` or `false` depending upon whether the input is successful. That allows such an expression to be used to control a loop.

EXAMPLE 6.6 Using the Extraction Operation to Control a Loop

```
int main()
{ int n;
  while (cin >> n)
    cout << "n = " << n << endl;
}
```

Here is a sample run (with the input shown in **boldface**):

```
46
n = 46
22    44    66    88
n = 22
n = 44
n = 66
n = 88
33, 55, 77, 99
n = 33
```

The loop continues iterating as long as the integer data is separated by only whitespace. The first non-whitespace character, the comma `','` causes the input to fail, thereby stopping the loop.

6.4 UNFORMATTED INPUT

The `<iostream>` files defines several functions inputting characters and C-strings that do not skip over whitespace. The most common are the `cin.get()` function for reading individual characters and the `cin.getline()` function for reading C-strings.

EXAMPLE 6.7 Inputting Characters with the `cin.get()` Function

```
while (cin.get(c))
{ if (c >= 'a' && c <= 'z') c += 'A' - 'a';  // capitalize c
  cout.put(c);
  if (c == '\n') break;
}
```

This loop is controlled by the input expression `(cin.get(c))`. When the input stream object `cin` detects the end-of-file (signaled interactively by **<Ctrl-D>** or **<Ctrl-Z>**), the expression evaluates to `false` and stops the loop. This loop also terminates with a `break` statement after reading and processing the newline character `'\n'`. The `if` statement simply capitalizes all lowercase letters, and the `cout.put(c)` statement prints the character.

Here is a sample run:

```
Cogito, ergo sum!
COGITO, ERGO SUM!
```

EXAMPLE 6.8 Inputting C-Strings with the `cin.getline()` Function

This program shows how to read text data line-by-line into an array of C-strings:

```
const int LEN=32;          // maximum word length
const int SIZE=10;         // array size
typedef char Name[LEN];    // defines Name to be a C-string type
int main()
{ Name king[SIZE];         // defines king to be an array of 10 names
  int n=0;
  while(cin.getline(king[n++], LEN) && n<SIZE)
    ;
  --n;                     // now n == the number of names read
  for (int i=0; i<n; i++)
    cout << '\t' << i+1 << ". " << king[i] << endl;
}
```

The object `king` is an array of 10 object of type `Name` which is defined to be a synonym for C-strings that hold up to 32 `chars` (31 non-null character). The function call `cin.getline(king[n++], LEN)` reads characters from `cin` until either it has extracted `LEN`-1 characters or it encounters the newline character, whichever comes first. It copies these characters into the C-string `king[n]`. If it encounters the newline character, it extracts it and ignores it (*i.e.*, it does not copy it into the C-string). Then it increments `n`. Note that the body of the `while` loop is empty. The loop stops when either `cin` detects the end-of-file or when `n` == `SIZE`. Since n starts at 0 and is incremented after the last name is read, its value is always 1 greater than the number of names read. So it gets decremented once at the end so that its value equals the number of names read. Then it is easy to print them or process them in other ways using a simple `for` loop.

When input was read from a text file that looks like this:

```
Kenneth II (971-995)
Constantine III (995-997)
Kenneth III (997-1005)
Malcolm II (1005-1034)
Duncan I (1034-1040)
Macbeth (1040-1057)
Lulach (1057-1058)
Malcolm III (1058-1093)
```

the output was

```
        1. Kenneth II (971-995)
        2. Constantine III (995-997)
        3. Kenneth III (997-1005)
        4. Malcolm II (1005-1034)
        5. Duncan I (1034-1040)
        6. Macbeth (1040-1057)
        7. Lulach (1057-1058)
        8. Malcolm III (1058-1093)
```

6.5 THE `string` TYPE

Standard C++ defines a `string` type in the `<string>` file. Objects of type `string` can be declared and initialized in several ways:

```
string s1;                 // s1 contains 0 characters
string s2 = "New York";    // s2 contains 8 characters
string s3(60, '*');        // s3 contains 60 asterisks
string s4 = s3;            // s4 contains 60 asterisks
string s5(s2, 4, 2);       // s5 is the 2-character string "Yo"
```

If the `string` is not initialized, like `s1` here, then it represents the empty string containing 0 characters. A `string` can be initialized the same way a C-string is, like `s2` here. Or a `string` can be initialized to hold a given number of the same character, like `s3` here which holds 60 stars. Unlike a C-string, C++ `string` objects can be initialized with a copy of another existing `string` object, like `s4` here, or with a substring of an existing string, like `s5`. Note that the standard substring designator has three parts: the parent string (`s2`, here), the starting character (`s2[4]`, here), and the length of the substring (`2`, here).

Formatted input works the same way for C++ `string`s as it does for C-strings: preceding whitespace is skipped, and input is halted at the end of the first whitespace-terminated word. C++ `string`s have a `getline()` function that works almost the same way as the `cin.getline()` function for C-strings:

```
string s = "ABCDEFG";
getline(cin, s);              // reads the entire line of characters into s
```

They also use the subscript operator the same way that C-strings do:

```
char c = s[2];                // assigns 'C' to c
s[4] = '*';                   // changes s to "ABCD*FG"
```

Note that the array index always counts how many characters precede the indexed character. C++ `string`s can be converted to C-strings like this:

```
const char* cs = s.c_str();   // converts s into the C-string cs
```

The `c_str()` function has return type `const char*`.

The C++ `string` class also defines a `length()` function that can be used like this to determine how many characters are stored in a `string`:

```
cout << s.length() << endl;   // prints 7 for the string s == "ABCD*FG"
```

C++ `string`s can be compared using the relational operators like fundamentals types:

```
if (s2 < s5) cout << "s2 lexicographically precedes s5\n";
while (s4 == s3) //...
```

You can also concatenate and append `string`s using the `+` and `+=` operators:

```
string s6 = s + "HIJK";       // changes s6 to "ABCD*FGHIJK"
s2 += s5;                      // changes s2 to "New YorkYo"
```

The `substring()` function is used like this:

```
s4 = s6.substr(5,3);          // changes s4 to "FGH";
```

The `erase()` and `replace()` function work like this:

```
s6.erase(4, 2);               // changes s6 to "ABCDGHIJK"
s6.replace(5, 2, "xyz");      // changes s6 to "ABCDGxyzJK"
```

The `find()` function returns the index of the first occurrence of a given substring:

```
string s7 = "Mississippi River basin";
cout << s7.find("si") << endl;   // prints 3
cout << s7.find("so") << endl;   // prints 23, the length of the string
```

If the `find()` function fails, it returns the length of the string it was searching.

EXAMPLE 6.9 Using the Standard C++ `string` Type

This code adds a nonsense syllable after each "t" that precedes a vowel. For example, it changes the sentence

```
The first step is to study the status of the C++ Standard.
```

into the sentence:

```
The first stegep is tego stegudy the stegatus of the C++ Stegandard.
```

It uses an auxiliary boolean function named `is_vowel()`:

```
string word;
int k;
while (cin >> word)
{ k = word.find("t") + 1;
  if (k < word.length() && is_vowel(word[k]))
    word.replace(k, 0, "eg");
  cout << word << ' ';
}
```

The `while` loop is controlled by the input, terminating when the end-of-file is detected. It reads one word at a time. If the letter `t` is found and if it is followed by a vowel, then `eg` is inserted between that `t` and the vowel.

6.6 FILES

File processing in C++ is very similar to ordinary interactive input and output because the same kind of stream objects are used. Input from a file is managed by an `ifstream` object the same way that input from the keyboard is managed by the `istream` object `cin`. Similarly, output to a file is managed by an `ofstream` object the same way that output to the monitor or printer is managed by the `ostream` object `cout`. The only difference is that `ifstream` and `ofstream` objects have to be declared explicitly and initialized with the external name of the file which they manage. You also have to `#include` the `<fstream>` file (or `<fstream.h>` in pre-Standard C++) that defines these classes.

EXAMPLE 6.10 Capitalizing All the Words in a Text File

Here is a complete program that reads words from the external file named `input.txt`, capitalizes them, and then writes them to the external file named `output.txt`:

```
#include <fstream>
#include <iostream>
using namespace std;
int main()
{ ifstream infile("input.txt");
  ofstream outfile("output.txt");
  string word;
  char c;
  while (infile >> word)
  { if (word[0] >= 'a' && word[0] <= 'z') word[0] += 'A' - 'a';
    outfile << word;
    infile.get(c);
    outfile.put(c);
  }
}
```

The picture below illustrates the process. Compare this with the picture on page 27.

Notice that the program has four objects: an `ifstream` object named `infile`, an `ofstream` object named `outfile`, a `string` object named `word`, and a `char` object named `c`.

The advantage of using external files instead of command line redirection is that there is no limit to the number of different files that you can use in the same program.

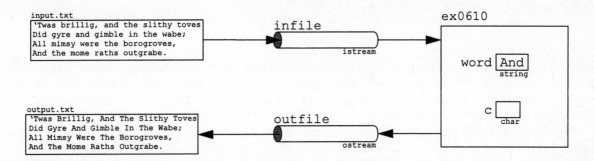

EXAMPLE 6.11 Merging Two Sorted Data Files

This program merges two files into a third file. The numbers stored in the files north.dat and
south.dat are sorted in increasing order. The program reads these two input files simultaneously and copies
all their data to the file combined.dat so that they are all together in increasing order:

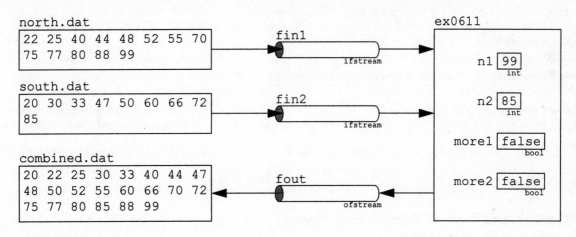

```
bool more(ifstream& fin, int& n)
{ if (fin >> n) return true;
  else return false;
}
bool copy(ofstream& fout, ifstream& fin, int& n)
{ fout << " " << n;
  return more(fin, n);
}
int main()
{ ifstream fin1("north.dat");
  ifstream fin2("south.dat");
  ofstream fout("combined.dat");
  int n1, n2;
  bool more1 = more(fin1, n1);
  bool more2 = more(fin2, n2);
  while (more1 && more2)
    if (n1 < n2) more1 = copy(fout, fin1, n1);
    else more2 = copy(fout, fin2, n2);
  while (more1)
    more1 = copy(fout, fin1, n1);
```

```
    while (more2)
      more2 = copy(fout, fin2, n2);
    fout << endl;
  }
```

The more() function is used to read the data from the input files. Each call attempts to read one integer from the fin file to the reference parameter n. It returns true if it is successful, otherwise false. The copy() function writes the value of n to the fout file and then calls the more() function to read the next integer from the fin file into n. It also returns true if and only if it is successful.

The first two calls to the more() function read 22 and 20 into n1 and n2, respectively. Both calls return true which allows the main while loop to begin. On that first iteration, the condition (n1 < n2) is false, so the copy() function copies 20 from n2 into the combined.dat file and then calls the more() function again which reads 30 into n2. On the second iteration, the condition (n1 < n2) is true (because 22 < 30), so the copy() function copies 22 from n1 into the combined.dat file and then calls the more() function again which reads 25 into n1. The next iteration writes 25 to the output file and then reads 40 into n1. The next iteration writes 30 to the output file and then reads 33 into n2. This process continues until 85 is written to the output file from n2 and the next call to more() fails, assigning false to more2. That stops the main while loop. Then the second while loop iterates three times, copying the last three integers from north.dat to combined.dat before it sets more1 to false. The last loop does not iterate at all.

Note that file objects (fin1, fin2, fout) are passed to function the same way any other objects are passed. However, they must always be passed by reference.

6.7 STRING STREAMS

A *string stream* is a stream object that allows a string to be used as an internal text file. This is also called *in-memory I/O*. String streams are quite useful for buffering input and output. Their types istringstream and ostringstream are defined in the <sstream> file.

EXAMPLE 6.12 Using an Output String Stream

Here is a complete Standard C++ program:

```
#include <iostream>
#include <sstream>
#include <string>
using namespace std;
int main()
{ ostringstream oss;
  int n = 44;
  float x = 3.14;
  oss << "Hello!\t" << n << '\t' << x;
  string s = oss.str();  // copies the stream's string to s
  oss << '\t' << &n;
}
```

The objects in this program can be visualized like this:

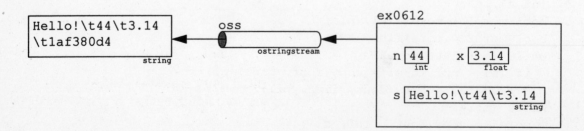

The stream object's anonymous string is drawn outside the program to emphasize its natural analogy with an external file. (See the drawings on pages 27 and 116.) But actually, both the stream object and its anonymous string are objects in the program.

The object `oss` is an output string stream. It serves as a conduit to an anonymous `string` which can be read with the built-in `oss.str()` function that is bound to the `oss` object. The insertion operator `<<` is used to insert the string literal `"Hello!\t"`, the integer `n`, the character `'\t'`, and the float `x`. Then the contents of `oss`'s anonymous string are copied to the local string `s`. Then the character `'\t'` and the address of the object `n` are inserted into `oss`.

EXAMPLE 6.13 Using an Input String Stream

Suppose that we append the following lines of code to the program in Example 6.12:

```
const string buffer = oss.str();
istringstream iss(buffer);      // binds the stream iss to the string
string word;
int m;
float y;
iss >> word >> m >> y;
```

The first line copies the current contents of `oss`'s string into `buffer`. Then the input string stream `iss` is defined and bound to `buffer`. This means that all extractions from `iss` will come from the contents of `buffer`, just as though it were an external text file. Then after declaring another `string`, `int`, and `float`, their values are read from `iss`.

The objects in this expanded program can be visualized like this:

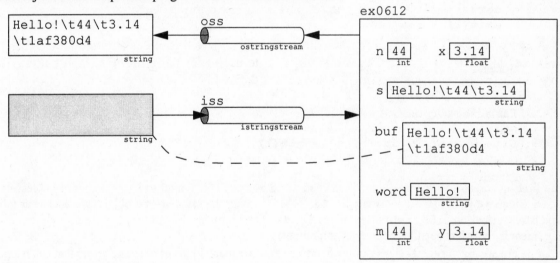

Note that the contents of buffer can be accessed two ways: as elements of a `string`, or by formatted input through the `iss` object.

```
char c = buffer[16];   // assigns 'f' to c
iss >> word;           // copies "1af380d4" into word
```

6.8 RANDOM ACCESS FILES

Files can be accessed directly like an array. This is called *direct access* or *random access*. The access location is set by using the file's `seekg()` function for reading and its `seekp()` function for writing.

EXAMPLE 6.14 Random Access of a Text File

This complete program creates a dummy text file and then allows the user to select a random location to rewrite a part of it.

```
#include <cstdlib>  // defines the exit() function
#include <fstream>
#include <iostream>
#include <string>
void load(fstream& f)
{ for (int i=1; i <= 5; i++)       // write 5 64-char lines
  { for (int j=1; j <= 60; j++)
      f << j%10;                    // write 60 digits
    f << "  " << i << '\n';        // write 4 chars
  }
}
void dump(fstream& f)
{ f.seekg(0);          // start at the beginning of the file
  char c;
  while (f.get(c))     // echo each character in f to cout
    cout.put(c);
  f.clear();           // resets the file's eofbit
}
int main()
{ fstream file("Demo.dat", ios::in | ios::out);
  if (!file)
  { cerr << "File Demo.dat could not be opened.\n";
    exit(1);
  }
  load(file);
  dump(file);
  int pos, len;
  cin >> pos >> len;
  file.seekp(pos);
  string s(len, '*');
  file.write(s.c_str(), s.length());
  dump(file);
}
```

The first line creates an external text file named `Demo.dat`. It is bound to an `fstream` object named `file`. Since we want to read and write to `Demo.dat` using the same stream object, we declare it to have type fstream (instead of `ifstream` or `ofstream`) and initialize it with the `ios::in | ios::out` flag (meaning that it is open for both input and output).

File processing in general is very prone to error. There are many kinds of run-time errors that can happen to programs that use files. For example, the system may be unable to create the new file because your directory is full or its file permissions prevent it. So it is recommended that whenever a file is opened (by declaring its file stream object), it should be checked for possible error before proceeding with its processing. This is usually done with an `if` statement like the one on lines 2–4 of the `main()` function here. The condition `(!file)` means that the file is not ready for processing. If so, we simply print an error message and quit the program. The exit() function is defined in the `<cstdlib>` file. Passing the integer `1` is simply a signal to the operating system that the program is terminating with an error.

If the file is ready for processing, we call the `load()` function to fill it with 5 lines of digits and then the `dump()` function to display the complete file on the screen. Then the program interactively reads a position number `pos` and a length number `len`. In the run shown below, we entered 200 for the position and 17 for the length.

The next three statement change the 17 characters in positions 201–217 to asterisks. The call `file.seekp(pos)` function moves its write pointer (the "p" in "seekp" stands for "put") to position `pos`;

i.e., it advances that many characters past the beginning of the file. Then `s` is defined to be a string of 17 asterisks. The call `file.write(cs, len)` replaces the file's `len` characters that are located by its write pointer with the same number of characters in the C-string `cs`. So the call

file.write(s.c_str(), s.length());

changes the next 17 digits to asterisks. Notice the use of the string's `c_str()` and `length()` functions.

Here is a sample run:

```
12345678901234567890123456789012345678901234567890123456789012345678901234567890  1
12345678901234567890123456789012345678901234567890123456789012345678901234567890  2
12345678901234567890123456789012345678901234567890123456789012345678901234567890  3
12345678901234567890123456789012345678901234567890123456789012345678901234567890  4
12345678901234567890123456789012345678901234567890123456789012345678901234567890  5
200 17
12345678901234567890123456789012345678901234567890123456789012345678901234567890  1
12345678901234567890123456789012345678901234567890123456789012345678901234567890  2
12345678901234567890123456789012345678901234567890123456789012345678901234567890  3
12345678************5678678901234567890123456789012345678901234567890  4
12345678901234567890123456789012345678901234567890123456789012345678901234567890  5
```

The arrangement of the (background) digits makes it easy to check that the correct 17 characters were "aster-isked out." The call to the `seekp()` function specified that writing begins after the 200th character. Since each line contains 64 characters (counting the newline character), the first 3 lines contain $3 \cdot 64 = 192$ characters, which means that the 200th character must be the 8th character of line 4. So the 9th – 25th digits on line 4 are replaced with asterisks.

The `seekp(pos)` and `write(cs, len)` functions are used to write the C-string `cs` of length `len` to a random access file at position `pos`. In the same way, the `seekg(pos)` and `read(cs, len)` functions are used to read the `len` characters starting at position `len` from a random access files into the C-string `cs`.

EXAMPLE 6.15 Processing Student Grades

Consider the two data files shown below. The `Students.dat` file contains students records, one per line, in four fields: the student's id number, name, total credits earned, and grade point average. The `Grades.dat` file contains grade records, one per line, in three fields: a student's id number, final grade in a course, and credit hours for that course. The following program processes these grades, updating the student records by adding the new credits and recomputing the grade point averages of those students whose ids appear in the `Grades.dat` file. Note that the records in both files are sorted by student id. Also in both files, each field is separated by a single tab character `'\t'`, and each record is terminated by the newline character `'\n'`.

```
#include <fstream.h>
#include <iomanip.h>
#include <iostream.h>
#include <sstream.h>
using namespace std;
int credit(string grade_rec);
void get(string& student_rec, fstream& students, string id);
void update(string& student_rec, char grade, int credit);
void put(string student_rec, fstream& students);
const int STUDENT_REC_SIZE=30;
int main()
{ fstream students("Students.dat", ios::in | ios::out);
  ifstream grades("Grades.dat");
  if (!students || !grades)
  { cerr << "One of the files could not be opened.\n";
    exit(1);
  }
```

Students.dat

```
017142031      Vance, Vera      85      3.06
027910908      Nixon, Nora      47      2.61
104148606      Allen, Adam      29      2.84
118229053      Tyson, Tara      37      2.80
129830779      Evans, Earl      92      3.21
370221320      Ogden, Owen      80      3.23
391235525      Chang, Carl      87      3.10
407890754      Gomez, Gary      50      2.35
413114410      Rosen, Raul      73      2.18
487072864      Davis, Dora      43      2.39
490130095      Ukrop, Urey      20      3.75
569844817      Singh, Sara      19      3.63
645378014      Paine, Perl      51      3.00
678206512      Jones, Judy      37      2.77
709404115      Hanes, Hope      94      3.44
724978457      Brown, Bill      63      2.17
861480354      Frost, Fred      17      1.63
863050853      Russo, Rose      95      1.99
907723489      Levin, Lisa      65      2.53
926311364      Irvin, Ivan      76      2.97
956733958      Moore, Mark      25      3.01
966739174      Knopp, Karl      41      1.88
```

Grades.dat

```
027910908      B      4
104148606      A      3
118229053      B      3
370221320      F      3
407890754      B      4
487072864      C      3
490130095      C      4
569844817      A      3
645378014      A      4
678206512      B      3
709404115      A      3
724978457      C      3
926311364      A      4
956733958      D      3
```

```
    string grade_rec;      // a line from the Grades.dat file
    string student_rec;    // a line from the Students.dat file
    string _id;            // the student id from the grade_rec
    char _grade;           // the student grade from the grade_rec
    int _credit;           // the student credit from the grade_rec
    while (getline(grades, grade_rec))
    { _id = grade_rec.substr(0,9);
      _grade = grade_rec[10];
      _credit = credit(grade_rec);
      get(student_rec, students, _id);
      update(student_rec, _grade, _credit);
      put(student_rec, students);
    }
  }
```

The Students.dat file is opened for both input and output because its records are to be updated. Each iteration of the main loop reads one grade_rec record from the grades file. It extracts the student _id and _grade directly from the string, and uses the credit() function to get the numeric _credit value from the string. Then it calls the get() function to get the student_rec record from the students file that matches the _id. That record is then updated by the update() function and written back to the students file by the put() function.

Here is the credit() function:

```
    int credit(string grade_rec)
    { string s = grade_rec.substr(12,1);
      istringstream ss(s);
      int n;
      ss >> n;
      return n;
    }
```

The credit integer is a single digit occupying the 13th character of the `grade_rec`. That is extracted as a substring, and then the input string stream `ss` is used to take advantage of the automatic formatting of the extraction operator `>>` to get the integer value into `n` so it can be returned.

Here is the `get()` function:

```
void get(string& student_rec, fstream& students, string id)
{ while (!students.eof())
    { getline(students, student_rec);
      if (student_rec.substr(0,9) == id) break;
    }
}
```

This continues reading records from the `student_rec` file until it finds the one that has the same `id` as that passed in to the function. Notice that it uses the string `substr()` function to extract the 9-character `id` from each student record.

Here is the `update()` function:

```
void update(string& student_rec, char grade, int credit)
{ int grade_points = 4 - int(grade - 'A');
  grade_points = (grade_points < 0 ? 0 : grade_points);
  string s = student_rec.substr(22,7);
  istringstream iss(s);
  int credits;
  iss >> credits;
  float gpa, points;
  iss >> gpa;
  points = credits*gpa + credit*grade_points;
  credits += credit;
  gpa = points/credits;
  ostringstream oss;
  oss << credits << '\t' << setprecision(3) << gpa;
  s = oss.str();
  student_rec.replace(22, 7, s.substr(0,7));
}
```

First it converts the letter grade into its numeric equivalent: 4 for an `'A'`, 3 for a `'B'`, 2 for a `'C'`, 1 for a `'D'`, and 0 for an `'F'`. Then it uses the input string stream `iss` to extract the numeric `credits` and `gpa` from the student record. These lie in columns 23–29 of the `student_rec`. It computes the student's new `credits` and `gpa`. Then it uses the output string stream `oss` to insert the new `credits` and `gpa` into the string `s`. Finally it uses the string `substr()` and `replace()` functions to insert these new values back into the `student_rec`.

Here is the `put()` function:

```
void put(string student_rec, fstream& students)
{ student_rec += string(1, '\n');   // append the newline character
  const char* p = student_rec.c_str();
  int location = students.tellg();
  location -= STUDENT_REC_SIZE;
  students.seekp(location);
  students.write(p, STUDENT_REC_SIZE);
}
```

The `student_rec` contains 29 characters. Each record in the Students.dat file is 30 characters long, the last being the newline character. So we have to append `'\'` to `student_rec` before writing it back to the file. Then we can update the file by re-writing the record. The `write()` function requires the equivalent C-string `p` to be passed.

Review Questions

6.1 What is the difference between a C-string and a C++ `string`?

6.2 What is the difference between formatted input and unformatted input?

6.3 Why can't whitespace be read with the extraction operator?

6.4 What is a stream?

6.5 How does C++ simplify the processing of strings, external files, and internal files?

6.6 What is the difference between sequential access and direct access?

6.7 What do the `seekg()` and `seekp()` functions do?

6.8 What do the `read()` and `write()` functions do?

Problems

6.9 Describe what the following code does:
```
char cs1[] = "ABCDEFGHIJ";
char cs2[] = "ABCDEFGH";
cout << cs2 << endl;
cout << strlen(cs2) << endl;
cs2[4] = 'X';
if (strcmp(cs1, cs2) < 0) cout << cs1 << " < " << cs2 << endl;
else cout << cs1 << " >= " << cs2 << endl;
char buffer[80];
strcpy(buffer, cs1);
strcat(buffer, cs2);
char* cs3 = strchr(buffer, 'G');
cout << cs3 << endl;
```

6.10 Describe what the following code does:
```
string s = "ABCDEFGHIJKLMNOP";
cout << s << endl;
cout << s.length() << endl;
s[8] = '!';
s.replace(8, 5, "xyz");
s.erase(6, 4);
cout << s.find("!");
cout << s.find("?");
cout << s.substr(6, 3);
s += "abcde";
string part(s, 4, 8);
string stars(8, '*');
```

6.11 Describe what happens when the code
```
string s;
int n;
float x;
cin >> s >> n >> x >> s;
```
executes on each of the following inputs:

a. ABC 456 7.89 XYZ
b. ABC 4567 .89 XYZ
c. ABC 456 7.8 9XYZ
d. ABC456 7.8 9 XYZ
e. ABC456 7 .89 XYZ

f. ABC4 56 7.89XY Z
g. AB C456 7.89 XYZ
h. AB C 456 7.89XYZ

6.12 Trace the execution of the merge program in Example 6.11 on page 117 on the following two data files:

```
north.dat
27 35 38 52 55 61 81 87
```

```
south.dat
31 34 41 45 49 56 63 74
92 95
```

Show each value of the variables n1, n2, more1, and more2, as they change.

Programming Problems

6.13 Write a program that reads full names, one per line, and then prints them in the standard telephone directory format. For example, the input

```
Johann Sebastian Bach
George Frederic Handel
Carl Phillipp Emanuel Bach
Joseph Haydn
Johann Christian Bach
Wolfgang Amadeus Mozart
```

would be printed as:

```
Bach, Johann S.
Handel, George F.
Bach, Carl P. E.
Haydn, Joseph
Bach, Johann C.
Mozart, Wolfgang A.
```

6.14 Write a program that counts and prints the number of lines, words, and letter frequencies in its input. For example, the input:

```
Two roads diverged in a yellow wood,
And sorry I could not travel both
And be one traveler, long I stood
And looked down one as far as I could
To where it bent in the undergrowth;
```

would produce the output:

```
The input had 5 lines, 37 words,
and the following letter frequencies:
    A: 10    B: 3    C: 2    D: 13   E: 15   F: 1    G: 3    H: 4
    I: 7     J: 0    K: 1    L: 8    M: 0    N: 12   O: 20   P: 0
    Q: 0     R: 11   S: 5    T: 11   U: 3    V: 3    W: 6    X: 0
    Y: 2     Z: 0
```

6.15 Implement and test the following function:

```
void reduce(string& s);
// Changes all capital letters in s to lowercase
// and removes all non-letters from the beginning and end.
// EXAMPLE: if s == "'Tis,", then reduce(s) makes it "tis"
```

Hint: First write and test the following three boolean functions:

```
bool is_uppercase(char c);
bool is_lowercase(char c);
bool is_letter(char c);
```

6.16 Modify your program from Problem 6.14 so that it counts the frequencies of words instead of letters. For example, the input

```
[I] then went to Wm. and Mary college, to wit in the spring of
1760, where I continued 2 years.  It was my great good fortune,
and what probably fixed the destinies of my life that Dr. Wm.
Small of Scotland was then professor of Mathematics, a man
profound in most of the useful branches of science, with a happy
talent of communication, correct and gentlemanly manners, & an
enlarged & liberal mind.  He, most happily for me, became soon
attached to me & made me his daily companion when not engaged in
the school; and from his conversation I got my first views of the
expansion of science & of the system of things in which we are
placed.
```

would produce the output

```
The input had 11 lines and 120 words,
with the following frequencies:
```

i:	3	then:	2	went:	1
to:	3	wm:	2	and:	4
mary:	1	college:	1	wit:	1
in:	4	the:	6	spring:	1
of:	11	:	6	where:	1
continued:	1	years:	1	it:	1
was:	2	my:	3	great:	1
good:	1	fortune:	1	what:	1
probably:	1	fixed:	1	destinies:	1
life:	1	that:	1	dr:	1
small:	1	scotland:	1	professor:	1
mathematics:	1	a:	2	man:	1
profound:	1	most:	2	useful:	1
branches:	1	science:	2	with:	1
happy:	1	talent:	1	communication:	1
correct:	1	gentlemanly:	1	manners:	1
an:	1	enlarged:	1	liberal:	1
mind:	1	he:	1	happily:	1
for:	1	me:	3	became:	1
soon:	1	attached:	1	made:	1
his:	2	daily:	1	companion:	1
when:	1	not:	1	engaged:	1
school:	1	from:	1	conversation:	1
got:	1	first:	1	views:	1
expansion:	1	system:	1	things:	1
which:	1	we:	1	are:	1
placed:	1				

6.17 Write a program that right-justifies text. It should read and echo a sequence of left-justified lines and then print them in right-justified format. For example, the input

```
Listen, my children, and you shall hear
Of the midnight ride of Paul Revere,
On the eighteenth of April, in Seventy-five;
Hardly a man is now alive
Who remembers that famous day and year.
```

would be printed as

```
            Listen, my children, and you shall hear
               Of the midnight ride of Paul Revere,
      On the eighteenth of April, in Seventy-five;
                     Hardly a man is now alive
         Who remembers that famous day and year.
```

6.18 Implement and test the following function:

```
string Roman(int n);
//   Returns the Roman numeral equivalent to the Hindu-Arabic
//   numeral n.
//   PRECONDITIONS: n > 0, n < 3888
//   EXAMPLES: Roman(1776) returns "MDCCLXXVI",
//      Roman(1812) returns "MDCCCXII", Roman(1945) returns
"MCMXLV"
```

6.19 Implement and test the following function:

```
int HindArabic(string s);
//   Returns the Hindu-Arabic numeral equivalent to the Roman
//   numeral given in the string s.
//   PRECONDITIONS: s contains a valid Roman numeral
//   EXAMPLES: HindArabic("MDCCLXXVI") returns 1776,
//      HindArabic("MDCCCXII") returns 1812
```

Note that this is the inverse of the `Roman()` function in Problem 6.18.

Hint: Write an auxiliary function `int v(string s, int i)` that returns the digit for the Roman numeral character `s[i]`; *e.g.*, `v("MDCCCXII", 1)` returns `500`.

6.20 Implement Algorithm 1.4 on page 6 to convert decimal numerals to hexadecimal:

```
string hexadecimal(int n);
//   Returns the hexadecimal numeral that represents n.
//   PRECONDITION: n >= 0
//   POSTCONDITION: each character in the returned string is a
//      hexadecimal digit and that string is the dexadecimal
//      equivalent of n
//   EXAMPLE: hexadecimal(11643) returns "2d7b"
```

Hint: Write an auxiliary function `char c(int k)` that returns the hexadecimal character for the hexadecimal digit `k`; *e.g.*, `c(14)` returns `'e'`.

6.21 Implement Algorithm 1.4 on page 6 to convert hexadecimal numerals to decimal:

```
int decimal(string s);
//   Returns the decimal numeral that represents the hexadecimal
//   numeral stored in the string s.
//   PRECONDITION: s.length() > 0 and each s[i] is a hexadecimal
//      digit
//   POSTCONDITION: the returns value is the decimal equivalent
//   EXAMPLE: decimal("2d7b") returns 11643
```

Note that this is the inverse of the `hexadecimal()` function in Problem 6.20.

Hint: Write an auxiliary function `int v(string s, int i)` that returns the decimal digit for the hexadecimal character `s[i]`; *e.g.*, `v("2d7b", 3)` returns `12`.

6.22 Implement and test the following function:

```
void reverse(string& s);
//   Reverses the string s.
//   POSTCONDITION: s[i] <--> s[len-i-1]
//   EXAMPLE: reverse(s) changes s = "ABCDEFG" into "GFEDCBA"
```

Hint: Use a temporary string.

6.23 Implement and test the following function:

```
bool is_palindrome(string s);
//   Returns true iff s is a palindrome
//   EXAMPLES: is_palindrome("RADAR") returns true,
//     is_palindrome("ABCD") returns false
```

6.24 Modify the program in Example 6.11 on page 117 so that it merges the following two files of sorted lines of text, writing the resulting sorted lines both to a file named `Presidents.dat` and to `cout`:

Democrats.dat

```
Carter, James Earl
Clinton, William Jefferson
Johnson, Lyndon Baines
Kennedy, John Fitzgerald
Roosevelt, Franklin Delano
Truman, Harry S
```

Republicans.dat

```
Bush, George Herbert Walker
Eisenhower, Dwight David
Ford, Gerald Rudolph
Nixon, Richard Milhous
Reagan, Ronald Wilson
```

Hint: Use `getline(fin, s)`.

6.25 A certain image file format stores graphic images using one byte per pixel (256 colors) It uses the first 8 bytes to store the image's dimensions: the first four-byte integers giving the number of rows and the second the number of columns. The remaining bytes represent the two-dimensional image stored in *row-major* form. For example, the first 8 bytes evaluate to the two integers 5000 and 6400, then the file will have 32,000,000 more bytes (a 32-MB file) for its 32,000,000 pixels, arranged in 5000 rows of 6400 pixels each. Write the following function that cleans up a noisy image file by smoothing erroneous pixels. If a pixel value differs from the average value of its four neighboring pixels by more than a given tolerance, then that value is changed to the average value. For example, the call `clean(f, 16)` would make the following change:

72	78	80	79	83
73	77	78	84	88
77	79	21	82	85
76	81	82	87	89
80	16	84	85	90

72	78	80	79	83
73	77	78	84	88
77	79	**80**	82	85
76	81	82	87	89
80	16	84	85	90

```
void clean(fstream& f, int tolerance);
//   Cleans the image file by averaging singularities.
//   PRECONDITIONS: f is bound to a file that contains mn+8 bytes,
//     where m and n are 4-byte unsigned integers stored in the
//     first 8 bytes; f is open for input and output
//   POSTCONDITION: no pixel value differs from the average of its
//     four neighbors by more than tolerance
```

Hint: The locations of the four neighbors of a pixel located at byte `x` are `x-n`, `x-1`, `x+1`, and `x+n` (north, west, east, and south).

6.26 Modify the program in Example 6.15 on page 121 so that assumes a 3-digit credits field (instead of 2 digits) in the `Students.dat` file. Then adjust the actual data file accordingly, change the record for `Hope Hanes` to 114 credits, and run your program.

Solutions

6.1 A C-string is an array of chars that uses the null character '\0' to mark the end of the string. A C++ string is an object whose `string` type is defined in the `<string>` file and which has a large repertoire of function, such as `length()` and `replace()`:

```
char cs[8] = "ABCDEFG";   // cs is a C-string
string s = "ABCDEFG";     // s is a C++ string
cout << s << " has " << s.length() << " characters.\n";
s.replace(4, 2, "yz");    // changes s to "ABCDyzG"
```

6.2 Formatted input uses the extraction operator `>>` which ignores whitespace. Unformatted input uses the `get()` and `getline()` functions. The `get()` function reads the next character in the input stream without ignoring whitespace. The `getline()` function reads all the rest of the characters in the input stream until it reaches the newline character `'\n'`, which it extracts and ignores.

6.3 Whitespace (blanks, tabs, newlines, *etc.*) cannot be read with the extraction operator because it ignores all whitespace.

6.4 A *stream* is an object that manages input and output between a program and a data source. C++ allows `<iostream>` objects for interactive I/O (*viz.*, `cin` and `cout`), `<fstream>` objects for external files, and `<sstream>` objects for internal files (string streams).

6.5 C++ simplifies the processing of strings, external files, and internal files, by defining the same family of functions and operations for all three. For example, the extraction operator `>>` works the same way for inputting a `double` from the keyboard, from an external file, or from a string stream.

6.6 Sequential access must begin at the beginning and access each element in order, one after the other. Direct access allows the access of any element directly by locating it by its index number or address. Arrays allow direct access. Magnetic tape has only sequential access, but CDs had direct access. If you are on a railroad train, to go from one car to another you must use sequential access. But when you board the train initially you have direct access. Direct access is faster than sequential access, but it requires some external mechanism (array index, file byte number, railroad platform).

6.7 The `seekg()` and `seekp()` functions position the get pointer and the put pointer, respectively, in an external file to allow direct access. For example, the call `input.seekg(24)` positions the get pointer at byte number 24 in the file bound to the file stream named `input`.

6.8 The `read()` and `write()` functions are used for direct access input and output, respectively, of external files. For example, the call `input.read(s.c_str(), n)` would copy n bytes to the string s directly from the file bound to the file stream named `input`.

6.9
```
char cs1[] = "ABCDEFGHIJ";    // defines cs1 to be that C-string
char cs2[] = "ABCDEFGH";      // defines cs1 to be that C-string
cout << cs2 << endl;                          // prints: ABCDEFGH
cout << strlen(cs2) << endl;                       // prints: 8
cs2[4] = 'X';                     // changes cs2 to "ABCDXFGH"
if (strcmp(cs1, cs2) < 0) cout << cs1 << " < " << cs2 << endl;
else cout << cs1 << " >= " << cs2 << endl;
                              // prints: ABCDEFGHIJ < ABCDXFGH
char buffer[80];  // defines buffer to be a C-string of < 80 chars
strcpy(buffer, cs1);          // changes buffer to "ABCDEFGHIJ"
strcat(buffer, cs2);   // changes buffer to "ABCDEFGHIJABCDXFGH"
char* cs3 = strchr(buffer, 'G');  // make cs3 point to buffer[6]
cout << cs3 << endl;                    // prints: GHIJABCDXFGH
```

6.10

```
string s = "ABCDEFGHIJKLMNOP";      // defines s to be that string
cout << s << endl;                     // prints: ABCDEFGHIJKLMNOP
cout << s.length() << endl;                         // prints: 16
s[8] = '!';                    // changes s to "ABCDEFGH!JKLMNOP"
s.replace(10, 5, "xyz");        // changes s to "ABCDEFGH!JxyzP"
s.erase(2, 4);                        // changes s to "ABGH!JxyzP"
cout << s.find("!") << endl;                        // prints: 4
cout << s.find("?") << endl;                       // prints: 10
cout << s.substr(3, 6) << endl;            // prints: H!Jxyz
s += "abcde";                   // changes s to "ABGH!JxyzPabcde"
string part(s, 1, 10);          // defines part to be "BGH!JxyzPa"
string stars(8, '*');           // defines stars to be "********"
```

6.11   ***a****.* ABC 456 7.89 XYZ
Assigns "ABC" to s, 456 to n, 7.89 to x, and then "XYZ" to s.

   b. ABC 4567 .89 XYZ
Assigns "ABC" to s, 4567 to n, 0.89 to x, and then "XYZ" to s.

   c. ABC 456 7.8 9XYZ
Assigns "ABC" to s, 456 to n, 7.8 to x, and then "9XYZ" to s.

   d. ABC456 7.8 9 XYZ
Assigns "ABC456" to s, and then crashes because 7.8 is not a valid integer literal.

   e. ABC456 7 .89 XYZ
Assigns "ABC456" to s, 7 to n, 0.89 to x, and then "XYZ" to s.

   f. ABC4 5 67.89XY Z
Assigns "ABC4" to s, 56 to n, and then crashes because 7.89XY is not a valid float literal.

   g. AB C456 7.89 XYZ
Assigns "AB" to s and then crashes because C456 is not a valid integer literal. (Note that the hexidecimal numeral c456, which can also be written C456, would qualify as a valid integer literal. But on input, hexadecimal numerals must be prefixed with "0x", as in 0xc456.)

   h. AB C 456 7.89XYZ
Assigns "ABC" to s and then crashes because C is not a valid integer literal.

6.12   Tracing the merge program:

n1	n2	more1	more2
27	31	true	true
35			
	34		
	41		
38			
52			
	45		
	49		
	56		
55			
61			
	63		
81			
	74		
	92		
87		false	
	95		false

6.13
```
int main()
{ string word, first, last;
  char c;
  bool is_first, is_last = true;
  string name[32];
  int n=0;
  while (cin >> word)
  { cin.get(c);           // should be either a blank or a newline
    is_first = is_last;         //  current word is a first name
    is_last = bool(c == '\n');    //  current word is a last name
    if (is_first) first = word;
    else if (is_last) name[n++] = word + ", " + first;
    else first += " " + word.substr(0,1) + ".";    // add initial
  }
  --n;
  for (int i=0; i<n; i++)
    cout << '\t' << i+1 << ". " << name[i] << endl;
}
```

6.14
```
int main()
{ string word;
  const int SIZE=91;       // for frequency array (int('Z') == 90)
  int lines=0, words=0, freq[SIZE] = {0}, len;
  char c;
  while (cin >> word)
  { ++words;
    cin.get(c);
    if (c == '\n') ++lines;
    len = word.length();
    for (int i=0; i<len; i++)
    { c = word[i];
      if (c >= 'a' && c <= 'z') c += 'A' - 'a';    // capitalize c
      if (c >= 'A' && c <= 'Z') ++freq[c];               // count c
    }
  }
  cout << "The input had " << lines << " lines, " << words
       << " words,\nand the following letter frequencies:\n";
  for (int i=65; i<SIZE; i++)
  { cout << '\t' << char(i) << ": " << freq[i];
    if (i > 0 && i%8 == 0) cout << endl;       // print 8 to a line
  }
  cout << endl;
}
```

6.15
```
bool is_upper(char c)
{ return bool(c >= 'A' && c <= 'Z');
}
bool is_lower(char c)
{ return bool(c >= 'a' && c <= 'z');
}
bool is_letter(char c)
{ return bool(is_upper(c) || is_lower(c));
}
void reduce(string& s)
{ while (s.length() > 0 && !is_letter(s[0]))
    s.erase(0, 1);
  int k = s.length() - 1;
  while (k > 0 && !is_letter(s[k--]))
    s.erase(k+1, 1);
  int len = s.length();
  if (len == 0) return;
  for (int i=0; i<len; i++)
    if (is_upper(s[i])) s[i] += 'a' - 'A';
}
```

6.16
```
int main()
{ string s;
  const int SIZE=1000;      // assume at most 1000 different words
  string word[SIZE];                          // holds words read
  int lines=0, words=0, n=0, freq[SIZE]={0};
  char c;
  while (cin >> s)
  { reduce(s);
    if (s.length == 0) continue;
    ++words;
    cin.get(c);
    if (c == '\n') ++lines;                            // count line
    for (int i=0; i<n; i++)
      if (word[i] == s) break;
    if (i == n) word[n++] = s;                  // add word to list
    ++freq[i];                                        // count word
  }
  cout << "The input had " << lines << " lines and " << words
       << " words,\nwith the following frequencies:\n";
  for (int i=0; i<n; i++)
  { s = word[i];
    if (i > 0 && i%3 == 0) cout << endl;     // print 3 to a line
    cout << setw(16) << setiosflags(ios::right)
         << s.c_str() << ": " << setw(2) << freq[i];
  }
  cout << endl;
}
```

6.17
```
int main()
{ const int SIZE=100;  // maximum number of lines stored
  string line[SIZE], s;
  int n=0, len, maxlen=0;
  while (!cin.eof())
  { getline(cin, s);
    len = s.length();
    if (len > 0) cout << s << endl;
    if (len > maxlen) maxlen = len;
    line[n++] = s;
  }
  --n;                         // n == number of lines read
  for (int i=0; i<n; i++)
  { s = line[i];
    len = s.length();
    cout << string(maxlen-len, ' ') << s << endl;
  }
}
```

6.18
```
string Roman(int n)
{ int d3 = n/1000;  // the thousands digit
  string s(d3, 'M');
  n %= 1000;
  int d2 = n/100;  // the hundreds digit
  if (d2 == 9) s += "CM";
  else if (d2 >= 5)
  { s += "D";
    s += string(d2-5, 'C');
  }
  else if (d2 == 4) s += "CD";
  else s += string(d2, 'X');
  n %= 100;
  int d1 = n/10;  // the tens digit
  if (d1 == 9) s += "XC";
  else if (d1 >= 5)
  { s += "L";
    s += string(d1-5, 'X');
  }
  else if (d1 == 4) s += "XL";
  else s += string(d1, 'X');
  n %= 10;
  int d0 = n/1;  // the ones digit
  if (d0 == 9) s += "IX";
  else if (d0 >= 5)
  { s += "V";
    s += string(d0-5, 'I');
  }
  else if (d0 == 4) s += "IV";
  else s += string(d0, 'I');
  return s;
}
```

6.19
```
int v(string s, int i)
{ char c = s[i];
  if (c == 'M') return 1000;
  if (c == 'D') return 500;
  if (c == 'C') return 100;
  if (c == 'L') return 50;
  if (c == 'X') return 10;
  if (c == 'V') return 5;
  if (c == 'I') return 1;
  return 0;
}
int HindArabic(string s)
{ int n = v(s,0);
  int len = s.length();
  for (int i=1; i<len; i++)
    if (v(s,i) <= v(s,i-1)) n += v(s,i);
    else n -= 2*v(s,i-1);
  return n;
}
```

6.20
```
char c(int k)
{ assert(k >= 0 && k <= 15);
  if (k < 10) return char(k + '0');
  return char(k - 10 + 'a');
}
string hexadecimal(int n)
{ if (n == 0) return string(1, '0');
  string s;
  while (n > 0)
  { s = string(1, c(n%16)) + s;
    n /= 16;
  }
  return s;
}
```

6.21
```
int v(string s, int i)
{ char c = s[i];
  assert(c >= '0' && c <= '9' || c >= 'a' && c <= 'f');
  if (c >= '0' && c <= '9') return int(c - '0');
  else return int(c - 'a' + 10);
}
int decimal(string s)
{ int len = s.length();
  assert(len > 0);
  int n=0;
  for (int i=0; i<len; i++)
    n = 16*n + v(s,i);
  return n;
}
```

6.22
```
void reverse(string& s)
{ string temp = s;
  int len = s.length();
  for (int i=0; i<len; i++)
    s[i] = temp[len-i-1];
}
```

6.23
```
bool is_palindrome(string s)
{ int len = s.length();
  for (int i=0; i<len/2; i++)
    if (s[i] != s[len-i-1]) return false;
  return true;
}
```

6.24
```
bool more(ifstream& fin, string& s)
{ cout << s << endl;
  fout << s << endl;
  return more(fin, s);
}
bool more(ifstream& fin, string& s)
{ if (getline(fin, s)) return true;
  else return false;
}
int main()
{ ifstream fin1("Democrats.dat");
  ifstream fin2("Republicans.dat");
  ofstream fout("Presidents.dat");
  string s1, s2;
  bool more1 = more(fin1, s1);
  bool more2 = more(fin2, s2);
  while (more1 && more2)
    if (s1 < s2) more1 = copy(fout, fin1, s1);
    else more2 = copy(fout, fin2, s2);
  while (more1)
    more1 = copy(fout, fin1, s1);
  while (more2)
    more2 = copy(fout, fin2, s2);
  fout << endl;
}
```

6.25
```
typedef unsigned short int Byte;
const int MAX = 4*255;              // 4* maximum value for a Byte
void clean(fstream& f, int tolerance);
{ long unsigned int m, n;                        // 4-byte integers
  string pixel(1,' ');        // each pixel is a 1-character string
  string north(1,' '), west(1,' '), east(1,' '), south(1,' ');
  int x, sum;
  Byte p, a, b, c, d, ave;
  f.seekg(0);
  f >> m >> n;  // read dimensions of image
  for (int i=1; i<m-1; i++)          // examine every interior pixel
    for (int j=1; j<n-1; j++)
    { x = i*n + j + 8;         // the address of the current pixel
      f.seekg(x);
      f.read(pixel.c_str(), 1);
      p = Byte(pixel[0]);    // convert string character to a Byte
      f.seekg(x-n);
      f.read(north.c_str(), 1);
      a = Byte(north[0]);
      f.seekg(x-1);
      f.read(west.c_str(), 1);
      b = Byte(west[0]);
      f.seekg(x+1);
      f.read(east.c_str(), 1);
```

```
c = Byte(east[0]);
f.seekg(x+n);
f.read(south.c_str(), 1);
d= Byte(south[0]);
sum = a + b + c + b;
sum = (sum > MAX ? MAX : sum);     // watch out for overflow
ave = sum/4;
if (p > ave + tolerance || p < ave - tolerance)
{ f.seekp(x);
  pixel[0] = char(ave);
  f.write(pixel.c_str(), 1);
}
}
```

Note: This solution is not optimized for speed.

Chapter 7

Abstract Data Types

In computer science the term "abstraction" refers to the idea of disregarding implementation details and imagining the ideal that is being represented. For example, when you click on a button to send your email message, you imagine some kind mechanism that transports your message. You don't want to think about the actual software code that is being executed by various computers in order to deliver your message. Instead, you imagine the abstraction of an email delivery device.

7.1 PROCEDURAL ABSTRACTION

The term *procedural abstraction* is used to describe the use of functions as fundamental actions without regard to the details of their implementation. For example, using a `sort()` function on an array is a procedural abstraction. When we use the function in a program, we assume that the function has already been written and tested thoroughly. This idea is often referred to as *off-the-shelf software*. It is like putting a battery in a camera: we know what the battery is supposed to do, and we assume that it will work properly. But we don't want to think about how the battery works. Instead, we depend upon our confidence that it will work properly so that we can concentrate on the task at hand (using the camera to take good photographs).

The discipline of *structured programming* requires that we decompose our programs into reliable functions that work like the batteries in a camera. These functions may be written by different people at different times. But it is their responsibility to ensure that they work properly.

To facilitate procedural abstraction, a function is often written in two parts: its interface and its implementation. To keep these two parts separate, they are often stored in different files. For example, on a UNIX system, the interface for a `sort()` function might be stored in a file named `sort.h` (called a *header file*) and the implementation might be stored in a file named `sort.cc` (the *source code file*).

The *interface* is the part that the user (called the *client*) sees. It contains all the information that the compiler needs in order to compile a program that calls the function. That includes the declaration of the function, called its *prototype*, and possibly other definitions and declarations. It also contains all the documentation that the client needs in order to use the function correctly.

The *implementation* is the actual complete definition of the function. This, of course, is the function's algorithm: the detailed instructions that the computer needs in order to perform the function. It is analogous to the internal workings of the battery that you put in your camera. It is essential for the program to work but irrelevant to the client who writes the program. Consequently, the implementation file is often compiled separately and provided to the user only as an *object module* in machine language. This is called *information hiding*. Preventing the client from viewing the function's implementation ensures that the programs that use the function will be independent of its algorithm. This is advantageous because it guarantees that, like replacing one battery with another, a newer version of the function could replace the current one without having to make any changes in the program that uses it. Such modularization is essential to structured programming.

EXAMPLE 7.1 Abstracting a `sort()` Function
    Here are four files:

program.cc

```
#include "sort.h"

int main()
{ int a, b, c;
  //...
  sort(a, b, c);
  //...
  return 0;
}
```

sort.h

```
void swap(int& x, int& y, int& z)
//  POSTCONDITION: x <= y <= z
```

sort.cc

```
void swap(int& x, int& y)
{ int t = x;
  x = y;
  y = t;
}

void sort(int& x, int& y, int& z)
{ if (y < x) swap(x, y);
  if (z < y) swap(y, z);
  if (y < x) swap(x, y);
}
```

sort.cc

```
#include <iostream>
#include "sort.h"

void print(int x, int y, int z)
{ cout << x << ", " << y << ", "
       << z << endl;
}

int main()
{ int a = 77;
  int b = 33;
  int c = 99;
  sort(a, b, c);
  print(a, b, c);
  sort(a, c, b);
  print(a, c, b);
  sort(b, a, c);
  print(b, a, c);
  sort(b, c, a);
  print(b, c, a);
  sort(c, a, b);
  print(c, a, b);
  sort(c, b, a);
  print(c, b, a);
  return 0;
}
```

The file named `my_program.cc` contains the client program which calls the `sort()` function. To compile successfully, it must include the precompiler directive `#include "sort.h"`.

The file named `sort.h` contains the function interface. This is the function prototype together with a comment that specifies what the function does.

The file named `sort.cc` contains the function implementation. This is the complete definition of the function. In this case, that includes an auxiliary `swap()` function.

The file named `test_sort.cc` contains the function test driver. It is a temporary program whose only purpose is to test the function thoroughly.

The implementors of the function write the function interface, implementation, and test driver. They could then compile the function on a UNIX system like this:

```
$ cc++ -c sort.cc
$ ls sort*
sort.cc   sort.h    sort.o
```

Here, the dollar sign ($) is taken to be the UNIX prompt, and `cc++` is the C++ compile command. The UNIX `-c` option on the compile command tells the compiler to compile but don't link the source code. This is necessary because the `sort.cc` file contains no `main()` function (it is not a complete C++ program). The UNIX `ls` command then shows the result of the compile-but-don't-link command: it produced the object module named `sort.o` which contains the machine language translation of the C++ code in `sort.cc`. This is where information hiding takes place: the function implementors can supply their customers with the function interface `sort.h` and this binary file without revealing the implementation algorithm.

The customers write the client program `my_program.cc` and then they could compile and run it in a UNIX environment like this:

```
$ cc++ -o my_program my_program.cc sort.o
$ ls my_program*
my_program  my_program.cc
$ my_program
```

The C++ compiler compiles the client program in the file `my_program.cc` and then links it with the object module `sort.o` to produce the executable file named `my_program`. This program is then run simply by using that file name as a UNIX command. (The UNIX option `-o my_program` tells the compiler to use the name `my_program` for the executable file.)

The implementors can compile and run their test driver the same way:

```
$ cc++ -o test_sort test_sort.cc sort.o
$ ls test_sort*
test_sort  test_sort.cc
$ test_sort
```

Of course, they should do this before they deliver their product to their clients.

EXAMPLE 7.2 Interchanging Modules

Suppose that some time after delivering their first version of their `sort()` function the implementors develop the following improved version: After testing this version thoroughly, they can produce an object

sort.cc
```
void sort(int& x, int& y)
{ if (x > y)
  { int t = x;
    x = y;
    y = t;
  }
}


void sort(int& x, int& y, int& z)
{ sort(x, y);
  sort(y, z);
  sort(x, y);
}
```

module for it and ship it out to their customers. If a customer had compiled her application program separately, like this:

```
$ cc++ -c my_program.cc
$ ls my_program*
my_program  my_program.cc  my_program.o
```

then she could upgrade her application without having to recompile it, like this:

```
$ cc++ -o my_program my_program.o sort.o
```

The big advantage here is that the program is improved without changing any of its source code.

When you implement a function you should take the point of view of fulfilling a contract which specifies exactly what the function is required to do. These specifications then become the documentation for the function's specification file. In the "real world" the specifications may be written by the customer.

Function specifications are often written in terms of preconditions and postconditions. A *precondition* is a statement about the function's parameters that is assumed to be true before the function is called. A *postcondition* is a statement about function's output (*i.e., its* return value and any arguments passed by reference) that is guaranteed to be true after the function returns.

EXAMPLE 7.3 Preconditions and Postconditions

```
double geometric_mean(double x, double y);
//   PRECONDITION: x >= 0.0 && y >= 0.0
//   POSTCONDITION: r*r == x*y, where r is the value returned
```

7.2 FUNCTION TEMPLATES

The `swap()` function (see Example 7.1) is widely used in sorting and other essential algorithms. The two values that it interchanges might have type `int` in some applications and type `float` or `string` in others. But the algorithm itself is the same regardless of the type of its two parameters. C++ provides a mechanism that saves the programmer from having to write separate definitions for different type versions of the same function. Called a *function template*, it provides the minimal information needed by the compiler to generate its own definitions of the function whenever it needs them.

EXAMPLE 7.4 A `swap()` Function Template

Here is a template for `swap()` functions, followed by a program that will use three instantiations of it:

```
template <class T>
void swap(T& x,  T& y)
{ T t = x;
  x = y;
  y = t;
}
int main()
{ int a = 44;
  int b = 66;
  swap(a, b);          // compiler generates void swap(int, int);
  float s = 4.4;
  float t = 6.6;
  swap(s, t);          // compiler generates void swap(float, float);
  string mr = "George";
  string ms = "Martha";
  swap(mr, ms);        // compiler generates void swap(string, string);
  return 0;
}
```

When the compiler reads `swap(a, b)` it recognizes that `a` and `b` have the (same) type `int` and uses the template to generate the function by substituting `int` for `T` in the three places where it occurs in the template. It does the same again when it reads `swap(s, t)` except that it substitutes `float` for `T` in the same three places. And when it reads `swap(mr, ms)` it substitutes `string` for `T`.

The only difference between a function definition and a function template definition is that the latter is preceded by the code `template <class T>` and the symbol `T` is used in place of a type. The symbol is called a *template parameter*.

7.3 DATA ABSTRACTION

Data abstraction is a generalization of procedural abstraction. The latter (see Section 7.1) facilitates the development of software by separating the interfaces of user-defined functions from their implementations. The former does the same for user-defined data types. C++ extends this facility by allowing the user to incorporate functions (operations) within the data types which are called *classes*.

EXAMPLE 7.5 A `Ratio` Class

Here is a C++ class definition for a type whose objects represent ratios (fractions):

```cpp
class Ratio
{ public:
    Ratio(int num, int den) { _num = num; _den = den; }
    void print() { cout << _num << '/' << _den; }
  private:
    int _num;              // numerator
    int _den;              // denominator
};
```

The definition block contains two parts, one labeled `public` and one labeled `private`. Data objects and functions declared in the `public` section may be used anywhere in the program: in `main()` or in any other function. But data and functions declared in the `private` section may only be used within the class itself. In this case, we have two function members (`Ratio()` and `print()`) in the `public` section and two data members (`_num` and `_den`) in the `private` section. Notice that the `private` data `_num` and `_den` are used within the class itself (in the `Ratio()` and `print()` functions) but not in `main()`. This is called *information hiding*: the internal details (`_num` and `_den`) of an object are "hidden" from the outside world. In most programmer-defined classes like this, most of the class functions are in the `public` section and most of the class data are in the `private` section.

Most C++ programmers follow the convention of capitalizing the name of a new class; *e.g.* `Ratio`; this distinguishes it as the name of a programmer-defined type. Another recommended method is to prefix an underscore to the name of each `private` member. This allows the same names without the underscore to be used in other places (*e.g.*, `_num = num` in the `Ratio()` function) to make the code easier to understand.

Note that the bodies of the class functions (`Ratio()` and `print()`) are set on the same lines as their heads. This is normally done only with very simple functions. More often, the function bodies will be defined elsewhere, even in a separate file, leaving only the function declarations within the class definition. Also note that the class data (`_num` and `_den`) are declared on separate lines, with a comment for each. That form is recommended, instead of simply declaring `int _num, _den;`.

Finally, note that the first member function has the same name as the class itself (`Ratio`) and that it has no return type. Such class functions are called constructors. A *constructor* is a special member function that is automatically invoked whenever an object of the class is declared (*i.e.*, "constructed").

Here is a little program that uses this `Ratio` class:

```cpp
int main()
{ Ratio x(3,4);       // constructs the object x representing 3/4
  x.print();          // calls the print() function for the object x
  cout << endl;
  return 0;
}
```

The first statement in `main()`, `Ratio x(3,4)` invokes this constructor, which creates the object `x` and passes the arguments 3 and 4 to the parameters `num` and `den`.

At this point, the object x can be visualized as shown at right. The name of
the object is x; its type is Ratio; it has two fields (data members) named _num
and _den, both of type int; and their values are 3 and 4, respectively.

The call x.print() produces the output 3/4.

To summarize, a class defines a new type in C++. The class contains
data and functions, with the data (also called *fields*) usually in the private
section and the functions (also called *methods* or *operations*) usually in the
public section of the class declaration, like this:

```
class ObjectType
{ public:
    ObjectType() { /* definition of constructor ObjectType() */ }
    void f(short k) { /* definition of function f() */ }
    int g() { /* definition of function g() */ }
  private:
    float a;
    char c;
};
```

In external functions (such as main()), class objects (also called *instances*) are declared as any other
objects are declared, like this:

```
ObjectType u, v;
```

The member functions of the class can only be called when "bound" to a specific object of the class,
like this:

```
u.f(44);                // the call f() is bound to the object u
int n = v.g();          // the call g() is bound to the object v
```

The class object to which a member function call is bound is called the *implicit argument* for the call.
For example, the call u.f(44)   actually has two arguments: the explicit argument 44 and the
implicit argument u.

A class constructor has the same name as the class itself, it has no return type, it is invoked
automatically when the class is *instantiated* (*i.e.*, an object of that class type is declared), and it
cannot be called explicitly.

EXAMPLE 7.6 Defining the Addition Operation for the Ratio Class

Like all numeric types, the Ratio type should "know" how to add. We can give it this ability by including a
sum() member function:

```
class Ratio
{ public:
    Ratio(int num, int den) { _num = num; _den = den; }
    void print() const { cout << _num << '/' << _den; }
    Ratio sum(Ratio y)
    { int num = _num*y._den + _den*y._num;
      int den = _den*y._den;
      Ratio temp(num, den);
      return temp;
    }
  private:
    int _num;                 // numerator
    int _den;                 // denominator
};
int main()
{ Ratio r(3,4), s(2,3), t(0,1);  // constructs objects r, s, and t
  t = r.sum(s);                   // assigns to t the sum of r and s
  t.print();            // calls the print() function for the object t
```

```
    cout << endl;
    return 0;
}
```

The first line of the `main()` function constructs the three `Ratio` objects `r`, `s`, and `t`, which represent 3/4, 2/3, and 0/1, respectively. The second line calls the `sum()` member function, passing the argument `s` and using `r` as the implicit argument (we say that `r` "owns" the call). This assigns 3·3 + 4·2 = 17 to the local variable `num` and 4·3 = 12 to the local variable `den`. Then it constructs the local `Ratio` object `temp` using the values 17 and 12 to represent the ratio 17/12, and returns that object's value to where the function was called in `main()`. Then that value (the pair {17,12}) is assigned to `t`, and then `t` is printed on the fourth line. The resulting output is `17/12`.

Notice that the member data values of the implicit argument `r` are references without the "dot" notation: `int den = _den*y._den;`. That is because whatever object "owns" the function call, its `_num` and `_den` fields are directly accessible. When the call is `r.sum(s)`, the line `int den = _den*y._den;` means `int den = r._den*s._den;`. If the call were `a.sum(s)`, then the same line would mean `int den = a._den*s._den;`.

Also note here that an object (`s`) of type `Ratio` is passed to a function, an object (`temp`) of type `Ratio` is used as a local variable within a function, and an (anonymous) object of type `Ratio` is assigned to another `Ratio` object (`t`). The point is that objects of programmer-defined types can be used the same way as objects of fundamental types (*e.g.*, `int`, `float`, *etc.*).

The `sum()` function in Example 7.6 is a bit awkward because it represents the addition operation + which takes two operands, but it must defined with only one (explicit) parameter. That is a result of the function being a member of the Ratio class, which requires it to have one implicit argument (the object that owns the call: `r` in `r.sum(s)`). The function would be more natural if it could be called using both operands (`r` and `s`) as explicit parameters like this:

```
    t = sum(r,s);
```

That would require the function to be declared as a non-member function, like this:

```
    Ratio sum(Ratio x, Ratio y)
    { int num = x._num*y._den + y._den*y._num;
      int den = x._den*y._den;
      Ratio temp(num, den);
      return temp;
    }
```

But that won't work because the function needs access to the private data members `_num` and `_den` of the objects `x` and `y`; only member functions are granted that access. Fortunately, C++ provides an exception to that rule, precisely for situations like this. The solution is to make the `sum()` function a "friend" of the `Ratio` class.

7.4 C++ `friend` Functions

A `friend` function of a class is a non-member function that has the privileges of a member function of the class, namely access to the class's private members. One reason for making a function a `friend` of a class instead of an actual member of the class is to eliminate the requirement of the implicit argument, making instead all arguments passed to the function explicit. This simplifies the syntax and makes the code more readable.

A function is declared to be a `friend` of a class simply by declaring the function within the class and preceding its declaration with the keyword `friend`:

EXAMPLE 7.7 Using friend Functions

This works the same as Example 7.6. The changes are shown in **boldface**:

```
class Ratio
{ public:
    Ratio(int num, int den) { _num = num; _den = den; }
    void print() const { cout << _num << '/' << _den; }
    friend Ratio sum(Ratio x, Ratio y)
    { int num = x._num*y._den + x._den*y._num;
      int den = x._den*y._den;
      Ratio temp(num, den);
      return temp;
    }
  private:
    int _num;              // numerator
    int _den;              // denominator
};
int main()
{ Ratio r(3,4), s(2,3), t(0,1);  // constructs objects r, s, and t
  t = sum(r,s);                   // assigns to t the sum of r and s
  t.print();           // calls the print() function for the object t
  cout << endl;
  return 0;
}
```

The form `t = sum(r, s)` is a notational improvement over the form `t = r.sum(s)` that was used in Example 7.6.

As mentioned earlier, the actual definitions of a class's member functions are usually specified separately. This is illustrated in the next example.

EXAMPLE 7.8 Separating the Definitions of Member Functions from Their declarations

This is the same class as in Example 7.7:

```
class Ratio
{    friend Ratio sum(Ratio, Ratio);
  public:
    Ratio(int, int);        // constructor
    void print() const;
  private:
    int _num;              // numerator
    int _den;              // denominator
};

Ratio sum(Ratio x, Ratio y)
{ int num = x._num*y._den + x._den*y._num;
  int den = x._den*y._den;
  Ratio temp(num, den);
  return temp;
}

Ratio::Ratio(int num, int den)
{ _num = num;
  _den = den;
}
void Ratio::print()
{ cout << _num << '/' << _den;
}
```

The only significant change here is that the bodies of the `friend` function `sum()` and of both member functions `Ratio()` and `print()` have been removed from the class, thereby separating the function definitions from their declarations. We have also shifted the `friend` function up to the beginning of the class definition to emphasize that it is not a member function. Its placement outside of the `public` and `private` declaration sections of the class is irrelevant since it is not a member of the class.

Notice the necessity of the *scope resolution operator* in the prefix `Ratio::` before the names of the member functions `Ratio()` and `print()` in their definitions. A class is like a namespace, restricting the scope of the names declared within. Of course, the definition of the `sum()` function does not need any scope resolution because it is not declared to be the member of any class; it is only a `friend` of the `Ratio` class.

The definitions of class functions are usually separated from their declarations that are given inside the class, like this:

```
// the interface for class ObjectType:
class ObjectType
{ public:
     ObjectType();           // constructor
     void f(short);
     int g();
  private:
     float a;
     char c;
};

// the implementation for class ObjectType:
ObjectType::ObjectType()
{ // definition of constructor ObjectType() goes here
}

void ObjectType::f(short k)
{ // definition of function f() goes here
}

int ObjectType::g()
{ // definition of function g() goes here
}
```

The first part is called the *class interface*, and the second part is called the *class implementation*. This separation makes it easier to use the class because all the information that the programmer needs to use the class is given in its interface, leaving its implementation details hidden typically in a separate file. It also allows the class's creator to change the class implementation without affecting its interface or the programs that use it.

7.5 OVERLOADING OPERATORS

An *operator* is a function that can be called with an alternative *infix* syntax form. For example, the *addition operator* + is usually used like this:

```
c = a + b;
```

But is can also be used in its formal form, like this:

```
c = operator+(a, b);
```

As a function, its name is `operator+`.

Recall that any function in C++ can be *overloaded*. That means that the same name can be used for different functions, as long as their parameter lists are different. For example, the following two distinct functions can be defined in the same scope:

```
    void swap(int x, int y) { int temp=x; x = y; y = temp; }
    void swap(float x, float y) { float temp=x; x = y; y = temp; }
```
Then the following code will execute as intended:
```
    int m=33, n=66;
    swap(m, n);  // swaps the integers m and n
    float a=4.44, b=8.88;
    swap(a, b);  // swaps the floats a and b
```
The calls are made to the separate functions, distinguished by their different parameter lists.

A class defines a new type. To give the new type functionality comparable to the operations that exist for fundamental types, we usually overload the operators used for those operations. For example, the addition operator defined for numeric types can be overloaded for our new Ratio type:

EXAMPLE 7.9 Overloading the Addition Operator

This class is equivalent to that defined in Example 7.8. The only changes are shown in **boldface**:
```
    class Ratio
    {    friend Ratio operator+(Ratio, Ratio);
      public:
         Ratio(int, int);       // constructor
         void print() const;
      private:
         int _num;              // numerator
         int _den;              // denominator
    };

    Ratio operator+(Ratio x, Ratio y)
    { int num = x._num*y._den + x._den*y._num;
      int den = x._den*y._den;
      Ratio temp(num, den);
      return temp;
    }
```
The implementations of the Ratio() and print() functions are omitted since they are identical to those in Example 7.8.

The advantage to naming the function operator+() instead of sum() is that the operator name allows the function to be called like this:
```
    Ratio r(3,4), s(2,3), t(0,1);
    t = r + s;
```
This is a significant improvement over the form t = sum(r,s) used in Example 7.7.

The other arithmetic operators, operator-(), operator*(), and operator/(), can be overloaded the same way.

In addition to overloading arithmetic operators, it is also convenient to overload the input and output operators operator>>() and operator<<().

EXAMPLE 7.10 Overloading the Input and Output Operators

This extends Example 7.9:
```
    class Ratio
    {    friend Ratio operator+(Ratio, Ratio);
         friend istream& operator>>(istream& istr, Ratio& r);
         friend ostream& operator<<(ostream& ostr, const Ratio& r);
      public:
         Ratio(int, int);        // constructor
```

```
    private:
      int _num;                // numerator
      int _den;                // denominator
  };

  istream& operator>>(istream& istr, Ratio& x)
  { char ch;            // used to eat the slash character '/'
    istr >> x._num;
    if (istr.peek() == '/') istr >> ch >> x._den;
    else x._den = 1;
    return istr;
  }

  ostream& operator<<(ostream& ostr, const Ratio& x)
  { if (x._den == 1) ostr << x._num;
    else ostr << x._num << '/' << x._den;
    return ostr;
  }
```

The implementation of the `Ratio()` constructor is omitted since it is the same as in Example 7.8.

Note that the output operator `operator<<` replaces the `print()` function.

With these overloaded operators, we can write the following more natural looking code:

```
  Ratio r(3,4), s(2,3), t(0,1);
  cin >> r >> s;              // calls operator>>(istream&,Ratio&) twice
  t = r + s;
  cout << t << endl;          // calls operator<<(ostream&,constRatio&) once
```

The second line first makes the call `operator>>(cin,r)`, passing the arguments `cin` and `r` to the parameters `ostr` and `x`, respectively, both by reference. If the input is `22/7`, then the function reads `22` into `r._num` and `7` into `r._den` (ignoring the slash character). Since r was passed by reference, the resulting ratio {22, 7} is stored in `r`.

Note how the third line uses the `peek()` function to determine whether the next character in the input stream is the slash character. If it is (as in the input `22/7`), then that character is read into `ch` and the next integer is read into `r._den`. This code allows integer input also to be accepted by the input function (*e.g.*, 250 would be read and stored as {250, 1}).

The input function returns the input stream as a reference. This allows it to be passed along to the next call to the input function when the operator >> is chained as in

```
  cin >> r >> s;
```

In fact, these two calls are actually implemented as

```
  operator>>( operator>>(cin, r), s );
```

so a second ratio can be read into the object `s`.

7.6 CLASS INVARIANTS

One problem that is likely to occur with ratios (fractions) is that they are likely to be stored in non-reduced form such as 24/40 and −11/−8. Even if they are always in reduced form when they are created, non-reduced forms can still result, as with 1/6 + 3/8 = 26/48. This can be confusing because a single ratio can have an unlimited number of different forms (*e.g.*, (−5)/4 = (−10)/8 = (−15)/12 = ⋯ = 5/(−4) = ⋯). This problem can be solved by specifying class invariants.

A *class invariant* is a condition that is forced upon all instances of the class. We shall specify the following two class invariants for the `Ratio` class:

  1. The data members `_num` and `_den` have no common factors greater than 1.
  2. The data member `_den` > 0.

These two conditions ensure that no two distinct `Ratio` objects are numerically equal unless they have the same values stored in their `_num` and `_den` fields; *i.e.*, that every fraction that can be represented as a `Ratio` object has a unique representation.

Class invariants are typically enforced by means of `private` utility functions.

EXAMPLE 7.11 Enforcing Class Invariants

This extends Example 7.10:

```cpp
class Ratio
{   friend Ratio operator+(Ratio, Ratio);
    friend istream& operator>>(istream&, Ratio&);
    friend ostream& operator<<(ostream&, const Ratio&);
  public:
    Ratio(int, int);        // constructor
  private:
    void _reduce();         // enforces the class invariants
    int _num;               // numerator
    int _den;               // denominator
};

Ratio operator+(Ratio x, Ratio y)
{ int num = x._num*y._den + x._den*y._num;
  int den = x._den*y._den;
  Ratio temp(num, den);
  temp._reduce();
  return temp;
}

istream& operator>>(istream& istr, Ratio& x)
{ char ch;          // used to eat the slash character '/'
  istr >> x._num;
  if (istr.peek() == '/') istr >> ch >> x._den;
  else x._den = 1;
  x._reduce();
  return istr;
}

Ratio::Ratio(int num, int den)
{ _num = num;
  _den = den;
  _reduce();
}

int gcd(int m, int n)
{ assert(m > 0 && n > 0);
  while (m > 0)
  { if (m < n) swap(m,n);
    m -= n;
  }
  return n;
}
```

```
    void Ratio::_reduce()
  { if (_num == 0 || _den == 0)
    { _num = 0;
      _den = 1;
      return;
    }
    if (_den < 0)                             // enforces constraint: _den > 0
    { _num *= -1;
      _den *= -1;
    }
    int abs_num = (_num < 0 ? -_num : _num);              // = |_num|
    int g = gcd(abs_num, _den);
    _num /= g;  // enforces constraint that ratio be in lowest terms
    _den /= g;
  }
```

The _reduce() function is a private member function of the Ratio class that is used by the addition operator operator+(), the input operator operator>>(), and the constructor Ratio(). The gcd() function does not need to be a member function because it does not access any private data and is used only by the _reduce() function. Note that the gcd() function does use the swap() function which would be defined just above it in the class implementation file.

The _reduce() function first checks for division by 0; if the denominator is 0, the ratio is changed to the default 0/1. Next it checks for a negative denominator to enforce the second class invariant. Then it uses the conditional expression operator to set up the absolute value of the numerator: if the condition (_num < 0) is true it assigns -_num to abs_num; otherwise it assigns _num to it. Then it uses the gcd() function to obtain the greatest common divisor g of abs_num and _den. Since the greatest common divisor is a multiple of all other common divisors, dividing _num and _den by the g guarantees that the resulting pair will have no common divisors greater than 1.

The assert() function used in the gcd() function is assumed to be defined elsewhere. Its single parameter accepts a condition (*i.e.*, an int). If the condition is false (*i.e.*, evaluates to 0), then the program aborts at that point. If the condition is true (*i.e.*, evaluates to non-zero), then the program continues. Such a function is defined in the old C header file assert.h, which is named cassert in Standard C++.

7.7 CONSTRUCTORS AND DESTRUCTORS

There is still room for improvement of the Ratio class. For example, we can use an *initialization list* for the constructor:

EXAMPLE 7.12 Initialization Lists for Constructors

```
    class Ratio
  {   friend Ratio operator+(Ratio, Ratio);
      friend istream& operator>>(istream&, Ratio&);
      friend ostream& operator<<(ostream&, const Ratio&);
    public:
      Ratio(int, int);        // constructor
    private:
      _reduce();                    // enforces the class invariants
      int _num;               // numerator
      int _den;               // denominator
  };

  Ratio::Ratio(int num, int den) : _num(num), _den(den)
  { _reduce();
  }
```

The only change here (shown in **boldface**) over Example 7.11 is the initialization list in the implementation of the constructor `Ratio()`:

```
:  _num(num), _den(den)
```

This is simply an alternative for the assignment statements

```
_num = num;
_den = den;
```

which were in the body of the function.

Initialization lists are very specialized: they can be used only in constructors and only for initializing member data. But they are convenient and are widely used.

A more significant improvement is to use *default values* for the constructor parameters:

EXAMPLE 7.13 Default Values for Parameters

```
class Ratio
{   friend Ratio operator+(Ratio, Ratio);
    friend istream& operator>>(istream&, Ratio&);
    friend ostream& operator<<(ostream&, const Ratio&);
  public:
    Ratio(int=0, int=1);    // constructor
  private:
    _reduce();               // enforces the class invariants
    int _num;                // numerator
    int _den;                // denominator
};
```

No change is needed here in the implementation. We have simply added (in **boldface**) "=0" and "=1" to the parameter list of the constructor's declaration. The effect is to use the value 0 for the parameter `num` and 1 for the parameter `den` if values are not passed in as arguments. For example:

```
Ratio x(5,7);    // creates the object x representing the ratio 5/7
Ratio x(5);      // creates the object x representing the ratio 5/1
Ratio x;         // creates the object x representing the ratio 0/1
```

By including these default values in the constructor's declaration, we have the equivalent of three different (overloaded) constructors, one with 2 parameters (`num` and `den`) as in Example 7.11, one with 1 parameter (`num`) and one with 0 parameters. Note that, unlike all other functions, a constructor with 0 parameters is called without using parentheses:

```
Ratio x;         // creates the object x representing the ratio 0/1
```

Also note that when arguments are passed to some of the parameters that have default values, they are matched to those parameters in the same way that all arguments are matched with parameters: in the order in which they are listed. Thus the call

```
Ratio x(5);      // creates the object x representing the ratio 5/1
```

matches the argument 5 to the first parameter (`num`), leaving the second parameter (`den`) to use its default value 1.

Finally note that these default values 0 and 1 help enforce the `Ratio` class invariant that `_den` never be 0 or negative, and they nicely allow whole numbers (`int`s like 5) to be represented as ratios.

Default values can be specified for the parameters of <u>any</u> function in C++ (not just class constructors). The only restrictions are (1) the values must be given in the parameter list of the function declaration but not its definition (if separate); (2) if only some of the parameters are given default values, they must be listed after all other parameters in the parameter list. If you include the names of the parameters in the function declaration (an option in C++), then the initial values are listed on their right, like this:

```
Ratio(int num=0, int den=1);
```

EXAMPLE 7.14 A Copy Constructor for the `Ratio` Class

A class may have many constructors. The one that can be invoked with no arguments is called the *default constructor*. The default constructor implemented here is also invoked when one or two integer arguments are used (see Example 7.13).

A constructor may also be invoked with an argument of the same class, like this:

```
Ratio x(22,7);   // invokes the default constructor
Ratio y(x);      // invokes the copy constructor, copying x into y
Ratio z=x;       // invokes the copy constructor, copying x into z
```

The copy constructor looks like the default constructor:

```
class Ratio
{   friend Ratio operator+(Ratio, Ratio);
    friend istream& operator>>(istream&, Ratio&);
    friend ostream& operator<<(ostream&, const Ratio&);
  public:
    Ratio(int=0, int=1);    // default constructor
    Ratio(const Ratio&);    // copy constructor
  private:
    _reduce();     // enforces the class invariants
    int _num;      // numerator
    int _den;      // denominator
};
Ratio::Ratio(const Ratio& r) : _num(r._num), _den(r._den)
{
}
```

The copy constructor's single parameter is passed by *constant reference*. This means that the function can access the argument passed but it cannot change it. In this implementation, it simply copies the values of the argument's _num and _den fields into the corresponding fields of the new object being constructed.

7.8 THE FOUR AUTOMATIC MEMBER FUNCTIONS

Every class in C++ must have four special member functions: a default constructor, a copy constructor, an assignment operator, and a destructor. Since these member functions are required, the compiler will create them automatically if they are not defined explicitly in the class.

The *default constructor* is the constructor that can be called with no arguments. It is invoked whenever a declaration without parameters is executed, like this:

```
ObjectType x;   // creates the object x of type ObjectType
```

The *copy constructor* is the constructor whose header has the special form:

```
ObjectType(const ObjectType&);
```

It is invoked automatically in three special cases:

(1) whenever a newly declared object is initialized:

```
ObjectType y=x;   // the copy constructor is invoked to initialize y
with x
```

(2) whenever an object is passed by value to a function:

```
void f(ObjectType x)
{ //...
}
f(y);   // the copy constructor is invoked to copy y into x
```

(3) whenever an object is returned by value from a function:

```
ObjectType f()
{ ObjectType y;
  // ...
  return y;
}
x = f();  // the copy constructor is invoked to copy y into x
```

The *assignment operator* is the overloaded operator whose header has the special form

```
ObjectType& operator=(const ObjectType&);
```

It is invoked whenever one object is assigned to another:

```
ObjectType x, y;
// ...
x = y;  // the assignment operator is called to copy y into x
```

The *destructor* is the function whose header has the special form:

```
~ObjectType();
```

It is invoked automatically whenever an object goes "out of scope":

```
if (t > 0)
{ ObjectType x;
  // ...
}  // the destructor is invoked for x
```

EXAMPLE 7.15 The Assignment Operator

Here are an assignment operator for the `Ratio` class:

```
Ratio& Ratio::operator=(const Ratio& r)
{ _num = r._num;
  _den = r._den;
  return *this;
}
```

Although it is not a constructor, the assignment operator is almost the same as the copy constructor (see Example 7.14): it copies the values of the argument's `_num` and `_den` fields into the corresponding fields of the implicit argument (the object that "owns" the call). Then the function returns that implicit argument with the statement:

```
        return *this;
```

The C++ keyword `this` can be used only within class member functions; it always refers to the implicit argument. For example, when the statement

```
y = x;
```

executes for the existing `Ratio` objects `x` and `y`, it is equivalent to the call

```
y.operator=(x);
```

which passes the <u>explicit</u> argument `x` to the parameter `r` and uses `y` as the <u>implicit</u> argument. In that case, `this` is a pointer to (*i.e.*, the memory address of) `y`, and `*this` is a synonym for `y` itself. So the complete effect of this call to the assignment operator is really

```
y._num = x._num;
y._den = x._den;
```

Remember that the assignment operator, like the default constructor, the copy constructor, and the destructor, will be created automatically by the compiler if it is not explicitly specified in the class definition. In that case, the compiler implements it in the simplest way possible: by copying the fields of the object on the right of the assignment into the fields of the object on the left. Since that is precisely what this implemented version does, it really does not need to be included at all in the class definition. In fact, the only times that the assignment operator, the default constructor, the copy constructor, or the destructor really need to be explicitly implemented is when they would do more than the obvious. In the `Ratio` class, that applies only to the default constructor which is implemented to work with optional `int` parameters. Example 7.18 illustrates a class where the destructor needs to be implemented explicitly.

7.9 ABSTRACT DATA TYPES

An abstraction is an idealization in the mathematical sense: it is an imaginary idea that usually can be only approximated in the "real world." One of the best example of this is the set of all integers $\mathbf{Z} = \{ ..., -2, -1, 0, 1, 2, 3, ... \}$. This set is essential to most mathematics. But it does not really exist because it is infinite. We can imagine it in our minds, but there is no way to represent it in the real world, by computer or any other means. The best we can do is approximate it. That is what the type `long` does. On a standard 32-bit workstation, a `long` object may assume any one of the 4,294,967,296 elements of the set $\mathbf{long} = \{ -2147483648, \cdots, -2, -1, 0, 1, 2, 3, \cdots, 2147483647 \}$. That is a big set and is quite adequate for most programs. But it is infinitesimal compared to $\mathbf{Z}$.

The point here is that the real set $\mathbf{long}$ is far different from the ideal set $\mathbf{Z}$, and the successful programmer must keep that difference in mind. In practice, the difference becomes painfully apparent when integer overflow occurs.

EXAMPLE 7.16 Integer Overflow

This program will produce erroneous output on most standard 32-bit PCs and workstations:

```
int main()
{ long n=1;
  for (int i=0; i < 20; i++)
  { n *= 4;
    cout << n << endl;
  }
  return 0;
}
```

Assuming that the largest value of type long is `2147483647` ($= 2^{31} - 1$), this program will suffer integer overflow as soon as `i` reaches 16. The actual output looks like this on one UNIX workstation:

```
4
16
64
256
1024
4096
16384
65536
262144
1048576
4194304
16777216
67108864
268435456
1073741824
0
0
0
0
0
```

On another workstation, the last 5 numbers output are negative! In both cases, those values are obviously incorrect. The problem simply is that the next number after 1073741824 ($= 2^{20}$) would ideally be 4294967296 ($= 2^{22}$); but that is greater than the largest value that `n` can have.

In computer science, we use the term *abstract data type* ("ADT") to describe the ideal which the real implemented data type represents: **Z** is the ADT which type `long` represents. Of course, there may be several different representations of the same ADT. For example, in C++ all the integer types (`bool`, `char`, `short`, `long`, `unsigned char`, `unsigned short`, `unsigned`, and `unsigned long`) are representations of **Z**.

An *ADT* is a description of an ideal type which could be implemented in different ways in a program. The description includes the set of all values that the ideal type could have, the set of operations that could be performed on objects of that type, and any other information (*e.g.*, class invariants) that should be imposed on the objects. The ADT serves as a "blueprint" for the programmer who implements the type. It also serves as a specification that can be used when deriving algorithms, so that they can be implemented after the ADT has been implemented.

An ADT may be based upon a mathematical abstraction (as **Z** is) or upon more practical considerations. For example, we may want to define an ADT for graphic images in order to build a type named `image` that could be used in computer graphics programs. Our choice of operations to define for the ADT would likely be based upon previous experience, both with computers and with real visual images.

EXAMPLE 7.17 An ADT for Stacks

A *stack* is a container that uses the "last-in-first-out" ("LIFO") method for insertions and removals. Imagine a stack of trays in a lunch room: when you "push" a tray onto the stack, it goes on top; when you "pop" a tray off the stack, you get the one that was on the top.

Here is a formal ADT specification for stack:

ADT: <u>Stack</u>

Represents:

A sequence of elements, all of the same type.

Access:

A stack allows access only at one end of the sequence, called the *top* of the stack. Both insertions and removals must be made at the top.

Constructors and Destructors:

create	Creates an empty stack of a given maximum size.
destroy	De-allocates the memory used for the stack.

Access Functions:

top	Returns the last element on the stack.
is_empty	Returns `true` if the stack is empty; otherwise returns `false`.
is_full	Returns `true` if the stack is full; otherwise returns `false`.

Mutator Functions:

push	Inserts a new element at the top of the stack.
pop	Removes and returns the element from the top of the stack.

EXAMPLE 7.18 An Implementation of the ADT: <u>Stack</u> with Element Type `char`

```
class Stack
{ public:
    Stack(int s=100);      // sets the default maximum number at 100
    ~Stack();
    char top() const;
    bool is_empty() const;
    bool is_full() const;
    void push(const char);
    char pop();
```

```
    private:
       char* _a;       // the stack itself: a dynamic array of char
       int _max;       // the maximum number of elements on the stack
       int _count;     // the number of elements on the stack
};

Stack::Stack(int m) : _max(m), _count(0)
{ _a = new char[_max];
  assert(_a != 0);
}

Stack::~Stack()
{ delete [] _a;
}

char Stack::top() const
{ assert (_count > 0);
  return _a[_count-1];
}

bool Stack::is_empty() const
{ return bool(_count == 0);
}

bool Stack::is_full() const
{ return bool(_count == _max);
}

void Stack::push(const char x)
{ assert(_count < _max);
  _a[_count++] = x;
}

char Stack::pop()
{ assert(_count > 0);
  return _a[--_count];
}
```

The class has three private data members: a dynamic array named _a, and two integers named _max and _count. A *dynamic array* in C++ is a pointer (*i.e.*, an address in memory) that can be used like an ordinary array (*i.e.*, with the subscript operator, as in _a[4]). But unlike an ordinary array, the size of a dynamic array may be declared at run-time by means of the new operator: _a = new char[_max], and whose memory allocation can be de-allocated (*i.e.*, returned to the "heap" of memory available for use by other dynamic objects) by means of the delete operator: delete [] _a.

The integer _max holds the maximum number of elements that can be pushed onto the stack, and the integer _count contains the actual number of elements that are currently on the stack. Note the class invariant: $0 \le$ _count $\le$ _max.

Note the use of the assert() function defined in the header <cassert>. This function will abort the program if the condition passed to it is false. In the constructor, the condition (_a != 0) means that the new operator was successful; *i.e.*, that there was enough dynamic memory available to allocate _max elements. The other conditions used in the calls to assert() will prevent the array index _count from going out of range; *i.e.*, they enforce the class invariant: $0 \le$ _count $\le$ _max.

Also note the effective use of the postincrement and predecrement operators in the push() and pop() functions. Since _count is always the location of the next element to be pushed onto the stack (the top of the stack is always _a[_count-1]), it has to be incremented after a new item is pushed onto the stack and it has to be decremented before the top element is popped off the stack.

After this code executes:

```
Stack s(20);
s.push('A');
s.push('B');
cout << s.pop() << endl;
s.push('C');
s.push('D');
cout << s.pop() << endl;
s.push('E');
```

the Stack object named s would look like this:

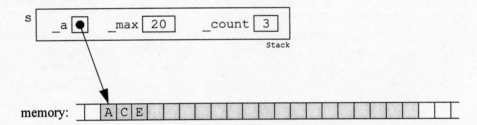

The shaded part of memory represents those bytes that have been allocated for the dynamic array _a. Its abstraction should be imagined as shown at right.

Review Questions

7.1 What is the difference between procedural abstraction and data abstraction?

7.2 What is an *implicit argument*?

7.3 What is a `friend` function?

7.4 What is the purpose of separating a class implementation from its interface?

7.5 Show how the line

```
cin >> r >> s >> t;
```

is actually implemented for `Ratio` objects. (See Example 7.10.)

Problems

7.6 Implement the multiplication operator `*` for the `Ratio` class.

7.7 A *queue* is a container that uses the "first-in-first-out" ("FIFO") method for insertions and removals. Imagine a line of people waiting to buy tickets to a movie: People enter the queue at the back and leave the queue from the front.

Implement the following ADT for queues, with element type `char`:

ADT: <u>Queue</u>

Represents:

A sequence of elements, all of the same type.

Access:

A queue allows access only at the ends of the sequence, called the *back* and the *front* of the queue. Insertions are allowed only at the back, and removals are allowed only at the front.

Constructors and Destructors:

create	Creates an empty queue of a given maximum size.
destroy	De-allocates the memory used for the queue.

Access Functions:

back	Returns the last element in the queue.
front	Returns the first element in the queue.
is_empty	Returns true if the queue is empty; otherwise returns false.
is_full	Returns true if the queue is full; otherwise returns false.

Mutator Functions:

enter	Inserts a new element at the back of the queue.
leave	Removes and returns the first element from the front of the queue.

7.8   Write a function that uses a stack to reverse a queue.

7.9   Clock arithmetic is based on the notion of a 12-hour clock which "wraps around" the time every 12 hours. The arithmetic operations are the same as with ordinary integers, except for the wraparound property that keeps all values within the finite range { 1, 2, 3, 4, 5, 6, 7, 8, 9, 10, 11, 12 }. Mathematicians call this *modulo 12 arithmetic*. (It is equivalent to the set named Z_{12} with the slight difference that "0" is used in place of "12".) For example, $7 + 9 = 4$, $7 - 9 = 10$, and $7*9 = 3$. (Division is omitted.)

Implement the following ADT for Z_{12}:

ADT: <u>Hour</u>

Represents:

An element from the finite set { 1, 2, 3, 4, 5, 6, 7, 8, 9, 10, 11, 12 }.

Constructors and Destructors:

create	Creates an object whose value is between 0 and 11, inclusive.

Arithmetic Operators:

sum	Returns the sum of two given hours.
difference	Returns the difference of two given hours.
product	Returns the product of two given hours.

Input/Output Operators:

input	Reads a value for an hour from standard input.
output	Prints the value of an hour to standard output.

7.10   Implement the following ADT for a random number:

ADT: <u>Random</u>

Represents:

An object represents a device that generates random numbers. It uses a "seed" integer that generates the random numbers and is changed after each generation.

Constructor:

create	Creates a random number generator. If no seed is passed to it, it accesses the system clock to initialize the seed.

Mutator Function:

reset	Changes the seed for the existing object. If no seed is passed to it, it accesses the system clock to initialize the seed.

Generator Functions:

integer	Generates an integer selected at random from a uniform distribution in the range $lo \leq n \leq hi$, where the default value for *hi* is INT_MAX and for *lo* is 1.
real	Generates a real number selected at random from a uniform distribution in the range $0.0 \leq x < 1.0$.

7.11 Implement the following ADT for a pair of dice:

ADT: <u>Dice</u>

Represents:
An object represents two dice, in terms of the sum of their values shown.

Domain:
The finite set { 2, 3, 4, 5, 6, 7, 8, 9, 10, 11, 12 }.

Constructor:

create   Creates an object whose value is between 2 and 12, inclusive.

Access Function:

toss   Simulates the tossing of the two dice. The value of each die is selected from a
                uniform distribution of integers from 1 to 6, and then their sum is returned.

7.12 Implement the following ADT for an address:

ADT: <u>Address</u>

Represents:
An object represents a mailing address.

Constructor:

create   Creates an address with optional given string values for the fields.

Access Functions:

street   Returns a string with the street component of the address.
city   Returns a string with the city component of the address.
state   Returns a string with the state or province of the address.
code   Returns a string with the postal code (*e.g.*, ZIP Code) of the address.
country   Returns a string with the country component of the address.

Mutator Function:

set_street   Sets the street field to a given string value.
set_city   Sets the city field to a given string value.
set_state   Sets the state field to a given string value.
set_code   Sets the code field to a given string value.
set_country   Sets the country field to a given string value.

Output Operator:

output   Prints the complete mailing address.

7.13 Implement the subtraction operator for the `Ratio` class. (See Example 7.9 on page 146.)

7.14 Implement the division operator `/` for the `Ratio` class.

7.15 Implement the following member function for the `Queue` class (Problem 7.7):

```
int size();
// returns the number of elements in the queue
```

7.16 The mathematical set $Z_n = \{ 0, 1, 2, ..., n-1 \}$ is used in abstract algebra with many important practical applications in coding theory and other sciences. The simplest version is the case where $n = 2$: $Z_2 = \{0, 1\}$, which is equivalent to the type `bool`. Another familiar version is the case where $n = 12$: Z_{12} is similar to the `Hour` class in Problem 7.7. Write up a complete ADT specification for Z_7. Then implement it. Call it `ModN`. Use a `const int N = 7`. Include all the arithmetic operations, including the *division* (`/`) and *remainder* (`%`) operators. (It is a mathematical fact that division works in Z_n only if n is a prime number. For example, it does not work in Z_{12} because 6/2 has more than one answer: $2*3 = 6$ but $2*9 = 18 = 6$ in Z_{12}, so 6/2 could be either 3 or 9!)

7.17 Implement the following ADT for a coin purse:

ADT: <u>Purse</u>

Description:

An object represents a coin changer or coin purse that can contain any number of pennies (1¢), nickels (5¢), dimes (10¢), and quarters (25¢).

Invariant:

The number of coins is minimal for the given monetary value.

Constructor:

create	Creates a purse with a given number of pennies, nickels, dimes, and quarters.

Access Functions:

pennies	Returns the number of pennies in the purse.
nickels	Returns the number of nickels in the purse.
dimes	Returns the number of dimes in the purse.
quarters	Returns the number of quarters in the purse.
value	Returns the total value of the coins in the purse.

Mutator Functions:

insert	Adds a given monetary value to the purse.
remove	Removes a given monetary value to the purse.
empty	Empties the purse.

7.18 Implement the following ADT for a measured distance:

ADT: <u>Distance</u>

Description:

An object represents a single (non-negative) measured distance.

Constructors and Destructors:

create	Creates an object that represents a single measured distance in a given number of meters.

Access Functions:

cm	Returns the distance measured in centimeters.
km	Returns the distance measured in kilometers.
in	Returns the distance measured in inches.
ft	Returns the distance measured in feet.
mi	Returns the distance measured in miles.

Mutator Functions:

set_cm	Resets the distance measured in centimeters.
set_km	Resets the distance measured in kilometers.
set_in	Resets the distance measured in inches.
set_ft	Resets the distance measured in feet.
set_mi	Resets the distance measured in miles.
add_cm	Adds a distance measured in centimeters.
add_km	Adds a distance measured in kilometers.
add_in	Adds a distance measured in inches.
add_ft	Adds a distance measured in feet.
add_mi	Adds a distance measured in miles.
subtract_cm	Subtracts a distance measured in centimeters.
subtract_km	Subtracts a distance measured in kilometers.
subtract_in	Subtracts a distance measured in inches.
subtract_ft	Subtracts a distance measured in feet.
subtract_mi	Subtracts a distance measured in miles.

Operators:

assignment	Assigns another distance to *this.
multiply	Multiplies *this by a non-negative real number.
divide	Divides *this by a positive real number.

Friend Operators:

multiply	Multiplies one distance by another.
divide	Divides one distance by another.

7.19 Write and implement a complete ADT similar to that in Problem 7.11 for a class named `Dice` that represents the sum of a <u>three</u> <u>four-sided</u> dice tossed. (Each die is a tetrahedron.)

7.20 Write and implement a complete ADT similar to that in Problem 7.11 for a class named `Tack` that uses the `Random` class (Problem 7.10) to represent the state of a tossed thumbtack. Assume that the thumbtack lands with its point up 60% of the time. The two outcomes are 0 (for point up) and 1 (for point down).

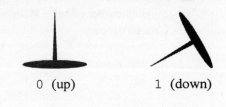

0 (up)   1 (down)

7.21 Implement the following ADT for a date:

ADT: <u>Date</u>

Description:

An object represents a specific date in history.

Invariants:

There was no year 0; the day after Dec 31 1 B.C. as Jan 1 1 A.D.
The month field can have only 12 different values.
The day field must be a positive integer that does not exceed the number of days in its month.

Constructor:

`create`   Creates an object representing a date given its era, year, month, and day.

Access Function:

`era`   Returns the date's era, either `BC` or `AD`.
`year`   Returns the card's year; *e.g.*, 1969.
`month`   Returns the card's month; *e.g.*, July.
`day`   Returns the card's day; *e.g.*, 26.

Arithmetic Functions:

`add`   Adds a given number of days to the date.
`subtract`   Subtracts a given number of days from the date.

Output Operator:

`output`   Prints the date; *e.g.*, "`July 26, 1969 A.D.`".

Hint: Use a `private` utility function named `is_leap()` that determines whether the year is a leap year.

7.22 Write and implement a complete ADT for a class named `Person` whose objects represent people. Then implement it. Include fields for `Address` (see Problem 7.10), date of birth, date of death, identification number (*e.g.*, Social Security Number in the U.S.A.), sex, telephone number, email address, and web page URL. Use the `Date` class (Problem 7.11) for DOB and DOD. Include an access function that returns the person's age in years on a given date.

7.23 We can imagine a queue as a row of seats, where the first person to arrive sits in the left-most seat, the second person sits to the right of him, *etc.*, each new arrival sitting to the right of the previous arrival. This is the same as a stack, except that the departure algorithm is different. If it were a stack, the first to leave would be the one at the right end (*i.e.*, the last one who arrived). But since it is a queue the first to leave is the one on the left end (*i.e.*, the first one who arrived). Dynamically, there is another distinction between a stack and a queue: When one leaves a stack, he or she is the only one who moves, but when one leaves a queue, all the others in the queue shift one seat to the left. That shifting requires much movement of data in the array implementation.

a. In the implementation in Problem 7.7, we chose not to shift the elements in the `leave()` function. This allows it to run faster, but it makes inefficient use of the allocated space. (Each seat is used only once!) Modify the `leave()` function so that after each departure, everyone remaining in the queue shifts one seat to the left. For example a `char` queue implemented as in Problem 7.7 with `max` = 20 would look like this after 18 arrivals, 16 departures, and then 8 more arrivals:

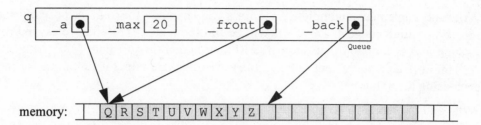

Note that in this implementation, the `_front` pointer is redundant and could be omitted.

b. Instead of shifting everyone to the left after each departure, we could simply "wrap around" the end whenever there are no more seats on the left. For example a `char` queue implemented as in Problem 7.7 with `max` = 20 would look like this after 18 arrivals, 16 departures, and then 8 more arrivals:

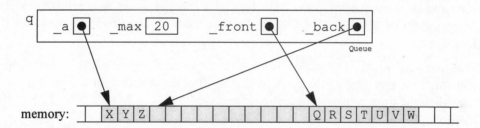

Implement this algorithm for the `leave()` function. This is the most efficient implementation of the `leave()` function when an array is used. It is called a *circular array*.

7.24 A *deque* (rhymes with "neck") is a container that allows insertions and removals at both ends. The word is a contraction for "double-ended queue." Here is how a deque could be implemented using dynamic arrays:

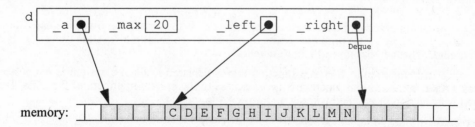

Array subscripts are shown here even though the actual memory addresses would be large hexadecimal numbers instead. The deque is allowed to grow and shrink on both the left and the right. Growth would start in the middle at `a[max/2]`. The `_left` pointer points to the last element inserted on the left, and the `_right` pointer points to the position where the next insertion would be made on the right. (This asymmetry is a result of maintaining the conventions used in all the other container classes that the difference between the two pointers equals the number of elements in the container.) Write a formal ADT for the deque data structure, and then implement it for elements of type `char`.

7.25 Write and implement a complete ADT for a class named `Angle` whose objects represent a specific plane angle measurement. This class will be similar to the `Distance` class in Problem 7.18. Include access functions that return the equivalent measure in degrees, radians, and grads. Also include mutator functions for increasing or decreasing the measure.

7.26 Write and implement a complete ADT for a class named `Numeral` whose objects represent specific positive integers. This class will be similar to the `Distance` class in Problem 7.18. Include access function that return the Roman numeral equivalent (*e.g.*, `MCMCDVIII`) and the Hindu-Arabic equivalent (*e.g.*, `1998`). Also include mutator functions for increasing or decreasing the value.

7.27 Write and implement a complete ADT for a class named `Money` whose objects represent a specific amount of money. This class will be similar to the `Distance` class in Problem 7.18. Include access functions that return the equivalent amount in primary currencies, such as dollars, pounds, marks, and yen. Also include mutator functions for increasing or decreasing the amount in dollars.

7.28 Write and implement a complete ADT for a class named `Book` whose objects represent published books. Include fields for author, title, publisher, year, and ISBN.

7.29 Write and implement a complete ADT for a class named `Complex` whose objects represent complex numbers (*e.g.*, $2.91 - 74.03i$). Include member functions like those for the `Ratio` class.

7.30 Write and implement a complete ADT for a class named `Time` whose objects represent specific times of day (*e.g.*, 7:52:29 p.m.). Also include mutator functions for increasing or decreasing the time by a given number of seconds.

Solutions

7.1 *Procedural abstraction* refers to the creation of an independent function whose use does not depend upon the knowledge of its implementation. *Data abstraction* refers to the creation of a programmer-defined data type (a `class` in C++) which may include operations that are specific to that type. Like procedural abstraction, data abstraction includes the assumption that the user of the type needs no knowledge of its implementation.

7.2 The *implicit argument* of a class member function call is the object that owns the call. For example, in the call `x.print()` to print the `Ratio` object `x` (in Example 7.5), the object `x` is the implicit argument. (That call has no explicit arguments.)

7.3 A `friend` function in C++ is a function that is declared inside a class but is not a member of the class. As a `friend`, the function is given access to the private members of the class. But as a non-member function, it is called without an implicit argument.

7.4 Separating a class's implementation from its interface has two main advantages:

a. It makes it easier to use the class because all the information that the programmer needs to use the class is given in its interface, leaving its implementation details hidden typically in a separate file.

b. It also allows the class's creator to change the class implementation without affecting its interface or the programs that use it. Indeed, the class's user can even compile the programs that use it before the class's implementation has been written.

7.5 The implementation of `cin >> r >> s >> t;` would be

```
operator>>( operator>>(operator>>(cin, r), s), t);
```

7.6   This is similar to the addition operator + given in Example 7.9:

```
Ratio operator*(const Ratio& x, const Ratio& y)
{ int num = x._num*y._num;
  int den = x._den*y._den;
  Ratio z(num, den);
  return z;
}
```

7.7   The implementation is quite similar to that for a stack of `chars` (see Example 7.18.):

```
class Queue
{ public:
    Queue(int s=100);   // sets the default maximum number at 100
    ~Queue();
    char front() const;  // returns the element at the front
    char back() const;    // returns the element at the back
    bool is_empty() const;
    bool is_full() const;
    void enter(const char&);
    char leave();
  private:
    char* _a;       // the queue itself: a dynamic array of char
    int _max;       // the maximum number of elements on the queue
    int _front;     // the location of the next element to leave
    int _back;      // the location for the next element to enter
};
Queue::Queue(int m) : _max(m), _front(0), _back(0)
{ _a = new char[_max];
  assert(_a != 0);
}
Queue::~Queue()
{ delete [] _a;
}
char Queue::front() const
{ assert (_back > _front);
  return _a[_front];
}
char Queue::back() const
{ assert (_back > _front);
  return _a[_back-1];
}
bool Queue::is_empty() const
{ return bool(_back == _front);
}
bool Queue::is_full() const
{ return bool(_back == _max);
}
void Queue::enter(const char& item)
{ assert(_back < _max);
  _a[_back++] = item;
}
char Queue::leave()
{ assert(_front < _back);
  return _a[_front++];
}
```

Following the execution of this code:

```
Queue q(20);
q.enter('A');
q.enter('B');
cout << q.leave() << endl;
q.enter('C');
q.enter('D');
cout << q.leave() << endl;
q.enter('E');
```

the Queue object named q would look like this:

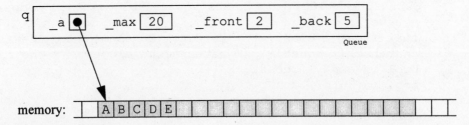

Its abstraction should be imagined like the picture at right. Note that the is_full() function will return true after _max elements have arrived, regardless of how many have left. Methods of correcting this inefficiency are given in Problem 7.23.

7.8
```
void reverse(Queue& q)
{ Stack s;
  while(!q.is_empty())
    s.push(q.leave());
  while(!s.is_empty())
    q.enter(s.pop());
}
```

This assumes that the Stack and Queue classes are both implemented with the same element type.

7.9 The implementation is similar to that for the Ratio class (see Example 7.18.):

```
class Hour
{    friend Hour operator+(const Hour&, const Hour&);
     friend Hour operator-(const Hour&, const Hour&);
     friend Hour operator*(const unsigned&, const Hour&);
     friend istream& operator>>(istream&, Hour&);
     friend ostream& operator<<(ostream&, const Hour&);
  public:
     Hour(int=0);    // constructor
  private:
     short _value;
     void _reduce();
};
Hour operator+(const Hour& h1, const Hour& h2)
{ Hour sum = h1 + h2;
  sum._reduce();
  return sum;
}
Hour operator-(const Hour& h1, const Hour& h2)
{ Hour difference = h1 - h2;
  difference._reduce();
  return difference;
}
```

```
        Hour operator*(const unsigned& n, const Hour& h)
        { Hour product = n*h;
          product._reduce();
          return product;
        }
        istream& operator>>(istream& istr, Hour& h)
        { istr >> h;
          h._reduce();
        }
        ostream& operator<<(ostream& ostr, const Hour& h)
        { ostr << h._value << ":00";
        }
        Hour::Hour(int value) : _value(value)
        { _reduce();
        }
        void Hour::_reduce()
        { while (_value < 1)
            _value += 12;
          while (_value > 12)
            _value -= 12;
        }
```

As in the `Ratio` class, the `_reduce()` function is a private utility function used to enforce the class constraint. If `_value` is out of range (*i.e.*, either < 1 or > 12), then we repeatedly add or subtract 12 until it is in range.

7.10   This solution is adapted from [Stroustrup2]:

```
        #include <iostream>
        #include <climits>
        #include <cmath>
        #include <ctime>
        typedef unsigned long ulong;
        const int MAX = INT_MAX;              // = 2,147,483,647 or 32,767
        class Random
        { public:
            Random(ulong seed=0);
            void seed(ulong seed=0);        // allows client to reset
        _seed
            int integer(ulong hi=MAX, ulong lo=1);
            double real();
          private:
            ulong _seed;                    // INVARIANT: 0 <= _seed <= ULONG_MAX
            void _randomize();                          // resets _seed
        };
        Random::Random(ulong s)
        { if (s > 0) _seed = s;
          else _seed = time(NULL);
          _randomize();
        }
        void Random::seed(ulong s)
        { if (s > 0) _seed = s;
          else _seed = time(NULL);
          _randomize();
        }
        int Random::integer(ulong hi, ulong lo)
        { _randomize();
          return _seed/10 % (hi - lo + 1) + lo;
        }
```

```
        double Random::real()
```

```
                        q C D E
                          Queue
```

```
        { _randomize();
          return double(_seed)/ULONG_MAX;
        }
        void Random::_randomize()
        { _seed = (1103515245*_seed + 123456789) % ULONG_MAX;
        }
```

Here is a test driver for the class:

```
        int main()
        { Random random;
          const int NUM=10;
          const int CNT=10000;
          const int MEAN=CNT/NUM;
          int bucket[NUM] = {0};
          int n, ssdev=0;
          for (int i=0; i < CNT; i++)
          { n = random.integer(NUM-1,0);   // 0 <= n <= 9
            bucket[n]++;                    // count n
            ssdev += (n-MEAN)*(n-MEAN);     // sum its deviation squared
          }
          for (int j=0; j < NUM; j++)
            cout << "\t" << j << ": " << bucket[j] << endl;
          cout << "Standard deviation = " << sqrt(ssdev/CNT) << endl;
          for (i=0; i < 25; i++)
            cout << random.integer(2) << ", ";
          cout << endl;
          for (i=0; i < 25; i++)
            cout << random.integer(6) << ", ";
          cout << endl;
          for (i=0; i < 20; i++)
            cout << random.integer(99,10) << "      "
                 << random.integer(9999,1000) << "       "
                 << random.integer(999999,100000) << "      "
                 << random.real() << endl;
          return 0;
        }
```

7.11   This solution uses the Random class given in Problem 7.10:

```
        #include "Random.h"
        class Dice
        { public:
            Dice() : _sum(2) { }
            void toss() { _sum = _random.integer(6) +_random.integer(6);
        }
            int sum() { return _sum; }
          private:
            Random _random;  // random number generator
            int _sum;        // the sum of the two dice
        };
```

When a Dice object is created (by the class constructor), it creates a Random object whose seed is initialized from the system clock. Then whenever the Dice object's toss() function is called, it makes two independent calls to the integer() function in the Random class. Each of those calls returns a random integer in the range from 1 to 6, thereby simulating two independent dice tosses. The sum is assigned to _sum. Note that the distribution of this sum is <u>not</u> uniform. For example, a 9 is twice as likely as an 11, because there are 4 ways ({3,6}, {4,5}, {5,4}, or {6,3}) that a 9 can occur but only 2 ways ({5,6}, {6,5}) that an 11 can occur.

7.12
```
     class Address
     { public:
         Address(string="",string="",string="",string="",string="");
         string street() { return _street; }
         string city() { return _city; }
         string state() { return _state; }
         string code() { return _code; }
         string country() { return _country; }
         void set_street(string street) { _street = street; }
         void set_city(string city) { _city = city; }
         void set_state(string state) { _state = state; }
         void set_code(string code) { _code = code; }
         void set_country(string country) { _country = country; }
       private:
         string _street;
         string _city;
         string _state;
         string _code;
         string _country;
     };
     Address::Address(string street, string city, string state,
       string code, string country) : _street(street), _city(city),
       _state(state), _code(code), _country(country) { }
```

7.13
```
     class Ratio
     { friend Ratio operator-(Ratio, Ratio);
       //...
     };
     Ratio operator-(Ratio x, Ratio y)
     { int num = x._num*y._den - x._den*y._num;
       int den = x._den*y._den;
       Ratio temp(num, den);
       return temp;
     }
```

7.14
```
     class Ratio
     { friend Ratio operator/(Ratio, Ratio);
       //...
     };
     Ratio operator/(const Ratio& x, const Ratio& y)
     { assert(y._num != 0);
       int num = x._num*y._den;
       int den = x._den*y._num;
       Ratio z(num, den);
       return z;
     }
```

7.15
```
     int Queue::size()
     { return _back - _front;
     }
```

7.16 ADT: <u>ModN</u>
Description:
An object represents one of these integers: 0, 1, 2, 3, 4, 5, or 6.
Invariant:
The private data _n is an integer in the range 0–6.

Constructor:

create   Creates an object with default value 0.

Access Functions:

value   Returns the value stored.

Friend Functions:

add   Adds two ModN objects.

subtract   Subtracts one ModN object from another.

multiply   Multiplies two ModN objects.

divide   Divides one ModN object by another.

remainder   Obtains the remainder from the division of one ModN object by another.

input   Extracts a ModN object from an input stream.

output   Inserts a ModN object into an output stream.

```cpp
const int N = 7;
class ModN
{    friend ModN operator+(ModN, ModN);
     friend ModN operator-(ModN, ModN);
     friend ModN operator*(ModN, ModN);
     friend ModN operator/(ModN, ModN);
     friend ModN operator%(ModN, ModN);
     friend istream& operator>>(istream&, ModN&);
     friend ostream& operator<<(ostream&, const ModN&);
  public:
     ModN(int n=0) : _n(n) { }
     ModN(const ModN& x) : _n(x._n) { }
     ModN& operator=(const ModN& x) { _n = x._n; return *this; }
     ModN& operator=(const int n) { _n = n%N; return *this; }
     int value() const { return _n; }
  private:
     int _n;
};
ModN operator+(ModN x, ModN y)
{ ModN z;
  z._n = (x._n + y._n)%N;
  return z;
}
ModN operator-(ModN x, ModN y)
{ ModN z;
  z._n = (x._n - y._n + N)%N;
  return z;
}
ModN operator*(ModN x, ModN y)
{ ModN z;
  z._n = (x._n * y._n)%N;
  return z;
}
ModN operator/(ModN x, ModN y)
{ assert(y._n != 0);
  ModN z;
  z._n = x._n / y._n;
  return z;
}
```

```
ModN operator%(ModN x, ModN y)
{ assert(y._n != 0);
  ModN z;
  z._n = x._n % y._n;
  return z;
}
istream& operator>>(istream& istr, ModN& x)
{ int n;
  istr >> n;
  x._n = n%N;
  return istr;
}
ostream& operator<<(ostream& ostr, const ModN& x)
{ ostr << x._n;
  return ostr;
}
```

7.17
```
class Purse
{ public:
    Purse(int p=0, int n=0, int d=0, int q=0)
      : _p(p), _n(n), _d(d), _q(q) { _reduce(); }
    int pennies() const { return _p; }
    int nickels() const { return _n; }
    int dimes() const { return _d; }
    int quarters() const { return _q; }
    int value() const { return _p + 5*_n + 10*_d + 25*_q; }
    void insert(int n) { _p += n; _reduce(); }
    void remove(int n) { _p -= n; _reduce(); }
    void empty() { _p = _n = _d = _q = 0; }
  private:
    int _p;  // number of pennies in the purse
    int _n;  // number of nickels in the purse
    int _d;  // number of dimes in the purse
    int _q;  // number of quarters in the purse
    void _reduce();
};
void Purse::_reduce()
{ int v = _p + 5*_n + 10*_d + 25*_q;
  assert(v >= 0);
  _q = v/25;   v %= 25;
  _d = v/10;   v %= 10;
  _n = v/5;    v %= 5;
  _p = v;
}
```

7.18
```
class Distance
{   friend Distance operator*(double, Distance);
    friend Distance operator/(Distance, double);
  public:
    Distance(double m=0) : _m(m) { }
    double cm() const { return 100*_m; }
    double km() const { return _m/100; }
    double in() const { return _m/0.0254; }   // 1 in == 0.0254 m
    double ft() const { return _m/0.0254/12; }
    double mi() const { return _m/0.0254/12/5280; }
    void add_cm(double cm) { _m = cm/100; }
    void add_km(double km) { _m = 100*km; }
    void add_in(double in) { _m = 0.0254*in; }
```

```
         void add_ft(double ft) { _m = 0.0254*12*ft; }
         void add_mi(double mi) { _m = 0.0254*12*5280*mi; }
         void add_cm(double cm) { _m += cm/100; }
         void add_km(double km) { _m += 100*km; }
         void add_in(double in) { _m += 0.0254*in; }
         void add_ft(double ft) { _m += 0.0254*12*ft; }
         void add_mi(double mi) { _m += 0.0254*12*5280*mi; }
         void subtract_cm(double cm) { _m -= cm/100; }
         void subtract_km(double km) { _m -= 100*km; }
         void subtract_in(double in) { _m -= 0.0254*in; }
         void subtract_ft(double ft) { _m -= 0.0254*12*ft; }
         void subtract_mi(double mi) { _m -= 0.0254*12*5280*mi; }
         Distance& operator=(const Distance&);
         Distance& operator*=(const double);
         Distance& operator/=(const double);
      private:
         double _m;  // meters
   };
   Distance operator*(double t, Distance x)
   { assert(t >= 0.0);
      Distance y(t*x._m);
      return y;
   }
   Distance operator/(Distance x, double t)
   { assert(t > 0.0);
      Distance y(x._m/t);
      return y;
   }
   Distance& Distance::operator=(const Distance& x)
   { _m = x._m;
      return *this;
   }
   Distance& Distance::operator*=(const double t)
   { assert(t >= 0.0);
      _m *= t;
      return *this;
   }
   Distance& Distance::operator/=(const double t)
   { assert(t > 0.0);
      _m /= t;
      return *this;
   }
```

7.19 ADT: <u>Dice</u>

Represents:

An object represents three four-sided dice, in terms of the sum of their values shown.

Domain:

The finite set { 3, 4, 5, 6, 7, 8, 9, 10, 11, 12 }.

Constructor:

create   Creates an object whose value is between 3 and 8, inclusive.

Access Function:

toss   Simulates the tossing of the three dice. The value of each die is selected from a uniform distribution of integers from 1 to 4, and then their sum is returned.

```
#include "Random.h"
class Dice
{ public:
    Dice() : _sum(3) { }
    void toss()
    { _sum = _r.integer(4) + _r.integer(4) + _r.integer(4);
    }
    int sum() { return _sum; }
  private:
    int _sum;   // the sum of the three dice
    Random _r;  // random number generator
};
```

7.20 ADT: <u>Tack</u>

Represents:

An object represents the position of a dropped thumbtack.

Domain:

The finite set { DOWN, UP }.

Constructor:

create   Creates an object whose state is UP.

Access Function:

toss   Simulates the tossing of the thumbtack. The state (DOWN or UP) is selected
                at random so that UP occurs 60% of the time..

```
#include "Random.h"
enum State { DOWN, UP };
class Tack
{ public:
    Tack() : _state(UP);
    State toss()
    { int n = _random.integer(5);
      if (n < 3) return DOWN;  // 2/5 = 40%
      else return UP;
    }
  private:
    State _state;
    Random _random;
};
```

7.21
```
const int FIRST_YEAR = 1601;
const int LAST_YEAR = 10000;
class Date
{   friend istream& operator>>(istream&, Date&);
    friend ostream& operator<<(ostream&, const Date&);
    friend bool operator==(const Date&, const Date&);
    friend bool operator!=(const Date&, const Date&);
    friend bool operator<(const Date&, const Date&);
    friend bool operator>(const Date&, const Date&);
    friend bool operator<=(const Date&, const Date&);
    friend bool operator>=(const Date&, const Date&);
    friend Date operator+(const Date&, const int);
    friend Date operator-(const Date&, const int);
    friend int operator-(const Date&, const Date&);
  public:
    Date(int =1601, int =1, int =1);
    int day_of_year() const;
    int year() const;
```

```
      int month() const;
      int day() const;
      int days() const;
      string weekday() const;
      Date operator++();
      Date operator--();
      Date& operator+=(const int);
      Date& operator-=(const int);
  private:
      int _days;  // number of days elapsed since Dec 31 1600
};
bool is_leap_year(int year)
{ if (year % 400 == 0) return true;    // 2000 is a leap year
  if (year % 100 == 0) return false;   // 1900 is not a leap year
  if (year % 4 == 0) return true;      // 1996 is a leap year
  return false;                        // 1999 is not a leap year
}
int days_in_month(int m, int y)
{ if (m == 2) return (is_leap_year(y) ? 29 : 28);
  if (m == 9 || m == 4 || m == 6 || m == 11) return 30;
  return 31;
}
int elapsed(int y, int m, int d)
// returns the number of days between 1600-12-31 and y-m-d
{ int n = 0;
  for (int yy=FIRST_YEAR; yy<y; yy++)
    n += (is_leap_year(yy) ? 366 : 365);
  for (int mm=1; mm<m; mm++)
    n += days_in_month(mm, y);
  return n + d;
}
istream& operator>>(istream& istr, Date& x)
{ int year, month, day;
  char c;  // to eact the '-'
  cin >> year >> c >> month >> c >> day;
  x._days = elapsed(year, month, day);
  return istr;
}
ostream& operator<<(ostream& ostr, const Date& x)
{ ostr << x.year() << "-";
  int m = x.month();
  if (m < 10) ostr << "0";
  ostr << m << "-";
  int d = x.day();
  if (d < 10) ostr << "0";
  ostr << d;
  return ostr;
}
inline bool operator==(const Date& x, const Date& y)
{ return bool(x._days == y._days);
}
inline bool operator!=(const Date& x, const Date& y)
{ return bool(x._days != y._days);
}
```

```cpp
inline bool operator<(const Date& x, const Date& y)
{ return bool(x._days < y._days);
}
inline bool operator<=(const Date& x, const Date& y)
{ return bool(x._days <= y._days);
}
inline bool operator>(const Date& x, const Date& y)
{ return bool(x._days > y._days);
}
inline bool operator>=(const Date& x, const Date& y)
{ return bool(x._days >= y._days);
}
inline Date operator+(const Date& x, const int n)
{ Date y = x;
  y._days += n;
  return y;
}
inline Date operator-(const Date& x, const int n)
{ Date y = x;
  y._days -= n;
  return y;
}
inline int operator-(const Date& x, const Date& y)
{ return x._days - y._days;
}
Date::Date(int y, int m, int d)
{ assert(y >= FIRST_YEAR);
  assert(1 <= m && m <= 12);
  assert(1 <= d && d <= days_in_month(m, y));
  _days = elapsed(y, m, d);
}
int Date::day_of_year() const
{ int diy;  // number of days in year
  int n = _days;
  for (int y=FIRST_YEAR; y<LAST_YEAR; y++)
  { diy = (is_leap_year(y) ? 366 : 365);
    if (n <= diy) return n;
    n -= diy;
  }
  return n;
}
int Date::year() const
{ int diy;  // number of days in year
  int n = _days;
  for (int y=FIRST_YEAR; y<LAST_YEAR; y++)
  { diy = (is_leap_year(y) ? 366 : 365);
    if (n <= diy) return y;
    n -= diy;
  }
  return LAST_YEAR;
}
int Date::month() const
{ int dim;  // number of days in month
  int y = year();
  int n = day_of_year();
```

```cpp
    for (int m=1; m<12; m++)
    { dim = days_in_month(m, y);
      if (n <= dim) return m;
      n -= dim;
    }
    return 12;
}
int Date::day() const
{ int dim;  // number of days in month
  int y = year();
  int n = day_of_year();
  for (int m=1; m<12; m++)
  { dim = days_in_month(m, y);
    if (n <= dim) return n;
    n -= dim;
  }
  return n;
}
inline int Date::days() const
{ return _days;
}
string Date::weekday() const
// Zeller's Algorithm (see Reilly & Federighi, p.309)
{ const string WEEKDAY[7]
    = { "Sun", "Mon", "Tue", "Wed", "Thu", "Fri", "Sat" };
  int y = year();
  int m = month();
  int d = day();
  m = 1 + (m + 9)%12;
  if (m > 10) --y;
  int c = y/100;
  y %= 100;
  int i = ((13*m - 1)/5 + d + y + y/4 + c/4 + 5*c)%7;
  return WEEKDAY[i];
}
inline Date Date::operator++()
{ ++_days;
  return *this;
}
inline Date Date::operator--()
{ --_days;
  return *this;
}
inline Date& Date::operator+=(const int n)
{ _days += n;
  return *this;
}
inline Date& Date::operator-=(const int n)
{ _days -= n;
  return *this;
}
```

7.22

```
class Person
  { public:
      Person(string lname, string fname, string id)
        : _lname(lname), _fname(fname), _id(id) { }
      string lname() const { return _lname; }
      string fname() const { return _fname; }
      string id() const { return _id; }
      Address address() const { return _address; }
      Date dob() const { return _dob; }
      Date dod() const { return _dod; }
      string sex() const { return _sex; }
      string phone() const { return _phone; }
      string email() const { return _email; }
      string url() const { return _url; }
      int age(Date date) const ( return (date - dob)/365.2425; }
      void set_lname(string lname) { _lname = lname; }
      void set_fname(string fname) { _fname = fname; }
      void set_id(string id) { _id = id; }
      void set_address(Address address) { _address = address; }
      void set_dob(Date dob) { _dob = dob; }
      void set_dod(Date dod) { _dod = dod; }
      void set_sex(string sex) { _sex = sex; }
      void set_phone(string phone) { _phone = phone; }
      void set_email(string email) { _email = email; }
      void set_url(string url) { _url = url; }
    private:
      string _lname;
      string _fname;
      string _id;
      Address _address;
      Date _dob;
      Date _dod;
      string _sex;
      string _phone;
      string _email;
      string _url;
  };
```

7.23 *a.* The code for the member functions in this implementation is the same as that given in the solution to Problem 7.7 except that each occurrence of `_front` is replaced with 0, and the `leave()` function is changed to

```
char Queue::leave()
{ assert(0 < _back);
  char temp = _a[0];
  for (int i=1; i < _back; i++)
    _a[i-1] = _a[i];
  return temp;
}
```

b. The code for the member functions in this implementation is the same as that given in the solution to Problem 7.7 except for the `enter()` function and the `leave()` function:

```
void Queue::enter(const char& item)
{ assert(_back != _max && _back != _front - 1);
  _a[_back++] = item;
  if (_back == _max) _back = 0;   // wrap around
}
```

```
char Queue::leave()
{ assert(_back != _front);
  return _a[_front++];
  if (_front = _max) _front = 0;   // wrap around
  if (_front == _back) _front = _back = 0;   // reset
}
```

7.24   ADT: Deque

Represents:

A double-ended sequence of elements, all of the same type.

Access:

A deque allows access only at the two ends of ends of the sequence, called the *left* and the *right* of the deque. Each end acts independently like a stack: last-in-first-out.

Constructors and Destructors:

create   Creates an empty deque of a given maximum size.
destroy   De-allocates the memory used for the deque.

Access Functions:

left   Returns the last element inserted at the left.
right   Returns the last element inserted at the right.
is_empty   Returns true if the deque is empty; otherwise returns false.
is_full   Returns true if the deque is full; otherwise returns false.

Mutator Functions:

enter_left   Inserts a new element at the left end of the deque.
enter_right   Inserts a new element at the right end of the deque.
leave_left   Removes and returns the left-most element from the deque.
leave_right   Removes and returns the right-most element from the deque.

```
class Deque
{ public:
    Deque(int s=100);   // sets the default maximum number at 100
    ~Deque() { delete [] _a; }
    char left() const { return _a[0]; }
    char right() const { return _a[_max-1]; }
    bool is_empty() const;
    bool is_full() const { return bool(_left == _right-1); }
    void enter_left(const char&);
    void enter_right(const char&);
    char leave_left();
    char leave_right();
  private:
    char* _a;       // the Deque itself: a dynamic array of char
    int _max;       // the maximum number of elements on the Deque
    int _left;      // the next available element of the left
    int _right;     // the next available element of the left
};
Deque::Deque(int m) : _max(m), _left(0), _right(m-1)
{ _a = new char[_max];
  assert(_a != 0);
}
inline bool Deque::is_empty() const
{ return bool(_left == 0 && _right == _max-1);
}
```

```
void Deque::enter_left(const char& item)
{ assert(_left != _right-1);
  for (int i=_left; i>0; i--)
    _a[i] = _a[i-1];  // shift all the left elements right
  ++_left;
  _a[0] = item;
}
void Deque::enter_right(const char& item)
{ assert(_left != _right-1);
  for (int i=_right; i < _max-1; i++)
    _a[i] = _a[i+1];  // shift all the right elements left
  --_right;
  _a[_max-1] = item;
}
char Deque::leave_left()
{ assert(_left > 0);
  char temp = _a[0];
  for (int i=0; i < _left-1; i++)
    _a[i] = _a[i+1];  // shift all the left elements left
  --_left;
  return temp;
}
char Deque::leave_right()
{ assert(_right < _max-1);
  char temp = _a[_max-1];
  for (int i=_max-1; i > _right+1; i--)
    _a[i] = _a[i-1];  // shift all the right elements right
  ++_right;
  return temp;
}
```

Chapter 8

Pointers

A *pointer* is an address of a byte in main memory. Pointers are widely used in C++ to facilitate efficient dynamic processing of data.

8.1 POINTERS

If `T` is any type, then `T*` is the derived type "pointer to `T`." The base type `T` may be a built-in type, such as `int` or `float`. Or it may be a user-defined type, such as `Date` or `Person`.

EXAMPLE 8.1 A Pointer to an `int`

```
int n = 22;     // defines the integer n initialized to 22
int* p = &n;    // defines the pointer p initialized to the address of n
```

This code defines two objects: the integer `n` and the pointer `p`. Both are initialized: `n` with the value 22, and `p` with the value `&n`, which means the memory address of the object `n`. We think of `p`

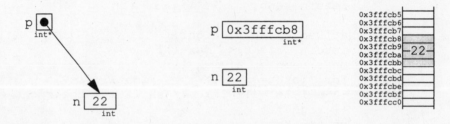

as an arrow that points to the object `n`, as shown here on the left. But really `p` is an object whose value is a memory address, perhaps the hexadecimal address `0x3fffcb6`, as shown above on the right.

Note that the pointer contains only the address of the first byte occupied by `n`. In this example, `n` is an integer occupying the four bytes `0x3fffcb8` to `0x3fffcbb`, but `p` contains only the address of the first byte `0x3fffcb8`.

8.2 THE DEREFERENCE OPERATOR

The asterisk symbol `*` has two related uses in C++. When used as a suffix on a type, as in Example 8.1, it defines the pointer type derived from the base type. It is also used as a prefix to the name of a pointer. In that context it is called the *dereference operator*. The resulting expression refers to the object to which the pointer points. This is called *dereferencing* the pointer.

EXAMPLE 8.2 Dereferencing a Pointer

```
Date x(1969,7,20);  // the object x represents the date Jul 20, 1969
Date* p = &x;       // the pointer p points to the object x
cout << "Man stepped onto the moon on " << *p << endl;
```

Here `p` points to a `Date` object, where `Date` is a user-defined class (see page 171). The pointer is dereferenced in the output statement: `*p` is the same as `x`, so `x` is inserted into the output stream, thereby printing

```
Man stepped onto the moon on 1969-07-20
```

178

The relationship between `p` and `x` is illustrated in
the picture at right. Note that `p` has type `Date*`
and `x` has type `Date`.

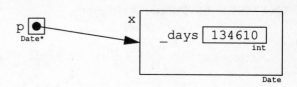

When a pointer points to a class object, as in
Example 8.2 above, there is an alternative nota-
tion for calling a member function bound to a dereferenced pointer. The following two forms are
equivalent:

```
(*p).f();
p->f();
```

The second of these two equivalent forms is generally preferred because it is simpler and because the
combination symbol `->` suggests the pointer relationships.

EXAMPLE 8.3 Binding a Function Call to a Dereferenced Pointer

This code continues from Example 8.2:

```
Date y(1972,12,17);
Date* q = &y;
cout << "Apollo 17 left the moon on " << q->weekday() << ", "
    << q->month() << "/" << (*q).day() << "/" << y.year() << endl;
cout << "The era of moon landings lasted " << y - *p << " days.\n";
```

The output is

```
Apollo 17 left the moon on Sun, 12/17/1972
The era of moon landings lasted 1246 days.
```

8.3 POINTER OPERATIONS

Pointer values may be output with the insertion operator `<<`.

EXAMPLE 8.4 Pointer I/O

```
Date x(1941,12,7);  // the object x represents the date Dec 7 1941
Date* p = &x;       // the pointer p points to the object x
cout << x << '\t' << p << '\t' << *p << endl;
```

The output is

```
1941-12-07        0x3fffcc4        1941-12-07
```

This shows that the `Date` object `x` is stored in memory beginning at byte number 0x3fffcc4.

However, pointers cannot be input:

```
cin >> p;  // ERROR: the insertion operator is not defined for pointers
```

Pointers may be assigned to other pointers of the same type.

EXAMPLE 8.5 Assigning Pointers

This code continues from Example 8.3:

```
q = p;  // now both p and q point to x
cout << "Apollo 11 landed on the moon on " << q->weekday() << ", "
    << q->month() << "/" << q->day() << "/" << q->year() << endl;
```

The output is

```
Apollo 11 landed on the moon on Sun, 7/20/1969
```

Pointers can also be incremented and decremented.

EXAMPLE 8.6 Pointer Arithmetic

```cpp
char s[] = "ABCDEFGH";
char* p = &s[3];            // p points to s[3]
cout << "*p = " << *p << endl;
++p;                        // p points to s[4]
cout << "*p = " << *p << endl;
p += 3;                     // p points to s[7]
cout << "*p = " << *p << endl;
p -= 6;                     // p points to s[1]
cout << "*p = " << *p << endl;
--p;                        // p points to s[0]
cout << "*p = " << *p << endl;
```

Here is the output:

```
*p = D
*p = E
*p = H
*p = B
*p = A
```

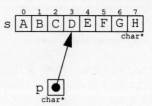
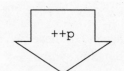
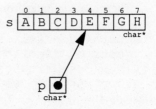
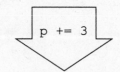
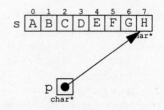
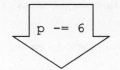
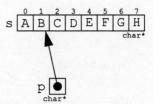

The pointer p is initialized to point to s[3] which contains 'D'. Incrementing p advances it to point to s[4] which contains 'E'. Adding 3 to p advances it to point to s[7] which contains 'H'. Subtracting 6 from p moves it back to point to s[1] which contains 'B'. Then decrementing it moves it back to point to s[0] which contains 'A':

Pointers can also be subtracted from other pointers:

EXAMPLE 8.7 Subtracting Pointers

```cpp
char s[] = "ABCDEFGHIJ";
char* p = &s[3];            // p points to s[3]
char* q = &s[6];            // q points to s[6]
cout << "*p = " << *p << ", *q = " << *q;
--p;                        // p points to s[2]
++q;                        // q points to s[7]
cout << "\t*p = " << *p << ", *q = " << *q;
cout << "\tq - p = " << q - p << endl;
```

The output is

```
*p = D, *q = G
*p = C, *q = H
q - p = 5
```

The pointer p is initialized to point to s[3] which contains 'D', and then the pointer q is initialized to point to s[6] which contains 'G'. Decrementing p makes it point to s[2] which contains 'C', and then incrementing q makes it point to s[7] which contains 'H'. Now q contains an address which is 5 bytes higher than the address in p, so q - p evaluates to 5.

Arithmetic on pointers depends upon the size of their base types. Incrementing a pointer to char increases its value by 1. But incrementing a pointer to double increases its value by 8. In general the unit used in arithmetic on pointers of type pointer to T is sizeof(T).

EXAMPLE 8.8 Pointer Arithmetic with Unit Size 4

```
int a[] = { 22, 33, 44, 55, 66, 77, 88, 99 };
int* p = &a[3];                    // p points to a[3]
cout << "p = " << p << ", *p = " << *p << endl;
++p;                               // p points to a[4]
cout << "p = " << p << ", *p = " << *p << endl;
p += 3;                            // p points to a[7]
cout << "p = " << p << ", *p = " << *p << endl;
p -= 6;                            // p points to a[1]
cout << "p = " << p << ", *p = " << *p << endl;
--p;                               // p points to a[0]
cout << "p = " << p << ", *p = " << *p << endl;
```

The output is

```
p = 0x3fffcb4, *p = 55
p = 0x3fffcb8, *p = 66
p = 0x3fffcc4, *p = 99
p = 0x3fffcac, *p = 33
p = 0x3fffca8, *p = 22
```

The pointer `p` is initialized to point to `a[3]` which contains 55. Incrementing `p` advances it to point to `a[4]` which contains 66. This changes the value of `p` from `0x3fffcb4` to `0x3fffcb8`, an increase of 4. Adding 3 to `p` advances it to point to `a[7]` which contains 99. This changes the value of `p` from `0x3fffcb8` to `0x3fffcc4`, an increase of 12. Subtracting 6 from `p` moves it back to point to `a[1]` which contains 33. This changes the value of `p` from `0x3fffcc4` to `0x3fffcac`, a decrease of 24. Then decrementing it moves it back to point to `a[0]` which contains 22. This changes the value of `p` from `0x3fffcac` to `0x3fffca8`, a decrease of 4.

Note that pointers in the same expression must point to the same type:

```
int n = 22;
double x = 3.141592653589793;
int* p = &n;
double* q = &x;
cout << p << endl;        // ok
cout << q << endl;        // ok
cout << q - p << endl;  // ILLEGAL: *p and *q have different types
```

Here `p` has type pointer to `int` and `q` has type pointer to `double`.

A pointer expression such as `p+5` makes sense and acts like a pointer. In particular, it can be dereferenced: `*(p+5)` refers to the object located at address `p + 5*sizeof(T)`, where `T` is the base type for the pointer `p`. If `p` has type pointer to `short`, then `p+5` points to the address `p+10`; but if `p` has type pointer to `double`, then `p+5` points to the address `p+40`.

EXAMPLE 8.9

```
int a[] = { 22, 33, 44, 55, 66, 77, 88, 99 };
int* p = &a[2];                    // p points to a[2]
cout << "p = " << p << ", *p = " << *p << endl;
int* q = p+3;                      // q points to a[5]
cout << "q = " << q << ", *q = " << *q << endl;
cout << "p+4 = " << p+4 << ", *(p+4) = " << *(p+4) << endl;
cout << "q-2 = " << q-2 << ", *(q-2) = " << *(q-2) << endl;
cout << "q - p = " << q - p << endl;
```

The output is

```
p = 0x3fffcb0, *p = 44
q = 0x3fffcbc, *q = 77
p+4 = 0x3fffcc0, *(p+4) = 88
```

```
q-2 = 0x3fffcb4, *(q-2) = 55
q - p = 3
```

The pointer `p` is initialized to point to `a[2]` which contains `44` at address `0x3fffcb0`. Then the pointer `q` is initialized to point to `a[5]` which contains `77` at address `0x3fffcbc`. Note that this is 12 bytes farther than `0x3fffcb0`. The expression `p+4` evaluates to `0x3fffcc0` which is 16 bytes farther than `0x3fffcb0`. It is the first of the four bytes that contain `a[6]` which is `88`, so the dereferenced expression `*(p+4)` evaluates to `88`. Similarly, the expression `q-2` evaluates to `0x3fffcb4` which is 8 bytes ahead of `0x3fffcbc`; that is the first of the four bytes that contain `a[3]` which is `55`, so the dereferenced expression `*(q-2)` evaluates to `55`. Finally, the expression `q - p` evaluates to `3` because the distance from `0x3fffcb0` to `0x3fffcbc` is 3 four-byte units:

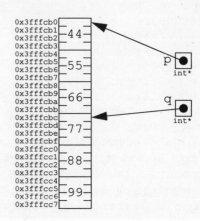

```
     0    1    2    3    4    5    6    7
a [ 22 | 33 | 44 | 55 | 66 | 77 | 88 | 99 ]
```

The array `a` is pictured above on the left. The diagram on the right shows a detail of memory where the array is stored. The pointer `p` points to byte number `0x3fffcb0` which is the first of the four bytes that hold `a[2]`, and the pointer `q` points to byte number `0x3fffcbc` which is the first of the four bytes that hold `a[5]`.

8.4 THE REFERENCE OPERATOR

Like the asterisk symbol `*`, the ampersand symbol `&` has two related uses in C++. When used as a prefix to the name of an object, it is called the *reference operator*. As the previous examples illustrate, the reference operator returns the address of the object:

```
p = &y;   // assigns the address of y to the pointer p
```

But we have also used the ampersand as suffix to a type:

```
void swap(float& x, float& y);
```

When used this way, the ampersand defines a derived type, called a *reference type*. For example, `float&` is the type "reference to `float`." This is the way reference parameters are declared in functions. (See Example 4.13 on page 75.)

A *reference* is a synonym or alias; *i.e.*, another name for an existing object. Chapter 4 describes how references are used for passing to and returning from functions. References are also used independently of functions.

EXAMPLE 8.10 Declaring References

This code uses the `Person` class defined on page 175:

```
Person student_6025("Lewis", "Lois", "491176025");
Person& assistant = student_6025;
```

```
    Person& lois = assistant;
    lois.set_phone("418-3306");
```
It defines a single `Person` object with three different names: `student_6025`, `assistant`, and `lois`.
Then it sets the phone number for that single object:

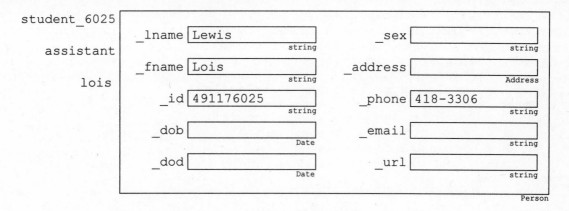

Like constants, references must be initialized. That should seem reasonable, since you couldn't
have an alternative name for something that doesn't exist.

Although not required, pointers should also be initialized.

The reference and dereference operators are inverses in the sense that each reverses the action of
the other.

EXAMPLE 8.11 The Reference and Dereference Operators
```
    Address x("72 N Main", "Troy", "NY", "12180", "USA");
    Address y("49 Elm St", "Troy", "MI", "48099", "USA");
    Address* p = &x;    // p points to x
    Address* q = &y;    // q points to y
    Address z = *p;     // initializes z to x
    z = *&y;            // assigns y to z
    p = &*q;            // assigns q to p
```
Note that although the reference operator can be applied to any lvalue, the dereference operator
can be applied only to pointers:
```
    Address** pp = &p;  // ok: p has type Address*
    z = *x;             // ERROR: x is not a pointer
```

8.5 NULL POINTERS

The number zero (0) is an integer literal that can be used as a pointer value. But as an address,
`0x0` would locate the first byte in memory, which is certainly outside any memory segment allocated
to a program. So 0 is a valid pointer value that cannot be dereferenced. It is called the *null value*, and
any pointer whose value is zero is called a *null pointer*.

Null pointers are often used to indicate the end of something, like a list or a tree. But since they
cannot be dereferenced, they are a common cause of run-time error.

EXAMPLE 8.12 Bus Errors
This program defines a version of the Standard C `strchr()` function for finding characters within C-
strings. The `locate()` function prints the index of the given character within the given string if it is found.

But if the character is not in the string, the program crashes on the dereference `*p` because in that case `p` is the null pointer:

```
char* strchr(char* s, char c)
{ for (char* p=s; *p; p++)
    if (*p == c) return p;
  return 0;
}


void locate(char* s, char c)
{ char* p = strchr(s, c);
    if (*p == 0) cout << "Not found" << endl;                        // ERROR
    else cout << "The first occurrence of the character '" << c
            << "'\n\tin the string \"" << s
            << "\"\n\tis at position: " << p - s << endl;
}


int main()
{ locate("Newton, Isaac, 1642-1727", 'a');
  locate("Leibniz, Gottfried Wilhelm, 1646-1716", 'l');
  locate("Gauss, Carl Friedrich, 1777-1855", 'k');
}
```

The output is

```
The first occurrence of the character 'a'
        in the string "Newton, Isaac, 1642-1727"
        is at position: 10
The first occurrence of the character 'l'
        in the string "Leibniz, Gottfried Wilhelm, 1646-1716"
        is at position: 21
Bus error
```

On the third call to the `locate()` function, the `strchr()` function returns 0 to `p`. Since the dereference `*p` is not possible when `p` is 0, the program crashes with a "Bus error." This code is repaired simply by changing the condition to `(p == 0)`.

Notice how the `for` loop works in the `strchr()` function. It is controlled by the pointer `p` which traverses the string `s`. The C-string variable `s` contains the address of the first character in the string, so the loop is initialized by setting `p = s`. The characters in the string reside in consecutive bytes in memory, so `++p` moves it down the string one character at a time. And since every C-string ends with the null character 0, the condition `*p != 0` can be used to continue the loop. But the condition `*p != 0` is equivalent to the condition `*p` because any non-zero integer value (or pointer values) is always interpreted as the `bool` value `true`, and the zero integer value (or null pointer) is always interpreted as the `bool` value `false`. Thus, the form

```
for (char* p=s; *p; p++)
```

neatly and succinctly traverses the C-string, giving access to each character of `s` through `*p`. This is a standard technique in C programs.

The bus error illustrated in Example 8.12 was caused by dereferencing the null pointer. A similar run-time error occurs when a dangling pointer is dereferenced. In that case, the diagnostic error message from the operating system is likely to be "Segmentation fault" because the dereference is an attempt to access a memory location that is outside the segment allocated to the running process.

8.6 DYNAMIC ARRAYS

A *dynamic array* is an array whose size can be changed dynamically while the program is running. We used dynamic arrays to implement the `Stack`, `Queue`, and `Deque` classes in Chapter 7.

EXAMPLE 8.13 Using a Dynamic Array in the `Stack` Class

Here are the relevant parts of the `Stack` class defined on page 154:

```
class Stack
{ public:
    Stack(int s=100);      // sets the default maximum number at 100
    ~Stack();
    //...
  private:
    char* _a;         // the stack itself: a dynamic array of char
    int _max;         // the maximum number of elements on the stack
    int _count;       // the number of elements on the stack
};
Stack::Stack(int m) : _max(m), _count(0)
{ _a = new char[_max];
  assert(_a != 0);
}
Stack::~Stack()
{ delete [] _a;
}
```

The dynamic array `_a` is declared to be a `char*` because the array's element type is `char`. If the class were for stacks of `Person` objects instead of stacks of `char`s, we would declare its dynamic array as

```
    Person* _a;
```

The default constructor uses the `new` operator to allocate space for `m` elements of type `char` to the array `_a`. This storage allocation occurs dynamically, at the moment a declaration such as

```
    Stack stack(500);   // creates a stack that can hold up to 500 chars
```

executes. Those 500 bytes of memory remain allocated to `_a` until the `stack` goes out of scope. At that moment, the destructor is invoked, which uses the `delete` operator to deallocate the storage.

Notice the call

```
    assert(_a != 0);
```

in the constructor. This is done to check whether the storage allocation was successful. If the operating system is unable to allocate the number of bytes requested, it sets the pointer `_a` to 0. That would likely happen upon a declaration such as

```
    Stack big_stack(5000000);   // asks for 5 MB of memory
```

The `new` and `delete` operators are used to allocate and deallocate dynamic arrays. But they can also be used to allocate and deallocate individual objects.

EXAMPLE 8.14 Dynamic Objects

This example uses the `Person` class defined on page 175 and the `Date` class defined on page 171.

```
    Person* p = new Person("Wells", "Ward", "614405927");
    p->set_dob(Date(1980,8,18));
```

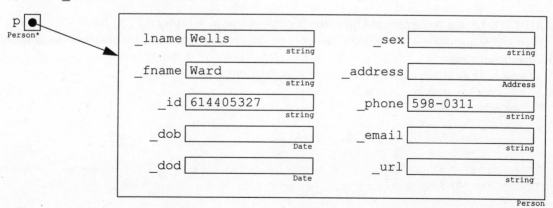

The first line uses the `new` operator to create an anonymous `Person` object. It initializes its `_lname`, `_fname`, and `_id` fields, and defines the pointer `p` to point to it. The second line dereferences the pointer `p` to call the `set_dob` member function to set the object's `_dob` field.

Note how the `Date` constructor is used in the second line to create an anonymous temporary `Date` object to represent the date Aug 18 1980. That object is passed to `set_dob()` member function of the `Person` class to set the `Person` object's `_dob` field. The `Date` object is passed by value, so the `Date` class copy constructor copies the data into the `_dob` field.

8.7 THE `this` POINTER

When a class member function is called, it must be bound to an instance of the class. For example,

```
Person sara("Smith", "Sara", "510880457");
sara.set_email("ssmith@richmond.edu");
```

The call `set_email("ssmith@richmond.edu")` is bound to the object `sara`. To carry out its instructions, the function needs access to both the explicit argument `"ssmith@richmond.edu"` and the implicit argument `sara`. Member functions can access their explicit arguments by means of their parameters. Member functions can access their implicit argument by means of the `this` pointer.

The C++ keyword `this` can be used only within member functions. It is a predefined pointer that always points to the object to which the member function call is bound.

EXAMPLE 8.15 Using the `this` Pointer

This member function for the `Purse` class (defined on page 169) determines whether a variable is a synonym for its implicit argument

```
bool is_same(Purse& x)
{ return bool(&x == this);
}
```

If `x` and `y` are Purse objects, this function could be called like this:

```
if (x.is_same(y)) cout << "It's the same purse.\n";
```

The function returns `true` if the address of `y` is the same as this which points to `x`; *i.e.*, if `x` and `y` have the same address. That condition determines, by definition, whether `x` and `y` are names for the same object.

Of course, this function is unnecessary. The call could be replaced by the condition `(&x == &y)`.

Whenever a class member function has to return a reference to its implicit argument, it should

```
return *this;
```

That is the standard code for the overloaded assignment operator.

EXAMPLE 8.16 An Assignment Operator for the `Stack` Class

This member function could be added to the `Stack` class (defined on page 154) to allow the assignment of one stack to another:

```
Stack& Stack::operator=(const Stack& x)
{ if (&x == this) return *this;
  _max = x._max;
  _count = x._count;
  _a = new char[_max];
  for (int i = 0; i < _count; i++ )
    _a[i] = x._a[i];
  return *this;
}
```

The function returns immediately if its explicit argument is the same object as its implicit argument. Otherwise, it copies the values of _max and _count, allocates the dynamic array _a, and then copies the stack elements from x to *this.

The assignment operator returns *this so that the operator can be used in a *cascade assignment*, like this:

```
z = y = x;
```
This calls the assignment operator twice, like this:
```
z.operator=(y.operator=(x));
```
The inside call assigns x to y and returns a reference to y. Then the outside call uses that reference as its explicit argument, and assigns y to z.

Warning: Without the explicit definition of the class assignment operator, the compiler will generate a default version of it. But this default version simply performs a *bitwise copy* of an object's data members. For classes like Person and Purse, a bitwise copy is completely adequate, so there is no need to include an explicit definition of the assignment operator. However, for classes like Stack whose member data are dynamic, a bitwise copy produces incorrect results. A bitwise copy of the data member _a will not duplicate the array; it simply duplicates its name. So the assignment of one Stack object to another would result in two separate objects using the same array to hold their data.

Any class whose member data use pointers should either include explicit definitions of the class's copy constructor and assignment operator, or those two member functions should be disabled by declaring them to be private, like this:

```
class Stack
{ public:
    Stack(int s=100);    // sets the default maximum number at 100
    ~Stack();
    //...
  private:
    char* _a;      // the stack itself: a dynamic array of char
    int _max;      // the maximum number of elements on the stack
    int _count;    // the number of elements on the stack
    Stack(const Stack& x) {}
    Stack& operator=(const Stack& x) { return *this; }
};
```
As private function members, they can be called only from within the class itself.

Review Questions

8.1 What is the difference between p and *p? (Assume that p is a pointer type.)

8.2 What is the difference between x and &x?

8.3 What is the difference between ++(*p) and *(++p)?

8.4 Why must a reference be initialized?

8.5 What boolean expression determines whether two names, x and y, are names for the same object?

8.6 What is a dangling pointer?

8.7 What's wrong with storing pointers in a file?

8.8 What is the difference between a static array and a dynamic array?

8.9 How are dynamic arrays better than static arrays?

8.10 What is the this pointer?

8.11 Why should the assignment operator of a class return `*this`?

8.12 Why is it important to define the copy constructor and the assignment operator explicitly `private` in a class whose data members include pointers, instead of allowing the compiler to generate its default versions of these two member functions?

8.13 What does the `new` operator do?

8.14 What does the `delete` operator do?

Problems

8.15 Tell what is wrong with each of the following:

a.
```
int n = 44;
int* p = &n;
++(*p);
int m = p;
```
b.
```
int* p = new int;
*p = 44;
int* q = p;
delete p;
```
c.
```
int* p = new int;
*p = 44;
int* q = new int;
p = q;
```
d.
```
int n = new int;
n = 44;
```

8.16 Trace the following code, showing each value of each variable:
```
int a[] = { 22, 33, 44, 55, 66, 77 };
int* p = &a[3];    // assume that p gets the value 0x3fffcbc here
int n = *p;
++(*p);
++p;
int* q = &a[5];
*(--q) = 88;
p -= 3;
n = q - p;
```

8.17 Draw pictures to show the effect of the following code:
```
double* p = new double;
*p = 3.141592653589793;
short* q = new short[5];
*q = 44;
*(q+4) = 88;
```

8.18 Draw pictures to show the effects of the following statements:
```
string* p = new string("ABCDEFG");
string s = *p;     // s is a copy of *p;
string& r = *p;    // r is a synonym for *p
string* q = &s;    // q points to s
r[5] = '?';
q->erase(3, 2);
s[1] = '!';
p->replace(2, 1, "$=$");
```

Programming Problems

8.19 Write declarations for each of the following
  a. A pointer to a `char`.
  b. A C-string wich can have up to 19 characters.
  c. A pointer to a C-string.
  d. A `string` object.
  e. A pointer to a `string` object.
  f. A static array of 8 `string` objects.
  g. A dynamic array of 8 `string` objects.

8.20 Write statements for each of the following:
  a. Initialize a pointer `p` to point to a `Person` object `x`.
  b. Assign the `Person` object `y` to the object to which `p` points.
  c. Initialize a pointer `q` to the address of the pointer `p`.
  d. Initialize a reference `r` to the `Person` object `x`.

8.21 Write and run a program that declares the following objects and then prints their addresses: a `bool`, a `short`, an `int`, a `float`, a `double`, a `string` of 5 characters, and an array of 5 `float`s:
  a. using static allocation;
  b. using dynamic allocation.

8.22 Implement the following function for the `Purse` class (defined on page 169):
```
int f(Purse* p, Purse* q);
// Returns 1 if p and q point to the same purse. Returns 0 if p
// and q point to different purses which have the same contents.
// Returns -1 if the two purses have different contents.
```

8.23 Implement the following function:
```
bool same(Person& x, Person& y);
// Returns true iff x and y are the same person.
```

8.24 Implement the following function from the `<cstring>` library for C-strings:
```
int strlen(const char* s);
// Returns the number of non-null characters in the C-string s.
```

8.25 Implement the following function from the `<cstring>` library for C-strings:
```
char* strcat(char* s1, const char* s2);
// Appends a copy of the C-string s2 to s1, and returns s1.
```

8.26 Implement the following function from the `<cstring>` library for C-strings:
```
char* strcpy(char* s1, const char* s2);
// Copies the non-null characters of s2 into s1, and returns s1.
```

8.27 Implement the following function from the `<cstring>` library for C-strings:
```
int strcmp(const char* s1, const char* s2);
// Compares s1 and s2 lexicographically. Returns a negative
// integer is s1 < s2, a positive integer if s1 > s2, and 0
// if the two strings have the same value.
```

8.28 Implement the following function from the `<cstring>` library for C-strings:
```
char* strstr(const char* s1, const char* s2);
// Searches s1 for the substring s2. If found, its address in s1
// is returned. Otherwise, 0 is returned.
```

Solutions

8.1 If p is a pointer, then the value stored in p is a memory address and the value of *p is the value stored at that address.

8.2 If x is an object, then the value of &x is the address of that object in memory.

8.3 If p is a pointer to an integer, then ++(*p) increments that integer, whereas the value of the expression *(++p) is whatever is stored in the memory location immediately after that integer. For example, if a is an array of short integers, and if p points to a[2], then ++(*p) increments a[2], while *(++p) refers to a[3].

8.4 A reference is a synonym for an existing object, so it must be bound to an existing object when it is declared.

8.5 Two names, x and y, are names for the same object iff (&x == &y).

8.6 A *dangling pointer* is a pointer whose value is an unallocated (or deallocated) address; *i.e.*, a pointer that does not point to any existing object.

8.7 Pointers are *volatile* data: as memory addresses, they are useful only during the execution of the program in which they were created. Once a program has terminated, all its data in memory are lost, and so any references to the memory locations at which they were stored is meaningless. Data is stored in files on disks so that they can be retrieved and reused by different programs at different times. If that reuse is not possible, then there is no reason to store it.

8.8 A static array is declared like this:
```
double x[N];
```
Its dimension (N) must be a constant, determined at compile-time. A dynamic array is declared like as:
```
double x = new double[n];
```
Its dimension (n) may be a variable whose value is set at run-time.

8.9 Dynamic arrays are more flexible than static arrays because their sizes can be variables.

8.10 The this pointer is a pointer that is available inside class member functions. It points to the object to which the function call is bound.

8.11 The assignment operator should return *this to allow cascade assignments, such as z = y = x;

8.12 The compiler-generated versions of the copy constructor and the assignment operator simply make a bitwise duplicate of each object being assigned or copied. If the class data members include pointers, the values to which they point will not be duplicated.

8.13 The new operator is used to allocate storage dynamically (at run-time) to arrays and anonymous objects. For example:
```
short* a = new short[10];   // allocates 20 bytes for the array a
float* p = new float;       // allocates 4 bytes for a float
```

8.14 The delete operator is used to deallocate storage dynamically. For example:
```
delete [] a; // deallocates the storage allocated to the array a
delete p;    // deallocates the storage allocated at p
```

8.15 *a.* The initialization
```
int m = p;
```
is illegal because m has type int and p has type pointer to int.

   b. The statement
```
delete p;
```
leaves q dangling. It deletes the only int allocated, so q has nothing to point to.

   c. The assignment
```
p = q;
```
renders the value 44 inaccessible. It remains allocated, but its "handle" p has been removed.

   d. The new operator returns a pointer, not an int. So the code should be written as in *b*.

8.16

a[0]	a[1]	a[2]	a[3]	a[4]	a[5]	p	n	q
22	33	44	55	66	77	0x3fffcbc	55	
			56			0x3fffcc0		
				88			.	0x3fffcc0
						0x3fffcb4	3	

8.17

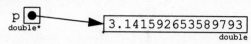

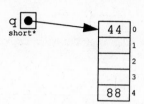

8.18

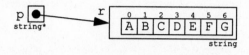

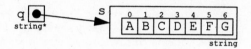

r[5] = '?'

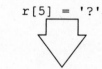

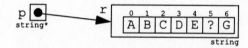

q->erase(3,2)

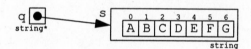

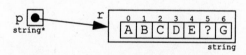

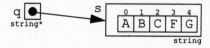

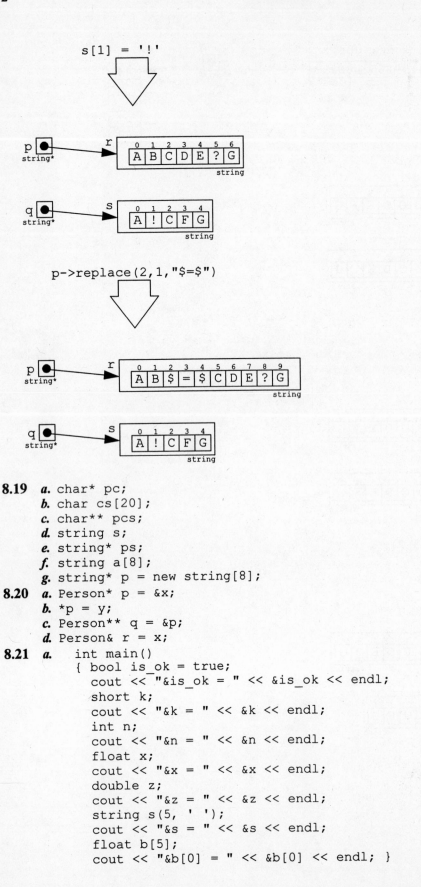

8.19 *a.* `char* pc;`
  b. `char cs[20];`
  c. `char** pcs;`
  d. `string s;`
  e. `string* ps;`
  f. `string a[8];`
  g. `string* p = new string[8];`

8.20 *a.* `Person* p = &x;`
  b. `*p = y;`
  c. `Person** q = &p;`
  d. `Person& r = x;`

8.21 *a.*
```
    int main()
    { bool is_ok = true;
      cout << "&is_ok = " << &is_ok << endl;
      short k;
      cout << "&k = " << &k << endl;
      int n;
      cout << "&n = " << &n << endl;
      float x;
      cout << "&x = " << &x << endl;
      double z;
      cout << "&z = " << &z << endl;
      string s(5, ' ');
      cout << "&s = " << &s << endl;
      float b[5];
      cout << "&b[0] = " << &b[0] << endl; }
```

b.
```
    int main()
    { bool* pb = new bool;
      cout << "pb = " << pb << endl;
      short* pk = new short;
      cout << "pk = " << pk << endl;
      int* pn = new int;
      cout << "pn = " << pn << endl;
      float* px = new float;
      cout << "px = " << px << endl;
      double* pz = new double;
      cout << "pz = " << pz << endl;
      string* ps = new string(5, ' ');
      cout << "ps = " << ps << endl;
      float* py = new float[5];
      cout << "py = " << py << endl;
    }
```

8.22
```
    int f(Purse* p, Purse* q)
    { if (p == q) return 1;
      if (p->pennies() != q->pennies()) return -1;
      if (p->nickels() != q->nickels()) return -1;
      if (p->dimes() != q->dimes()) return -1;
      if (p->quarters() != q->quarters()) return -1;
      return 0;
    }
```

8.23
```
    int same(Person& x, Person& y)
    { return bool(&x == &y);
    }
```

8.24
```
    int strlen(const char* s)
    { for (const char* p=s; *p; p++)
        ;
      return int(p - s);
    }
```

8.25
```
    char* strcat(char* s1, const char* s2)
    { char* p;
      for (p=s1; *p; p++)
        ;
      for (; *s2; p++, s2++)
        *p = *s2;
      *p = *s2;
      return s1;
    }
```

8.26
```
    char* strcpy(char* s1, const char* s2)
    { while(*s2)
        *s1++ = *s2++;
      *s1 = 0;
      return s1;
    }
```

8.27
```
    int strcmp(const char* s1, const char* s2)
    { while (*s1 && *s1++ == *s2++)
        ;
      return *s1 - *s2;
    }
```

8.28

```
char* strstr(const char* s1, const char* s2)
{ if (*s2 == 0) return (char*)(s1);
  for (; *s1; s1++)
  { char* p = (char*)(s1);
    char* q = (char*)(s2);
    while (*p == *q && *p)
      if (*p++ == 0) return 0;
      else if (*q++ == 0) return (char*)(s1);
    if (*q++ == 0) return (char*)(s1);
  }
  return 0;
}
```

Chapter 9

Lists

A *list* is a sequence of elements of the same type. A list is like an array, with one essential distinction: arrays provide direct access to their elements; lists provide only sequential access. For example, the 100th element of an array `a` can be changed directly: `a[99] = 65432;` But in a sequential access list, the 100th element cannot be changed until it has been located, typically by traversing through its preceding 99 elements. The trade-off for this slower access time is the more efficient methods that lists have for inserting and deleting elements. To insert a new element into the 100th element of a 1000-element array would require shifting the following 900 elements. But the same insertion can be made to a linked list without moving any elements.

9.1 LINKED STRUCTURES

Arrays are inefficient when an element needs to be inserted or deleted from the sequence. That is because arrays are stored contiguously in memory. Linked lists overcome the problem by storing their elements in non-contiguous memory locations. For this strategy to work, each element has to be stored together with the memory address of the next element in the list. These two items are encapsulated together into an object called a *node*. A *linked list* is then a sequence of nodes, each node containing an element and the address of the next node in the list:

This shows a linked list containing the sequence of integers (22, 33, 44, 55). It consists of four `Node` objects, each containing an integer data member and a pointer to the next node. Since the pointer in the last node doesn't point to anything, it is the null pointer (0) indicated by a "grounded" arrow.

Here is a definition for a `Node` class to implement liked lists of `ints`:

```
class Node
{ public:
    Node(int data, Node* next) : _data(data), _next(next) { }
  private:
    int _data;
    Node* _next;
};
```

Then the linked list shown above could be constructed like this:

```
Node* list = new Node(55, 0);
list = new Node(44, list);
list = new Node(33, list);
list = new Node(22, list);
```

Recall that the `new` operator uses the class's constructor to build the new node. So the expression

```
new Node(44, list)
```

constructs a new `Node` object, assigns 44 to its `_data` field, and copies the address from the list pointer into its `_next` field.

To make any practical use of such a list, we need functions that have access to the nodes' _data and _next fields. Since they are declared to be private members of the Node class, such functions would have to be either members too or friends of the Node class. Both of those design options are unwieldy. A preferred method is to declare the functions members of a separate List class which is then declared to be a friend of the Node class. This is done by many authors. But it has the disadvantage of leaving the Node class as an independent class. Since these nodes are used only to construct lists (in Chapter 12 we use a different type of node to implement trees), it is better to *nest* the Node class inside the List class, like this:

```
class List
{ private:
    class Node
    { //...
    };
    //...
};
```

That allows only members of the List class access to the Node class members.

The List class functions could include a print() function that works like this:

```
for (Node* p = list; p != 0; p = p->_next)
    cout << p->_data << " ";
```

The output would be

```
22 33 44 55
```

An insert() function could insert the new element 50 in front of 55 like this:

```
Node* pre;
for (Node* p = list; p != 0 && p->_data != 55; p = p->_next)
    pre = p;
pre->_next = new Node(50, p);
```

This uses a *pre-pointer* named pre to keep access to the node that precedes the node located by p. This is necessary because when the loop terminates, p is pointing to the node that contains 55, and it is its predecessor (the one containing 44) that has to be changed to point to the new node being inserted. Here's how the list looks after this insertion:

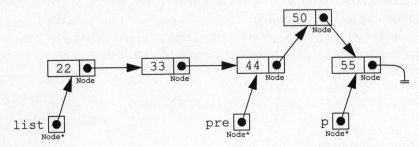

This illustrates the real value of linked lists: the insertion of the new element can be made without moving any of the list's element. Deletions are just as efficient.

9.2 C++ structs

C++ inherits from the C language a type called struct (for "structure"). In C++, a struct is the same as a class except for the minor distinction:

   • The default access category is private for classes and public for structs.

The "default access category" means the access category (public, protected, or private) that is used if you do not specify one explicitly in your definition.

EXAMPLE 9.1 The Default Access Category Is `private` for `classes`

```
class X
{   void f();   // private access
    char c;     // private access
  public:
    void g();   // public access
    int n;      // public access
  private:
    void h();   // private access
    float z;    // private access
};
```

This class has six members: `X::f()`, `X::c`, `X::h()`, and `X::z` have `private` access; `X::g()` and `X::n` have `public` access.

EXAMPLE 9.2 The Default Access Category Is `public` for `structs`

```
struct Y
{   void f();   // public access
    char c;     // public access
  public:
    void g();   // public access
    int n;      // public access
  private:
    void h();   // private access
    float z;    // private access
};
```

This structure has six members: `Y::f()`, `Y::c`, `Y::g()`, and `Y::n` have `public` access; `Y::h()` and `Y::z` have `private` access.

So unless you use inheritance, the only difference between a `struct` and a `class` is the access category of those data members that are declared without an explicit access category. Of course, if you always explicitly specify the access categories of all your data members (as we have done throughout this book), then there is no difference.

Most C++ programmers prefer to use `classes` instead of `structs`. But Bjarne Stroustrup, the creator of C++, recommends using a `struct` instead of a `class` if all its members are `public`:

```
struct Node
{ Node(int data, Node* next) : _data(data), _next(next) { }
  int _data;
  Node* _next;
};
```

This makes the code simpler.

The `List` class then looks like this:

```
class List
{ private:
    struct Node
    { Node(int data, Node* next) : _data(data), _next(next) { }
      int _data;
      Node* _next;
    };
  public:
    List();
    //...
};
```

Warning: Some older pre-Standard C++ compilers do not support nested classes and structures.

9.3 LINKED INPLEMENTATION OF THE <u>Stack</u> ADT

Here is our abstract type definition for stacks (from page 154):

ADT: <u>Stack</u>

Represents:

A sequence of elements, all of the same type.

Access:

A stack allows access only at one end of the sequence, called the *top* of the stack.

Constructors and Destructors:

create	Creates an empty stack of a given maximum size.
destroy	De-allocates the memory used for the stack.

Access Functions:

top	Returns the last element on the stack.
is_empty	Returns true if the stack is empty; otherwise returns false.
is_full	Returns true if the stack is full; otherwise returns false.

Mutator Functions:

push	Inserts a new element at the top of the stack.
pop	Removes and returns the element from the top of the stack.

In Chapter 7 we used a dynamic array to implemented this ADT. That required the specification of the maximum stack size. We can avoid that restriction now by using a linked list instead.

Here is a linked implementation of this ADT for stacks of char elements:

```
class Stack
{ private:
    struct Node
    { Node(int data, Node* next) : _data(data), _next(next) { }
      char _data;
      Node* _next;
    };
  public:
    Stack() : _top(0) { }
    ~Stack();
    char top() const { assert(_top != 0); return _top->_data; }
    bool is_empty() const { return bool(_top == 0); }
    bool is_full() const { return false; }
    void push(const char c) { _top = new Node(c, _top); }
    char pop();
  private:
    Node* _top;
};
Stack::~Stack()
{ for (Node* p = _top; p;)
  { _top = p->_next;
    delete p;
  }
}
char Stack::pop()
{ assert(_top != 0);
  Node* p = _top;
  char ch = p->_data;
  _top = p->_next;
  delete p;
  return ch;
}
```

A `Stack` class of any type `T` would have the same definition with **char** replaced by **T**.

The definition of the `Node` structure is completely encapsulated as a `private` declaration nested inside the `Stack` class. Consequently, all members of the `Stack` class can access the `_data` and `_next` members of the `Node` class, but nothing outside of the `Stack` class can.

EXAMPLE 9.3 Using the `Stack` Class's `push()` Function

After the execution of the code

```
Stack x;
x.push('A');
x.push('B');
x.push('C');
x.push('D');
```

the `Stack` object `x` would look like this:

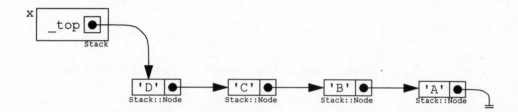

The details of each `Stack::Node` object look are shown shown at right.

The call `x.push('A')` executes the statement

```
_top = new Node(c, _top);
```

where `c` contains the char `'A'`. This is an assignment statement, so the system first evaluates the expression

```
new Node(c, _top)
```

This expression invokes the `new` operator which calls the `Node` constructor to create a new `Node` object. The `Node` constructor is defined as

```
Node(int data, Node* next) : _data(data), _next(next) { }
```

so the parameter `data` is matched to the argument `c`, and the parameter `next` is matched to the argument `_top`. Then the constructor's initialization list

```
_data(data), _next(next)
```

executes, initializing the new node's `_data` field with the value of the `data` parameter and its `_next` field with the value of the `next` parameter. The value of the `data` parameter is the value of the argument c which is the character `'A'`, so the new node's `_data` field is initialized with the character `'A'`. The value of the `next` parameter is the value of the argument `_top` which was initialized to be `0` by the `Stack` constructor, so the new node's `_next` field is initialized with the pointer value `0` which is the null pointer. This is indicated by the "grounded" arrow in the diagram above. Finally, the `Node` constructor executes the statements in its function body. But that body is empty, so the `Node` constructor has finished its work. The `new` operator then returns the address of the new `Node` object as the value of the expression

```
new Node(c, _top)
```

This value, the address of the new node, is then assigned to `_top`.

The successive calls `x.push('B')`, `x.push('C')`, and `x.push('D')` execute the same way. Each time, a new `Node` object is constructed with its `_data` field initialized with the character passed and its `_next` field initialized with the address stored in the `Stack` object's `_top` field. That address is always the address of the last node inserted into the list, so the nodes get linked as illustrated in the picture above. Note that nearly all the work is done each time by the `Node` constructor.

EXAMPLE 9.4 Using the `Stack` Class's `top()` and `pop()` Functions

Assume that the following statements execute after those in Example 9.3:

```
char ch = x.top();
x.pop();
```

The call `x.top()` executes the `assert()` macro first to ensure that the stack is not empty. If it is, the program will abort at that point. (Better no answer than the wrong answer!) If the condition (`_top != 0`) is `true`, then the `_top` field must contain the memory address of a `Node` object. Then the expression `_top->_data` will return the character stored in the `_data` field of that node pointed. In this case, that character is `'D'`. It is then returned by the `top()` function and consequently assigned to the object `ch`.

The call `x.pop()` executes the `assert()` macro again to ensure that the stack is not empty. If the condition (`_top != 0`) is `true`, then the local pointer `p` is initialized with the address stored in `_top`; *i.e.*, it is set to point to the same thing to which `_top` points: the node containing `'D'`:

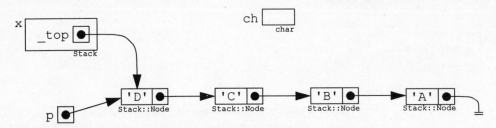

This saves that node's address temporarily so that `_top` can be reassigned to point to the next node (the one containing `'C'`). Then the local `char` object `ch` is initialized with the (`'D'`) that is stored in `*p`:

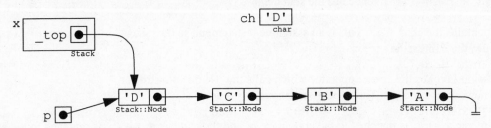

Finally, the `delete` operator is invoked to deallocate the memory space occupied by the node `*p`, and the character stored in `ch` is returned (but not used).

9.4 ITERATORS

Linked structures like the `Stack` implementation shown above differ from arrays in that they have no built-in mechanism for direct access. A stack does not need direct access; it is meant to allow access only at its top, which was implemented as the front of the list. But to take advantage of the efficient means that linked lists enjoy for insertions and deletions, we need some kind of mechanism for accessing any node in the list. One popular method is to assign ordinal numbers to the nodes: the 3rd node, the 8th node, *etc.*, analogous to an array index. However the more modern approach, employed extensively in the ISO C++ Standard Library, is to use iterators.

An *iterator* is an object that locates a node in a linked data structure. It works just like a pointer into an array. Here is an abstract data type for general iterators:

ADT: <u>Iterator</u>

Represents:

A locator and accessor for the elements of a linked data structure.

Constructors and Destructors:

create   Creates an iterator initialized by a node pointer.

Access Functions:

is_inactive Returns true iff the iterator is not currently locating an element.
dereference Returns a reference to the element located by the iterator.

Mutator Functions:

increment   Advances the iterator so that is locates the next element.
decrement   Backs the iterator up so that it locates the preceding element.
assignment   Assigns one iterator to another.

Operators:

equality   Returns true if the two given iterators locate the same element.
inequality   Returns true if the two given iterators locate different elements.

Here is a general iterator interface for this ADT:

```
class Iterator
{ public:
    Iterator(Node*);
    bool operator!() const;
    T& operator*() const;
    Iterator& operator++();
    Iterator& operator--();
    Iterator& operator=(const Iterator&);
    friend bool operator==(const Iterator&, const Iterator&);
    friend bool operator!=(const Iterator&, const Iterator&);
  private:
    Node* _p;   // points to the node that contains the element
};
```

Not surprisingly, the iterator class is implemented as a node pointer.

We can visualize a `List` iterator like this:

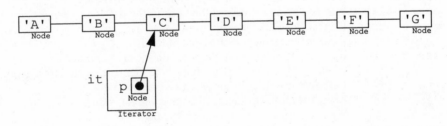

This shows an iterator named `it` that is bound to a list of `chars` and is currently locating the element `'C'`. It could have been declared as

```
List::Iterator it;
```

provided that the `Iterator` class is defined inside the `List` class. This iterator is not initialized; it is created by the default constructor generated by the compiler. It would need some mechanism provided by the `List` class itself to attach itself to a particular list node. The Standard approach is to define the following member function in the `list` class for this purpose:

```
Iterator begin();
```

This function returns an iterator that locates the first node of the list. The following code could be used to initialize it and then position it to the third element of a list `x` shown in the picture above:

```
it = x.begin();   // now it locates element 'A'
++it;             // now it locates element 'B'
++it;             // now it locates element 'C'
cout << "The current element is " << *it << endl;
```

This would print

```
The current node is C
```

9.5 A List ADT

Here is an abstract data type definition for lists:

ADT: List

Represents:

A sequence of elements, all of the same type.

Access:

Elements are accessed and modified through iterators that are bound to the list. At any time during its existence, an iterator either locates a single element in the list, or it locates the end of the list which is defined to be the null position that follows the last element. Iterators may be set to the beginning or the end of the list, they can be advanced to the next element or backed up to the previous element, and they can be tested for locating the end of the list.

Constructors and Destructors:

create	Creates an empty list.
copy	Create a duplicate of another list.
destroy	Destroys the list.

Access Functions:

size	Returns the number of elements in the list.
empty	Returns `true` if the list is empty; otherwise returns `false`.
front	Returns the first element in the list.
back	Returns the last element in the list.
begin	Returns an iterator locating the first element in the list.
end	Returns an iterator locating the null position that follows the last element.

Mutator Functions:

push_front	Inserts a given element at the front of the list.
push_back	Inserts a given element at the back of the list.
pop_front	Deletes the element at the front of the list.
pop_back	Deletes the element at the back of the list.
assign	Replace the elements in the list with those of another list.
insert	Inserts a given element in front of the element located by a given iterator.
erase	Removes the element located by a given iterator.
remove	Removes all the elements that have a given value.
clear	Removes all the elements from the list.

These 18 operations are actually defined by the ISO C++ Standard for the standard library `list` class which covered in Chapter 10.

EXAMPLE 9.5 List Processing

Here is some code that uses the list operations specified in the ADT:

```
List x;                 // constructs the empty list x
x.push_front('C');      // inserts 'C' at the front of the list x
x.push_front('B');      // inserts 'B' at the front of the list x
x.push_front('A');      // inserts 'A' at the front of the list x
x.push_front('X');      // inserts 'X' at the front of the list x
x.push_back('D');       // inserts 'D' at the back of the list x
x.push_back('E');       // inserts 'E' at the back of the list x
x.push_back('F');       // inserts 'F' at the back of the list x
```

```
x.pop_front();          // removes 'X' from the front of the list x
x.pop_back();           // removes 'F' from the back of the list x
```

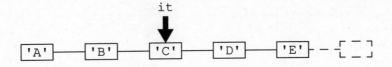

```
List y = x;             // constructs the list y as a copy of the list x
x.clear();              // removes the remaining 5 elements from x
x = y;                  // assigns y to a, making x a duplicate of y
List::Iterator it;      // constructs the detached iterator it
it = x.begin();         // assigns it to locate the first element of x
++it;                   // advances it to locate the second element of x
++it;                   // advances it to locate the third element of x
```

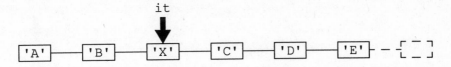

```
x.insert(it, 'X');   // inserts 'X' in front of the third element of x
```

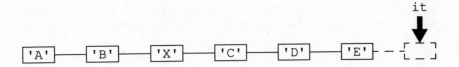

```
it = x.end();           // assigns it to locate the null end of x
```

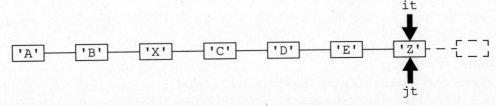

```
List::Iterator jt;   // constructs the detatched iterator jt
jt = x.insert(it, 'Z');   // inserts 'Z' at end of x, locating jt there
```

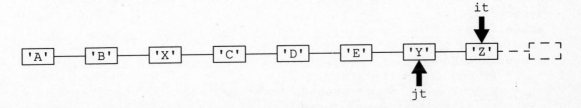

```
x.insert(jt, 'Y');   // inserts 'Y' in front of 'Z' in x
```

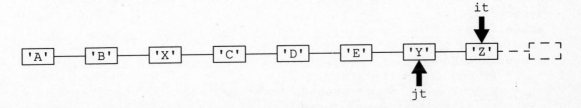

```
--jt;                   // backs up jt to locate the sixth element 'E'
--jt;                   // backs up jt to locate the fifth element 'D'
```

```
                                                                    it
                                                                    ↓
'A' —— 'B' —— 'X' —— 'C' —— 'D' —— 'E' —— 'Y' —— 'Z' – [ _ _ ]
                              ↑
                             jt
```

```
x.erase(jt);            // removes the fifth element 'D'
```

```
                                                              it
                                                              ↓
'A' —— 'B' —— 'X' —— 'C' —— 'E' —— 'Y' —— 'Z' – [ _ _ ]
                                                              ↑
                                                             jt
```

```
x.remove('X');          // removes the third element 'X'
```

```
                                                        it
                                                        ↓
'A' —— 'B' —— 'C' —— 'E' —— 'Y' —— 'Z' – [ _ _ ]
                                                        ↑
                                                       jt
```

```
it = x.begin();         // assigns it to locate the first element of x
*it = 'G'               // changes the first element to 'G'
```

```
  it
  ↓
'G' —— 'B' —— 'C' —— 'E' —— 'Y' —— 'Z' – [ _ _ ]
                                                        ↑
                                                       jt
```

9.6 A List CLASS

Here is a `List` class that implements the ADT defined above for lists of `ints`. It begins with a `typedef` that allows the use of the symbol `T` in place of the element type `int`. This is done so that the class definition can be modified to any element type simply by changing the `typedef`.

```
typedef int T;
class List
{ private:
    struct Node
    { friend class Iterator;
      Node(T data, Node* prev=0, Node* next=0)
      : _data(data), _prev(prev), _next(next) { }
```

```
        T _data;
        Node* _prev;
        Node* _next;
     };
  public:
    class Iterator
    {   friend class List;
      public:
        Iterator(Node* p) : _p(p) { }
        bool operator!() const { return (_p ? false : true); }
        T& operator*() const { return _p->_data; }
        Iterator& operator++() { _p = _p->_next; return *this; }
        Iterator& operator--() { _p = _p->_prev; return *this; }
        Iterator& operator=(const Iterator& it)
           { _p = it._p; return *this; }
        friend bool operator==(const Iterator& it, const Iterator& jt)
           { return bool(it._p == jt._p); }
        friend bool operator!=(const Iterator& it, const Iterator& jt)
           { return bool(it._p != jt._p); }
      private:
        Node* _p;  // points to list node
     };
  public:
    List() : _front(0), _back(0), _size(0) { }
    List(const List&);
    ~List() { clear(); }
    List& operator=(const List&);
    int size() const { return _size; }
    bool empty() const { return bool(_size == 0); }
    T& front() const { return _front->_data; }
    T& back() const { return _back->_data; }
    void push_front(const T&);
    void push_back(const T&);
    void pop_front();
    void pop_back();
    Iterator begin() { return Iterator(_front); }
    Iterator end() { return Iterator(0); }
    Iterator insert(Iterator&, const T&);
    void erase(Iterator&);
    void remove(const T&);
    void clear();
  private:
    Node* _front;
    Node* _back;
    int _size;
};
```

This class interface has four parts: the `private` definition of the `Node` structure, the `public` definition of the `Iterator` class, the `public` declarations of the 18 `List` member functions, and the `private` declarations of the three `List` data members `_front`, `_back`, and `_size`.

This implementation of the `List` class uses a *doubly linked list*. Think of a list as a sequence of linked elements, like a train of railroad cars on a track. We should be able to move from any node forward or backward. We obtain that double mobility by using a `_prev` (for "previous") pointer and a `_next` pointer in each node. Then a `List` object looks like this:

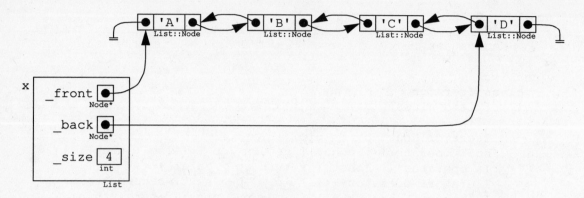

The details of a `Node` object can be visualized as shown at right.

Here is the implementation of the `List` copy constructor:

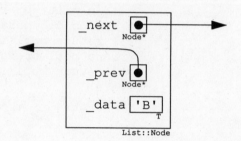

```
List::List(const List& x)
: _front(0), _back(0), _size(x._size)
{ if (x._size == 0) return;
  Node* p = x._front;
  Node* q = _front = new Node(p->_data);
  for (int i=1; i<_size; i++)
  { p = p->_next;
    q = q->_next = new Node(p->_data, q);
    assert(q);
  }
  _back = q;
}
```

This copies the nodes in `x` into the list being constructed. It uses two `Node` pointers, `p` and `q`, to traverse the two lists, `x` and `*this`. For each node that `p` points to in `x` it creates a `new` node and assigns its address to `q->_next`. The two lists are traversed by assigning `p->_next` to `p` and `q->_next` to `q` in each iteration of the `for` loop. The `assert(q)` call checks to ensure that the `new` operator was successful; it will fail in the unlikely event that the system runs out of memory.

Here is the assignment operator:

```
List& List::operator=(const List& x)
{ clear();
  if (x._size == 0) return *this;
  _size = x._size;
  Node* p = x._front;
  Node* q = _front = new Node(p->_data);
  for (int i=1; i<_size; i++)
  { p = p->_next;
    q = q->_next = new Node(p->_data, q);
    assert(q);
  }
  _back = q;
  return *this;
}
```

It works just like the copy constructor. The only differences are that it must `clear()` the `*this` list at the beginning and it has to return `*this` at the end of the call.

The `push_front()` function inserts the element `t` at the beginning of the list:

```
    void List::push_front(const T& t)
    { if (_size == 0) _front = _back = new Node(t);
      else _front = _front->_prev = new Node(t, 0, _front);
      ++_size;
    }
```

If the list is empty, the new node becomes both the _front and _back node. Otherwise, it becomes the new _front node and it in turn points to the old _front node.

The push_back() function works the same way as the push_front() function except that it becomes the _back node of a non-empty list:

```
    void List::push_back(const T& t)
    { if (_size == 0) _front = _back = new Node(t);
      else _back = _back->_next = new Node(t, _back);
      ++_size;
    }
```

The pop_front() function removes the _front element if the list is not empty:

```
    void List::pop_front()
    { if (_size == 0) return;
      Node* p = _front;
      if (_size == 1) _front = _back = 0;
      else
      { _front = _front->_next;
        _front->_prev = 0;
      }
      delete p;
      --_size;
    }
```

If the list contains only one element, then it is emptied by setting _front = _back = 0. Otherwise the _front pointer is advanced.

The pop_back() function works the same way as the pop_front() function; just substitute _back for _front and _prev for _next:

```
    void List::pop_back()
    { if (_size == 0) return;
      Node* p = _back;
      if (_size == 1) _front = _back = 0;
      else
      { _back = _back->_prev;
        _back->_next = 0;
      }
      delete p;
      --_size;
    }
```

The insert() function inserts the given element in front of the node located by the given iterator:

```
    Iterator List::insert(Iterator& pos, const T& t)
    { if (!pos)  // null iterator means insert at end of list
      { push_back(t);
        pos._p = _back;
      }
      else
      { Node* p = pos._p;
        if (p == _front) _front = p->_prev = new Node(t, p->_prev, p);
        else p->_prev = p->_prev->_next = new Node(t, p->_prev, p);
        ++_size;
```

```
        --pos;  // pos should point to newly inserted element
    }
    return pos;
}
```

If the null iterator is passed, then the `push_back()` function is called to insert the new element at the end of the list. Otherwise, the new node is hooked up between `*p` and `*(p->_prev)`, where `p` is the `Node` pointer defined in the iterator `pos`.

The `erase()` function is the inverse of the `insert()` function. It removes the element located by the given iterator:

```
    void List::erase(Iterator& pos)
    { if (!pos || _size == 0) return;
      Node* p = pos._p;
      pos._p = p->_next;        // pos locates next element, after erasure
      p->_prev->_next = p->_next;
      p->_next->_prev = p->_prev;
      delete p;
      --_size;
    }
```

If the iterator is null or the list is empty the function returns immediately.

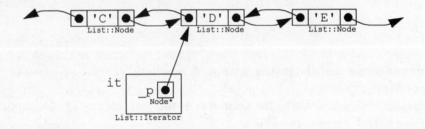

The given iterator is reset to locate the next element. Then the `_next` pointer of the previous element and the `_prev` pointer of the next element are reset to keep the list connected after the current element is deleted:

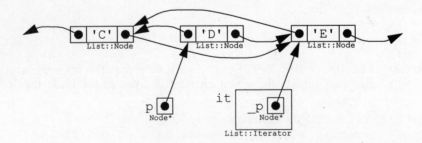

Then `*p` is deleted:

The `remove()` function removes all the elements that equal the given value `t`:

```
    void List::remove(const T& t)
    { if (_front == 0) return;
      Node* p_next = _front->_next;
```

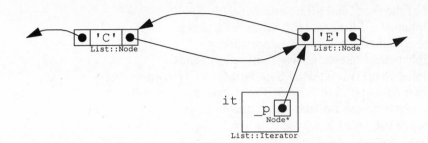

```
for (Node* p=_front; p; p = p_next, p_next = p->_next)
   if (p->_data == t)
   { if (p == _front) _front = p->_next;
     else p->_prev->_next = p->_next;
     if (p == _back) _back = p->_prev;
     else p->_next->_prev = p->_prev;
     delete p;
     --_size;
   }
}
```

If the list is empty, the function returns immediately. Otherwise, it traverses the entire list with a `for` loop. At each node, if the `_data` matches the given value `t`, then the node is removed using the same code as in the `erase()` function.

Since `*p` may be deleted at the end of an iteration, `p->_next` must be saved before the `delete` can execute. This is done with the `p_next` variable, which is assigned right after `p` is updated in the control of the `for` loop. The expression `p = p_next, p_next = p->_next` uses the *comma operator*, which has nearly the same effect as a compound statement. This comma expression first assigns `p = p_next` and then assigns `p_next = p->_next`.

The `clear()` function removes all the elements from the list, leaving it empty:

```
void List::clear()
{ Node* p=_front;
  while (p)
  { _front = p->_next;
    delete p;
    p = _front;
  }
  _back = 0;
  _size = 0;
}
```

The pointer `p` traverses the list, from `_front` to `_back`, deleting each node in succession.

Review Questions

9.1   What is the difference between arrays and linked lists, in terms of:
   a. the relative memory locations of their elements?
   b. the kind of access allowed?
   c. the efficiency of insertions and deletions?
   d. the efficiency of traversing the entire list?

9.2   For each of the following lists, decide which implementation would be better, an array or a linked list:

a. a list of the first 1000 prime numbers;

b. an alphabetized list of all the words on a page;

c. a chronological list of the U.S. presidents;

d. an alphabetical telephone list of all your friends;

e. an alphabetical list of the 63 Standard C++ keywords;

f. a numerical list of the 127 ASCII characters;

g. a list of passengers booked for an airline flight;

h. a grocery list.

9.3 What is the difference between a `class` and a `struct` in C++?

9.4 When is it better to use a `struct`?

9.5 Why were the `Node` structs declarations nested inside the `Stack` and `List` classes?

9.6 What is an iterator?

9.7 Describe the effect of each of the following operations on an iterator `it`:

a. `!it`

b. `*it`

c. `++it`

d. `--it`

e. `it = jt`

9.8 What is the difference between the `erase()` and `remove()` functions in the `List` class?

Problems

9.9 Draw pictures to show the effects of the statements in the following code fragment when it executes:

```
List x;
x.push_back('A');
x.push_back('B');
x.push_back('C');
x.push_back('D');
x.push_back('E');
List::Iterator it = x.begin();
*it = 'V';
++it;
x.insert(it, 'W');
it = x.end();
x.insert(it, 'Z');
--it;
--it;
List::Iterator jt = x.begin();
*jt = *it;
jt = it;
x.erase(it);
x.remove('C');
x.pop_front();
x.pop_back();
```

Programming Problems

9.10 Implement the `Queue` class (page 163) as a linked structure.

9.11   The implementation of the `List::remove()` function on page 208 is inefficient inside its `for` loop because it checks every node pointer for being the `_front` pointer and for being the `_back` pointer. Modify this code to make it more efficient.

9.12   The code for the implementation of many of the `List` functions is a little simpler if the List class itself is implemented using a circular list with a dummy node instead of a linear list:

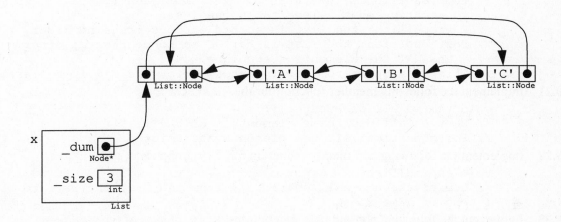

One big advantage is that no null pointers are used. Re-implement the `List` class using circular lists.

9.13   Implement the following constructor for the `List` class defined above in

```
List(int n, T& t);
// Constructs a list containing n copies of the element t.
// This is a Standard Library function for the C++ list class.
```

9.14   Implement the following member function for the `List` class defined in Problem 9.12:

```
void insert(Iterator& pos, int n, T& t);
// Inserts n copies of the element t at the position pos.
// This is a Standard Library function for the C++ list class.
```

9.15   Implement the following member function for the `List` class defined in Problem 9.12:

```
void erase(Iterator& pos1, Iterator& pos2);
// Removes all the elements from position pos1 up to but not
// including the element at position pos2.
// This is a Standard Library function for the C++ list class.
```

9.16   Implement the following member function for the `List` class defined in Problem 9.12:

```
void swap(List& x);
// Swaps the contents of *this with those in the list x.
// This is a Standard Library function for the C++ list class.
```

9.17   Implement the following member function for the `List` class defined in Problem 9.12:

```
void splice(Iterator& pos, List& x);
// Moves all the elements from the list x to *this in front of
// the element located at position pos.
// This is a Standard Library function for the C++ list class.
```

9.18   Implement the following member function for the `List` class defined in Problem 9.12:

```
void reverse();
// Reverses the contents of the list.
// This is a Standard Library function for the C++ list class.
```

9.19 Implement the following member function for the `List` class:

```
void sort();
// Sorts the elements of the list into nondecreasing order.
// This is a Standard Library function for the C++ list class.
```

9.20 Implement the following member function for the `List` class:

```
void unique();
// Removes all but the first element from each run of
// consecutive equal elements in the list.
// Precondition: the list is sorted in nondecreasing order
// Postcondition: the list is sorted in nondecreasing order,
//    and all the elements are unique.
// This is a Standard Library function for the C++ list class.
```

9.21 Implement the following member function for the `List` class:

```
void remove_all_duplicates();
// Removes all duplicate elements from the list.
// Postcondition: all the elements are unique.
```

9.22 Implement the following non-member function for `List` objects of type `char`:

```
void append(List& x, const char* cs);
// Copies the non-null characters from the C-string cs into the
// end of list x.
```

9.23 Implement the following non-member function for `List` objects of type `char`:

```
void copy(List& x, List::Iterator& pos, const char* cs);
// Copies the contents of the C-string cs into the list x at
// position pos.
```

9.24 Implement the following non-member function for `List` objects of type `char`:

```
void copy(char* cs, List& x);
// Copies the contents of the list x into the C-string cs
```

9.25 Implement the following non-member function for `List` objects of type `char`:

```
void copy(char* cs, List& x, List::Iterator& pos1,
          List::Iterator& pos2);
// Copies the contents of the sublist x from position pos1 up
// to but excluding position pos2 into the C-string cs
```

9.26 Implement the following member function for `List` objects of type `char`:

```
void halve(List& y);
// Divides *this in half, making y its second half.
// Postconditions: *this contains only its first half;
//    y contains the second half of *this.
// Example: if x = ABCDEFG, then x.halve(y) changes x to ABC
//    and y to DEFG.
```

9.27 Implement the following non-member function for `List` objects of type `char`:

```
// Divides x in half, making y its second half.
// Postconditions: x contains only its first half;
//    y contains the second half of x.
// Example: if x = ABCDEFG, then x.halve(y) changes x to ABC
//    and y to DEFG.
```

9.28 Implement the following member function for `List` objects of type `char`:

```
void split(List& y);
// Splits *this, moving every other element to y.
// Postconditions: *this contains only its first, third, fifth,
//    etc., elements; y contains the second, fourth, sixth, etc.,
//    elements that were in x.
// Example: if x = ABCDEFG, then x.split(y) changes x to ACEG
//    and y to BDF.
```

9.29 Implement the following non-member function for `List` objects of type `char`:

```
void split(List& x, List& y);
// Splits x, moving every other element to y.
// Postconditions: x contains only its first, third, fifth,
etc.,
//    elements; y contains the second, fourth, sixth, etc.,
//    elements that were in x.
// Example: if x = ABCDEFG, then split(x, y) changes x to ACEG
//    and y to BDF.
```

9.30 Implement the following non-member function for `List` objects of type `char`:

```
void intersection(List& z, List& x, List& y);
// Makes z the set-theoretic intersection of lists x and y.
// Postconditions: z contains only copies of elements that are in
//    x and y; z contains no duplicates; x and y are unchanged.
// Example if x = (1, 2, 3, 1, 5, 4) and y = (4, 6, 5, 7, 6)
// then z becomes (        5, 4).
```

9.31 Implement the following non-member function for `List` objects of type `char`:

```
void complement(List& z, List& x, List& y);
// Makes z the set-theoretic complement of list y in list x.
// Postconditions: z contains only copies of elements that are in
//    x but not y; z contains no duplicates; x and y are
unchanged.
```

9.32 Implement the following non-member function for `List` objects of type `char`:

```
List::Iterator find(List::Iterator& pos1,
                    List::Iterator& pos2, T& t);
// Searches for element t from position pos1 up to but excluding
// position pos2. If found, the position of its first occurrence
// is returned; otherwise, pos2 is returned.
// This is a Standard Library function.
```

9.33 Implement the following non-member function for `List` objects of type `char`:

```
List::Iterator adjacent_find(List::Iterator& pos1,
                             List::Iterator& pos2);
// Searches for an adjacent pair of equal elements from position
// pos1 up to but excluding position pos2. If found, the position
// of the first element of the first pair is returned; otherwise,
// pos2 is returned.
// This is a Standard Library function.
```

9.34 Implement the following non-member function for `List` objects of type `char`:

```
void count(List::Iterator& pos1, List::Iterator& pos2,
           T& t, int& n);
// Counts the number of occurrences of the value t in the range
// from position pos1 up to but excluding position pos2.
// The number of occurrences is added to n.
// This is a Standard Library function.
```

9.35 Implement the following non-member function for `List` objects of type `char`:

```
bool equal(List::Iterator& pos1, List::Iterator& pos2,
           List::Iterator& pos3);
// Returns true iff the elements from position pos1 up to but
// excluding position pos2 are the same as the same number of
// elements that begin at position pos3.
// This is a Standard Library function.
```

9.36 Implement the following non-member function for `List` objects of type `char`:

```
List::Iterator search(List::Iterator& pos1, List::Iterator& pos2,
                 List::Iterator& pos3, List::Iterator& pos4);
// The four iterators define two segments of elements, the first
// from position pos1 up to but excluding position pos2, and the
// second from position pos3 up to but excluding position pos4.
// If the second segment is found as a subsequence of the first
// segment, then that position in the first segment where the
// subsequence begins is returned; otherwise, pos2 is returned.
// This is a Standard Library function.
```

9.37 Implement the following non-member function for `List` objects of type `char`:

```
void shuffle(List& x);
// Performs a perfect shuffle on list x.
// For example, it transforms the list (1, 2, 3, 4, 5, 6, 7, 8)
// into (1, 5, 2, 6, 3, 7, 4, 8).
```

9.38 Implement the following non-member function for `List` objects of type `char`:

```
void remove_all_duplicates(List& x);
// Removes all duplicate elements from the list x.
// For example, it transforms the list (1, 2, 6, 4, 1, 5, 2, 5, 3)
// into (1, 2, 6, 4, 5, 3).
```

Solutions

9.1 *a.* The elements of an array are stored contiguously (next to each other) in memory; the elements of a linked list may be scattered about in non-contiguous locations.

b. Arrays allow direct access; linked lists allow only sequential access.

c. Insertions and deletions are very inefficient with arrays because they have to shift existing elements to maintain order; insertions and deletions are very efficient with linked lists because only one pointer has to be changed.

d. Arrays and linked lists are equally efficient in traversing the structure, because traversal only requires moving from each element to the next adjacent element.

9.2 *a.* A list of the first 1000 prime numbers should be stored in an array because the list is static (*i.e.*, the total number of elements is known in advance and does not change), it can be created in order, and the array index can be used to number the elements.

b. An alphabetized list of all the words on a page should be stored in a linked list because each word should be inserted in its correct alphabetical location.

c. A chronological list of the U.S. presidents should be stored in an array because the list is static, it can be created in order, and the array index can be used to number the elements.

d. An alphabetical telephone list of all your friends should be stored in a linked list because it is dynamic (*i.e.*, it changes frequently) and has to be maintained in order.

e. An alphabetical list of the 63 Standard C++ keywords should be stored in an array because the list is static, it can be created in order, and a binary search can be used to find elements quickly.

f. A numerical list of the 127 ASCII characters should be stored in an array because the list is static, it can be created in order, and the array index can be used to number the elements.

g. An alphabetical list of passengers booked for an airline flight should be stored in a linked list because it is dynamic and has to be maintained in order.

h. A grocery list can be stored in an array because the order is irrelevant: new items simply can be added to the end of the list.

9.3 There is no difference between a `class` and a `struct` except when some members are not given an explicit access category (`public`, `protected`, or `private`). The default access category for `classes` is `private`, while for `structs` it is `public`.

9.4 Use a `struct` instead of a `class` if no members (neither functions nor data) need to be `private` (or `protected`).

9.5 The `Node` struct declarations were nested inside the `Stack` and `List` classes because (1) the `Node` definition depends upon what kind of linked data structure (`Stack`, `Queue`, `List`, `Tree`, *etc.*) is using it; (2) the members of the enclosing class (`Stack`, `Queue`, *etc.*) need public access to all the `Node` class's data members (`_data`, `_next`, *etc.*), but at the same time their scope should be limited to the enclosing class.

9.6 An iterator is an object that is used to locate elements in a linked data structure.

9.7 *a.* The operation `!it` determines whether `it` is active. The boolean expression evaluates to `true` if `it` currently locates a node, and `false` if the iterator is null.

   b. The operation `*it` returns the `_data` value stored in the node to which `it` points.

   c. The operation `++it` advances the iterator to the next node in the data structure.

   d. The operation `--it` backs the iterator up to the preceding node in the data structure.

   e. The operation `it = jt` resets `it` to point to the same node to which the iterator `jt` points.

9.8 The `erase()` function deletes the element located by a given iterator. The `remove()` function deletes all (zero or more) the elements that equal a given `_data` value.

9.9
```
List x;
x.push_back('A');
x.push_back('B');
x.push_back('C');
x.push_back('D');
x.push_back('E');
```

```
List::Iterator it = x.begin();
```

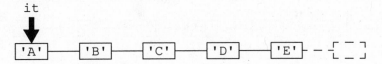

```
*it = 'V';
```

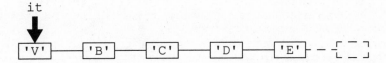

```
++it;
```

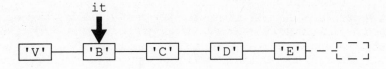

```
x.insert(it, 'W');
```

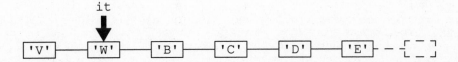

```
it = x.end();
```

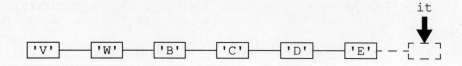

```
x.insert(it, 'Z');
```

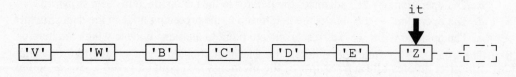

```
--it;
--it;
```

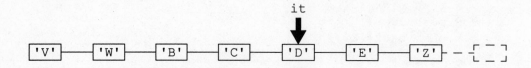

```
List::Iterator jt = x.begin();
```

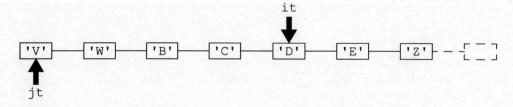

```
*jt = *it;
```

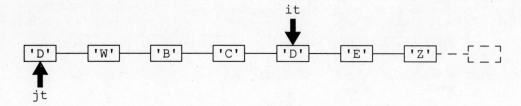

```
jt = it;
```

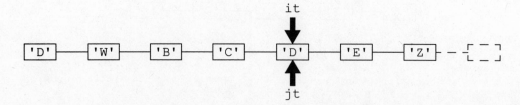

```
x.erase(it);
```

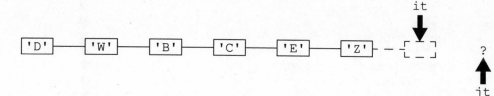

```
x.remove('C');
```

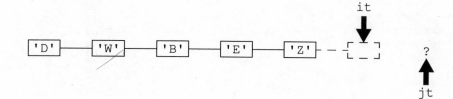

```
x.pop_front();
```

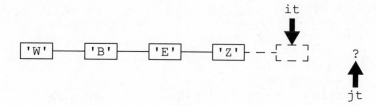

```
x.pop_back();
```

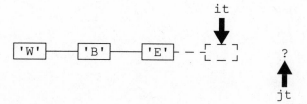

9.10

```
class Queue
{ private:
    struct Node
    { Node(int data, Node* next) : _data(data), _next(next) { }
      char _data;
      Node* _next;
    };
  public:
    Queue() : _top(0) { }
    ~Queue();
    char front() const { return _front->_data; }
    char back() const { return _back->_data; }
    bool is_empty() const { return bool(_front == 0); }
    bool is_full() const { return false; }
    void enter(const char c) { _back = new Node(c, _back); }
    char leave();
```

```
          private:
            Node* _front;
            Node* _back;
        };
        Queue::~Queue()
        { if (_front == 0) return;
          for (Node* p = _front->_next; p; p = p->_next)
            delete _front;
        }
        char Queue::leave()
        { assert(_front != 0);
          Node* p = _front;
          _front = p->_next;
          char ch = p->_data;
          delete p;
          return ch;
        }
```

9.11

```
        void List::remove(const T& t)
        { Node* p=_front;
          if (p == 0) return;
          while (p->_data == t && p != _back)
          { delete _front;
            --_size;
            _front = p = p->_next;
          }
          while (p != _back)
            if (p->_data == t)
            { p->_prev->_next = p->_next;
              p->_next->_prev = p->_prev;
              delete p;
              --_size;
              p = p->_next;
            }
          if (p->_data == t)
          { delete _back;
            --_size;
            _back = p->_prev;
          }
        }
```

9.12

```
        typedef char T;
        class List
        { private:
            struct Node
            { friend class Iterator;
              Node(T data=0, Node* prev=0, Node* next=0) : _data(data)
                { _prev = (prev?prev:this); _next = (next?next:this); }
              T _data;
              Node* _prev;
              Node* _next;
            };
          public:
            class Iterator
            { friend class List;
            public:
              Iterator(Node* p) : _p(p) { }
              bool operator!() const { return bool(!_p || !_p->_data); }
```

```
        T& operator*() const { return _p->_data; }
        Iterator& operator++() { _p = _p->_next; return *this; }
        Iterator& operator--() { _p = p->_prev; return *this; }
        Iterator& operator=(const Iterator& it)
           { _p = it._p; return *this; }
      friend bool operator==(const Iterator& i, const Iterator& j)
           { return bool(i._p == j._p); }
      friend bool operator!=(const Iterator& i, const Iterator& j)
           { return bool(i._p != j._p); }
    private:
      Node* _p;   // points to list node
    };
  public:
    List() : _size(0) { _dum = new Node(); }
    List(const List&);
    ~List() { clear(); }
    List& operator=(const List&);
    int size() const { return _size; }
    bool empty() const { return bool(_size == 0); }
    T& front() const { return _dum->_next->_data; }
    T& back() const { return _dum->_prev->_data; }
    void push_front(const T&);
    void push_back(const T&);
    void pop_front();
    void pop_back();
    Iterator begin() { return Iterator(_dum->_next); }
    Iterator end() { return Iterator(_dum); }
    Iterator insert(Iterator&, const T&);
    void erase(Iterator&);
    void remove(const T&);
    void clear();
  private:
    Node* _dum;
    int _size;
};
List::List(const List& x) : _size(x._size)
{ _dum = new Node();
  if (x._size == 0) return;
  Node* p = x._dum->_next;
  Node* q = _dum->_prev = _dum->_next
           = new Node(p->_data, _dum, _dum);
  for (int i=1; i<_size; i++)
  { p = p->_next;
    q = q->_next = _dum->_prev = new Node(p->_data, q, _dum);
    assert(q);
  }
}
List& List::operator=(const List& x)
{ clear();
  _size = x._size;
  _dum = new Node();
  if (x._size == 0) return *this;
  Node* p = x._dum->_next;
  Node* q = _dum->_prev = _dum->_next
           = new Node(p->_data, _dum, _dum);
```

```
      for (int i=1; i<_size; i++)
      { p = p->_next;
        q = q->_next = _dum->_prev = new Node(p->_data, q, _dum);
        assert(q);
      }
      return *this;
}
void List::push_front(const T& t)
{ if (_size == 0)
     _dum->_next = _dum->_prev = new Node(t, _dum, _dum);
   else
     _dum->_next = _dum->_next->_prev
                 = new Node(t, _dum, _dum->_next);
   ++_size;
}
void List::push_back(const T& t)
{ if (_size == 0)
     _dum->_next = _dum->_prev = new Node(t, _dum, _dum);
   else
     _dum->_prev = _dum->_prev->_next
                 = new Node(t, _dum->_prev, _dum);
   ++_size;
}
void List::pop_front()
{ if (_size == 0) return;
  Node* p = _dum->_next;
  _dum->_next->_next->_prev = _dum;
  _dum->_next = _dum->_next->_next;
  delete p;
  --_size;
}
void List::pop_back()
{ if (_size == 0) return;
  Node* p = _dum->_prev;
  _dum->_prev->_prev->_next = _dum;
  _dum->_prev = _dum->_prev->_prev;
  delete p;
  --_size;
}
Iterator List::insert(Iterator& pos, const T& t)
{ if (!pos || _size == 0) return pos;
  Node* p = pos._p;
  pos._p = p->_prev = p->_prev->_next = new Node(t, p->_prev, p);
  ++_size;
  return pos;
}
void List::erase(Iterator& pos)
{ if (!pos || _size == 0) return;
  Node* p = pos._p;
  p->_prev->_next = p->_next;
  p->_next->_prev = p->_prev;
  pos._p = 0;
  delete p;
  --_size;
}
```

```
                void List::remove(const T& t)
                { Node* p_next;
                  for (Node* p=_dum->_next; p != _dum; p = p_next)
                  { p_next = p->_next;
                    if (p->_data == t)
                    { p->_prev->_next = p->_next;
                      p->_next->_prev = p->_prev;
                      delete p;
                      --_size;
                    }
                  }
                }
                void List::clear()
                { Node* p_next;
                  for (Node* p=_dum->_next; p != _dum; p = p_next)
                  { p_next = p->_prev->_next = p->_next;
                    p->_next->_prev = p->_prev;
                    delete p;
                  }
                  _size = 0;
                }
```

9.13
```
                List::List(int n, T& t) : _size(n)
                { _dum = new Node();
                  for (int i=0; i<n; i++)
                  _dum->_next = _dum->_next->_prev = new Node(t, _dum, _dum->_next);
                }
```

9.14
```
                void List::insert(Iterator& pos, int n, T& t)
                { Node* p = pos._p;
                  for (int i=0; i<n; i++)
                    p->_prev = p->_prev->_next = new Node(t, p->_prev, p);
                }
```

9.15
```
                void List::erase(Iterator& pos1, Iterator& pos2)
                { if (!pos1 || !pos2) return;
                  Node* p_next = pos1._p->_next;
                  for (Node* p = pos1._p; p != pos2._p;
                       p = p_next, p_next = p->_next)
                  { p->_prev->_next = p->_next;
                    p->_next->_prev = p->_prev;
                    delete p;
                    --_size;
                  }
                }
```

9.16
```
                void List::swap(List& x)
                { Node* p = x._dum;
                  x._dum = _dum;
                  _dum = p;
                  int temp = x._size;
                  x._size = _size;
                  _size = temp;
                }
```

9.17
```
                void List::splice(Iterator& pos, List& x)
                { Node* p = pos._p;
                  for (Iterator itx = x.begin(); !!itx; ++itx)
                    p->_prev = p->_prev->_next = new Node(*itx, p->_prev, p);
                }
```

9.18
```
void List::reverse()
{ Node* p;
  Node* temp;
  for (p = _dum; p->_next != _dum; p = p->_prev)
  { temp = p->_next;
    p->_next = p->_prev;
    p->_prev = temp;
  }
  temp = p->_next;
  p->_next = p->_prev;
  p->_prev = temp;
}
```

9.19
```
void List::sort()
// implements the Bubble Sort
{ if (_size < 2) return;
  T temp;
  for (Node* end=_dum; end->_prev != _dum->_next; end = end->_prev)
  { Node* q = _dum->_next->_next;
    for (Node* p=_dum->_next; q != end; p = q, q = q->_next)
    { if (p->_data > q->_data)
      { temp = p->_data;
        p->_data = q->_data;
        q->_data = temp;
      }
    }
  }
}
```

9.20
```
void List::unique()
{ if (_size < 2) return;
  T pt;
  Node* q;
  Node* q_next;
  for (Node* p=_dum->_next; p->_next != _dum; p = p->_next)
  { pt = p->_data;
    q = p->_next;
    q_next = q->_next;
    for (; q != _dum && q->_data == pt;
           q = q_next, q_next = q->_next)
    { q->_prev->_next = q->_next;
      q->_next->_prev = q->_prev;
      delete q;
    }
  }
}
```

9.21
```
void List::remove_all_duplicates()
{ if (_size < 2) return;
  T pt;
  Node* q;
  Node* q_next;
  for (Node* p=_dum->_next; p->_next != _dum; p = p->_next)
  { pt = p->_data;
    q = p->_next;
    q_next = q->_next;
```

```
            for (; q != _dum; q = q_next, q_next = q->_next)
            { if (q->_data == pt)
              { q->_prev->_next = q->_next;
                q->_next->_prev = q->_prev;
                delete q;
              }
            }
          }
        }
```

9.22
```
        void append(List& x, List::Iterator pos, const char* cs)
        { for (char* p=(char*)(cs); *p; p++)
            x.push_back(*p);
        }
```

9.23
```
        void copy(List& x, List::Iterator& pos, const char* cs)
        { for (char* p=(char*)(cs); *p; p++)
          { x.insert(pos, *p);
            ++pos;
          }
        }
```

9.24
```
        void copy(char* cs, List& x)
        { for (List::Iterator it = x.begin(); it != x.end(); ++it)
            *cs++ = *it;
          *cs = 0;  // C-strings must be terminated with the null character
        }
```

9.25
```
        void copy(char* cs, List& x, List::Iterator& pos1,
                            List::Iterator& pos2)
        { for (List::Iterator it = pos1; it != pos2; ++it)
            *cs++ = *it;
          *cs = 0;  // C-strings must be terminated with the null character
        }
```

9.26
```
        void List::halve(List& x)
        { x.clear();
          x._size = _size - _size/2;
          _size /= 2;
          Node* p = _dum;
          for (int i=0; i<=_size; i++)  // find middle node:
            p = p->_next;
          p->_prev->_next = _dum;
          _dum->_prev->_next = x._dum;
          x._dum->_prev = _dum->_prev;
          _dum->_prev = p->_prev;
          p->_prev = x._dum;
          x._dum->_next = p;
        }
```

9.27
```
        void halve(List& x, List& y)
        { y.clear();
          int n = x.size();
          n -= n/2;
          char c;
          for (int i=0; i<n; i++)  // locate the middle of x:
          { c = x.back();
            x.pop_back();
            y.push_front(c);
          }
        }
```

9.28
```
void List::split(List& x)
{ x.clear();
  x._size = _size - _size/2;
  _size /= 2;
  Node* p = _dum->_next;
  Node* q = x._dum;
  for (; p != _dum && p->_next != _dum; p = p->_next, q = q->_next)
  { q->_next = p->_next;
    p->_next->_prev = q;
    p->_next = q->_next->_next;
    p->_next->_prev = p;
    q->_next->_next = x._dum;
    x._dum->_prev = q->_next;
  }
}
```

9.29
```
void split(List& x, List& y)
{ y.clear();
  char c;
  for (List::Iterator it = x.begin(); it != x.end();)
  { ++it;
    if (it == x.end()) return;
    c = *it;
    y.push_back(c);
    x.erase(it);
  }
}
```

9.30
```
List intersection(List& x, List& y)
{ List z;
  List xx = x;
  xx.remove_all_duplicates();
  for (List::Iterator it = xx.begin(); it != xx.end(); ++it)
    for (List::Iterator jt = y.begin(); jt != y.end(); ++jt)
      if (*it == *jt)
      { z.push_back(*it);
        break;
      }
  return z;
}
```

9.31
```
List complement(List& x, List& y)
{ List z = x;
  z.remove_all_duplicates();
  for (List::Iterator it = y.begin(); it != y.end(); ++it)
    z.remove(*it);
  return z;
}
```

9.32
```
List::Iterator find(List::Iterator& pos1,
                    List::Iterator& pos2, T& t)
{ for (List::Iterator it = pos1; it != pos2; ++it)
    if (*it == t) return it;
  return pos2;
}
```

9.34
```
void count(List::Iterator& pos1, List::Iterator& pos2, T& t, int& n)
{ n = 0;
  for (List::Iterator it = pos1; it != pos2; ++it)
    if (*it == t) ++n;
}
```

9.35
```
bool equal(List::Iterator& pos1, List::Iterator& pos2,
           List::Iterator& pos3)
{ List::Iterator it = pos1;
  List::Iterator jt = pos3;
  while (it != pos2)
  { if (*it != *jt) return false;
    ++it;
    ++jt;
  }
  return true;
}
```

9.36
```
List::Iterator search(List::Iterator& pos1, List::Iterator& pos2,
                      List::Iterator& pos3, List::Iterator& pos4)
{ List::Iterator it=pos1;
  List::Iterator jt=pos1;
  List::Iterator kt=pos3;
  while (it != pos2)
  { jt = it;
    kt = pos3;
    while (jt != pos2 && kt != pos4 && *kt == *jt)
      ++jt, ++kt;
    if (kt == pos4) return it;
    ++it;
  }
  return pos2;
}
```

Chapter 10

Standard Container Classes

10.1 CONTAINERS

A *container* is an object that contains other objects. The contained objects, called the *elements* of the container, must have the same type. Arrays, stacks, queues, and lists are containers.

A *container class* is a class whose instances are containers. The `Stack` class defined on page 154, the `Queue` class defined on page 163, and the `List` class defined on page 204 are container classes. The new ISO C++ Standard Library defines a collection of container classes including `stack`, `queue`, and `list`. (Note that we capitalized the names of our own container classes to distinguish them from the standard classes.) This chapter summarizes the standard container classes.

10.2 TEMPLATES

The `Stack`, `Queue`, and `List` classes in Chapters 7 and 9 define containers whose element type is `char`. With slight modification, these definitions can be changed for other element types. However C++ provides a better method for being able to change the underlying element type without having to change the container definition. This is done with a template.

A *template* is an outline for the definition of a function or class that uses parameters in place of types or objects. The template can then be *instantiated* by substituting types and objects for the template parameters. In C++, both functions and classes can be defined from templates.

EXAMPLE 10.1 The `swap()` Function Template

```
template <class T>
void swap(T& x, T& y)
{ T temp = x;
  x = y;
  y = temp;
}
```

This function template can be used to define a `swap()` function for any argument type:

```
int m=22, n=44;
cout << "m = " << m << ", n = " << n << endl;
swap(m, n);
cout << "m = " << m << ", n = " << n << endl;
string r="Washington", s="Jefferson";
cout << "r = " << r << ", s = " << s << endl;
swap(r, s);
cout << "r = " << r << ", s = " << s << endl;
```

The output is

```
m = 22, n = 44
m = 44, n = 22
r = Washington, s = Jefferson
r = Jefferson, s = Washington
```

When the compiler encounters the first call to swap(), it uses the fact that the arguments m and n have type int to generate the following function definition:

```
void swap(int& x, int& y)
{ int temp = x;
  x = y;
  y = temp;
}
```

Note that this is done simply by substituting the type int for the template parameter T.

When the compiler encounters the second call to swap(), it uses the fact that the arguments r and s have type string to generate the following function definition:

```
void swap(string& x, string& y)
{ string temp = x;
  x = y;
  y = temp;
}
```

This is done simply by substituting the type string for the template parameter T.

The effect of the function template is to shorten the source code by having a single template in place of several different function definitions. The compiler uses the template to generate the definitions based upon the calls that it finds in the source code. Note that the efficiency provided by the template occurs only within the source code file. The resulting executable file is no more efficient than if the source code had included two separate non-template definitions.

Note the required code

```
template <class T>
```

that precedes the function header. The symbol T is the name of the *template parameter*. Any valid identifier may be used for the name; the letter "T" stands for "type."

EXAMPLE 10.2 A Stack Class Template

This template is the same as the definition on page page 154 except with T in place of char:

```
template <class T>
class Stack
{ public:
    Stack(int m=100) : _max(m), _size(0) { _a = new T[_max]; }
    ~Stack() { delete [] _a; }
    bool is_empty() const { return bool(_size == 0); }
    bool is_full() const { return bool(_size == _max); }
    int size() const { return _size; }
    T top() const { return _a[_size-1]; }
    void push(const T& t) { _a[_size++] = t; }
    T pop() { return _a[--_size]; }
  private:
    T* _a;        // a dynamic array of elements of type T
    int _max;     // the maximum number of elements on the stack
    int _size;    // the number of elements on the stack
};
```

This class template can be used to define a Stack class for any element type:

```
Stack<int> int_stack;
int_stack.push(66);
int_stack.push(88);
cout << "int_stack.top() = " << int_stack.top() << endl;
Stack<string> string_stack;
string_stack.push("Madison");
string_stack.push("Monroe");
cout << "string_stack.top() = " << string_stack.top() << endl;
```

The output is
```
int_stack.top() = 88
string_stack.top() = Monroe
```
Note that, unlike a function template, the instantiation of a class template requires the extra < > syntax (*e.g.,* <int>, <string>) as a suffix onto the template name (*e.g.,* Stack<int>, Stack<string>) to indicate what type is to be substituted for the template parameter T. Function templates don't need this extra syntax because the type is already specified as the argument type.

10.3 THE STANDARD C++ CONTAINER CLASSES AND THEIR OPERATIONS

The C++ Standard Library defines the following ten container class templates:
```
stack<T>
queue<T>
deque<T>
vector<T>
list<T>
priority_queue<T>
set<T>
multitiset<T>
map<K,T>
multimap<K,T>
```
In each case, the template parameter T stands for the container's element type. For example the type vector<double> would be used to declare a vector whose elements have type double.

The map and multimap templates have two template parameters, K and T, which stand for the *key type* and the data type. For example the type map<string,Student> would be used to declare a map object (*a.k.a.* a *table* or an *associative array*) each of whose elements contains a string object paired with a Student object. The string object would be the student's identification code (*e.g.,* Social Security Number), and the Student object would be the data record for the student identified by that code. (The Student class would be user-defined, similar to the Person class in Problem 7.22 on page 160.) The ID code is called the *key* value for the record.

The common *fundamental operations* for these classes include:

Constructors and Destructors:
x()	Default constructor: creates an empty container x.
x(y)	Copy constructor: creates a duplicate x of container y.
x(n)	Creates a container x with n copies of the default element.
x(n,t)	Creates a container x with n copies of the element t.
x(p,q)	Creates a container x with the q-p elements *p...*(q-1).
~x()	Destructor: destroys the container x and all of its elements.

Assignment Functions:
assign(n)	Replaces current contents with n copies of the default element.
assign(n,t)	Replaces current contents with n copies of the element t.
assign(p,q)	Replaces current contents with the q-p elements *p...*(q-1).
operator=(y)	Assignment operator: replaces current contents with those of container y.

Iterators:
begin()	Returns the position of the first element of the container.
end()	Returns the position the dummy element at the end of the container.

Access Functions:
front()	Returns the first element of the container.
back()	Returns the last element of the container.
operator[](i)	Subscript operator: *e.g.,* x[4] = 99.
at(i)	Range-checked subscript function: *e.g.,* x.at(4) = 99.

`size()`	Returns the number of elements in the container.
`empty()`	Returns `true` if the container is empty otherwise, `false`.

Mutator Functions:

`push_front(t)`	Inserts the element `t` at the beginning of the container.
`pop_front()`	Removes the first element in the container.
`push_back(t)`	Inserts the element `t` at the end of the container.
`pop_back()`	Removes the last element in the container.
`insert(p)`	Inserts the default element in front of element `*p`.
`insert(p,t)`	Inserts the element `t` in front of element `*p`.
`insert(p,n,t)`	Inserts `n` copies of the element `t` in front of element `*p`.
`insert(p,q,r)`	Inserts `r-q` elements copied from another container in front of element `*p`.
`erase(p)`	Removes the element `*p`.
`erase(p,q)`	Removes the `q-p` elements `*p...*(q-1)`.
`swap(y)`	Swaps all of its elements with those in container `y`.

Relational Operators:

`operator==(y)`	Returns `true` if the container's contents are the same as those of `y`.
`operator!=(y)`	Returns `true` if the container's contents are not the same as those of `y`.
`operator<(y)`	Returns `true` if the container lexicographically precedes container `y`.

Here, `x` and `y` are container objects, `n` and `i` are non-negative integers, `t` is an element for the container, and `p`, `q`, and `r` are iterators that locate positions in the containers.

Iterators on containers work the same way as pointers on arrays. If `p` and `q` are iterators on the same container and `k` is a positive integer, then:

`*p`	is the element at position `p`;
`++p`	advances `p` to the next position;
`--p`	moves `p` back to the preceding position;
`p+k`	locates the position `k` elements after `p`;
`p-k`	locates the position `k` elements before `p`;
`q-p`	is the number of elements in the subsequence from `*p` to `*(q-1)`;

We use the notation `*p...*(q-1)` to denote the subsequence from element `*p` to the element `*(q-1)`. For example, if `p` locates the third element and `q` locates the eighth element of a `list` object `x`, then the value of the expression `q-p` is 5, which is the number of elements in the subsequence from the element `*p` (the third element) to `*(q-1)` (the seventh element).

In computer science, elements of sequences are always numbered beginning with the number zero. This is called *zero-based indexing*. The inescapable consequence of this protocol is that the ordinal number of an element is always one more than the index of the element. The 8th element is element number 7:

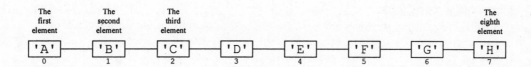

This is consistent with the fact that the number of elements in a subsequence is one more than the difference between the first and last element numbers. The sequence pictured above has 8 elements, which is one more than the difference $7 - 0 = 7$. The subsequence CDEFG has 5 elements, which is one more than the difference $6 - 2 = 4$, as shown in the figure below. Because of this intrinsic anomaly between cardinal and ordinal numbers, the C++ Standard Library always delineates a subsequence by specifying the position of its first element and the position of the element that

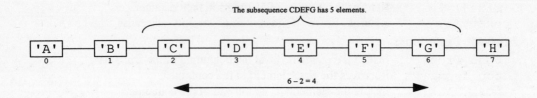

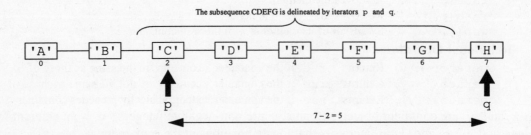

follows its last element. So the subsequence CDEFG would be delineated by the two iterators p and q that locate elements C and H:

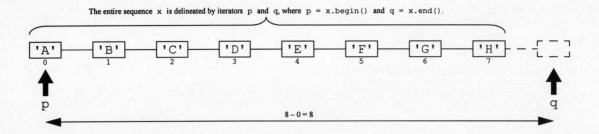

Then the notation *p...*(q-1) correctly represents the subsequence CDEFG because p locates C and q-1 locates G.

Consistency may be, as Henry David Thoreau wrote, "the hobgoblin of little minds," but it is essential to good software. It is the hallmark of the C++ Standard Library. To remain consistent to the protocol described above for subsequences, the Standard Library always includes a dummy element appended to the end of every sequence. This element cannot be accessed, but it can be located by an iterator. Indeed, if ContainerClass<ElementType> is any container class, then the code

```
ContainerClass<ElementType> x;
ContainerClass<ElementType>::iterator p = x.begin();
ContainerClass<ElementType>::iterator q = x.end();
```

declares x to be a container of that type and p and q to be iterators on x that locate the beginning and the end of the sequence:

The entire sequence x is delineated by iterators p and q, where p = x.begin() and q = x.end().

Then element number i can be located as *(p+i).

Note that the access *(p+i) appears to be direct access, just like x[i]. But the actual implementation of the iterator function operator+() depends upon the container class. If ContainerClass is vector, it will be direct access. But for the container classes that are implemented as linked structures, p+i is done by sequential access: i calls to ++p.

10.4 THE C++ STANDARD stack CLASS TEMPLATE

A *stack* is a "last-in-first-out" container (see Example 7.17 on page 154). The C++ Standard Library defines the stack<T> class template in the <stack> file. Here is a (simplified) partial listing of its interface:

```
template <class T>
class stack
{ public:
    stack();                            // default constructor
    stack(const stack&);                // copy constructor
    ~stack();                           // destructor
    stack& operator=(const stack&);     // assignment operator
    bool empty() const;                 // returns true iff empty
    int size() const;                   // return number of elements
    T& top();                           // returns the top element
    void push(const T&);                // pushes element onto stack
    void pop();                         // removes top element
  private:
    //...
};
```

Note that the pop() function does not return the element removed by it. It has to be accessed separately by the top() function. Also note that the top() function returns by reference (see Section 4.9 on page 76) so it can be used to change the top element without removing it, like this:

```
s.top() = 44;
```

EXAMPLE 10.3 Using the Standard stack<T> Class Template

Here is a complete C++ program that uses a stack of strings:

```
#include <iostream>
#include <stack>
using namespace std;
typedef stack<string> string_stack;

void load(string_stack& s)
{ s.push("alpha");
  s.push("beta");
  s.push("gamma");
  s.push("delta");
  s.push("epsilon");
}
void dump(string_stack& s)
// Postcondition: the stack s is empty
{ int n = s.size();
  for (int k=1; k <= n; k++)
  { cout << '\t' << k << ". " << s.top() << endl;
    s.pop();
  }
}
void transfer(string_stack& s1, string_stack& s2)
{ while (!s2.empty())
  { s1.push(s2.top());
    s2.pop();
  }
}
```

```
int main()
{ string_stack letters;
  load(letters);
  string_stack backup = letters;   // uses the copy constructor
  cout << "In reverse order:\n";
  dump(letters);
  transfer(letters, backup);
  cout << "In order:\n";
  dump(letters);
}
```

The output is

```
In reverse order:
        1. epsilon
        2. delta
        3. gamma
        4. beta
        5. alpha
In order:
        1. alpha
        2. beta
        3. gamma
        4. delta
        5. epsilon
```

The `letters` stack is loaded with the names of the first six Greek letters. Then the copy constructor is used to construct a clone named `backup`. The `dump()` function empties and prints in reverse order the contents of the stack passed to it. Next, the `transfer()` function transfers the contents of stack `s2` into `s1`. Since stack access is last-in-first-out, the transfer from the `backup` stack to the `letters` stack loads the names into the `letters` stack in reverse order. Consequently, the second call to `dump()` prints the letter names in their proper order.

10.5 THE C++ STANDARD `queue` CLASS TEMPLATE

A *queue* is a "first-in-first-out" container (see Problem 7.7 on page 156). The C++ Standard Library defines the `queue<T>` class template in the `<queue>` file. Its class interface is essentially the same as that for the `stack<T>` template, using the same names for its member functions. The difference, of course, is that the `pop()` function for queue classes removes elements from the other end. Here is a (simplified) partial listing of its interface:

```
template <class T>
class queue
{ public:
    queue();                             // default constructor
    queue(const queue&);                 // copy constructor
    ~queue();                            // destructor
    queue& operator=(const queue&);// assignment operator
    bool empty() const;                  // returns true iff empty
    int size() const;                    // return number of elements
    T& front();                          // returns the front element
    T& back();                           // returns the back element
    void push(const T&);                 // inserts element at back
    void pop();                          // removes element from front
  private:
    //...
};
```

Note that, like the `stack::top()` function, the `front()` and `back()` functions return by reference so they can be used to change those two elements without removing them.

EXAMPLE 10.4 Using the Standard `queue<T>` Class Template

Here is a complete C++ program that uses a queue of strings:

```
#include <iostream>
#include <queue>
using namespace std;
typedef queue<string> string_queue;

void load(string_queue& s)
{ s.push("alpha");
  s.push("beta");
  s.push("gamma");
  s.push("delta");
  s.push("epsilon");
}

void dump(string_queue& s)
// Postcondition: the stack s is empty
{ int n = s.size();
  for (int k=1; k <= n; k++)
  { cout << '\t' << k << ". " << s.front() << endl;
    s.pop();
  }
}

void transfer(string_queue& s1, string_queue& s2)
{ while (!s2.empty())
  { s1.push(s2.front());
    s2.pop();
  }
}

int main()
{ string_queue letters;
  load(letters);
  string_queue backup = letters;   // uses the copy constructor
  cout << "In order:\n";
  dump(letters);
  transfer(letters, backup);
  cout << "In order:\n";
  dump(letters);
}
```

The output is

```
In order:
        1. alpha
        2. beta
        3. gamma
        4. delta
        5. epsilon
```

```
In order:
        1. alpha
        2. beta
        3. gamma
        4. delta
        5. epsilon
```

This is the program from Example 10.3, except using queues in place of stacks. The only difference in its output is that, reflecting the first-in-first-out nature of queues, this dumps the letters in their proper order the first time.

10.6 THE C++ STANDARD `vector` CLASS TEMPLATE

A *vector* is a sequence of elements that supports direct access. As an abstract type, it simply generalizes the ordinary array type. The C++ Standard Library defines the `vector<T>` class template in the `<vector>` file. Its class interface is the prototype for all the Standard container class templates. With few exceptions, for each member function of the `vector` class there is an equivalent member function for each of the other container classes (`stack`, `queue`, `list`, `set`, `map`, *etc.*). Here is a (simplified) partial listing of its interface:

```
template <class T>
class vector
{    friend bool operator==(const vector&, const vector&);
     friend bool operator<(const vector&, const vector&);
  public:
     typedef T* iterator;
     vector();                              // default constructor
     vector(const vector&);                 // copy constructor
     vector(int, const T&);                 // auxiliary constructor
     vector(iterator, iterator);            // auxiliary constructor
     ~vector();                             // destructor
     vector& operator=(const vector&);      // assignment operator
     void assign(int, const T&);            // assigns a given value
     void assign(iterator, iterator);       // copies elements from object
     void resize(int);                      // changes size of vector
     void swap(vector&);                    // swaps elements with object
     bool empty() const;                    // returns true iff empty
     int size() const;                      // return number of elements
     iterator begin();                      // locates first element
     iterator end();                        // locates dummy element at end
     T& operator[](int);                    // subscript operator
     T& at(int);                            // range-checked access
     T& front();                            // accesses the first element
     T& back();                             // accesses the last element
     void push_back(const T&);              // inserts element at end
     void pop_back();                       // removes last element
     iterator insert(iterator, const T&);
     void insert(iterator, int, const T&);
     void insert(iterator, iterator, iterator);
     iterator erase(iterator);
     iterator erase(iterator, iterator);
     void clear();                          // removes all the elements
  private:
     //...
};
```

EXAMPLE 10.5 Using the Standard `vector<T>` Class Template

Here is a complete C++ program that uses the Standard `vector<T>` class template::

```
#include <iostream>
#include <vector>        // defines the Standard vector<T> class template
using namespace std;
typedef vector<double> vec;
typedef vector<bool> bits;

template <class T>
void copy(vector<T>& v, const T* x, int n)
{ vector<T> w;
  for (int i=0; i<n; i++)
    w.push_back(x[i]);
  v = w;
}

vec projection(vec& v, bits& b)
{ int v_size = v.size();
  assert(b.size() >= v_size);
  vec w;
  for (int i=0; i<v_size; i++)
    if (b[i]) w.push_back(v[i]);
  return w;
}

void print(vec& v)
{ int v_size = v.size();
  for (int i=0; i<v_size; i++)
    cout << v[i] << "  ";
  cout << endl;
}

int main()
{ double x[8] = { 22.2, 33.3, 44.4, 55.5, 66.6, 77.7, 88.8, 99.9 };
  vec v;
  copy(v, x, 8);
  bool y[8] = { false, true, false, true, true, true, false, true };
  bits b;
  copy(b, y, 8);
  vec w = projection(v, b);
  print(v);
  print(w);
}
```

The output is

```
22.2  33.3  44.4  55.5  66.6  77.7  88.8  99.9
33.3  55.5  66.6  77.7  99.9
```

This illustrates the `vector` class `push_back()` and `size()` member functions.

The purpose of the `projection(v, b)` function is to use the bit vector `b` as a *mask* to remove selected elements of the vector `v`. The resulting vector `w` is called the *projection* of `v` onto the subspace determined by `b`.

10.7 THE C++ STANDARD `list` CLASS TEMPLATE

A *list* is a sequence of elements that do not have direct access. A definition of the ADT **List** is given in Chapter 9 along with an implementation for lists of elements of type `char`.

The C++ Standard Library defines the `list<T>` class template in the `<list>` file. It is distinguished from the `vector<T>` class template class by the following features:

- it lacks the direct access provided by the subscript operator and the `at()` function;
- it includes `push_front()`, `pop_front()`, and `remove()` functions;
- its `insert()` and `erase()` functions are much faster than those for vectors.

These distinctions reflect the fundamental trade-off between the fast direct access provided by contiguous storage (vectors) and the fast insertions and deletions provided by linked storage (lists).

Due to the special nature of its linked implementation, the `list<T>` class template includes some other member functions not included in the `vector<T>` class template:

```
template <class T>
class list
{    // same functions as in vector<T>
  public:
     class iterator;                      // defined elsewhere
     void push_front(const T&);           // inserts element at beginning
     void pop_front();                    // removes first element
     void remove(const T&);               // removes elements
     void sort();                         // sorts the list
     void unique();                       // removes all duplicates
     void merge();                        // removes all duplicates
     void splice(iterator, list&);        // inserts elements from other list
     void reverse();                      // reverses the elements
  private:
     //...
};
```

Unlike `vector` iterators which are just pointers to elements, `list` iterators are separate objects, as defined in Chapter 9. The `list` classes can push and pop both at the end (like the `vector` classes) and at the beginning of the sequence. The other member functions declared here for `list` classes are defined as non-member generic functions for the `vector` classes. (See Section 10.8.)

Note that the subscript operator is defined for `list` classes; but it does not give direct access. The reference `x[6]` is implemented by 6 increments `++p` of an iterator initialized at `x.begin()`.

EXAMPLE 10.6 Using the Standard `list<T>` Class Template

This program uses a list of strings to find the most popular fruit among a group of people. The program reads a sequence of names of fruit and stores them in a list. Each item is inserted so that the list is maintained in alphabetical order. No name is inserted more than once. Instead, each name is stored together with its ordinal number within the input. For example, "pear" was the 1st, 15th, and 22nd name input, so it is stored in the list like this:

```
pear        01, 15, 22
```

This is one of the list elements.

```
#include <iomanip.h>
#include <iostream.h>
#include <vector>        // defines the Standard vector<T> class template
using namespace std;

typedef list<string> SL;               // string list type
typedef list<string>::iterator SLI;    // string list iterator type
```

```
string extract_word(SLI& it)
// returns the word stored in *it:
{ string element = *it;          // the complete element *it
  int k = element.find('\t');    // location of the tab
  return element.substr(0, k);   // the substring ahead of the tab
}
bool found(SL& x, SLI& it, string& new_word)
// searches the list x for the new_word:
{ for (it=x.begin(); it != x.end(); ++it)
  { string word = extract_word(it);
    if (word == new_word) return true;
    if (word > new_word) return false;
  }
}
string literal(int n)
// returns the string literal for the integer n:
{ string s(2);                   // a 2-character string
  s[0] = char('0' + n/10);       // the tens digit
  s[1] = char('0' + n%10);       // the ones digit
  return s;
}
void print(SL& x)
// prints the entire list, numering each element:
{ int i=1;
  for (SLI it=x.begin(); it != x.end(); ++it, ++i)
    cout << setw(4) << i << ". " << *it << endl;
}
int main()
{ SL x;                    // x is an empty list of strings
  SLI it = x.begin();      // it is an iterator on x
  string new_word;
  int count=0;
  while (cin >> new_word)
  { ++count;
    if (found(x, it, new_word)) *it += ", " + literal(count);
    else x.insert(it, new_word + "\t" + literal(count));
  }
  print(x);
}
```

Each iteration of the main `while` loop reads one word from `cin`, counts it, and searches for it in the list `x`. If it is found to be already in the list, then the string `*it` at that element is appended with the current `count`. Otherwise the `new_word` and its `count` are inserted into a new element in the list. The `while` loop terminates when the end-of-file is detected. Then the entire list is printed.

Here is the input:

pear	peach	prune	orange	plum	lemon	lime	banana
peach	raisin	grape	date	lemon	mango	pear	lime
apple	fig	orange	peach	mellon	pear	orange	apple
cherry	lemon	cherry	grape	raisin	orange	peach	mango
apple	cherry	date	peach				

And here is the output:

```
   1. apple    17, 24, 33
   2. banana   08
   3. cherry   25, 27, 34
   4. date     12, 35
   5. fig      18
   6. grape    11, 28
```

```
 7. lemon      06, 13, 26
 8. lime       07, 16
 9. mango      14, 32
10. mellon     21
11. orange     04, 19, 23, 30
12. peach      02, 09, 20, 31, 36
13. pear       01, 15, 22
14. plum       05
15. prune      03
16. raisin     10, 29
```

This shows that peaches are the most popular fruit among these 36 people, being the favorite of persons number 2, 9, 20, 31, and 36. Notice that the list elements are in alphabetical order. Also notice that the output forms a *histogram* (a frequency chart), from which the *mode* (most frequent item) is easily discernible.

The `extract_word()` function is passed a reference to the iterator `it`. It assigns the element `*it` to the string `element`, and then uses the `find()` function from the `string` class to locate the position of the tab character `'\t'` within the string. This character follows the last letter of the fruit name in each list element, so its index number `k` can be used to extract that name from the element. This is done with the string class's `substr()` function. The parameters `(0, k)` tell it to extract the first `k` characters (from position `0` to position `0+k`). That is the fruit name which is then returned.

The `found()` function is passed a reference to the list `x`, a reference to the iterator `it`, and a reference to the string `new_word`. It uses a `for` loop to traverse the list, searching for an element that contains `new_word`. It applies the `extract_word()` function to the iterator at each element to extract the fruit name in that element. If that `word` is the same as `new_word`, then the `found()` function returns `true`. Otherwise, it either returns `false` or continues to the next iteration of the `for` loop, depending upon whether the `word` in the current list element is greater (lexicographically) than `new_word`. This way, if the function does return `false`, then the iterator `it` is positioned at the correct location in the list at which the `new_word` should be inserted to maintain alphabetical order. On the other hand, if the function returns `true`, meaning that the `new_word` is already in the list, then again the iterator `it` returns locating that particular element, thereby allowing `main()` to update it. The iterator `it` must be passed by reference for this to work.

The `literal()` function simply constructs a `string` that is the literal equivalent to the integer passed to it. For example, if `n` has the value `27`, then the function returns the string `"27"`. This is done by extracting the ten's digit (the `2`) and the one's digit (the `7`) separately and then assigning them to `s[0]` and `s[1]`, respectively. This returned string is used by `main()`.

If the `new_word` was `found`, then the element `*it` is updated simply by appending `", "` and the string literal. For example, the 27th word is `cherry`. When that word is input, the list looks like this:

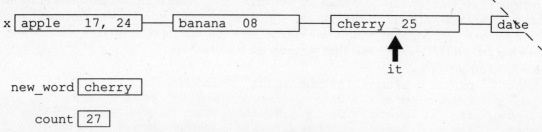

new_word `cherry`

count `27`

The `found()` function positions the iterator it at the third element and returns `true`. Then the statement
```
    *it += ", " + literal(count);
```
appends the string `", 27"` to the string stored in that element, changing the list to

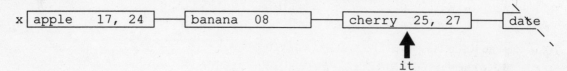

10.8 GENERIC ALGORITHMS

The C++ Standard Library is the result of the 1998 ISO standardization of the C++ programming language, which expanded its library by including a collection of classes and functions that were developed in the early 1990s by Alexander Stepanov and Meng Lee. Before the conclusion of the ISO standardization process, this separate collection was knows as the Standard Template Library. Because it is primarily a collection of classes, iterators, and implemented algorithms, Bjarne Stroustrup suggested the acronym CIA for the library. Regardless of the name, the implementation of the generic algorithms in the library are one of its most distinctive features.

The generic algorithms are defined in the Standard Library file `<algo>`. These algorithms are implemented as non-member functions (also called *free* functions). The file includes over 70 of these functions, most of which apply to most of the standard container classes. Here is a listing of some of the most useful:

```
find(start, stop, t);                          // find t in subseq
adjacent_find(start, stop);        // find adjacent equal pair in subseq
count(start, stop, t, n);           // count occurrences of t in subseq
equal(start, stop, pos);            // return true iff subseq1 == subseq2
search(start1, stop1, start2, stop2);      // find subseq2 in subseq1
copy(start, stop, pos);              // replace subseq2 with subseq1
swap(t, u);                                   // interchange t and u
swap_ranges(start, stop, pos);      // interchange subseq1 with subseq2
replace(start, stop, t, u);          // replace every t in subseq with u
fill(start, stop, t);          // replace every element in subseq with t
remove(start, stop, t);             // remove every element t in subseq
unique(start, stop);                 // remove all duplicates in subseq
reverse(start, stop);               // reverse the elements in subseq
rotate(start, mid, stop);    // shift subseq (mid-start) to left & wrap
random_shuffle(start, stop);             // randomly permute subseq
sort(start, stop);                              // sort the subseq
nth_element(start, nth, stop);       // partition the subseq about nth
binary_search(start, stop, t);             // search subseq for t
min(t, u);                               // return ( t < u ? t : u )
max(t, u);                               // return ( t > u ? t : u )
min_element(start, stop);        // return smallest element in subseq
max_element(start, stop);         // return largest element in subseq
next_permutation(start, stop);              // permute the subseq
```

Here, `start`, `stop`, `pos`, and `mid` are iterators, `t` and `u` are elements, and `n` is a positive integer. In the comments, `subseq` and `subseq1` refer to the elements `*start...*(stop-1)` or `*start1...*(stop1-1)`, and `subseq2` refers to the elements `*start2...*(stop2-1)` or `*pos...*(pos+(stop1-start1)-2)`.

The details of these algorithms are explained in the Problems below.

Review Questions

10.1 What is the difference between a class template and a template class?

10.2 What, if anything, is wrong with the following code. Explain.

```
Stack<Stack<short>> s;
```

10.3 Is the Ratio class (see Chapter 3) a container class?

10.4 What is the difference between a vector and an array?

10.5   What are the differences between C strings and C++ strings?

10.6   What is "fragmented memory" and why is it bad?

10.7   *a.* What is the difference between the subscript operator and the `at()` function?
           b. Why is one preferred over the other?

10.8   What is the difference between the `stack`, `queue`, `deque`, and `vector` template classes?

Programming Problems

10.9   Omit the member function `is_full()` in the definition for class template `Stack<T>` in Example 10.2 on page 227. Replace it with a private utility function named `_expand()` that dynamically doubles the size of the stack and copies the entire contents of the old stack into the first half of the new stack. Then use that utility function in the `push()` function to prevent overflow.

10.10 Convert the `Ratio` class (see Chapter 7) into a template that allows ratios of numbers other than `int`s. For example, `Ratio<long>` and even `Ratio<double>` would be valid classes.

10.11 Use the Standard `list` template defined in the `<list>` file to implement a `Deque<T>` class template. (See Problem 7.7 on page 156) Declare a list as the (only) data member and then call the appropriate list member functions to implement the corresponding deque member functions. For example, the deque's `push_back()` function is the same as the `push_back()` function defined in the Standard `list` class.

10.12 Use the Standard `deque` template defined in the `<deque>` file to implement the `Stack<T>` class template. Declare a deque as the (only) data member and then call the appropriate deque member functions to implement the corresponding stack member functions. For example, the stack's `pop()` function is simply the `pop_back()` function defined in the `deque` class. This is how `stack` is defined in the C++ Standard Library.

10.13 Use the Standard `deque` template defined in the `<deque>` file to implement the `Queue<T>` class template. Declare a deque as the (only) data member and then call the appropriate deque member functions to implement the corresponding queue member functions. For example, the queue's `pop()` function is simply the `pop_front()` function defined in the `deque` class. This is how `queue` is defined in the C++ Standard Library.

10.14 Use the Standard `queue` template defined in the `<queue>` file and the `Person` class (Problem 7.22 on page 160) to simulate a line of people waiting for movie tickets.

10.15 Modify the `projection()` function in Example 10.5 on page 235 so that it returns the vector `v` after erasing the elements in the slots where `b[i]` is false. Use the `erase()` function defined in the `vector` class. Use iterators instead of integers.

10.16 Add the following function to the program in Example 10.5 on page 235:
```
int freq(SL& x, string& word)
// returns the number of times word appeared in the input
```
Locate the word in the list `x` and then count how many numbers are in that element.

10.17 Implement the following generic Standard Library function defined in `<algo>`:
```
template <class Src, class T>
Src find(Src i, Src j, const T& t)
// Searches for t in the subsequence *i...*(j-1); if found, its
// position k is returned; otherwise, j is returned.
// Invariant: no elements are changed.
```

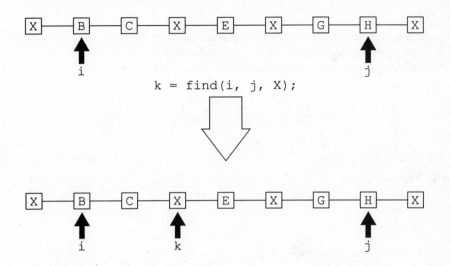

$$k = \text{find}(i, j, X);$$

10.18 Implement the following generic Standard Library function defined in `<algo>`:

```
template <class Src, class T>
Src adjacent_find(Src i, Src j);
// Returns the position k of the first occurrence of a pair of
// adjacent equal elements among the elements *i...*(j-1).
// If no equal adjacent elements are found, j is returned.
// Invariant: no elements are changed.
```

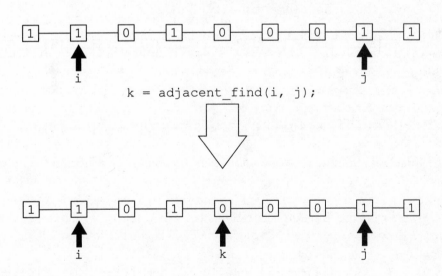

$$k = \text{adjacent\_find}(i, j);$$

10.19 Implement the following generic Standard Library function defined in `<algo>`:

```
template <class Src, class T>
void count(Src i, Src j, const T& t, int& n);
// Increments n for each occurrence of the value t among the
// elements *i...*(j-1).
// Invariant: no elements are changed.
```

10.20   Implement the following generic Standard Library function defined in `<algo>`:

```
template <class Src>
bool equal(Src i, Src j, Src p);
// Returns true iff the subsequence *i...*(j-1) is the same as the
// subsequence *p...*(p+n-1) where n = i - j.
// Invariant: no elements are changed.
```

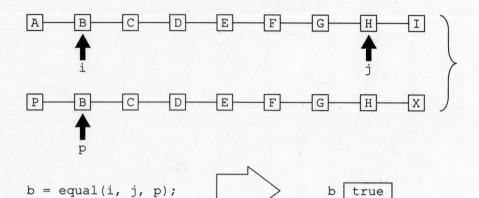

10.21   Implement the following generic Standard Library function defined in `<algo>`:

```
template <class Src1, class Src2>
Src1 search(Src1 i, Src1 j, Src2 p, Src2 q);
// Searches the sequence *i...*(j-1) for a subsequence that equals
// the sequence *p...*(q-1). If found, position k where it begins
// is returned; otherwise, j is returned.
// Invariant: no elements are changed.
```

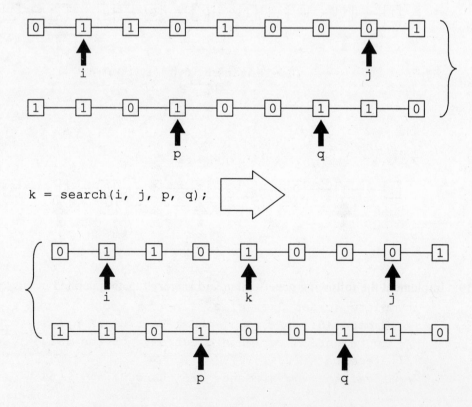

10.22 Implement the following generic Standard Library function defined in `<algo>`:

```
template <class Src, class Dst>
Dst copy(Src i, Src j, Dst p);
// Replaces the n elements *p...*(p+n-1) with the n elements
// *i...*(j-1), where n = j-i. Returns the position k = p+n.
// Invariant: size is unchanged.
```

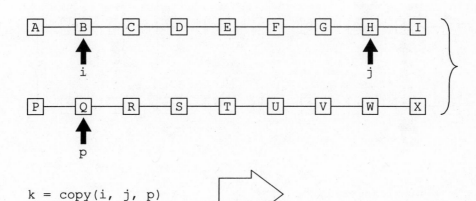

`k = copy(i, j, p)`

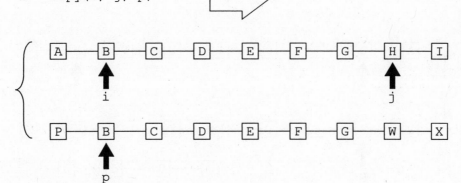

10.23 Implement the following generic Standard Library function defined in `<algo>`:

```
template <class Src, class T>
void replace(Src i, Src j, const T& t, const T& u);
// Replaces each occurrence of the value t with the value u in the
// sequence *i...*(j-1).
// Invariant: size is unchanged.
```

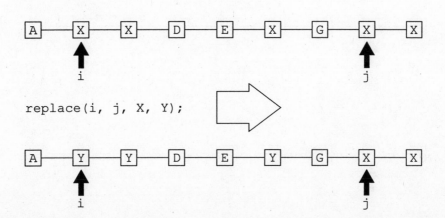

`replace(i, j, X, Y);`

10.24 Implement the following generic Standard Library function defined in `<algo>`:

```
template <class Src, class Dst>
Dst swap_ranges(Src i, Src j, Dst p);
// Interchanges the n elements *p...*(p+n-1) with the n elements
// *i...*(j-1), where n = j-i. Returns the position k = p+n.
// Invariant: size is unchanged.
```

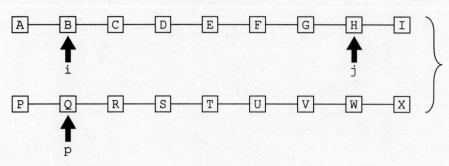

k = swap_ranges(i, j, p)

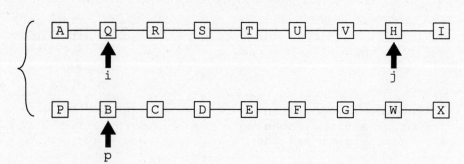

10.25 Implement the following generic Standard Library function defined in `<algo>`:

```
template <class Src, class T>
void fill(Src i, Src j, const T& t);
// Replaces each of the elements *i...*(j-1) with a copy of the
// value t.
// Invariant: size is unchanged.
```

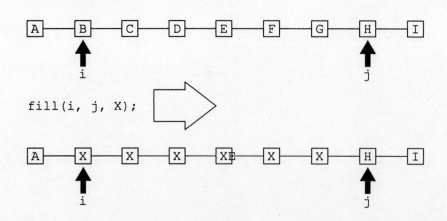

fill(i, j, X);

10.26 Implement the following generic Standard Library function defined in `<algo>`:

```
template <class Src, class T>
Src remove(Src i, Src j, const T& t);
// Shifts to the left the n elements among *i...*(j-1) that are
// not equal to t. Returns the position k = i+n.
// Postconditions: none of the elements among *i...*(k-1) are
//   equal to t; all the other elements are left unchanged.
// Invariant: size is unchanged.
```

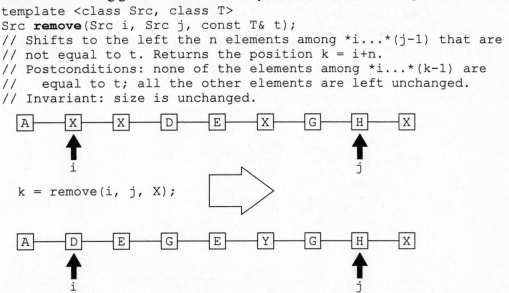

Warning: The `remove()` function does not remove any elements. Instead, it overwrites some of the elements in the subrange `*i...*(k-1)` range removing the `t` values.

10.27 Implement the following generic Standard Library function defined in `<algo>`:

```
template <class Src, class T>
Dst remove_copy(Src i, Src j, Dst p, const T& t);
// Replaces the first n elements of the sequence at *p with the n
// elements in the sequence *i...*(j-1) that are not equal to t.
// Returns the position k = p+n.
// Postconditions: none of the elements among *p...*(k-1) are
//   equal to t; all the other elements are left unchanged.
```

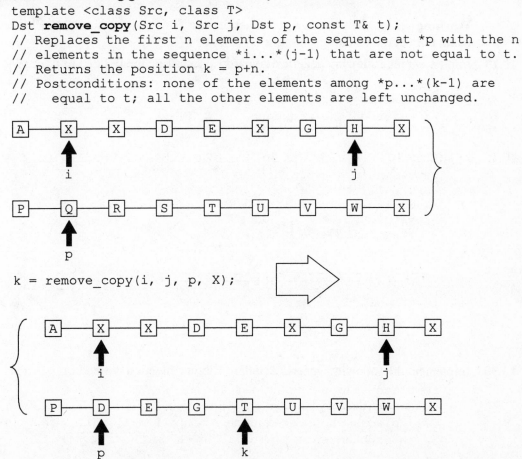

10.28 Implement the following generic Standard Library function defined in `<algo>`:

```
template <class Src, class T>
Src unique(Src i, Src j);
// Overwrites up to n-1 elements starting with element *i among
// the sequence *i...*(j-1), where n is the number of distinct
// elements in that range. Returns: the position k = i+n.
// Postconditions: all of the elements among *i...*(k-1) are
//   distinct; all the other elements are left unchanged.
```

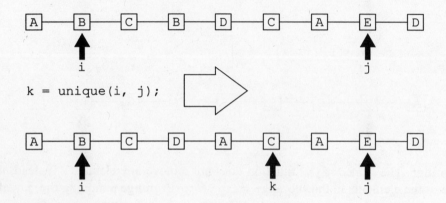

Warning: Like the `remove()` function, the `unique()` function achieves its desired result only in the resulting subsequence `*i...*(k-1)`.

10.29 Implement the following generic Standard Library function defined in `<algo>`:

```
template <class Src, class T>
void reverse(Src i, Src j);
// Reverses the sequence *i...*(j-1).
```

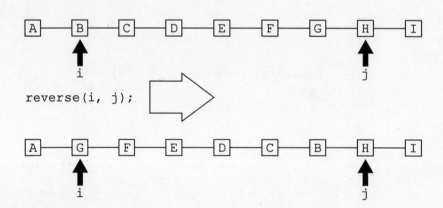

10.30 Implement the following generic Standard Library function defined in `<algo>`:

```
template <class Src, class T>
void rotate(Src i, Src k, Src j);
// Replaces the subsequence *i...*(i+n-1) with *k...*(j-1), and
// the subsequence *(i+n)...*(j-1) with *i...*(k-1),
// where n = j-k.
```

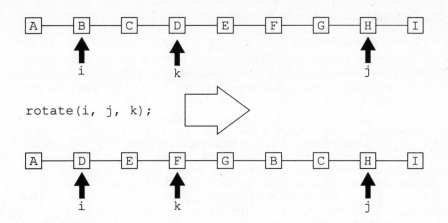

```
rotate(i, j, k);
```

Solutions

10.1   A *class template* is only an outline for a class; it includes one or more template parameters. A *template class* is a specific class that is generated by the compiler from a class template; it specifies what type(s) are to be substituted in for the template parameter(s). For example,

```
template<class T> class Stack ( //... );        // a class tem-
plate
Stack<int> s1;    // a template class used to declare the stack
s1
Stack<double> s2; // a template class used to declare the stack
s2
```

Here `s1` is declared to be a stack whose elements have type `int` and `s2` is declared to be a stack whose elements have type `double`. Note that when the declaration of `s1` is compiled, the compiler uses the template to create a complete class definition for the `Stack<int>` type, and when the declaration of `s2` is compiled, the compiler uses the template to create a separate class definition for the `Stack<double>` type.

10.2   There is nothing wrong with this code (although some compilers may not yet be able to compile it). It declares `s` to be a stack whose elements are stacks whose elements are `shorts`. It is equivalent to

```
typedef Stack<short> short_stack_type;
Stack<short_stack_type> s;
```

The object `s` could be used like this:

```
Stack<short> ss1, ss2;
ss1.push(22);   // now ss1 contains 1 element: 22
ss2.push(44);   // now ss2 contains 1 element: 44
s.push(ss1);    // now s contains 1 element: ss1
s.push(ss2);    // now s contains 2 elements: ss1 and ss2
```

The object `s` is a container of containers.

10.3   The `Ratio` class (Chapter 3) a not really a container class. Although `Ratio` objects (*i.e.*, fractions) do contain pairs of numbers, they themselves are used as numbers with the usual arithmetic operations (+, −, *, and /) being defined for them. Containers do not interact with other containers that way: one doesn't subtract a stack from a queue or even from another stack. Moreover, a ratio always contains exactly two numbers (its numerator and its denominator), whereas containers allow the insertion and removal of many elements.

10.4   A `vector` is a container object; an array is a built-in structured type. A `vector` has all the extra functionality provided by the `vectot<T>` class template and the free functions defined in the Standard Library. In the context of object-oriented programming, arrays are like linked lists; they provide a method of implementation.

10.5   A C-string is just a null-terminated array of `chars`. A C++ `string` is an object that has all the functionality provided by the Standard C++ `string` class.

10.6   Fragmented memory occurs when the memory allocated to a process consists of small, disconnected segments. This renders the unallocated memory less usable because it is "fragmented;" *i.e.*, broken into little pieces. Requests from the `new` operator for large contiguous blocks are more likely to fail.

10.7   *a.* The `at()` function checks the range on the subscript value and rejects it if it is out of range.

    b. So this function is safer to use than ordinary subscripting. But checking the index range takes extra time. So the programmer wanting fast code should opt for using the subscript operator and ensure that the code itself prevents the subscript from going out of range.

10.8   The `stack`, `queue`, `deque`, and `vector` templates all have the same functionality. The only difference between deques and vectors is the efficiency of their operations. Since a deque is meant to be changed only at its ends, insertions and deletions there are much faster than they are for vectors. On the other hand, the subscript operator and `at()` function are much faster for vectors than for deques. The only differences between stacks, queues, and deques are their names for the functions used to read, insert, and delete at their ends. Both the `stack` and the `queue` templates use `push()` for `push_back()`. The `stack` templates uses `pop()` for `pop_back()` and the `queue` templates uses `pop()` for `pop_front()`. The `stack` template also uses `top()` for the `back()` function. (Technically, the `stack` and `queue` templates are *adaptors* that use the `deque` template as their default implementation. They can also use the `vector` template or the `list` template. These alternate implementations change the efficiency of certain operations.)

10.9   Here are the changes:

```
template<class T>
class Stack
{ public:
    Stack(int);
    ~Stack();
    bool is_empty() const;
    void push(const T);
    T pop();
  private:
    void _expand();  // used to prevent stack overflow
    T* _a;            // the stack itself: a dynamic array of type T
    int _max;         // the maximum number of elements on the stack
    int _count;       // the actual number of elements on the stack
};
template<class T>
void Stack<T>::push(const T x)
{ if (_count == _max) _expand();
  _a[_count++] = x;
}
template<class T>
void Stack<T>::_expand()
{ T* new_a = new T[2*_max];     // allocate storage for array new_a
  assert(new_a != 0);                      // abort if not enough memory
  for (int i=0; i < _count; i++)       // copy all of _a into new_a
    new_a[i] = _a[i];
  T* temp_a = _a;                          // hold address _a in temp_a
  _a = new_a;                              // copy address new_a into _a
  _max *= 2;                                            // double _max
  delete [] temp_a;                // return old storage back to heap
}
```

The execution of the `_expand()` function looks like the picture shown below.
The object `s` would have been created by

```
Stack<char> s;
s.push('A');
s.push('B');
s.push('C');
```

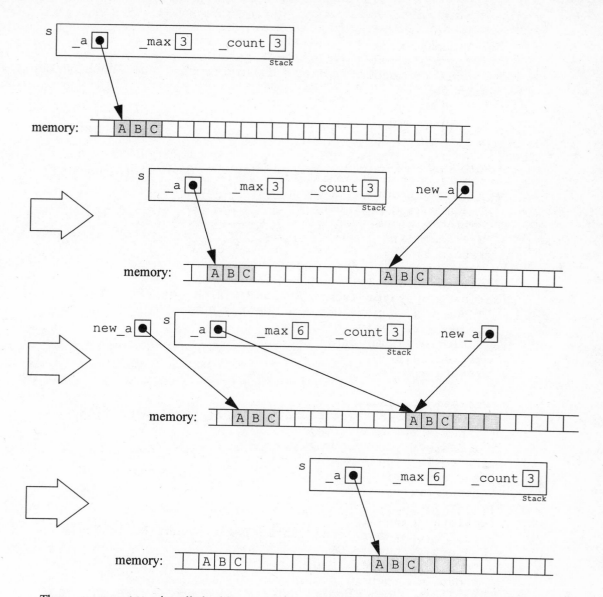

Then `_expand()` is called with `s._a[0]` containing `'A'`, `s._a[1]` containing `'B'`, `s._a[2]` containing `'C'`, `s._max` containing 3, and `s._count` containing 3. The array `new_a` is created and allocated 6 bytes in memory. The 3 elements (`'A'`, `'B'`, and `'C'`) in `_a` are then copied into the first 3 elements of `new_a`. Then the pointer `temp_a` is created and initialized to point to the same memory location to which `_a` points. This is done so that access to that location can be kept after `_a` is reassigned to point to the new array `new_a`. Finally the space used by the old array is returned to the heap so that it can be reused later by other processes.

10.10

```
#include "algo"      // defines swap()
#include <assert.h>  // defines assert()
template <class T>
class Ratio
{   friend Ratio operator+(const Ratio&, const Ratio&);
    friend Ratio operator-(const Ratio&, const Ratio&);
    friend Ratio operator*(const Ratio&, const Ratio&);
    friend Ratio operator/(const Ratio&, const Ratio&);
  public:
    Ratio(T num=0, T den=1): _num(num), _den(den) { _reduce(); }
    Ratio(const Ratio& x): _num(x._num), _den(x._den) {_reduce();}
```

```cpp
      Ratio& operator-() { _num *= -1; }
      T num() const { return _num; }
      T den() const { return _den; }
      operator double() const { return double(_num)/double(_den); }
  private:
    T _num;
    T _den;
    void _reduce();   // reduces fraction to lowest terms
};
template <class T>
Ratio<T> operator+(const Ratio<T>& x, const Ratio<T>& y)
{ T num = x._num*y._den + x._den*y._num;
  T den = x._den*y._den;
  Ratio<T> z(num, den);
  z._reduce();
  return z;
}
template <class T>
Ratio<T> operator-(const Ratio<T>& x, const Ratio<T>& y)
{ T num = x._num*y._den - x._den*y._num;
  T den = x._den*y._den;
  Ratio<T> z(num, den);
  z._reduce();
  return z;
}
template <class T>
Ratio<T> operator*(const Ratio<T>& x, const Ratio<T>& y)
{ T num = x._num*y._num;
  T den = x._den*y._den;
  Ratio<T> z(num, den);
  z._reduce();
  return z;
}
template <class T>
Ratio<T> operator/(const Ratio<T>& x, const Ratio<T>& y)
{ assert(y._num != 0);
  T num = x._num*y._den;
  T den = x._den*y._num;
  Ratio<T> z(num, den);
  z._reduce();
  return z;
}
template <class T>
T gcd(T m, T n)
{ assert(m > 0 && n > 0);
  while (m > 0)
  { if (m < n) swap(m,n);
    m %= n;
  }
  return n;
}
template <class T>
void Ratio<T>::_reduce()
{ if (_num == 0 || _den == 0) { _num = 0; _den = 1; return; }
  if (_den < 0) { _num *= -1; _den *= -1; }
  int sgn = ( _num < 0 ? -1 : 1 );
```

```
        _num *= sgn;
        T g = gcd(_num, _den);
        _num /= g;
        _den /= g;
        _num *= sgn;
    }
```

10.11 This conforms to the Standard C++ `deque` class template defined in `<deque>`:

```
        template <class T>
        class Deque
        { public:
            Deque(const list& x) : _list(x);        // auxiliary constructor
            int size() const { return _list.size(); }
            bool empty() const { return bool(_list.size() == 0); }
            T& front() const { return _list.front(); }
            T& back() const { return _list.back(); }
            void push_front(const T& t) { _list.push_front(t); }
            void push_back(const T& t) { _list.push_back(t); }
            void pop_front() { _list.pop_front(); }
            void pop_back() { _list.pop_back(); }
          private:
            list<T> _list;
        };
```

10.12 This conforms to the Standard C++ `stack` class template defined in `<stack>`:

```
        template <class T>
        class Stack
        { public:
            Stack(const deque& deque) : _deque(deque); // aux. constructor
            int size() const { return _deque.size(); }
            bool empty() const { return bool(_deque.size() == 0); }
            T& top() const { return _deque.back(); }
            void push(const T& t) { _deque.push_back(t); }
            void pop() { _deque.pop_back(); }
          private:
            deque<T> _deque;
        };
```

10.13 This conforms to the Standard C++ `queue` class template defined in `<queue>`:

```
        template <class T>
        class Queue
        { public:
            Queue(const deque& deque) : _deque(deque); // aux. constructor
            int size() const { return _deque.size(); }
            bool empty() const { return bool(_deque.size() == 0); }
            T& front() const { return _deque.front(); }
            T& back() const { return _deque.back(); }
            void push(const T& t) { _deque.push_back(t); }
            void pop() { _deque.pop_front(); }
          private:
            deque<T> _deque;
        };
```

10.14
```
        int main()
        { queue<Person> line;
          line.push(Person("Clinton", "William"));
          Address whitehouse("1600 Pennsylvania Avenue", "Washington");
          line.front().set_address(whitehouse);
          line.push(Person("Clinton", "Hillary"));
          line.push(Person("Gore", "Albert"));
```

```
cout << "There are " << line.size() << " people in line.\n";
cout << "The name of the first person in line is "
     << line.front().fname() + " " + line.front().lname()<<endl;
cout << "His street address is "
     << line.front().address().street() << endl;
cout << "The name of the last person in line is "
     << line.back().fname() + " " + line.back().lname() <<
endl;
}
```

The output from this program is

```
There are 3 people in line.
The name of the first person in line is William Clinton
His street address is 1600 Pennsylvania Avenue
The name of the last person in line is Albert Gore
```

10.15 Note that this alternative function requires that v be passed by value because it changes v:

```
vec projection(vec v, bits& b)
{ vec::iterator itv = v.begin();
  bits::iterator itb = b.begin();
  while (itv != v.end())
  { if (*itb++) v.erase(itv);
    ++itv;
  }
  return v;
}
```

10.16
```
int number_of_numbers(SLI& it)
{ int count=0;
  string element = *it;
  int k = element.find('\t');
  return (element.length() - k + 1)/4;
}
int freq(SL& x, string& word)
{ string x_word;
  for (SLI it=x.begin(); it != x.end(); ++it)
  { string x_word = extract_word(it);
    if (word == x_word) return number_of_numbers(it);
  }
  return 0;
}
```

10.17
```
template <class Src, class T>
Src find(Src i, Src j, const T& t)
{ while (i != j && *i != t)
    ++i;
  return i;
}
```

10.18
```
template <class Src, class T>
Src adjacent_find(Src i, Src j)
{ if (i == j) return j;
  for (Src k = i+1; k != j; ++i)
  { if (*k == *i) return i;
    k = i;  // with linked lists, this would be faster than ++k
  }
  return j;
}
```

10.19
```
template <class Src, class T>
void count(Src i, Src j, const T& t, int& n)
{ while (i != j)
    if (*i++ == t) ++n;
}
```

10.20
```
template <class Src>
bool equal(Src i, Src j, Src p)
{ while (i != j)
    if (*i++ != *p++) return false;
  return true;
}
```

10.21
```
template <class Src1, class Src2>
Src1 search(Src1 i, Src1 j, Src2 p, Src2 q)
{ while (i != j)
    return equal(p, q, i++);
  return j;
}
```

10.22
```
template <class Src, class Dst>
Dst copy(Src i, Src j, Dst p)
{ while (i != j)
    *p++ = *i++;
  return p;
}
```

10.23
```
template <class Src, class T>
void replace(Src i, Src j, const T& t, const T& u)
{ for (; i != j; ++i)
    if (*i == t) *i = u;
}
```

10.24
```
template <class Src, class Dst>
Dst swap_ranges(Src i, Src j, Dst p)
{ while (i != j)
    swap(*i++, *p++);
  return p;
}
```

10.25
```
template <class Src, class T>
void fill(Src i, Src j, const T& t)
{ while (i != j)
    *i++ = t;
}
```

10.26
```
template <class Src, class T>
Src remove(Src i, Src j, const T& t)
{ Src k=i;
  while (i != j)
  { if (*i != t) *k++ = *i;
    ++i;
  }
  return k;
}
```

10.27
```
template <class Src, class Dst, class T>
Dst remove_copy(Src i, Src j, Dst p, const T& t)
{ while (i != j)
  { if (*i != t) *p++ = *i;
    ++i;
  }
  return p;
}
```

Chapter 11

Recursion

11.1 INTRODUCTION

Some functions are naturally *self-referential*: they can be expressed easily in terms of themselves. For example, the *factorial function n*! can be defined using the recurrence formula:

$$n! = n(n-1)!$$

This is called *recursion* because the function being defined on the left of the equals sign recurs (appears again) on the right side.

The factorial function can also be defined iteratively, as it was in Example 4.4 on page 68. However some functions cannot be implemented easily without recursion. Other functions, which do admit both iterative and recursive solutions, are easier to understand in their recursive form. So recursion is an essential tool of the computer scientist.

11.2 THE BASIS FOR A RECURSIVE DEFINITION

The recurrence formula

$$n! = n \cdot (n-1)!$$

describes how each value of the factorial function can be computed in terms of the previous value. For example,

$$5! = 5 \cdot 4!$$

Then since $4! = 24$, it follows that $5! = 5 \cdot 24 = 120$.

But how do we know that $4! = 24$? By the same recurrence formula:

$$4! = 4 \cdot 3!$$

And this depends upon the knowledge that $3! = 6$.

So recursion causes a chain of similar computations. Each computation uses the same function on a previous value. The chain must end at some point. That ending is called the *basis* for the recursion.

The basis for the factorial function is

$$0! = 1$$

From that definition, we can use the recurrence formula

$$n! = n \cdot (n-1)!$$

to compute all other values of the factorial function:

$$1! = 1 \cdot 0! = 1 \cdot 1 = 1$$
$$2! = 2 \cdot 1! = 2 \cdot 1 = 2$$
$$3! = 3 \cdot 2! = 3 \cdot 2 = 6$$
$$4! = 4 \cdot 3! = 4 \cdot 6 = 24$$
$$5! = 5 \cdot 4! = 5 \cdot 24 = 120$$

etc.

Every recursive definition must have two parts: a basis and a recurrence relation. The two parts are often expressed together in a combination formula like this:

$$n! = \begin{cases} 1, \text{ if } n = 0 \\ n \cdot (n-1), \text{ if } n > 0 \end{cases}$$

This simply combines the basis formula

$n! = 1$, if $n = 0$

with the recurrence formula

$n! = n \cdot (n-1)!$, if $n > 0$

into a single expression that completely defines the factorial function.

11.3 IMPLEMENTATIONS OF THE `factorial()` FUNCTION

In Example 4.5 on page 69 we computed the factorial function iteratively; *i.e.*, with an explicit loop. Now we can compare the two implementations.

EXAMPLE 11.1 Recursive Implementation of the Factorial Function

Here is a direct translation of the above recursive definition into C++:

```
long factorial(int n)
{ if (n == 0) return 1;
   else return n*factorial(n-1);
}
```

The essential feature of this recursive implementation is that <u>the function calls itself</u> if n > 0, and it calls itself <u>repeatedly</u> if n > 1. For example, the call `factorial(5)` will generate the 5 recursive calls: `factorial(4)`, `factorial(3)`, `factorial(2)`, `factorial(1)`, and `factorial(0)`.

EXAMPLE 11.2 Iterative Implementation of the Factorial Function

Here is the iterative implementation from Chapter 3:

```
long factorial(int n)
{ long f=1;
   for (int i=2; i <= n; i++)
     f *= i;
   return f;
}
```

Note that if n < 2, the loop never iterates and 1 is returned.

The important difference between the two implementations is that the call `factorial(n-1)` in the recursive implementation replaces the `for` loop in the iterative implementation. On most computer systems, function calls take much longer to execute than loop iterations. Therefore, recursion generally is much slower than iteration. The advantages of recursive code are that it is often more intuitive and simpler to implement when the problem being solved is naturally recursive. There are examples in Chapter 12 where a non-recursive implementation is not feasible.

EXAMPLE 11.3 Summing Recursively

This function recursively adds the first n elements of an array of `floats`:

```
float sum(float a[], int n)
{ if (n == 0) return a[0];
   else return a[n] + sum(a, n-1);
}
```

The next example shows that, in some cases, the basis of a recursive function may do nothing.

11.4 ACTIVATION FRAMES

When a function is called, the current environment (non-static local variables, values, types, *etc.*) is saved by the operating system in a data structure called an *activation frame*. This structure is pushed onto the *run-time stack* which is another data structure maintained by the system while the program is running. When the function returns, its activation frame is popped from the run-time stack and its contents are used to restore the environment which it left when it was called. The data stored in an activation frame include the address of the statement where the function is called. This is the *return address* which the system needs to continue executing the program after the function returns.

EXAMPLE 11.4 Reversing a String

This function recursively reads a string from standard input and prints it in reverse:

```
void reverse()
{ char c;
  cin.get(c);
  if (c == '\n') return;
  reverse();
  cout << c;
  return;
}

int main()
{ cout << "Enter a string:\n";
  reverse();
}
```

Here is the output:

```
Enter a string:
Ciao!
!oaiC
```

There are two calls to the reverse() function here: one from main() and a recursive call from reverse() itself. Suppose that the address of the next instruction after the call from main() is 0x0120b4, and that the address after the call from reverse() is 0x012006. Then during the execution of this program, the run-time stack would progress like this:

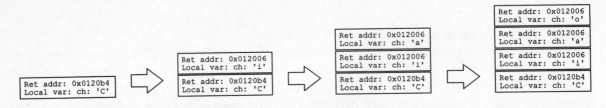

This shows the run-time stack after each of the five calls to the print() function. Note how the individual characters 'C', 'i', 'a', 'o', and '!' are stored: each in its own local version of the variable c.

When the user presses the **Return** key, the newline character '\n' is read into the variable c. This prevents another recursive call to reverse(). The newline character is read and the function returns. This pops the top activation record off the run-time stack, telling the system to return to the address 0x012006 and reassign the value '!' to c. Then that call to the reverse() function finishes by printing the '!' and returning. This pops the next activation record off the run-time stack, telling the system to return to the address 0x012006 and reassign the value 'o' to c. Then the 'o' is printed and that call returns. As the successive calls return, the run-time stack progresses like this:

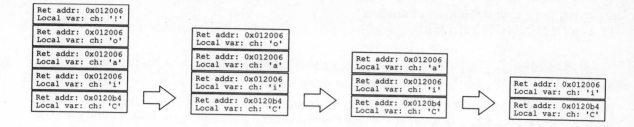

11.5 THE FIBONACCI SEQUENCE

A function may include more than one recursive call. The best example of this is the *Fibonacci sequence*, defined by

$$n! = \begin{cases} 0, \text{ if } n = 0 \\ 1, \text{ if } n = 1 \\ f(n-1) + f(n-2), \text{ if } n > 1 \end{cases}$$

So

$f(0) = 0,$
$f(1) = 1,$
$f(2) = f(0) + f(1) = 0 + 1 = 1,$
$f(3) = f(1) + f(2) = 1 + 1 = 2,$
$f(4) = f(2) + f(3) = 1 + 2 = 3,$
$f(5) = f(3) + f(4) = 2 + 3 = 5,$
etc.

Here are the first 18 Fibonacci numbers:

n	f(n)
0	0
1	1
2	1
3	2
4	3
5	5
6	8
7	13
8	21
9	34
10	55
11	89
12	144
13	233
14	377
15	610
16	987
17	1597

It can be shown that the Fibonacci sequence increases exponentially.

EXAMPLE 11.5 The Fibonacci Function

This recursive function is a direct translation of the definition of the Fibonacci numbers:

```
int f(int n)
{ if (n < 2) return n;
  else return f(n-1) + f(n-2);
}
```

The function returns `0` for `f(0)` and `1` for `f(1)` because in those two initial cases the `(n < 2)` condition in the `if` statement is true. For `f(2)` the function returns `f(1) + f(0)` which is $0 + 1 = 1$.

For larger values of `n`, the function makes a cascade of recursive function calls. Here is the calling tree for `f(5)`. The calls are indicated with dashed arrows:

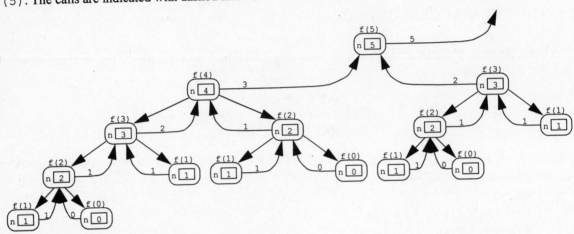

After cascading 14 recursive calls, the original call f(5) returns 5. This clearly is not an efficient way to compute the 5th Fibonacci number.

11.6 THE EUCLIDEAN ALGORITHM

A positive integer d is a *divisor* of a larger integer n if n is some multiple of d; *i.e.*, $n = k \cdot d$ for some integer k. For example, 7 is a divisor of 812 because $812 = 116 \cdot 7$.

A positive integer d is a *common divisor* of two larger integers m and n if it is a divisor of both m and n. For example, 7 is a common divisor of 812 and 924 because $812 = 116 \cdot 7$ and $924 = 132 \cdot 7$.

A positive integer d is the *greatest common divisor* of two larger integers m and n if it is a common divisor of m and n, and no other common divisor of m and n is greater than d. For example, 28 is the greatest common divisor of 812 and 924 because the only common divisors that 812 and 924 have are 1, 2, 4, 7, 14, and 28. You can also see that 28 is the greatest common divisor of 812 and 924 from the facts that $812 = 29 \cdot 28$ and $924 = 33 \cdot 28$. If there were a common divisor larger than 28, then the multipliers 29 and 33 would have to have a common divisor. The greatest common divisor of two integers m and n is often denoted by gcd(m, n). Thus gcd(812, 924) = 28.

Greatest common divisors are useful for reducing fractions. For example, to reduce the fraction 812/924, we first find the gcd(812, 924) = 28, and then we simply divide the numerator and denominator by the gcd: 812/28 = 29, 924/28 = 33, so 812/924 = 29/33.

It might seem that finding gcds of large integers could be very tedious and time-consuming. But fortunately the ancient Greeks discovered a clever algorithm for finding the gcd(m, n) without having to compute all the divisors of m and n. The algorithm was described in Euclid's great mathematical encyclopedia, the *Elements*,[*] and so it has come to be known as the Euclidean Algorithm.

---

[*] Book VII, Proposition 2.

The algorithm is most easily understood from an example. Consider the numbers $m = 528$ and $n = 936$. Euclid says to repeatedly subtract the smaller number from the larger number until you end up with 0; then the last positive number in the sequence must be the greatest common divisor:

$$936 - 528 = 408$$
$$528 - 408 = 120$$
$$408 - 120 = 288$$
$$288 - 120 = 168$$
$$168 - 120 = 48$$
$$120 - 48 = 72$$
$$72 - 48 = 24$$
$$48 - 24 = 24$$
$$24 - 24 = 0$$

Thus: gcd(528, 936) = 24.

Euclid's proof that this algorithm is correct is based entirely on the recurrence relation:

$$\gcd(m, n) = \gcd(n - m, m)$$

This, together with the facts that $\gcd(m, n) = \gcd(n, m)$ and $\gcd(g, g) = g$, guarantee that every pair of numbers in the progression have the same gcd which must be the last number in the progression. In the example above, this means: gcd(528, 936) = gcd(408, 528) = gcd(120, 408) = gcd(120, 288) = gcd(120, 168) = gcd(48, 120) = gcd(48, 72) = gcd(24, 48) = gcd(24, 24) = 24.

EXAMPLE 11.6 The Euclidean Algorithm

The modern computer version of the Euclidean Algorithm uses the remainder operator `n % m` in place of the subtraction `n - m`. This is valid because division is the same as repeated subtraction.

This recursive function finds the greatest common divisor of its two arguments:

```
int gcd(int m, int n)
{ if (m > n) return gcd(n, m);
  if (m == 0) return n;
  return gcd(n%m, m);
}
```

Here is a trace of the call `gcd(936, 528)`:

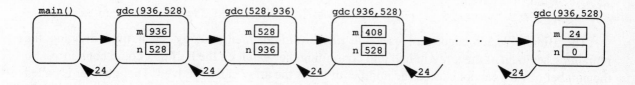

11.7 THE RECURSIVE BINARY SEARCH

The Binary Search for an element `x` in a sorted array `a[]` looks at the middle element of the array. If that is not `x`, then it continues the search in the half that could contain it. The process continues this recursive step until either `x` is found or the sub-array is empty.

EXAMPLE 11.7 The Recursive Binary Search

If x is among the first n elements of the sorted array a[] its location is returned; otherwise, -1 is returned:

```
int find(float* a, int start, int stop, float x)
{ if (start > stop) return -1;
  int mid = (start + stop)/2;
  if (x == a[mid]) return mid;
  if (x < a[mid]) return find(a, start, mid-1, x);
  if (x > a[mid]) return find(a, mid+1, stop, x);
}
```

Here is a test driver:

```
int main()
{ float a[] = { 22.2, 33.3, 44.4, 55.5, 66.6, 77.7, 88.8, 99.9 };
  int k = find(a, 0, 8, 77.7);
  cout << "k = " << k << endl;
  k = find(a, 0, 8, 50);
  cout << "k = " << k << endl;
}
```

The first call from main() searches for 77.7 in the array a. Two recursive calls are made before x is found at position 5:

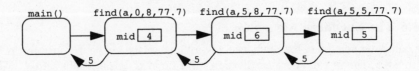

The second call from main() searches for 50. Three recursive calls are made before it is determined that x is not in the array:

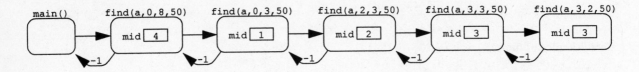

The Binary Search algorithm uses the *divide-and-conquer* strategy, each time dividing the remaining segment of the array in half and continuing the search on the half that could contain x. So the number of calls cannot exceed the number of times the array can be halved. That number is called the *binary logarithm* of n, written lg$n$, where n is the size of the array. This is called the *complexity function* for the algorithm, and is written $O(\lg n)$. It is a relative measure of how fast the algorithm can be executed. It means that the execution time is roughly proportional to lg$n$. So, for example, if you have two arrays of sizes n_1 and n_2, and if $n_2 = n_1^2$, then it should take the Binary Search only about twice as long to run on the larger array. That is because $\lg(n^2) = 2 \cdot \lg n$. For example, if it takes 3 milliseconds to run on an array of 200 elements, then it shouldn't take more than 6 milliseconds to run on an array of 40,000 elements.

The Binary Search algorithm requires that the array be sorted first.

11.8 THE TOWERS OF HANOI

We have seen important examples of functions that are more naturally defined and more easily understood using recursion. The Towers of Hanoi game is a classic example of a problem whose solution demands recursion. The game consists of a board with three vertical pegs labeled "A", "B",

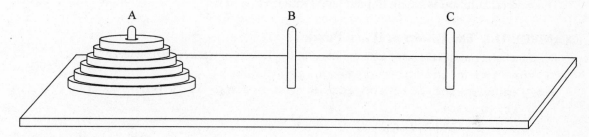

and "C", and a sequence of n disks with holes in their centers. The radii of the disks are in an arithmetic progression (*e.g.*, 6 cm, 7 cm, 8 cm, 9 cm, ...) and are mounted on peg A. The rule is that no disk may be above a smaller disk on the same peg. The objective of the game is to move all the disks from peg A to peg C, one disk at a time, without violating the rule.

The solution to the Towers of Hanoi game is naturally recursive:
- Move the smaller $n - 1$ disks from peg A to peg B.
- Move the remaining disk from peg A to peg C.
- Move the smaller $n - 1$ disks from peg B to peg C.

The first and third steps are recursive: apply the complete solution to $n{-}1$ disks. The basis to this recursive solution is the case where $n = 0$: in this case, do nothing. That makes the expanded solution for the case of $n = 1$ disk:
- Move the disk from peg A to peg C.

Then the expanded solution for the case of $n = 2$ disks becomes
- Move the top disk from peg A to peg B.
- Move the second disk from peg A to peg C.
- Move the top disk from peg B to peg C.

And then the expanded solution for the case of $n = 3$ disks becomes
- Move the top disk from peg A to peg C.
- Move the second disk from peg A to peg B.
- Move the top disk from peg C to peg B.
- Move the remaining disk from peg A to peg C.
- Move the top disk from peg B to peg A.
- Move the second disk from peg B to peg C.
- Move the top disk from peg A to peg C.

Note that the use of the general recursive solution here requires the substitution of different peg labels. So it is better to express the general solution using variables

To move n disks from peg x to peg y using the auxiliary peg z:
- Move the smaller $n - 1$ disks from peg x to peg z.
- Move the remaining disk from peg x to peg y.
- Move the smaller $n - 1$ disks from peg z to peg y.

If we name this three-step algorithm hanoi(n, x, y, z), then we can see that our solution for the case $n = 2$ was hanoi(2, A, C, B), and our solution for the case $n = 3$ was:

- hanoi(2, A, B, C).
- Move the top disk from peg A to peg C.
- hanoi(2, B, C, A).

The general solution is easily implemented into C++:

EXAMPLE 11.8 The Towers of Hanoi Puzzle

This function prints all the steps to the solution of the Towers of Hanoi puzzle with n disks:

```
void print(int n, char x, char y, char z)
// prints the solution for moving n disks from peg x to peg y:
  if (n > 0)
  { hanoi(n-1, x, z, y);
    cout << "Move top disk from peg " << x " to peg " << y << endl;
    hanoi(n-1, z, y, x);
  }
}
```

Here is a sample run for four disks:

```
#include <iostream>

void print(int n, char x, char y, char z);
// prints the solution for moving n disks from peg x to peg y:

int main()
{ print(4, 'A', 'C', 'B');
}
```

Here is the output:

```
Move the top disk from peg A to peg B.
Move the top disk from peg A to peg C.
Move the top disk from peg B to peg C.
Move the top disk from peg A to peg B.
Move the top disk from peg C to peg A.
Move the top disk from peg C to peg B.
Move the top disk from peg A to peg B.
Move the top disk from peg A to peg C.
Move the top disk from peg B to peg C.
Move the top disk from peg B to peg A.
Move the top disk from peg C to peg A.
Move the top disk from peg B to peg C.
Move the top disk from peg A to peg B.
Move the top disk from peg A to peg C.
Move the top disk from peg B to peg C.
```

11.9 MUTUAL RECURSION

In some cases there is computational advantage to having two (or more) functions call each other recursively. This is called *mutual recursion*. As with ordinary recursion, this requires that each function have a basis and that each recursive call reduce the order of the problem.

A classic example is the mutually recursive definitions of the sine and cosine functions. These functions satisfy the identities

$$\sin x = 2 \sin(x/2) \cos(x/2)$$
$$\cos x = 1 - 2 \sin^2(x/2)$$

and the approximate identities

$$\sin x \approx x - x^3/6$$
$$\cos x \approx 1 - x^2/2$$

for very small values of x. The two identities provide the mutually recursive calls, and the two approximate identities provide the bases for the two functions. The recursive calls reduce the order of the problem by replacing x with $x/2$.

EXAMPLE 11.9 Mutually Recursive Sine and Cosine

The following `s()` and `c()` functions compute the sine and cosine:

```cpp
#include <iomanip>    // defines the setprecision() function
#include <iostream>   // defines cin and cout objects
#include <cmath>      // defines the sin() and cos() functions
const double EPSILON=0.005;
double s(double x);  // computes the sine of x
double c(double x);  // computes the cosine of x

int main()
{ double x;
  cout << setprecision(10);
  do
  { cin >> x;
    cout << "\ts =       " << s(x)   << ", c =       " << c(x) << endl;
    cout << "\tsin(x) = " << sin(x) << ", cos(x) = " << cos(x) <<endl;
  } while (x != 0.0);
}
double s(double x)
{ if (x < EPSILON && -x < EPSILON) return x*(1 - x*x/6);
  return 2*s(x/2)*c(x/2);
}

double c(double x)
{ if (x < EPSILON && -x < EPSILON) return 1 - x*x/2;
  return 1 - 2*s(x/2)*s(x/2);
}
   int main()
   { double x;
     do
     { cin >> x;
       cout << "\ts = " << s(x) << ", c = " << c(x) << endl;
     } while (x != 0.0);
   }
```

Here is a test run:

```
1.2
          s =        0.932039086, c =       0.3623577545
          sin(x) = 0.932039086, cos(x) = 0.3623577545
1.5
          s =        0.9974949866, c =       0.07073720167
          sin(x) = 0.9974949866, cos(x) = 0.07073720167
```

```
3.14159265358979
        s =        1.392019833e-11, c =        -1
        sin(x) = 3.231085104e-15, cos(x) = -1
0.01
        s =        0.009999833334, c =        0.9999500004
        sin(x) = 0.009999833334, cos(x) = 0.9999500004
-1.2
        s =        -0.932039086, c =        0.3623577545
        sin(x) = -0.932039086, cos(x) = 0.3623577545
0
        s =        0, c =        1
        sin(x) = 0, cos(x) = 1
```

The test driver reads `x` interactively and then prints the values of `s(x)` and `c(x)` and also the values of `sin(x)` and `cos(x)` to 10 significant digits. The accuracy of these functions is remarkable, especially considering how simply their code is. The power of recursion is evident here.

Note that the expression $x - x^3/6$ is coded as `x*(1 - x*x/6)`. This is done to reduce roundoff error. When x is small, x^3 is much smaller than x^2. So $x^3/6$ could be insignificant (smaller than the computer's machine number) while $x^2/6$ is not. In this case, $x - x^3/6$ will be the same as x, but $x(1 - x^2/6)$ will not be; *i.e.*, the factored expression will have a more accurate computational value.

11.10 BACKUS-NAUR FORM

Although recursive definitions may seem like circular reasoning, they are frequently used in computer science to specify programming language grammars. This use of recursion was developed by John Backus and Peter Naur in the 1950s to define the Algol programming language, and so it is generally referred to as *Backus-Naur Form*, or *BNF*. A BNF grammar consists of a sequence of explicit and recursive definitions. The explicit definitions define new symbols in terms of existing symbols. The recursive definitions define new symbols in terms of themselves and other existing symbols. For example, the grammar rules of the C++ language ([Ellis] p. 388) define the new term *unary-operator* to be one of the symbols `*`, `&`, `+`, `-`, `!`, or `~`. This explicit definition would be expressed in BNF as

```
<unary-operator> ::= * | & | + | - | ! | ~
```

Here, the meta-symbol `::=` means that the object on its left is being defined, and the meta-symbol `|` means "or".

The symbols `*`, `&`, `+`, `-`, `!`, and `~` are called *terminals* because they are not defined in terms of any other symbols. The symbol `<unary-operator>` is called a *nonterminal* because it is defined in terms of other symbols. BNF definitions are called *productions* because they "produce" new terms from existing terms.

Here is the BNF production for the C++ nonterminal `<statement-list>`:

```
<statement-list> ::= <statement> | <statement-list> <statement>
```

This recursive definition means that a `statement-list` is either a `statement` or a `statement-list` followed by a `statement`. The C++ compiler would use this production to verify that the expression

```
x = 22; y = 44; z = 66;
```

is a valid `statement-list` by means of the following logic:

- "`x = 22;`" is a valid `statement`.
- Therefore, "`x = 22;`" is a valid `statement-list`.
- "`y = 44;`" is a valid `statement`.
- Therefore, "`x = 22; y = 44;`" is a valid `statement-list`.

•"z = 66;" is a valid statement.

• Therefore, "x = 22; y = 44; z = 66;" is a valid statement-list.

Here is the BNF production for the C++ nonterminal <compound-statement>:

   <compound-statement> ::= { [<statement-list>] }

This production includes the terminals { and }. It also uses the meta-symbol [ ], which means that whatever is listed inside the brackets is optional. So this production could also be expressed as

   <compound-statement> ::= { } | { <statement-list> }

meaning that a compound-statement is either just a pair of empty braces { } or it is a statement-list enclosed in braces. Thus, for example,

   { x = 22; y = 44; z = 66; }

is a valid compound-statement.

EXAMPLE 11.10 A BNF Grammar for Simple Expressions with Binary Digits

Given the eight terminals +, -, *, /, (,), 0, and 1 and the five nonterminals <bit>, <num>, <factor>, <term>, and <expr> defined by the BNF grammar

   <expr> ::= <term> | <expr> + <term> | <expr> - <term>
   <term> ::= <factor> | <term> * <factor> | <term> / <factor>
   <factor> ::= (<expr>) | <num>
   <num> ::= <bit> | <num> <bit>
   <bit> ::= 0 | 1

verify that the string (101 + 1)/10 is a valid expression.

We use the metasymbol →☐ to denote the application of one of the productions:

   <expr> →☐ <term>
     →☐ <term> / <factor>
     →☐ <factor> / <factor>
     →☐ (expr) / <factor>
     →☐ (expr + <term>) / <factor>
     →☐ (<term> + <term>) / <factor>
     →☐ (<factor> + <factor>) / <factor>
     →☐ (<num> + <num>) / <num>
     →☐ (<num> <bit> + <num>) / <num> <bit>
     →☐ (<num> <bit> <bit> + <num>) / <num> <bit>
     →☐ (<bit> <bit> <bit> + <bit>) / <bit> <bit>
     →☐ (<bit> <bit> <bit> + <bit>) / <bit> <bit>
     →☐ (1 0 1 + 1) / 1 0 = (101+1)/10

Note that the first four productions in the grammar use mutual recursion: <expr> is defined in terms of <term>, which is defined in terms of <factor>, which is defined in terms of <expr>.

Review Questions

11.1 A recursive function must have two parts: its *basis*, and its *recursive part*. Explain what each of these is and why it is essential to recursion.

11.2 How many recursive calls will the call factorial(10) generate?

11.3 How many recursive calls will the call f(6) to the Fibonacci function generate?

11.4 What are the advantages and disadvantages of implementing a recursive solution instead of an iterative solution?

11.5 How many recursive calls could the Binary Search make on an array of 1000 elements if the item being sought is not in the list?

11.6   If the Binary Search takes 7 ms to run on an array of 250 elements, how long would you expect it to take to run on any array of 62,500 elements?

Problems

11.7   Use the BNF grammar defined in Example 11.3 on page 255 to verify that the string `10*110+1` is a valid expression.

11.8   Write a BNF grammar for valid C++ identifiers.

11.9   Write a BNF grammar for a valid hexadecimal numerals.

11.10 Produce some valid sentences from this BNF grammar:
```
<sentence> ::= <subject> <predicate> .
<subject> ::= <noun-phrase>
<predicate> ::= <verb> | <verb> <noun-phrase>
<noun-phrase> ::= <article> [ <adjective> ] <noun>
<article> ::= my | your | his | hers | someone's
<adjective> ::= loyal | big | dumb | clever | immodest | dirty
<noun> ::= dog | sister | boyfriend | girlfriend | roommate
<verb> ::= bit | bumped into | threw up on | insulted | kissed
```

Programming Problems

11.11 Recursion is expensive because each recursive function call carries a lot of overhead. Modify the recursive implementation of the `factorial()` function (Example 11.1 on page 255) by handling the cases for `n` < 4 separately.

11.12 Write a recursive function that returns the sum of the first `n` squares.

11.13 Write a recursive function that reads lines of text from one file and then prints the lines in reverse order in another file.

11.14 Write a recursive function that returns the power x^n.

11.15 Write a recursive function that returns the power x^n, using at most 2 lg n recursive calls.

11.16 Write a recursive function that returns the maximum element in an array.

11.17 Write a recursive function that returns the maximum among the first n elements of an array, using at most lg n recursive calls.

11.18 Write a recursive function that prints the binary numeral for a positive integer.

11.19 Write a recursive function that prints the octal numeral for a positive integer. In your test driver, use the `oct` manipulator (defined in `<iomanip>`), like this:
```
cout << oct << n << dec << endl;
```
to compare check function's results.

11.20 Write a recursive function that prints the hexadecimal numeral for a positive integer. In your test driver, use the `hex` manipulator (defined in `<iomanip>`), like this:
```
cout << hex << n << dec << endl;
```
to compare check function's results.
[Hint: use a separate function `hex(n)` that returns the hexadecimal character for an integer in the range $0 \le n < 16$.]

11.21 Write an iterative implementation of the Fibonacci function.

11.22 The *binomial coefficient* $c(n,k)$ for integer parameters n and k is defined to equal 1 for $k = 0$ or n, and equal to $c(n-1, k-1) + c(n-1, k)$ for $0 \le k \le n$. Implement this recursive function.

11.23 Write a recursive function that returns the integer binary logarithm of a positive integer.

11.24 Draw the calling tree for the call `c(5,2)` to the recursive binomial coefficient function.

11.25 Implement an iterative version of the Euclidean Algorithm.

11.26 Implement an iterative version of the Binary Search.

11.27 *Ackermann's function A(m,n)* is defined recursively by

$$A(m, n) = \begin{cases} n+1, & \text{if } m = 0 \\ A(m-1, 1), & \text{if } n = 0 \text{ and } m > 0 \\ A(m-1, A(m, n-1)), & \text{if } m \cdot n > 0 \end{cases}$$

a. Implement and test Ackermann's function for $0 \le m \le 3$ and $0 \le n \le 8$.
b. Prove that $A(3,n) = 2^{n+3} - 3$, for all $n \ge 0$.
c. Compute $A(4,4)$.
d. Assuming that the largest value an `int` can have is 2,147,483,647 ($= 2^{31} - 1$), determine the computable domain of the Ackermann function.
Note that this function has no practical use. It's value is the insight into recursive functions that its study brings.

11.28 Write a recursive function to find a path through a maze. Represent the maze by an *n*-by-*n* array of 0s and 1s, where a 0 means occupied (part of the maze wall) and a 1 means unoccupied (open path). Use a vector `d` whose values 0, 1, 2, and 3 mean that the last move was left, down, right, or up, respectively.

11.29 Write a recursive function that prints all $n!$ permutations of the first n integers. For example, the call `print(s, 0, 3)` would print the 6 permutations: 012, 021, 102, 120, 201, 210.

11.30 Write and test a recursive function that returns the sum of the first `n` integers. Compare your results with the values given by the closed form function $n(n+1)/2$.

11.31 Write and test a recursive function that returns the sum of the first `n` cubes. Compare your results with the values given by the closed form function $n^2(n+1)^2/4$.

11.32 Write and test a recursive function that prints `n` stars in a row.

11.33 Write and test a recursive function that returns the integer logarithm with base b of a positive integer n. Use the `log()` function defined in `<cmath>` and the algebraic identity

$$\log_b x = \frac{\log x}{\log b}$$

to check your answers. (Hint: see Problem 11.33.)

11.34 The inefficiency of the recursive Fibonacci function can be overcome by storing previously computed values instead of recomputing them. Modify and test the function in Example 11.5 on page 258 by storing each computed value in an array named `fib[]`.

11.35 Re-implement and test the Fibonacci function (Example 11.5 on page 258) using the following close form formula:

$$f(n) = \frac{\varphi^n - \psi^n}{\sqrt{5}}$$

where $\varphi = (1 + \sqrt{5})/2 = 1.618033988749895...$ and $\psi = 1 - \varphi = -0.618033988749895....$ The mathematical constant φ is called the *Golden Mean*.

11.36   Determine empirically (*i.e.*, by running a test-driver on different inputs) the largest value of n for which your system will compute `factorial(n)` correctly. Then modify the solution to Problem 11.11 so that the function returns the value –1 to signal an error if n is out of range (*i.e.*, either too big or too small).

11.37   Write and test the following function:

```
int lcm(int m, int n);
// returns the least common multiple of m and n.
```

Hint: use the Euclidean Algorithm (Example 11.3 on page 255) and the identity:

$$\gcd(m, n) \cdot \mathrm{lcm}(m, n) = m \cdot n$$

11.38   Write and test the following recursive function:

```
int is_increasing(float a[], int n);
// returns 1 if the first n elements of the array a[] are
// increasing; otherwise returns 0.
```

11.39   Write and test a program that reads lines of text from an external file and then prints the same text but with each word written backwards. (See Example 11.3 on page 255.) For example:

meno.txt

```
Can you tell me, Socrates, whether virtue
is acquired by teaching or by practice;
or if neither by teaching nor practice,
then whether it comes to man by nature,
or in what other way?
```

```
naC uoy llet em, setarcoS, rehtehw eutriv
si deriuqca yb gnihcaet ro yb ecitcarp;
ro fi rehtien yb gnihcaet ron ecitcarp,
nrht rehtehw ti semoc ot nam yb erutan,
ro ni tahw rehto yaw?
```

11.40   Write and test a program that reads lines of text from an external file and then prints the same words but in reverse order on each line. (See Example 11.3 on page 255.) For example:

meno.txt

```
Can you tell me, Socrates, whether virtue
is acquired by teaching or by practice;
or if neither by teaching nor practice,
then whether it comes to man by nature,
or in what other way?
```

```
virtue whether Socrates, me, tell you Can
practice; by or teaching by acquired is
practice, nor teaching by neither if or
nature, by man to comes it whether then
way? other what in or
```

11.41   Write and test a recursive function that implements the *Interpolation Search*. This is the same as the Binary Search (Example 11.3 on page 255), except that the division point `div` (named `mid` in the Binary search) is selected each time so that the ratio `(div - first)/ (last - first)` is the same as the ratio `(x - a[first])/(a[last] - a[first])`. Note that this is the "common sense" algorithm that most people use when they look up a word in the dictionary.

11.42   Run the Towers of Hanoi solution for 5 and for 6 disks.

11.43   Modify the Towers of Hanoi function so that it counts and prints the number of disk moves made. Then extend this sequence {0, 1, 3, 5, 11, ...} up to the case of 10 disks. Use this empirical data to obtain a formula for the number of moves for *n* disks.

11.44   Modify Example 11.3 on page 255 using the alternative identities

$$\sin x = (4 \cos^2(x/3) - 1) \sin(x/3)$$

$$\cos x = (1 - 4 \sin^2(x/3)) \cos(x/3)$$

11.45 Implement the hyperbolic sine and cosine (sinh x and cosh x) using mutual recursion and the identities:

$$\sinh x = 2 \sinh(x/2) \cosh(x/2)$$
$$\cosh x = 1 + 2 \sinh^2(x/2)$$
$$\sinh x \approx x + x^3/6$$
$$\cosh x \approx 1 + x^2/2$$

Solutions

11.1 The *basis* of a recursive function is its starting point in its definition and its final step when it is being called recursively; it is what stops the recursion. The *recursive part* of a recursive function is the assignment that includes the function on the right side of the assignment operator, causing the function to call itself; it is what produces the repetition. For example, in the factorial function, the basis is $n! = 1$ if $n = 0$, and the recursive part is $n! = n \cdot (n-1)$ if $n > 0$.

11.2 The call `factorial(10)` will generate 10 recursive calls.

11.3 The call `f(6)` to the Fibonacci function will generate $14 + 8 = 22$ recursive calls because it calls `f(5)` and `f(4)`, which generate 14 and 8 recursive calls, respectively.

11.4 A recursive solution is often easier to understand than its equivalent iterative solution. But recursion runs more slowly than iteration.

11.5 The number of recursive calls that the Binary Search function will make on an array of 1000 elements is the number of times the list can be divided in half: $\lg n = \lg 1000 = 10$. If the item is not in the list, the function has to make one more call to stop the recursion. So the maximum number of possible recursive calls is 11.

11.6 The Binary Search has $O(\lg n)$ complexity, which means that its running time is roughly proportional to $\lg n$, where n is the number of elements in the array. Since $\lg(n^2) = 2 \cdot \lg n$, squaring the size of the array should double the running time of the search. Therefore, it should take about 14 milliseconds to run the Binary Search on the array of 62,500 elements (since $62,500 = 250^2$).

11.7
```
<expr> → <term>
       → <term> + <term>
       → <term> * <factor> + <term>
       → <factor> * <factor> + <factor>
       → <num> * <num> + <num>
       → <num> <bit> * <num> <bit> + <bit>
       → <bit> <bit> * <num> <bit> <bit> + <bit>
       → <bit> <bit> * <bit> <bit> <bit>  + <bit>
       → 1 0 * 1 1 0 + 1 = 10*110+1
```

11.8
```
<identifier> ::= <alpha/num-char> <digit>
<alpha/num-char> ::= <alpha> | _ | <digit>
<alpha> ::= <upper-alpha> | <lower-alpha>
<upper-alpha> ::= A | B | C | D | E | F | G | H | I | J | K | L
                  M | N | O | P | Q | R | S | T | U | V | W | X
                  Y | Z
<lower-alpha> ::= a | b | c | d | e | f | g | h | i | j | k | l
                  m | n | o | p | q | r | s | t | u | v | w | x
                  y | z
<digit> ::= 0 | 1 | 2 | 3 | 4 | 5 | 6 | 7 | 8 | 9
```

11.9
```
<hexa-num> ::= <hexa-digit> | <hexa-num> <hexa-digit>
<hexa-digit> ::= <hexa-alpha> | <digit>
<hexa-alpha> ::= A | B | C | D | E | F | a | b | c | d | e | f
<digit> ::= 0 | 1 | 2 | 3 | 4 | 5 | 6 | 7 | 8 | 9
```

11.10 <sentence> →☐ <subject> <predicate>.

   →☐ <noun-phrase> <predicate> .

   →☐ <noun-phrase> <verb> <noun-phrase> .

   →☐ <article> <noun> <verb> <article> <adjective> <noun>.

   →☐ my brother kissed your sister.

11.11 Just handle some more of the lower-value cases non-recursively:
```
int factorial(int n)
{ if (n == 0 || n == 1) return 1;
  if (n == 2) return 2;
  if (n == 3) return 6;
  return n*factorial(n-1);
}
```

11.12 This is similar to Example 11.3 on page 255:
```
int sumOfSquares(int n)
{ if (n == 0) return 0;
  return n*n + sumOfSquares(n-1);
}
```

11.13 This is similar to Example 11.3 on page 255:
```
void reverse(ofstream& output, ifstream& input)
{ char buffer[80];
  if (input.getline(buffer, 80))
  { reverse(output, input);
    output << buffer << endl;
  }
}
```

11.14 This is similar to Example 11.3 on page 255:
```
float power(float x, int n)
{ if (n == 0) return 1;
  return x*power(x, n-1);
}
```

11.15 This modifies the solution to Problem 11.14:
```
float power(float x, int n)
{ if (n == 0) return 1;
  if (n%2) return x*power(x, n-1);
  float y = power(x, n/2);
  return y*y;
}
```
Note the need here for the local variable y. Without it, two (identical) recursive calls would be required.

11.16 This is similar to Example 11.3 on page 255:
```
float max(float a[], int n)
{ if (n == 1) return a[0];
  float m = max(a, n-1);
  if (a[n-1] > m) return a[n-1];
  return m;
}
```

11.17
```
float max(float a[], int lo, int hi)
{ if (lo == hi) return a[lo];
  int mid = (lo + hi)/2;
  float maxlo = max(a, lo, mid), maxhi = max(a, mid+1, hi);
  return (maxlo > maxhi ? maxlo : maxhi);
}
```

11.18
```
void print_binary(int n)
{ if (n >= 2) print_binary(n/2);
  cout << n%2;
}
```

11.19
```
void print_octal(int n)
{ if (n >= 8) print_octal(n/8);
  cout << n%8;
}
```

11.20
```
char hex(int n)                 // returns the hexadecimal digit for n
{ assert(n >= 0 && n < 16);
  if (n < 10) return char('0' + n);
  else return char('a' + n - 10);
}
void print_hexadecimal(int n)
{ if (n >= 16) print_hexadecimal(n/16);
  cout << hex(n%16);
}
```

11.21
```
int f(int n)
{ if (n < 2) return n;
  int f0=0, f1=1, f2;
  for (int i=2; i < n; i++)
  { f2 = f0 + f1;
    f0 = f1;
    f1 = f2;
  }
  return (f0 + f1);
}
```

11.22
```
int c(int n, int k)
{ if (k < 0 || k > n) return 0;
  if (k == 0 || k == n) return 1;
  return c(n-1, k-1) + c(n-1, k);
}
```

11.23
```
int lg(int n)
{ if (n < 2) return 0;
  return lg(n/2) + 1;
}
```

11.24 The calling tree is shown on the next page.

11.25
```
int gcd(int m, int n)
{ while (m != n)
  { if (m > n)
    { int temp = m;
      m = n;
      n = temp;
    }
    n -= m;
  }
  return n;
}
```

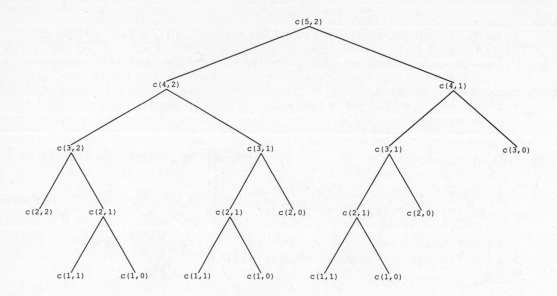

11.26
```
int find(float* a, int start, int stop, float x)
{ while (start <= stop)
   { int mid = (start + stop)/2;
     if (x == a[mid]) return mid;
     if (x < a[mid]) stop = mid - 1;
     if (x > a[mid]) start = mid + 1;
   }
   return -1;
}
```

11.27 *a.*
```
int ackermann(int m, int n)
{ if (m == 0) return n+1;
   else if (n == 0) return ackermann(m-1, 1);
   else return ackermann(m-1, ackermann(m, n-1));
}
int main()
{ for (int m=0; m <= 3; m++)
   { for (int n=0; n <= 8; n++)
     { cout.width(8);
       cout << ackermann(m, n);
     }
     cout << endl;
   }
}
```
The output is

1	2	3	4	5	6	7	8
2	3	4	5	6	7	8	9
3	5	7	9	11	13	15	17
5	13	29	61	125	253	509	1021

b. By definition $A(1,1) = A(0, A(1,0)) = A(0, A(0,1)) = A(0,2) = 3$, so for $n = 0$:
$A(3,n) = A(3,0) = A(2,1) = A(1, A(2,0)) = A(1, A(1,1)) = A(1,3) = A(0, A(1,2)) = A(0, A(0, A(1,1)))$
$= A(0, A(0,3)) = A(0, 4) = 5$, and $2^{n+3} - 3 = 2^{0+3} - 3 = 2^3 - 3 = 8 - 3 = 5$.

c. $A(4,4) = A(3, A(4,3))$, $A(4,3) = A(3, A(4,2))$, $A(4,2) = A(3, A(4,1))$, $A(4,1) = A(3, A(4,0))$,

$A(4,0) = A(3,1) = 13$, $\therefore A(4,1) = A(3, A(4,0)) = A(3, 13) = 2^{13+3} - 3 = 2^{16} - 3 = 65536 - 3 = 65533$,

$\therefore A(4,2) = A(3, A(4,1)) = A(3, 65533) = 2^{65533+3} - 3 = 2^{65536} - 3 \approx 2^{65536} = 2\text{^}65536 = 2\text{^}2\text{^}16$,

$\therefore A(4,3) = A(3, A(4,2)) \approx A(3, 2\text{^}2\text{^}16) = 2^{2\text{^}2\text{^}16+3} - 3 \approx 2^{2\text{^}2\text{^}16} = 2\text{^}2\text{^}2\text{^}16$,

$\therefore A(4,4) = A(3, A(4,3)) \approx A(3, 2\text{^}2\text{^}2\text{^}16) = 2^{2\text{^}2\text{^}2\text{^}16+3} - 3 \approx 2^{2\text{^}2\text{^}2\text{^}166} = 2\text{^}2\text{^}2\text{^}2\text{^}16$.

If we introduce the notation $b^{\wedge\wedge}n$ to represent $b^\wedge b^\wedge b^\wedge b^\wedge b^\wedge \cdots ^\wedge b$ (n bs), then we can express

$A(4,0) = 13 \approx 16 = 2\text{^}2\text{^}2 = 2^{\wedge\wedge}3$,

$A(4,1) = 65535 \approx 65536 = 2\text{^}2\text{^}2\text{^}2 = 2^{\wedge\wedge}4$,

$A(4,2) = 2^{65536} - 3 \approx 2^{2^{\wedge\wedge}4} = 2^{\wedge\wedge}5$,

$A(4,3) \approx 2^{2^{\wedge\wedge}5} = 2^{\wedge\wedge}6$,

$A(4,4) \approx 2^{2^{\wedge\wedge}6} = 2^{\wedge\wedge}7$.

This is called *super exponentiation.*

Note that $A(4,2) \approx 2^{\wedge\wedge}5$ is far greater than the estimated number (10^{81}) of particles in the universe.

d. From the definition and from parts *a–c* above, we can conclude

$A(0, n) = n + 1$,

$A(1, n) = n + 2$,

$A(2, n) = 2n + 3$,

$A(3, n) = 2^{n+3} - 3$,

$A(4, n) \approx 2^{\wedge\wedge}(n + 3)$

$A(5, 0) = A(4, 1) = 2^{\wedge\wedge}5$

Then, since $A(m, n)$ increases with m and with n, it follows that $A(m, n) \leq 2,147,483,647$ only for:

$m = 0$ and $n \leq 2,147,483,646$,

$m = 1$ and $n \leq 2,147,483,645$,

$m = 2$ and $n \leq 1,073,741,822$,

$m = 3$ and $n \leq 14$,

$m = 4$ and $n \leq 1$.

11.28
```
void print(Maze m, int n, int i, int j, int d)
{ if (d != 0 && m[i+1,j])
  { cout << " -> (" << i+1 << ", " << j << ")";
    print(m, n, i+1, j, 0);
  } else if (d != 1 && m[i,j+1])
  { cout << " -> (" << i << ", " << j+1 << ")";
    print(m, n, i, j+1, 1);
  } else if (d != 2 && m[i-1,j])
  { cout << " -> (" << i-1 << ", " << j << ")";
    print(m, n, i-1, j, 2);
  } else if (d != 3 && m[i,j-1])
  { cout << " -> (" << i << ", " << j-1 << ")";
    print(m, n, i, j-1, 3);
  }
}
```

11.29 This function prints permutations:
```
void print(string s, int k, int n)
{ if (k == n)
  { for (int i=0; i<=n; i++)
      cout << s[i];
    cout << endl;
  }
  else
    for (int i=k; i <= n; i++)
    { swap(s[i], s[k]);
      print(s, k+1, n);
      swap(s[i], s[k]);
    }
}
```

Here is a test driver for it:
```
int main()
{ int n;
  cin >> n;
  print("ABCDEFG", 0, n-1);
}
```

11.30
```
int sum(int n)
{ if (n < 2) return n;
  return n + sum(n-1);
}
```

11.31
```
int sum(int n)
{ if (n < 2) return n;
  return n*n*n + sum(n-1);
}
```

11.32
```
void print(int n)
{ if (n == 0) return;
  print(n-1);
  cout << "*";
}
```

11.33
```
int log(int b, int n)
{ if (n < b) return 0;
  return 1 + log(b, n/b);
}
```

Here is a test driver for it:
```
int main()
{ for (int n=10; n<260; n += 10)
  { cout << "\t" << n << "\t" << log(3, n) << endl;
    cout << "\t\t" << int(log(n)/log(3)) << endl;
  }
}
```

11.34
```
int fib[100];
int f(int n)
{ if (n < 2) return fib[n] = n;
  return fib[n] = f(n-1) + f(n-2);
}
```

11.35
```
const double PHI = 1.618033988749895;   // the Golden Mean
const double PSI = 1.0 - PHI;   // the conjugate of the Golden Mean
double recip_sqrt5 = 1.0/sqrt(5.0);
double f(int n)
{ return recip_sqrt5*(pow(PHI,n) - pow(PSI,n));
}
```

11.36 This test driver finds the first positive integer for which the `factorial()` function overflows:
```
int main()
{ long fact, pre=1;
  for (int n=1; n < 100; n++)
  { fact = factorial(n);
    cout << setw(4) << setiosflags(ios::right) << n << "! = "
         << setw(12) << factorial(n)
         << setw(20) << fact << "/" << pre << " = "
            << fact/pre << endl;
```

```
        if (fact/pre != n) break;
      pre = fact;
    }
  }
```

The condition `(fact/pre != n)` will be false when `factorial(n)` $\neq n!$. On the author's UNIX workstation, this happens when $n = 13$. Here is the revised function:

```
int factorial(int n)
{ assert(n >= 0 && n <= 12);
  // 12! =          479,001,600
  // 13! =        6,227,020,800
  // LONG_MAX == 2,147,483,647
  if (n == 0 || n == 1) return 1;
  if (n == 2) return 2;
  if (n == 3) return 6;
  return n*factorial(n-1);
}
```

11.37
```
int lcm(int m, int n)
// returns the least common multiple of m and n
{ return m*n/gcd(m,n);
}
```

Chapter 12

Trees

12.1 GENERAL TREES

A *tree of order k* is either the empty set or a pair (r, S), where r is a single element and S is a sequence of k disjoint trees. The single element r is called the *root* of the tree and the elements of the set S are called its *subtrees*. If all the subtrees of a root are empty then the root is called a *leaf*.

In general, roots are called *nodes*. If x is a node and y is the root of a subtree of x, then we call y a *child* of x and x the parent of y. More generally, if there is a sequence of nodes $x_0, x_1, x_2, ..., x_n$ where each x_i is the parent of x_{i+1}, then we call x_0 an *ancestor* of x_n and x_n a *descendant* of x_0. In this case, we call the sequence $(x_0, x_1, x_2, ..., x_n)$ a *path* from x_0 to x_n. Note that the root of a tree is the only node that has no parents, and the leaves are the nodes that have no children (*i.e.*, all their subtrees are empty). Nodes that do have children are called *interior* nodes. The *depth* of a node is the number of its ancestors. The *height* of a tree is the maximum depth of its nodes. The empty tree is defined to have height -1.

EXAMPLE 12.1 A Tree of Height 3 and Order 4

The tree shown at right has 15 nodes, 6 interior nodes (A, B, C, E, G, H), and 9 leaf nodes (D, F, J, K, L, M, N, O). Node A is its root. Node C is the parent of node H. The tree has height 3 because the deepest leaves (K, L, M, N, O, and P) have depth 3. The tree has order 4 because the node with the most children, C, has 4 children.

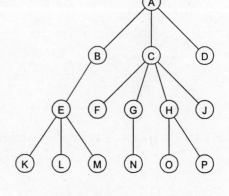

EXAMPLE 12.2 A Tree of Height 3 and Order 6

The tree shown below has 16 nodes, 1 at level 0, 6 at level 1, 4 at level 2, and 5 at level 3. It has height 3 and order 6.

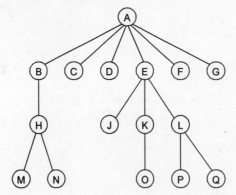

276

Sometimes it helps to partition a tree into its various levels. The subset of all nodes of depth d form the *level d* for a tree. A tree of height h has the $h + 1$ levels 0, 1, 2, ..., h. The tree in Example 12.2 has its 4 levels labeled.

12.2 BINARY TREES

A *binary tree* is a tree of order 2. This means that every node has exactly two subtrees, either one of which may be empty. They are called the *left subtree* and the *right subtree* of the node. If they are non-empty, their roots are called the *left child* and the *right child* of the node.

EXAMPLE 12.3 A Binary Tree of Height 4
This binary tree has 14 nodes, 5 leaves, and height 4:

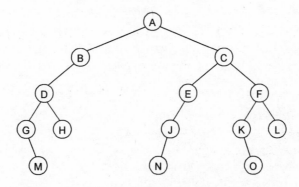

The left child of node B is node D. Node B has no right child because its right subtree is empty.

A binary tree is *full* if all its leaves are at the same level and every interior node has two children.

EXAMPLE 12.4 The Full Binary Tree of Height 3
The tree shown at right is the full binary tree of height 3.
Note that it has 15 nodes: 7 interior nodes and 8 leaves.

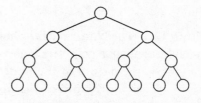

Theorem 12.1 The full binary tree of height h has $2^{h+1} - 1$ nodes: $2^h - 1$ internal nodes and 2^h leaves.
Proof: The full binary tree of height $h = 0$ is a single leaf node; so it has $2^h - 1 = 2^0 - 1 = 1 - 1 = 0$ internal nodes and $2^h = 2^0 = 1$ leaf. More generally, assume (the inductive hypothesis) that the theorem is true for all full binary trees of height less than $h > 0$. Then consider a full binary tree of height h. Both of its subtrees has height $h - 1$, so we apply the formulas to them: $m_L = 2^{h-1} - 1$, $m_R = 2^{h-1} - 1$, $l_L = 2^{h-1}$, and $l_R = 2^{h-1}$. Then
$$m = m_L + m_R + 1 = (2^{h-1} - 1) + (2^{h-1} - 1) + 1 = 2 \cdot 2^{h-1} - 1 = 2^l - 1,$$
and
$$l = l_L + l_R = 2^{h-1} + 2^{h-1} = 2 \cdot 2^{h-1} = 2^h.$$

Q.E.D.

Corollary 12.1 The full binary tree of height h has $n = 2^{h+1} - 1$ nodes, so $h + 1 = \lg(n+1)$.

Corollary 12.2 In any binary tree with n nodes and height h: $h + 1 \le n \le 2^{h+1} - 1$ and $\lfloor \lg n \rfloor \le h \le n - 1$.

A *complete binary tree* is either a full binary tree or one that can be made into a full binary tree by adding leaves on the right at the bottom level.

EXAMPLE 12.5 A Complete Binary Tree of Height 3

The tree shown at right can be made into the full binary tree of height 3 by adding 5 leaves on the right at level 3.

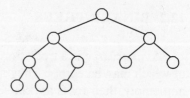

Theorem 12.2 In a complete binary tree with n nodes of height h: $2^h \le n \le 2^{h+1} - 1$, and $h = \lfloor \lg n \rfloor$.

Complete binary trees are important because of the simple way in which they can be stored in an array. This is achieved by assigning index numbers to the tree nodes by level, as shown in the picture below. The beauty in this natural mapping lies in simple way that it allows array locations of the children and parent nodes of a node stored in the array.

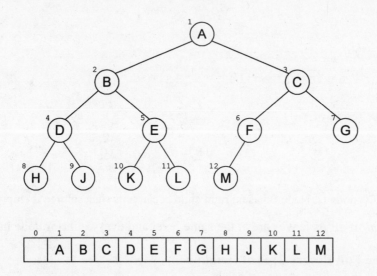

Algorithm 12.1 The Natural Mapping of a Complete Binary Tree into an Array

To navigate about a complete binary tree stored by its natural mapping in an array:
1. the parent of the node stored at location k is stored at location $k/2$;
2. the left child of the node stored at location k is stored at location $2k$;
3. the right child of the node stored at location k is stored at location $2k + 1$.

For example, node E is stored at location $k = 5$ in the array; its parent (node B) is stored at location $k/2 = 5/2 = 2$ in the array, its left child (node K) is stored at location $2k = 2 \cdot 5 = 10$ in the array, and its right child (node L) is stored at location $2k + 1 = 2 \cdot 5 + 1 = 11$ in the array.

The use of the adjective "complete" should now be clear: The defining property for complete binary trees is precisely the condition that guarantees that the natural mapping will store its nodes in an array with no empty elements. A binary tree that is not complete, such as the one shown in Example 12.3 above would leave gaps in the array. (See Problem 12.12.)

Warning: Some authors use the term "almost complete binary tree" for a complete binary tree and the term "complete binary tree" for a full binary tree.

12.3 TREE TRAVERSALS

Trees are nonlinear data structures. So it is not obvious how to *traverse* a tree; *i.e.*, to move systematically from one node to the next, visiting each node exactly once.

The most obvious way to traverse a general tree is the same method used above in the natural mapping of a complete binary tree: move from left to right, level by level. This is called the *level order traversal*.

Algorithm 12.2 The Level Order Traversal of a General Tree

To traverse a non-empty tree of height *h*:

1. Visit the root.
2. For each level, from level 1 to level *h*, visit the nodes from left to right.

EXAMPLE 12.6 A Level Order Traversal

The level order traversal of the tree shown in Example 12.1 visits the nodes in the order A, B, C, D, E, F, G, H, J, K, L, M, N, O, P.

There are two other standard traversal algorithms for general trees: the *preorder traversal* and the *postorder traversal*. They are very similar. They are also both recursive.

Algorithm 12.3 The Preorder Traversal of a General Tree

To traverse a non-empty tree:

1. Visit the root.
2. Do a preorder traversal on each subtree.

EXAMPLE 12.7 The Preorder Traversal of a Tree of Order 4

The preorder traversal of the tree shown in Example 12.1 visits the nodes in the order A, B, E, K, L, M, C, F, G, N, H, O, P, J, D.

Algorithm 12.4 The Postorder Traversal of a General Tree

To traverse a non-empty tree:

1. Do a postorder traversal on each subtree.
2. Visit the root.

EXAMPLE 12.8 The Postorder Traversal of a Tree of Order 4

The level order traversal of the tree shown in Example 12.1 visits the nodes in the order K, L, M, E, B, F, N, G, O, P, H, J, C, D, A.

Both the preorder and the postorder algorithms are usually expressed in their specialized versions for binary trees:

Algorithm 12.5 The Preorder Traversal of a Binary Tree

To traverse a non-empty binary tree:

1. Visit the root.
2. If the left subtree is non-empty, do a preorder traversal on it.
3. If the right subtree is non-empty, do a preorder traversal on it.

EXAMPLE 12.9 The Preorder Traversal of a Binary Tree

The picture below shows the preorder traversal on the full binary tree of height 3. The nodes are visited in the order A, B, D, H, J, E, K, L, C, F, M, N, G, O, P.

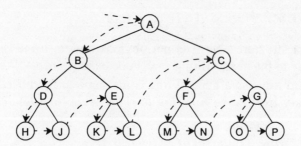

Note that the preorder traversal of a binary tree can be obtained by circum-navigating the tree, beginning at the root and visiting each node the first time it is encountered on the left side of the route. This is illustrated by the picture here.

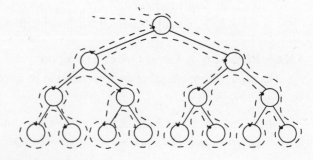

Algorithm 12.6 The Postorder Traversal of a Binary Tree
To traverse a non-empty binary tree:
      1. If the left subtree is non-empty, do a postorder traversal on it.
      2. If the right subtree is non-empty, do a postorder traversal on it.
      3. Visit the root.

EXAMPLE 12.10 The Postorder Traversal of a Binary Tree
Here is how the preorder traversal looks on the full binary tree of height 3:

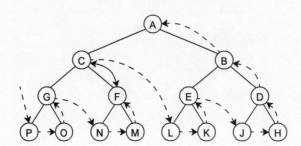

The nodes are visited in the order P, O, G, N, M, F, C, L, K, E, J, H, D, B, A.

The Preorder Traversal visits the root first and the Postorder Traversal visits the root last. This suggests a third alternative for binary trees: visit the root in between the traversals of the two subtrees. That is called the *inorder traversal*.

Algorithm 12.7 The Inorder Traversal of a Binary Tree
To traverse a non-empty binary tree:
      1. If the left subtree is non-empty, do a preorder traversal on it.
      2. Visit the root.
      3. If the right subtree is non-empty, do a preorder traversal on it.

EXAMPLE 12.11 The Inorder Traversal of a Binary Tree

Here is how the preorder traversal looks on the full binary tree of height 3:

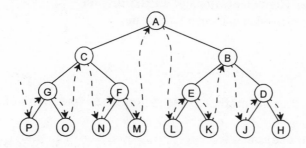

The nodes are visited in the order P, G, O, C, N, F, M, A, L, E, K, B, J, D, H.

12.4 EXPRESSION TREES

An *arithmetic expression* such as `(5 - x)*y + 6/(x + z)` is a combination of *arithmetic operators* (+, -, *, /, *etc.*), *operands* (5, x, y, 6, z, *etc.*), and parentheses to override the precedence of operations. Each expression can be represented by a unique binary tree whose structure is determined by the precedence of operations in the expression. Such a tree is called an *expression tree*.

EXAMPLE 12.12 An Expression Tree

Here is the expression tree for the expression `(5 - x)*y + 6/(x + z)`:

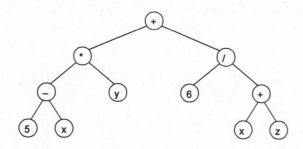

Here is an recursive algorithm for building an expression tree:

Algorithm 12.8 Build an Expression Tree

The expression tree for a given expression can be built recursively from the following rules:

      1. The expression tree for a single operand is a single root node containing that operand.

      2. If E_1 and E_2 are expressions represented by expression trees T_1 and T_2, and if *op* is an operator, then the expression tree for the expression E_1 *op* E_2 is the tree with root node containing *op* and subtrees T_1 and T_2.

An expression has three representations, depending upon which traversal algorithms is used to traverse its tree. The preorder traversal produces the *prefix representation*, the inorder traversal produces the *infix representation*, and the postorder traversal produces the *postfix representation* of the expression. The postfix representation is also called *reverse Polish notation* or *RPN*.

EXAMPLE 12.13 The Three Representations of an Expression

The three representations for the expression in Example 12.12 are:

Prefix:`+*-5xy/6+xz`

Infix:`5-x*y+6/x+z`

Postfix (RPN): `5x-y*6xz+/+`

Ordinary function syntax uses the prefix representation. The expression in Example 12.13 could be evaluated as

`sum(product(difference(5, x), y), quotient(6, sum(x, z)))`

Some scientific calculators use RPN, requiring both operands to be entered before the operator.

An expression can be evaluated by applying the following algorithm to its postfix representation:

Algorithm 12.9 Evaluating an Expression from Its Postfix Representation

To evaluate an expression represented in postfix, scan the representation from left to right:

```
create a stack for operands;
while (not at end of representation)
{ read the next token x from the representation;
  if (op is an operand) push its value onto the stack;
  else
  { pop a from the stack;
    pop b from the stack;
    evaluate c = b op a;
    push c onto the stack;
  }
the top element on the stack is the value of the expression;
```

EXAMPLE 12.14 Evaluating an Expression from Its Postfix Representation

Evaluate the expression in Example 12.13 using 2 for *x*, 3 for *y*, and 1 for *z*:

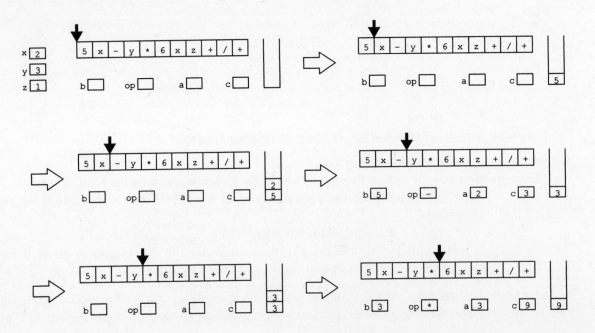

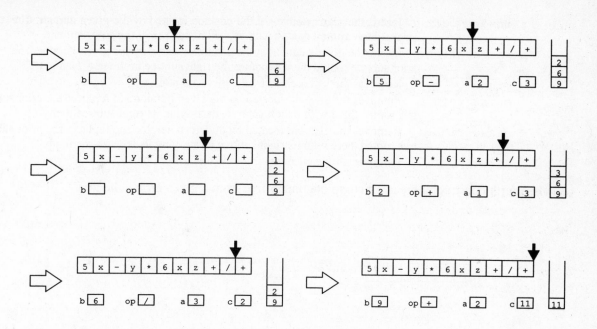

12.5 ADTs FOR BINARY TREES AND THEIR ITERATORS

Since trees are nonlinear structures, they have fewer elementary operations than lists. More of their functionality is managed by their iterators. Here is an ADT for binary trees:

ADT: BinaryTree

Represents:

A container that either is empty or consists of a root element and two disjoint binary trees, called its left subtree and its right subtree.

Access:

Elements are accessed sequentially by means of iterators.

Constructors and Destructors:

create	Creates an empty binary tree.
create	Creates a binary tree with a single given root element.
create	Creates a binary tree with given root, left subtree, and right subtree.
create	Creates a complete binary tree from a given array.
destroy	De-allocates all the memory used for the binary tree.

Access Functions:

is_empty	Returns `true` if the binary tree is empty; otherwise returns `false`.
size	Returns the number of elements in the binary tree.
height	Returns the height of the binary tree.
preorder	Returns a preorder iterator initialized at the root.
inorder	Returns an inorder iterator initialized at the root.
postorder	Returns a postorder iterator initialized at the root.
levelorder	Returns a level-order iterator initialized at the root.
end	Returns an iterator initialized at the dummy end node.

Mutator Functions:

grow_left	Inserts the given element as the left child of the leaf located by the given iterator. Returns an iterator locating the new element.
grow_right	Inserts the given element as the right child of the leaf located by the given iterator. Returns an iterator locating the new element.

insert_left   Inserts the given element at the position located by the given iterator. The prior subtree rooted there becomes the left subtree of the new element.

insert_right   Inserts the given element at the position located by the given iterator. The prior subtree rooted there becomes the right subtree of the new element.

prune   Removes the leaf located by the given iterator.

erase_left   Removes the element located by the given iterator and replaces the prior subtree rooted there with its left subtree, destroying its right subtree if any.

erase_right   Removes the element located by the given iterator and replaces the prior subtree rooted there with its right subtree, destroying its left subtree if any.

clear   Removes all the elements from the tree.

The fourth constructor creates a complete binary tree from a given array, like this:

The actions of the mutator function are illustrated by the diagrams shown below. Note that the grow and prune functions affect only the leaves of the tree, whereas the insert and erase functions can be applied to any element in the tree. The grow and insert functions leave the given iterator unchanged and return an iterator locating the new element. The given iterator is lost with the prune and erase functions. The prune function removes one element, but the erase functions will remove an entire subtree.

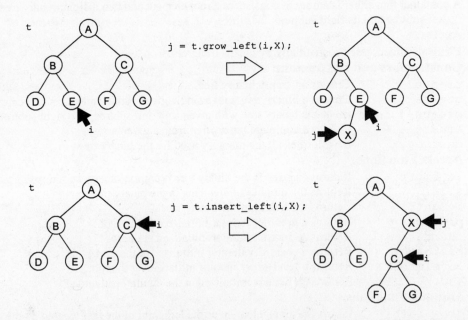

There are four kinds of binary tree iterators, one for each of the four traversal algorithms: preorder, inorder, postorder, and level-order.

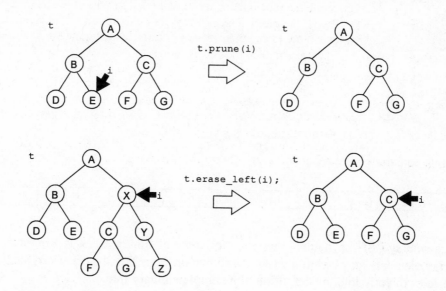

ADT: <u>BinaryTreeIterator</u>

Constructors and Destructors:

`create`	Creates an iterator for a given binary tree and a given traversal order.
`destroy`	De-allocates the memory used by the iterator.

Access Functions:

`order`	Returns an `enum` constants `PRE`, `IN`, `POST`, `LEVEL`, or `END`, indicating what kind of iterator it is.
`reset`	Resets the iterator to the root of the tree.
`is_null`	Returns `true` iff the iterator is not locating an element.
`is_root`	Returns `true` iff the current element is the root of the tree.
`is_leaf`	Returns `true` iff the current element is a leaf.
`dereference`	Returns a reference to the current element.
`parent`	Returns an iterator that locates the parent of the current element.
`left_child`	Returns an iterator that locates the left child of the current element.
`right_child`	Returns an iterator that locates the right child of the current element.

Mutator Functions:

`increment`	Moves the iterator to the next element.
`decrement`	Moves the iterator to the previous element.
`assign`	Assigns a given iterator to it.

Operators:

`equality`	Returns `true` iff the given iterator is equal to it.
`inequality`	Returns `true` iff the given iterator is not equal to it.

Compare these ADTs with those for lists (page 202) and their iterators (page 200).

12.6 CONTIGUOUS IMPLEMENTATION

Like lists, binary trees can be implemented using either contiguous storage or linked storage. The contiguous implementation depends upon the natural level-order numbering of the tree elements: This "linearizes" the tree, designating a unique location in the array for each element.

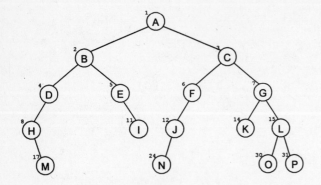

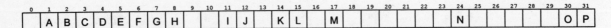

The disadvantage of the natural mapping for general binary trees is obvious: many of the allocated array elements may be left unused. As shown on page 278, the criterion that no elements be unused translates directly into the definition of a complete binary tree.

Theorem 12.3 A binary tree with n elements is complete if and only if its natural mapping maps it into the array elements `a[1]` through `a[n]`, leaving no gaps.

Because of this fact, we use the contiguous implementation only for complete binary trees.

This version uses a `typedef` for the element type instead of a template:

```cpp
typedef short T;
class CompleteBinaryTree
{ public:
    class Iterator
    { public:
        enum Order { END, PRE, IN, POST, LEVEL };
        Iterator(CompleteBinaryTree&, Order=IN);
        Order order();
        bool reset();
        bool operator!();          // returns true iff iterator is null
        bool is_root();
        bool is_leaf();
        T& operator*();        // read-write access to current element
        Iterator parent();
        Iterator left_child();
        Iterator right_child();
        void operator++();
        void operator--();
        friend bool operator==(Iterator&, Iterator&);
        friend bool operator!=(Iterator&, Iterator&);
      private:
        CompleteBinaryTree* _p;           // the tree being traversed
        int _k;              // index locating current element in _p->_v
        Order _order;                 // END, PRE, IN, POST, or LEVEL
        int _start(int);
        int _next_pre(int, int);
        int _next_in(int, int);
        int _next_post(int, int);
    };
```

```
        friend class Iterator;
        CompleteBinaryTree();
        CompleteBinaryTree(T*, int);
        ~CompleteBinaryTree();
        bool is_empty();
        int size();
        int height();
        Iterator preorder();
        Iterator inorder();
        Iterator postorder();
        Iterator levelorder();
        Iterator end();
    protected:
        const int _CAP=2;                          // initial capacity
        T* _v;                            // the dynamic array of elements
        int _size;                         // the number of elements in _v
        int _cap;                   // the number of elements allocated to _v
        _reallocate();                      // doubles the capacity _cap
    };
```

The `Iterator` class is a subclass of the `CompleteBinaryTree` class, so any external reference to its members must include the scope resolution prefix `CompleteBinaryTree::Iterator::` For example, the enumeration constant `CompleteBinaryTree::Iterator::LEVEL` specifies that an iterator uses the level-order traversal algorithm to traverse the tree.

The enumeration type `Order` defines five constants that are used to characterize each `iterator` object. An iterator object whose `_order` field has the value `PRE` will traverse the tree following the preorder traversal algorithm. Similarly, the `IN`, `POST`, and `LEVEL` constants indicate inorder, postorder, or level-order traversal iterators, respectively. The special `END` constant is used to indicate that the iterator is positioned at the "end" of the tree; *i.e.*, at the imaginary position that would follow the last element in any traversal. This provides a return type for the `end()` function that can be used in a loop like this:

```
    CompleteBinaryTree::Iterator it;
    for (it = x.postorder(); it != x.end(); ++it)
        cout << *it << " ";
```

This would print the contents of the tree using a postorder traversal. It is consistent with the `end()` functions defined in the C++ Standard Library. Note that, using the type definition

```
    typedef CompleteBinaryTree::Iterator CBTI;
```

the three lines could be written more simply as

```
    for (CBTI it(x, CBTI::POST); it != x.end(); ++it)
        cout << *it << " ";
```

The `Iterator` subclass leaves its default constructor, its copy constructor, its destructor, and its assignment operator to be defined by the compiler. The constructor declared here takes two arguments: a pointer to the tree to which it is bound, and one of the five enumeration constants to indicate what traversal order algorithm it uses or if it is an "end" iterator.

The picture below shows a preorder iterator `i` bound to a tree `x` and their implementations. The iterator object's pointer `_p` points to the `CompleteBinaryTree` object to which it is bound. Its data member `_k` is the array index of the iterator's current element (66), and its `_order` member has the value `PRE`, indicating that it is a preorder traversal iterator. The tree object contains the dynamic array `_v` and the two `int`s `_size` and `_cap`. The array elements `_v[1]` through `_v[_size]` contain the actual tree elements. The member `_cap` (for "capacity") contains the actual number (8) of elements allocated to the array. When `_size == _cap-1`, the array is automatically

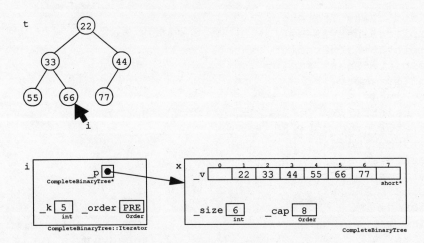

resized, doubling its capacity. That maintenance activity is handled by the `_reallocate()` function.

The mutator functions defined in the **BinaryTree** ADT are not implemented for the `CompleteBinaryTree` class because their actions do not preserve completeness, as the pictures on page 284 show.

EXAMPLE 12.15 Testing the `CompleteBinaryTree` Class

This program illustrates the use of the `CompleteBinaryTree` Class:

```
const int SIZE=20;
void print_family(CBTI& it)
{ CBTI pt = it.parent();
  CBTI lt = it.left_child();
  CBTI rt = it.right_child();
  cout << *it << " has";
  if(!pt) cout << " no parent ";
  else cout << " parent " << *pt;
  if(!lt) cout << ", no left child ";
  else cout << ", left child " << *lt;
  if(!rt) cout << ", and no right child.\n";
  else cout << ", and right child " << *rt << ".\n";
}
int main()
{ short a[SIZE+1];
  for (int i=1; i<SIZE+1; i++)
    a[i] = i;
  CBT x(a, SIZE);
  cout << "\nPreorder traversal:\n";
  for (CBTI it(x, CBTI::PRE); it != x.end(); ++it)
    cout << *it << " ";
  cout << "\nInorder traversal:\n";
  for (it = x.inorder(); it != x.end(); ++it)
    cout << *it << " ";
  cout << "\nPostorder traversal:\n";
  for (it = x.postorder(); it != x.end(); ++it)
    cout << *it << " ";
```

```
    cout << "\nLevel-order traversal:\n";
    for (it = x.levelorder(); it != x.end(); ++it)
      cout << *it << " ";
    cout << endl;
    cout << "The tree has " << x.size() << " elements.\n";
    cout << "The tree has " << leaves(x) << " leaves.\n";
    cout << "The height of the tree is " << height(x) << ".\n";
    it = x.preorder();  print_family(it);
    ++it;  print_family(it);
    ++it;    ++it;    ++it;    ++it;
    ++it;  print_family(it);
    ++it;  print_family(it);
    ++it;  print_family(it);
    ++it;  print_family(it);
    ++it;  print_family(it);
  }
```

The output is

```
    Preorder traversal:
    1 2 4 8 16 17 9 18 19 5 10 20 11 3 6 12 13 7 14 15
    Inorder traversal:
    16 8 17 4 18 9 19 2 20 10 5 11 1 12 6 13 3 14 7 15
    Postorder traversal:
    16 17 8 18 19 9 4 20 10 11 5 2 12 13 6 14 15 7 3 1
    Level-order traversal:
    1 2 3 4 5 6 7 8 9 10 11 12 13 14 15 16 17 18 19 20
    The tree has 20 elements.
    The tree has 10 leaves.
    The height of the tree is 4.
    1 has no parent , left child 2, and right child 3.
    2 has parent 1, left child 4, and right child 5.
    9 has parent 4, left child 18, and right child 19.
    18 has parent 9, no left child , and no right child.
    19 has parent 9, no left child , and no right child.
    5 has parent 2, left child 10, and right child 11.
    10 has parent 5, left child 20, and no right child.
```

The complete binary tree looks like this:

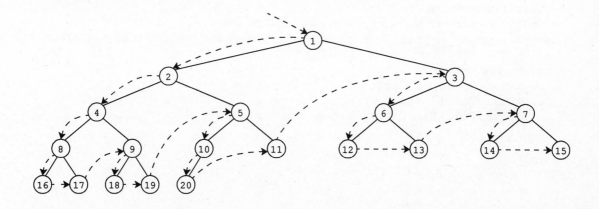

The 20-element tree is created from a 21-element array by the second declared constructor. Then four different iterators are used to traverse the tree by the four traversal algorithms. Next, the `size()`, `leaves()`, and `height()` member functions are tested. Then a special `print_family()` function is used to test the `parent()`, `left_child()`, and `right_child()` member functions.

12.7 LINKED IMPLEMENTATION

Most applications of binary trees require the more general insertion and deletion functions defined in the **BinaryTree** ADT. These are using links, similar to the List implementation on page 204. Again, we use a `typedef` instead of a template:

```
typedef short T;
class BinaryTree
{ private:
    struct Node
    { Node(T& data, Node* left=0, Node* right=0) : _data(data) { }
      T _data;
      Node* _pre;        // points to parent
      Node* _left;
      Node* _right;
    };
  public:
    class Iterator
    {   friend class BinaryTree;
      public:
        enum Order { END, PRE, IN, POST, LEVEL };
        Iterator(BinaryTree&, Order =IN);
        Order order();
        bool reset();
        bool operator!();
        T& operator*();
        bool is_root();
        bool is_leaf();
        Iterator parent();
        Iterator left_child();
        Iterator right_child();
        void operator++();
        friend bool operator==(Iterator&, Iterator&);
        friend bool operator!=(Iterator&, Iterator&);
      private:
        const BinaryTree& _tree;
        Node* _p;
        Order _order;  // END, PRE, IN, POST, or LEVEL
        Node* _start();  // returns the index of starting element
    };
    friend class Iterator;
    BinaryTree() : _root(0) { }
    BinaryTree(T&);
    BinaryTree(T&, BinaryTree&, BinaryTree&);
    BinaryTree(T*, int);
    bool is_empty();
    int size();
    int height();
    Iterator preorder();
    Iterator inorder();
    Iterator postorder();
    Iterator levelorder();
    Iterator end();
    Iterator grow_left(Iterator, const T&);
    Iterator grow_right(Iterator, const T&);
```

```
        Iterator insert_left(Iterator, const T&);
        Iterator insert_right(Iterator, const T&);
        void prune(Iterator);
        void erase_left(Iterator);
        void erase_right(Iterator);
        void clear(Iterator);
    protected:
        Node* _root;
    };
```

The `BinaryTree::Node` type defines three pointers, one to each child and one to the parent. The resulting `BinaryTree` objects that use these nodes are called *threaded trees*.

The `BinaryTree::Iterator` class is nearly the same as the `Iterator` class defined within the `CompleteBinaryTree` class on page 286. The only essential difference is that this version uses `Node` pointers instead of `int`s.

This picture shows the implementation of a preorder iterator `i` bound to a tree `x`:

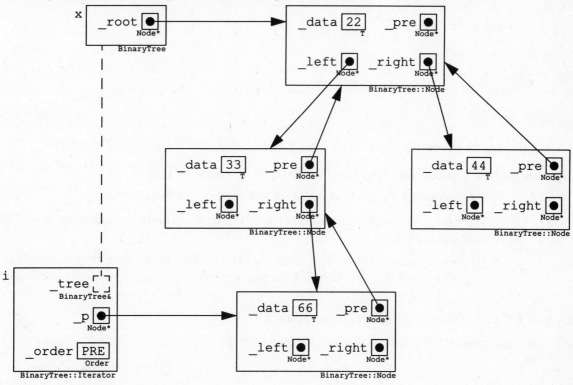

The dashed line indicates that `i._tree` is a reference (*i.e.*, a synonym) for `x`. The black dots without arrows represent null (*i.e.*, 0) pointers.

The implementation shown above represents the BinaryTree object `x` and the Iterator object `i` that we normally would draw as shown in the picture on the right. Compare this with the picture on page 287.

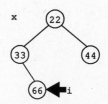

12.8 FORESTS

A *forest* is a collection of trees.

EXAMPLE 12.16 A Forest

Here is a forest consisting or three trees:

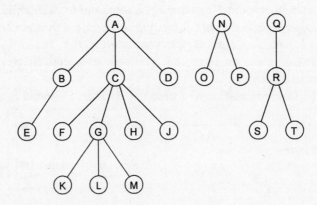

A forest can be represented by a single binary tree by means of the following algorithm:

Algorithm 12.10 The Natural Mapping of a Forest into a Binary Tree

1. Map the root of the first tree into the root of the binary tree.

2. If node X maps into X' and node Y is the first child of X, then map Y into the left child of X'.

3. If node X maps into X' and node Z is the sibling of X, then map Z into the right child of X'. The roots of the trees themselves are considered siblings.

EXAMPLE 12.17 Mapping a Forest into a Binary Tree

Here is the mapping of the forest shown in Example 12.16:

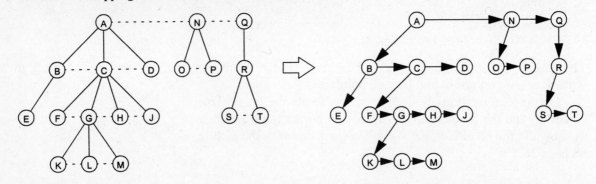

For example, in the original forest, C has oldest child F and next sibling D; so in the resulting binary tree, C has left child F and right child D.

Review Questions

12.1   How many ancestors can the root of a tree have?

12.2   How many descendants can a tree leaf have?

12.3   How many leaf nodes does the full binary tree of height $h = 3$ have?

12.4   How many internal nodes does the full binary tree of height $h = 3$ have?

12.5   How many nodes does the full binary tree of height $h = 3$ have?

12.6   How many leaf nodes does a full binary tree of height h have?

12.7   How many internal nodes does a full binary tree of height h have?

12.8   How many nodes does a full binary tree of height h have?

12.9   What is the range of possible heights of a binary tree with $n = 100$ nodes?

12.10   Why is there no inorder traversal for general trees?

Problems

12.11   Prove Corollary 12.12.2 (on page 277).

12.12   Show the array obtained by using the natural mapping to store the binary tree shown in Example 12.3.

12.13   Give the order of visitation for each of the three standard traversal algorithms (level order, preorder, and postorder) of the tree of order 6 shown in Example 12.2.

12.14   Give the order of visitation for each of the three standard traversal algorithms (level order, preorder, and postorder) of each of the five trees shown in Problem 12.20.

12.15   Give the order of visitation for each of the four standard traversal algorithms (level order, preorder, inorder, and postorder) for the   full binary tree shown here.

12.16   Write the expression tree for the expression $a*(b + c)*(d*e + f)$.

12.17   Write the prefix and the postfix representations for the expressions in Problem 12.16.

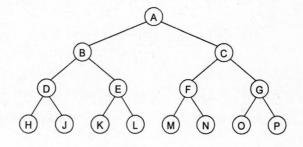

12.18   Draw the binary tree that represents the forest that consists of the single tree that is shown in Example 12.1 on page 276.

12.19   Draw the forest that is represented by the binary tree shown on the right.

12.20   For each of the five trees given below, list the leaf nodes, the children of node C, the depth of node F, all the nodes at level 3, the height of the tree, and the order of the tree.

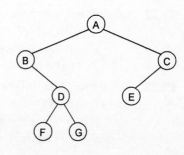

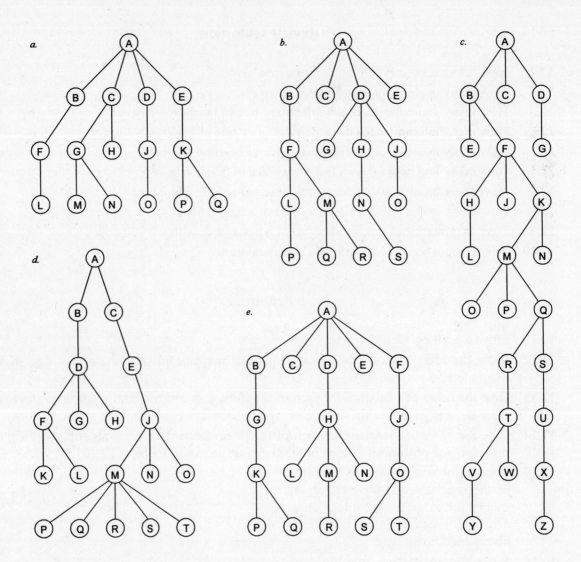

Programming Problems

12.21 Implement the following member function of the `CompleteBinaryTree::Iterator`
class (page 286):

```
bool operator!();
// Returns true iff the iterator is not locating an element.
```

12.22 Implement the following member function of the `BinaryTree::Iterator` class
(page 290):

```
bool operator!();
// Returns true iff the iterator is not locating an element.
```

12.23 Implement the following member function of the `CompleteBinaryTree::Iterator`
class (page 286):

```
bool is_root();
// Returns true iff the current element is the root of the tree.
```

12.24 Implement the following member function of the `BinaryTree::Iterator` **class** (page 290):
```
bool is_root();
// Returns true iff the current element is the root of the tree.
```

12.25 Implement the following member function of the `CompleteBinaryTree::Iterator` class (page 286):
```
bool is_leaf();
// Returns true iff the current element is a leaf of the tree.
```

12.26 Implement the following member function of the `BinaryTree::Iterator` **class** (page 290):
```
bool is_leaf();
// Returns true iff the current element is a leaf of the tree.
```

12.27 Implement the following member function of the `CompleteBinaryTree::Iterator` class (page 286):
```
T& operator*();
// Returns a reference to the current element.
```

12.28 Implement the following member function of the `BinaryTree::Iterator` **class** (page 290):
```
T& operator*();
// Returns a reference to the current element.
```

12.29 Implement the following member function of the `CompleteBinaryTree::Iterator` class (page 286):
```
Iterator parent();
// Returns the location of the parent of the current element.
```

12.30 Implement the following member function of the `CompleteBinaryTree::Iterator` class (page 286):
```
Iterator left_child();
// Returns the location of the left child of the current element.
```

12.31 Implement the following member function of the `CompleteBinaryTree::Iterator` class (page 286):
```
int _start();
// Returns the index of the first element in a traversal.
```

12.32 Implement the following member function of the `CompleteBinaryTree::Iterator` class (page 286):
```
void operator++();
// Advances the iterator to the next element.
```

12.33 Implement the following member function of the `CompleteBinaryTree` class (page 286):
```
bool is_empty();
// Returns true iff the tree is empty.
```

12.34 Implement the following non-member function for the `CompleteBinaryTree` class:
```
int leaves(CompleteBinaryTree& x);
// Returns the number of leaves in the tree x.
```

12.35 Implement the following non-member function for the `CompleteBinaryTree` class:
```
int depth(Iterator& it);
// Returns the depth of *it.
```

12.36 Implement the following non-member function for the `CompleteBinaryTree` class:
```
int height(CompleteBinaryTree& x);
// Returns the height of x.
```

12.37 Implement the following member function of the `BinaryTree::Iterator` class (page 290):

```
Iterator parent();
// Returns the location of the parent of the current element.
```

12.38 Implement the following member function of the `BinaryTree::Iterator` class (page 290):

```
Iterator left_child();
// Returns the location of the left child of the current element.
```

12.39 Implement the following member function of the `BinaryTree::Iterator` class (page 290):

```
Node* _start();
// Returns a pointer that points to the first traversal element.
```

12.40 Implement the following member function of the `BinaryTree::Iterator` class (page 290):

```
void operator++();
// Advances the iterator to the next element.
```

12.41 Implement the following member function of the `CompleteBinaryTree` class (page 286):

```
int size();
// Returns the number of elements in the tree.
```

12.42 Implement the following member function of the `BinaryTree` class (page 290):

```
int size();
// Returns the number of elements in the tree.
```

12.43 Implement the following member function of the `BinaryTree` class (page 290):

```
bool is_empty();
```

12.44 Implement the following member function of the `CompleteBinaryTree` class (page 286):

```
int height();
// Returns the height of the tree.
```

12.45 Implement the following member function of the `BinaryTree` class (page 290):

```
int height();
// Returns the height of the tree.
```

12.46 Implement the following member function of the `CompleteBinaryTree` class (page 286):

```
Iterator preorder();
// Returns an iterator on the tree with PRE _order.
```

12.47 Implement the following member function of the `BinaryTree` class (page 290):

```
Iterator preorder();
// Returns an iterator on the tree with PRE _order.
```

12.48 Implement the following member function of the `BinaryTree` class (page 290):

```
Iterator grow_left(Iterator i, const T& t);
// Inserts the element t as the left child of the leaf element
*i.
// Returns an iterator locating the new element.
```

12.49 Implement the following member function of the `BinaryTree` class (page 290):

```
Iterator insert_left(Iterator i, const T& t);
// Inserts the element t at the position i. The prior subtree
// rooted there becomes the left subtree of the new element.
// Returns an iterator locating the new element.
```

12.50 Implement the following member function of the `BinaryTree` class (page 290):

```
void prune(Iterator i);
// Removes the leaf element *i.
```

12.51 Implement the following member function of the `BinaryTree` class (page 290):

```
void erase_left(Iterator i);
// Removes the element *i and replaces it with its left subtree,
// destroying its right subtree.
```

12.52 Implement the following member function of the `CompleteBinaryTree` class (page 286):

```
void clear();
// Removes all the elements from the tree.
```

12.53 Implement the following member function of the `BinaryTree` class (page 290):

```
void clear();
// Removes all the elements from the tree.
```

12.54 Implement the following member function of the `CompleteBinaryTree` class (page 286):

```
BinaryTree& operator=(const BinaryTree&);
// Assignment operator.
```

12.55 Implement the following member function of the `BinaryTree` class (page 290):

```
BinaryTree& operator=(const BinaryTree&);
// Assignment operator.
```

12.56 Implement the following non-member function for the `BinaryTree` class (page 290):

```
int leaves(BinaryTree& x);
// Returns the number of leaves in the tree x.
```

12.57 Implement the following non-member function for the `BinaryTree` class (page 290):

```
int depth(Iterator& it);
// Returns the depth of *it.
```

12.58 Implement the following non-member function for the `BinaryTree` class (page 290):

```
int height(BinaryTree& x);
// Returns the height of x.
```

12.59 Implement the following non-member function for the `BinaryTree` class (page 290):

```
Iterator grandparent(Iterator& it);
// Returns the location of the grandparent of *it.
```

12.60 Implement the following non-member function for the `BinaryTree` class (page 290):

```
Iterator sibling(Iterator& it);
// Returns the location of the sibling of *it.
```

12.61 Implement the following non-member function for the `BinaryTree` class (page 290):

```
Iterator uncle(Iterator& it);
// Returns the location of the uncle (aunt) of *it.
```

12.62 Implement the following non-member function for the `BinaryTree` class (page 290):

```
int ancestors(Iterator& it);
// Returns the number of ancestors of *it.
```

12.63 Implement the following non-member function for the `BinaryTree` class (page 290):

```
int descendants(Iterator& it);
// Returns the number of descendants of *it.
```

12.64 Implement the following non-member function for the `BinaryTree` class (page 290):

```
void reflect(BinaryTree& x);
// Transforms x into its mirror image.
```

12.65 Implement the following non-member function for the `BinaryTree` class (page 290):

```
void defoliate(BinaryTree& x);
// Removes all of the leaves of x.
```

12.66 Implement the following non-member function for the `BinaryTree` class (page 290). A binary tree is *balanced* if at every node, the difference between the heights of the two subtrees is no more than 1:
```
bool is_balanced(BinaryTree& x);
// Returns true iff x is balanced.
```

12.67 Implement the following non-member function for the `BinaryTree` class (page 290):
```
bool is_full(BinaryTree& x);
// Returns true iff x is full.
```

12.68 Implement the following non-member function for the `BinaryTree` class (page 290):
```
bool is_complete(BinaryTree& x);
// Returns true iff x is complete.
```

12.69 Modify the contiguous implementation of the `CompleteBinaryTree` class on page 286, using the Standard type `vector<T>` in place of the array `_v`.

Solutions

12.1 The root of a tree cannot have any ancestors because it has no parents.

12.2 A leaf cannot have any descendants because it has no children.

12.3 The full binary tree of height h has 2^h leaves. So the full binary tree of height 3 has $2^3 = 8$ leaves.

12.4 The full binary tree of height h has $2^h - 1$ internal nodes. So the full binary tree of height 3 has $2^3 - 1 = 7$ internal nodes.

12.5 The full binary tree of height h has $2^{h+1} - 1$ nodes. So the full binary tree of height 3 has $2^{3+1} - 1 = 2^4 - 1 = 16 - 1 = 15$ nodes.

12.6 The full binary tree of height h has 2^h leaves.

12.7 The full binary tree of height h has $2^h - 1$ internal nodes.

12.8 The full binary tree of height h has $2^{h+1} - 1$ nodes.

12.9 By Corollary 12.12.2 (on page 277), in any binary tree: $\lfloor \lg n \rfloor \le h \le n-1$. Thus in a binary tree with 100 nodes $\lfloor \lg 100 \rfloor \le h \le 100-1 = 99$. Since $\lfloor \lg 100 \rfloor = \lfloor (\log 100)/(\log 2) \rfloor = \lfloor 6.6 \rfloor = 6$, it follows that the height must be between 6 and 99, inclusive: $6 \le h \le 99$.

12.10 The inorder traversal algorithm for binary trees recursively visits the root in between traversing the left and right subtrees. This presumes the existence of exactly two (possibly empty) subtrees at every (non-empty) node. In general trees, a node may have any number of subtrees, so there is no simple algorithmic way to generalize the inorder traversal.

12.11 For a given height $h > 0$, the binary tree with the most nodes is the full binary tree. Corollary 12.12.1 (on page 277) states that that number is $n = 2^{h+1} - 1$. Therefore, in any binary tree of height h, the number n of nodes must satisfy $n \le 2^{h+1} - 1$. The binary tree with the fewest nodes for a given height h is the one in which every internal node has only one child; that linear tree has $n = h + 1$ nodes because every node except the single leaf has exactly one child. Therefore, in any binary tree of height h, the number n of nodes must satisfy $n \ge h + 1$.
The second pair of inequalities follows from the first by solving for h.

12.12 The picture below shows the natural mapping of the binary tree shown in Example 12.3.

12.13 Level order traversal: A, B, C, D, E, F, G, H, J, K, L, M, N, O, P, Q.
Preorder traversal: A, B, H, M, N, C, D, E, J, K, O, L, P, Q, F, G.
Postorder traversal: M, N, H, B, C, D, J, O, K, P, Q, L, E, F, G, A.

12.14 *a.* Level order traversal: A, B, C, D, E, F, G, H, J, K, L, M, N, O, P, Q.
    Preorder traversal: A, B, F, L, C, G, M, N, H, D, J, O, E, K, P, Q.
    Postorder traversal: L, F, B, M, N, G, H, C, O, J, D, P, Q, K, E, A.
b. Level order traversal: A, B, C, D, E, F, G, H, J, L, M, N, O, P, Q, R, S.
    Preorder traversal: A, B, F, L, P, M, Q, R, C, D, G, H, N, S, J, O, E.
    Postorder traversal: P, L, Q, R, M, F, B, C, G, S, N, H, O, J, D, E, A.
c. Level order traversal: A, B, C, D, E, F, G, H, J, K, L, M, N, O, P, Q, R, S, T, U, V, W, X, Y, Z.
    Preorder traversal: A, B, E, F, H, L, J, K, M, O, P, Q, R, T, V, Y, W, S, U, X, Z, N, C, D, G.
    Postorder traversal: E, L, H, J, O, P, Y, V, W, T, R, Z, X, U, S, Q, M, N, K, F, B, C, G, D, A.

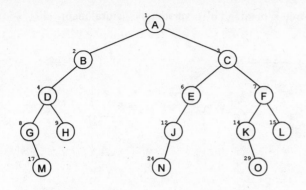

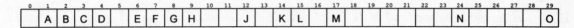

0	1	2	3	4	5	6	7	8	9	10	11	12	13	14	15	16	17	18	19	20	21	22	23	24	25	26	27	28	29
	A	B	C	D		E	F	G	H			J		K	L		M							N					O

   d. Level order traversal: A, B, C, D, E, F, G, H, J, K, L, M, N, O, P, Q, R, S, T.
      Preorder traversal: A, B, D, F, K, L, G, H, C, E, J, M, P, Q, R, S, T, N, O.
      Postorder traversal: K, L, F, G, H, D, B, P, Q, R, S, T, M, N, O, J, E, C, A.
   e. Level order traversal: A, B, C, D, E, F, G, H, J, K, L, M, N, O, P, Q, R, S, T.
      Preorder traversal: A, B, G, K, P, Q, C, D, H, L, M, R, N, E, F, J, O, S, T.
      Postorder traversal: P, Q, K, G, B, C, L, R, M, N, H, D, E, S, T, O, J, F, A.

12.15 Level order traversal: A, B, C, D, E, F, G, H, J, K, L, M, N, O, P.
     Preorder traversal: A, B, D, H, J, E, K, L, C, F, M, N, G, O, P.
     Inorder traversal: H, D, J, B, K, E, L, M, F, N, C, O, G, P.
     Postorder traversal: H, J, D, K, L, E, B, M, F, N, O, G, P, C, A.

12.16 The expression tree for $a*(b + c)*(d*e + f)$ is
     shown at right.

12.17 The prefix representation is $*a*+bc+*def$, and
     the postfix representation is $abc+de*f+**$.

12.18 The binary tree that represents the tree shown in
     Example 12.1 on page 276 is shown below.

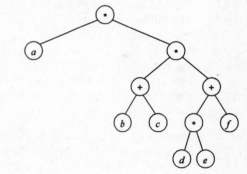

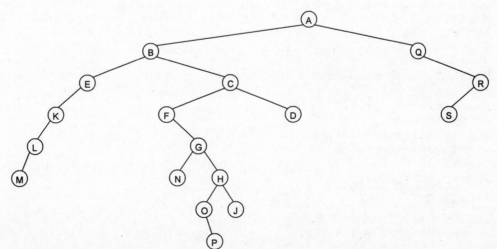

12.19   The forest that produced the given binary tree is obtained by reversing the natural map:

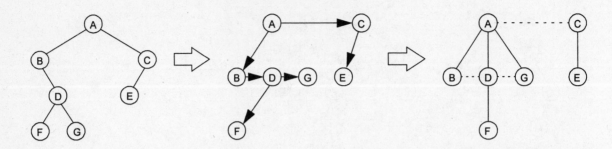

12.20   *a.* the leaf nodes are L, M, N, H, O, P, Q; the children of node C are G and H; node F has depth 2; the nodes at 3 three are L, M, N, O, P, and Q; the height of the tree is 3; the order of the tree is 4;

   b. the leaf nodes are C, E, G, O, P, Q, R, and S; node C has no children; node F has depth 2; the nodes at level 3 are L, M, N, and O; the height of the tree is 4; the order of the tree is 4;

   c. the leaf nodes are C, E, G, J, L, N, O, P, W, Y, and Z; node C has no children; node F has depth 2; the nodes at level 3 are H, J, and K; the height of the tree is 9; the order of the tree is 3;

   d. the leaf nodes are G, H, K, L, N, O, P, Q, R, S, and T; the only child node C has is node E; node F has depth 3; the nodes at level 3 are F, G, H, and J; the height of the tree is 5; the order of the tree is 5;

   e. the leaf nodes are D, E, L, N, P, Q, R, S, and T; node C has no children; node F has depth 1; the nodes at level 3 are K, L, M, N, and O; the height of the tree is 4; the order of the tree is 5;

12.21
```
bool operator!()
{ return bool(_k == 0);
}
```

12.22
```
bool operator!()
{ return bool(_k < 1 || _k > _p->_size);
}
```

12.23
```
bool is_root()
{ return bool(_k == 1);
}
```

12.24
```
bool is_root()
{ return bool(_p == _tree._root);
}
```

12.25
```
bool is_leaf()
{ return bool(2*_k > _p->_size);
}
```

12.26
```
bool is_leaf()
{ return bool(_p->_left == 0 && -p->_right == 0);
}
```

12.27
```
T& operator*()
{ return (_p->_v)[_k];
}
```

12.28
```
T& operator*()
{ return _p->_data;
}
```

12.29
```
Iterator parent()
{ CBTI it(*_p);
  it._k = _k/2;
  return it;
}
```

12.30
```
Iterator left_child()
{ CBTI it(*_p);
  it._k = 2*_k;
  return it;
}
```

12.31
```
int _start(int size)
// returns number of start node:
{ if (_order == PRE || _order == LEVEL) return 1;
  else return last_power(size);
}
```

12.32
```
void CBTI::operator++()
{ if (_order == PRE)
  { if (size+1 == 2*last_power (size)
    || (_k >= last_power (size)  && _k < size))
    { if (_k == size) return 0;        // last is youngest daughter
      if (2*_k <= size) return 2*_k;   // interior node returns son
      ++_k;                                  // male leaf's sister
      while (_k%2 == 0)                    // while male
       _k /= 2;                            //    move to parent
    }
    else                  // tree is not full
    { if (_k == last_power (size) - 1) return 0;
      if (_k >= last_power (size) && _k%2 == 0)
      { _k += 2;
        while (_k%2 == 0)                       // while male
         _k /= 2;                              //    move to parent
      }
      else
      { if (_k == size) return 0;        // last is youngest daughter
        if (2*_k <= size) return 2*_k;  // interior node returns son
        ++_k;                                 // male leaf's sister
        while (_k%2 == 0)                   // while male
         _k /= 2;                          //    move to parent
      }
    }
    else if (_order == IN)
    { if (size+1 == 2*last_power (size))  // tree is full
      { if (_k == size) return 0;        // last is youngest daughter
        if (2*_k <= size)                  // interior node:
        { _k = 2*_k + 1;                   // move to daughter
          while (2*_k <= size)            // while not a leaf
           _k *= 2;                       //    move to son
        }                                  //    male leaf descendant
        if (_k%2 == 0) return _k/2;      // male leaves return parent
        ++_k;                              // move to male cousin
        while (_k%2 == 0)                 // while male
         _k /= 2;                         //    move to parent
        _k /= 2;                          // return aunt
      }
```

```
                else      // tree is not full
                { if (_k == last_power (size) - 1) return 0;
                  if (_k >= size/2 && _k < last_power (size))
                  { ++_k;                                // move to male cousin
                    while (_k%2 == 0)                    // while male
                     _k /= 2;                            //    move to parent
                   _k /= 2;                              // return aunt
                  }
                  else
                  { if (_k == size) return _k/2;
                    if (2*_k <= size)                    // interior node:
                    { _k = 2*_k + 1;                     // move to daughter
                      while (2*_k <= size)               // while not a leaf
                       _k *= 2;                          //    move to son
                  }                                      //    male leaf descendant
                  if (_k%2 == 0) return _k/2;     // male leaves return parent
                    ++_k;                                // move to male cousin
                   while (_k%2 == 0)                     // while male
                    _k /= 2;                             //    move to parent
                  _k /= 2;                               // return aunt
                  }
                }
              }
            else if (_order == POST)
            { if (size+1 < 2*last_power (size) && _k == size) return _k/2;
              if (_k == 1) return 0;                     // last is root
             if (_k%2 == 1) return _k/2;         // return parent of females
             ++_k;                                       // move to sister
              if (2*_k > size) return _k;                // return leaf
              while (2*_k <= size)                       // while not a leaf
               _k *= 2;                                  //    move to son
            }
            else _k = (_k + 1)%(_p->_size + 1);
          }
```

12.33
```
        bool is_empty() const
        { return bool(_root == 0);
        }
```

12.34
```
        int leaves(CBT& x)
        { int count=0;
          for (CBTI it = x.preorder(); it != x.end(); ++it)
            if (it.is_leaf()) ++count;
          return count;
        }
```

12.35
```
        int depth(CBTI& it)
        { if (it.is_root()) return 0;
          return 1 + depth(it.parent());
        }
```

12.36
```
        int height(CBT& x)
        { int max=0, depth_it;
          for (CBTI it(x); !!it; ++it)
          { depth_it = depth(it);
            if (depth_it > max) max = depth_it;
          }
          return max;
        }
```

Chapter 13

Sorting

This chapter outlines the six standard sorting algorithms: the Bubble Sort, the Selection Sort, the Insertion Sort, the Merge Sort, the Quick Sort, and the Heap Sort. The first three are $O(n^2)$ sorts and the second three are $O(n \lg n)$ sorts.

13.1 PRELIMINARIES

Each of these algorithms is defined as a C++ function template on an array `a` of `n` elements of type `T`, where `T` is the template parameter. The function prototype is:

```
template<class T>
void sort(T* a, int n);
// Precondition: a has at least n elements.
// Postcondition: a[0] <= a[1] <= a[2] <= ... <= a[n-1].
```

Each sorting function should be tested with the same test driver:

```
int main()
{ int a[] = { 77, 44, 99, 66, 33, 55, 88, 22, 44 };
  print(a, 9);
  sort(a, 9);
  print(a, 9);
}
```

This uses the following `print()` function template:

```
template<class T>
void print(T* a, int n)
{ for (int i=0; i < n; i++)
    cout << a[i] << ", ";
  cout << endl;
}
```

Some of the sorting algorithms move data by swapping elements in the array. The following `swap()` function template is used to perform that task:

```
template<class T>
void swap(T& x, T& y)
{ T temp=x;
  x = y;
  y = temp;
}
```

13.2 THE BUBBLE SORT

The Bubble Sort is probably the simplest of the sorting algorithms. Its name come from the idea that the larger elements "bubble up" to the top (the high end) of the array like the bubbles in a carbonated beverage.

Algorithm 13.1 The Bubble Sort

```
template<class T>
void sort(T* a, int n)
{ for (int i=1; i < n; i++)
    for (int j=1; j <= n-i; j++)
      if (a[j-1] > a[j]) swap(a[j-1], a[j]);
    // Invariant: the i largest elements are in the correct locations.
}
```

EXAMPLE 13.1 Tracing the Bubble Sort

Here is a trace of the Bubble Sort on the array of 9 integers listed above:

a[0]	a[1]	a[2]	a[3]	a[4]	a[5]	a[6]	a[7]	a[8]
77	44	99	66	33	55	88	22	44
44	77							
		66	99					
			33	99				
				55	99			
					88	99		
						22	99	
							44	99
	66	77						
		33	77					
			55	77				
					22	88		
						44	88	
	33	66						
		55	66					
				22	77			
					44	77		
33	44							
			22	66				
				44	66			
		22	55					
			44	55				
	22	44						
22	33							

On each iteration of the outside `i` loop, the next largest element "bubbles up" to the right. On the first iteration, 99 bubbles up, bouncing off of 11, 33, 55, 88, 22, and 66. On the second iteration, **88** bubbles up, bouncing off of 66. Also notice that 77 bubbles up to `a[4]` on the second iteration.

Theorem 13.1 The Bubble Sort is correct.

Proof: The loop invariant can be used to prove that the Bubble Sort does indeed sort the array. After the first iteration of the main `i` loop, the largest element must have moved to the last position. Wherever it began, it had to be moved step-by-step all the way to the right, because on each comparison the larger element is moved right. For the same reason, the second largest element must have been moved to the second-from-last position in the second iteration of the main `i` loop. So the two largest elements are in the correct locations. This reasoning verifies that the loop invariant is true at the end of every iteration of the main `i` loop. But then, after the last iteration, the `n-1` largest elements must be in their correct locations. That forces the nth largest (*i.e.*, the smallest) element also to be in its correct location, so the array must be sorted.   **Q.E.D.**

Theorem 13.2 The complexity of the Bubble Sort is $O(n^2)$.

Proof: The complexity function $O(n^2)$ means that, for large values of n, the number of loop iterations is proportional to n^2. That means that, if one large array is twice the size of another, it should take about four times as long to sort.

The inner j loop iterates $n-1$ times on the first iteration of the outside i loop, $n-2$ times on the second iteration of the i loop, $n-3$ times on the third iteration of the i loop, *etc.* For example, when $n = 7$, there are 6 comparisons made on the first iteration of the i loop, 5 comparisons made on the second iteration of the i loop, 4 comparisons made on the third iteration of the i loop, *etc.*, so the total number of comparisons is $6 + 5 + 4 + 3 + 2 + 1 = 21$. In general, the total number of comparisons will be $(n-1) + (n-2) + (n-3) + \cdots + 3 + 2 + 1$. From Theorem 13.3, this sum is $n(n-1)/2$. For large values of n, that expression is nearly $n^2/2$ which is proportional to n^2.   **Q.E.D.**

Theorem 13.3 The sum $1 + 2 + 3 + \cdots + (n-3) + (n-2) + (n-1) = n(n-1)/2$.

Proof: If n is odd, we can add the $n-1$ numbers in pairs so that each pair sums to n: add the first to the last to get $(1 + (n-1)) = n$; add the second to the second-from-last to get $(2 + (n-2)) = n$; add the third to the third-from-last to get $(3 + (n-3)) = n$; *etc.* There are $(n-1)/2$ pairs and each pair sums to n, so the total must be $((n-1)/2)(n) = n(n-1)/2$.

If n is even, then $n+1$ is odd and we can apply the previous argument to the sum $1 + 2 + 3 + \cdots + (n-2) + (n-1) + (n)$ to get the expression on the right with $(n+1)$ in place of n:

$$1 + 2 + 3 + \cdots + (n-2) + (n-1) + (n) = (n+1)(n)/2$$

Then simply subtract n from both sides:

$$1 + 2 + 3 + \cdots + (n-2) + (n-1) = (n+1)(n)/2 - n = (n^2+n)/2 - (2n)/2 = n(n-1)/2. \quad \textbf{Q.E.D.}$$

The simple formula in Theorem 13.3 is widely used in computer science. Here is an easy way to visualize it:

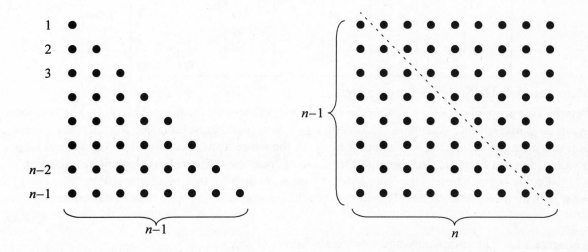

The dots on the left accumulate to $1 + 2 + 3 + \cdots + (n-2) + (n-1)$. The total number of dots on the right is $n(n-1)$. There are twice as many dots on the right as on the left. Therefore:

$1 + 2 + 3 + \cdots + (n-2) + (n-1) = (1/2)(n-1)(n) = n(n-1)/2.$

13.3 THE SELECTION SORT

The Selection Sort works like the Bubble Sort: on each iteration of the main `i` loop, the next largest element is moved into its correct position. But instead of "bubbling" these elements into position, the Selection Sort finds the element to be moved without first moving any elements. Then it is put into place with a single swap. This is more efficient than the Bubble Sort.

This implementation of the Selection Sort puts the next smallest element (instead of the next largest element) in place on each iteration of the main `i` loop. Both versions work equally well.

Algorithm 13.2 The Selection Sort

```
template<class T>
void sort(T* a, int n)
{ for (int i=0; i < n-1; i++
  { int min=i;
    for (int j=i+1; j < n; j++)
      if (a[j] < a[min]) min = j;
    // Invariant: a[min] <= a[j] for i <= j < n.
    swap(a[min], a[i]);
    // Invariant: the subarray a[0:i] is sorted.
  }
}
```

EXAMPLE 13.2 Tracing the Selection Sort

Here is a trace of the Selection Sort on the same array of 9 integers:

a[0]	a[1]	a[2]	a[3]	a[4]	a[5]	a[6]	a[7]	a[8]
77	44	99	66	33	55	88	22	44
22							88	
	33			44				
		44		99				
			44					66
				55	99			
					66			99
						77	88	

Theorem 13.4 The Selection Sort is correct.

Proof: This proof is similar to that for the corresponding theorem for the Bubble Sort. The first loop invariant is true because each time an element `a[j]` was found to be less than `a[min]`, the value of min was changed to `j`. That was done for all `j` in the range from `i` up to `n-1`. The second loop invariant follows from the first, because the `swap()` puts the `i`th smallest element into position `a[i]`. On the last iteration of the outer loop, `i == n-2`. So after that, elements a[0] up to `a[n-2]` must be in their correct positions. That forces the nth element, `a[n-1]` also to be in its correct position.

Q.E.D.

Theorem 13.5 The complexity of the Selection Sort is $O(n^2)$.

Proof: Again, the proof is essentially the same as that for the corresponding theorem for the Bubble Sort. On the first iteration of the outer `i` loop, the inner `j` loop iterates $n-1$ times. On the second, it iterates $n-2$ times. This progression continues, giving a total of

$$(n-1) + (n-2) + \cdots + 2 + 1 = n(n-1)/2.$$

Q.E.D.

13.4 THE INSERTION SORT

The Insertion Sort is so named because on each iteration of its main loop it inserts the next element in its correct position relative to the subarray that has already been processed. This is the common method people use to sort playing cards dealt to them in card games. Unlike the Bubble Sort and the Quick Sort, the Insertion Sort does not use the `swap()` function. Instead, it shifts elements over to make room for each new element inserted. In the ith iteration of the main loop, all the elements on the left of `a[i]` that are less than `a[i]` are shifted one position to the right, making room for the insertion of `a[i]` into is correct position relative to the previously processed `i-1` elements.

Algorithm 13.3 The Insertion Sort

```
template<class T>
void sort(T* a, int n)
{ for (int i=1; i < n; i++)
  { T temp = a[i];
    for (int j=i; j > 0 && a[j-1] > temp; j--)
      a[j] = a[j-1];
    a[j] = temp;
    // Invariant: a[0] <= a[1] <= ... <= a[i].
  }
}
```

EXAMPLE 13.3 Tracing the Insertion Sort

Here is a trace of the Insertion Sort on the same array of 9 integers:

a[0]	a[1]	a[2]	a[3]	a[4]	a[5]	a[6]	a[7]	a[8]
77	44	99	66	33	55	88	22	44
44	77							
		66	77	99				
33	44	66	77	99				
		55	66	77	99			
					88	99		
22	33	44	55	66	77	88	99	
			44	55	66	77	88	99

Theorem 13.6 The Insertion Sort is correct.

Proof: As with the previous two correctness theorems, this too will be proved as soon as the algorithm's loop invariant is verified. On the first iteration of the main `i` loop, `a[1]` is compared with `a[0]` and interchanged if necessary. So `a[0] <= a[1]` after the first iteration. If we assume that the loop invariant is true prior to some `k`th iteration, then it must also be true after that iteration has finished, because during it `a[k+1]` is inserted between the elements that are less than or equal to it and those that are greater. It follows from the Principle of Mathematical Induction then that the loop invariant is true for all `k`.   **Q.E.D.**

Theorem 13.7 The complexity of the Insertion Sort is $O(n^2)$.

Proof: The proof is similar to that for the corresponding theorems for the Bubble Sort and the Selection Sort. On the first iteration of the outer `i` loop, the inner `j` loop iterates once. On the second, it iterates once or twice, depending upon whether `a[1] > a[2]`. On the third iteration, the inner `j` loop iterates at most three times, again depending upon how many of the element on the left of `a[3]` are greater than a[3]. This pattern continues, so that on the kth iteration of the outer loop, the inner loop iterates at most k times. Therefore, the total number of iterations is

$$1 + 2 + 3 + \cdots + (n-2) + (n-1) = n(n-1)/2.$$ **Q.E.D.**

Theorem 13.8 If the array is already sorted, the Insertion Sort has complexity $O(n)$.

Proof: In this case, the inner loop will iterate only once for each iteration of the outer loop. So the total number of iterations of the inner loop is

$$1 + 1 + 1 + \cdots + 1 + 1 = n-1.$$ **Q.E.D.**

An algorithm that has complexity function $O(n)$ is said to be *linear*, or to "run in linear time." The term "linear" is used because the graph of the equation $y = x$ is a straight line. Similarly, an algorithm that has complexity function $O(n^2)$ is said to be *quadratic* because $y = x^2$ is a quadratic equation. We can summarize the last two theorems by saying that the Insertion Sort is a quadratic algorithm whose "best case" performance is linear.

At first glance, Theorem 13.8 seems silly: why would anyone re-sort an array that is already sorted? Of course, one wouldn't. But one might often need to sort an array that is already *nearly* sorted. In those cases, Theorem 13.8 suggests that the Insertion Sort will be almost linear. It certainly will be faster than the Bubble Sort or the Selection Sort.

13.5 THE MERGE SORT

The Merge Sort is a recursive algorithm. It works by splitting the array into sorted 2-element subarrays, merging them pairwise into sorted 4-element subarrays, merging them into sorted 8-element subarrays, *etc.*, until the are only two sorted subarrays to be merged. After that last merge, a single sorted "subarray" remains.

The C++ code exploits the fact that an array name is actually a pointer that supports pointer arithmetic. For example, a+4 is the subarray of a that begins with element a[4]. So the call

```
sort(a+4, m);
```

applies the sort() function to the subarray { a[4], a[5], ..., a[4+m-1] } containing m elements.

The Merge Sort is noticeably more complicated than any of the three previous algorithms. It is recursive and it uses an auxiliary function that has four separate loops. But these complicating factors produce an algorithm that is much faster than the others.

Algorithm 13.4 The Merge Sort

```
template<class T>
void merge(T* a, int n1, int n2)
{ T* temp = new T[n1+n2];
  int i=0, j1=0, j2=0;
  while (j1 < n1 && j2 < n2)
    temp[i++] = ( a[j1] <= a[n1+j2] ? a[j1++] : a[n1+j2++] );
  while (j1 < n1)
    temp[i++] = a[j1++];
  while (j2 < n2)
    temp[i++] = (a+n1)[j2++];
  for (i=0; i < n1+n2; i++)
    a[i] = temp[i];
  delete [] temp;
}
```

```
template<class T>
void sort(T* a, int n)
{ if (n > 1)
  { int n1 = n/2;
    int n2 = n - n1;
    sort(a, n1);
    sort(a+n1, n2);
    merge(a, n1, n2);
  }
}
```

Here is a trace of the Merge Sort on the same array of 9 integers:

a[0]	a[1]	a[2]	a[3]	a[4]	a[5]	a[6]	a[7]	a[8]
77	44	99	66	33	55	88	22	44
44	77							
		66	99					
	66	77						
						22	44	88
				22	33	44	55	
22	33	44	44	55	66	77	88	99

Here is the calling tree for this example:

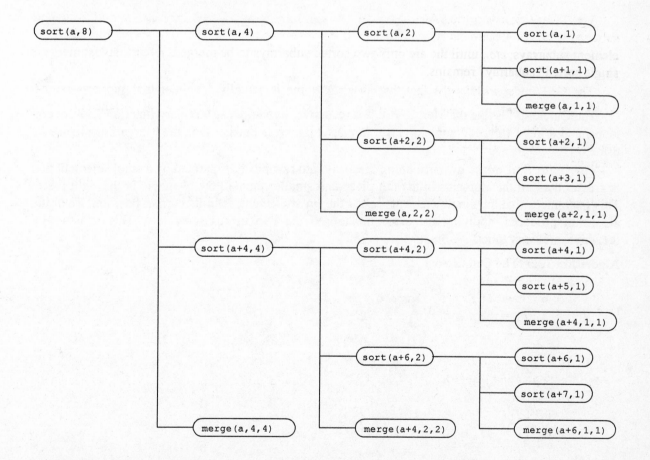

The Merge Sort is correct, but its proof is beyond the scope of this outline.

Theorem 13.9 The complexity of the Merge Sort is $O(n \lg n)$.

Proof: In general, the Merge Sort works by repeatedly dividing the array in half until the pieces are singletons, and then it merges the pieces pairwise until a single piece remains. The number of iterations in the first part equals the number of times n can be halved: that is $\lg n$, the binary logarithm of n. In terms of the number and sizes of the pieces, the second part of the process reverses the first; merging two pieces reverses halving them. So the second part also has $\lg n$ steps. So the entire algorithm has $2 \cdot \lg n$ steps. Each step compares all n elements. So the total number of comparisons is $2n \lg n$, which is proportional to $n \lg n$.   **Q.E.D.**

This analysis can be visualized like this:

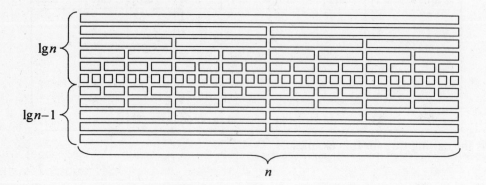

13.6 THE QUICK SORT

The Quick Sort is like the Merge Sort: it is recursive, it requires an auxiliary function with several loops, and it has $O(n \lg n)$ complexity. But in mast cases, it is quicker than the Merge Sort; hence its name.

The Quick Sort works by partitioning the array into two pieces separated by a single element that is greater than all the elements in the left piece and smaller than all the elements in the right piece. This guarantees that the single element, called the *pivot* element, is in its correct position. Then the algorithm proceeds, applying the same method to the two pieces separately. This is naturally recursive, and very quick.

Algorithm 13.5 The Quick Sort

```
template<class T>
void quicksort(T* a, int lo, int hi)
{ if (lo >= hi) return;
  T pivot = a[hi];
  int i = lo - 1;
  int j = hi;
  while (i < j)
  { while (a[++i] < pivot) ;
    while (j >= 0 && a[--j] > pivot) ;
    if (i < j) swap(a[i], a[j]);
  }
  swap(a[i], a[hi]);
  // Invariant: a[j] <= a[i] <= a[k] for lo <= j < i < k <= hi
```

```
    quicksort(a, lo, i-1);
    quicksort(a, i+1, hi);
}

template<class T>
void sort(T* a, int n)
{ quicksort(a, 0, n-1);
}
```

EXAMPLE 13.4 Tracing the Quick Sort

Here is a trace of the Quick Sort on the same array of 9 integers:

a[0]	a[1]	a[2]	a[3]	a[4]	a[5]	a[6]	a[7]	a[8]
77	44	99	66	33	55	88	22	44
22							77	
		33		99				
			44					66
	33	44						
				55	99			
					66			99
						77	88	

Warning: Some authors write the Quick Sort algorithm so that the pivot element is chosen each time to be the first element of the subarray instead of the last element. Other authors choose the middle element. These versions work equally well.

The Quick Sort is correct, but its proof is beyond the scope of this outline.

Theorem 13.10 The complexity of the Quick Sort is $O(n \lg n)$.

The proof of the general statement in this theorem is beyond the scope of this outline. However, the analysis of the "best case" is not.

The Quick Sort proceeds through a series of steps. At each step, each piece of the array is split in two pieces. In the best case, each pivot element will be the median value among those in its piece. So the partition of each piece will result in its being split into two pieces of equal length. Thus, on each step, each piece is halved, like this:

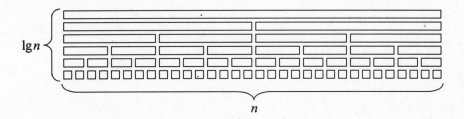

With the splitting balanced this way, the number of steps is $\lg n$. Since each step compares all n elements, the entire process takes $n \lg n$ comparisons.

13.7 HEAPS

A binary tree is said to have the *heap property* if the elements along any path from root to leaf are non-increasing. A *heap* is a complete binary tree that has the heap property.

EXAMPLE 13.5 A Heap

The binary tree shown at right has the heap property. It has six root-to-leaf paths, one for each leaf: 88-66-55-33, 88-66-55-55, 88-66-66-11, 88-66-66-33, 88-77-55-22, and 88-77-44. Each one is non-increasing (*i.e.*, $x \geq y$ if y follows x in the sequence).

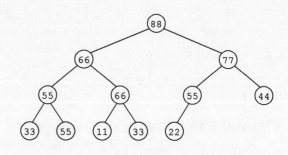

Note that the heap property is consistent with ordinary family trees of people: each child is younger than his/her parent.

Theorem 13.11 In a heap, every element is the maximum value of all the elements in its subtree.
Proof: Every element y in the subtree rooted at a given element x is in a path from x to a leaf. That path can be extended back up to the root of the whole tree. In that path, y follows x. So by the heap property, $x \geq y$.   **Q.E.D.**

Corollary 12.3 In a heap, the largest element is at the root, and the smallest element is at some leaf.

Warning: Some authors define a heap by the opposite condition: the elements along any path from root to leaf are non-decreasing. The two versions are equally useful. In this version, the root of every subtree contains the minimum value in the subtree.

Warning: The word "heap" is also frequently used to describe the collection of unallocated bytes in memory. Other authors refer to this as the *free store*. It is not related to the heap property of binary trees.

By definition, a heap is a complete binary tree. This means that a heap can be stored naturally in an array. (See Section 12.2.)

EXAMPLE 13.6 A Heap Stored as an Array
Here is the heap from Example 13.5, stored in an array of 13 elements:

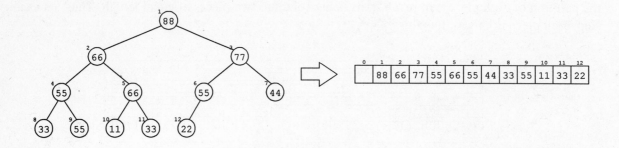

Note that the heap property is easy to see in the tree structure, but it is not clear at all in the linearized array.

13.8 THE HEAP SORT

A heap is, by definition, partially sorted, because each linear string from root to leaf is sorted. This leads to an efficient general sorting algorithm called the Heap Sort. As with all sorting algorithms, it applies to an array (or `vector`). But the underlying heap structure which the array represents is used to define this algorithm.

Like the Merge Sort and the Quick Sort, the Heap Sort uses an auxiliary function which is called from the `sort()` function. And also like the Merge Sort and the Quick Sort, the Heap Sort has complexity function $O(n \lg n)$. But unlike the Merge Sort and the Quick Sort, the Heap Sort is not recursive.

The natural mapping (see EXAMPLE 12.1 on page 276) of a complete binary tree into an array maps the n elements of the tree into array elements `a[1]` through `a[n]`. But to be consistent with all our other sorting algorithms, the n elements should be stored in positions `a[0:n-1]` in the array. So for this reason, we modify the natural mapping so that the correspondence looks like this:

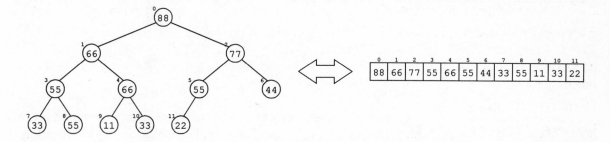

The only consequences of this modification are that now:

- the children of element k are elements $2k+1$ and $2k+2$;

- the parent of element k is elements $(k-1)/2$;

These recurrence relations are used in the algorithm to traverse paths back and forth between root and leaves.

Algorithm 13.6 The Heap Sort

```
template<class T>
void heapify(T* a, int k, int n)
{ T t = a[k];
  while (k < n/2)
  { int j = 2*k + 1;                    // make j the oldest child of k
    if (j+1 < n && a[j] < a[j+1]) ++j;
    if (t > a[j]) break;
    a[k] = a[j];
    k = j;
  }
  a[k] = t;
}


template<class T>
void sort(T* a, int n)
{ for (int i= n/2 - 1; i >= 0; i--)
    heapify(a, i, n);
  for (i = n-1; i > 0; i--)
  { swap(a[0], a[i]);
    // Invariant: the elements a[i:n-1] are in the correct positions.
    heapify(a, 0, i);
    // Invariant: the subarray a[0:i-1] has the heap property.
  }
}
```

The `sort()` function first converts the array so that its underlying complete binary tree is transformed into a heap. This is done by applying the `heapify()` function to each nontrivial subtree.

The nontrivial subtrees (*i.e.*, those having more than one element) are the subtrees that are rooted above the leaf level. In the array, the leaves are stored at positions `a[n/2]` through `a[n]`. So the first `for` loop in the `sort()` function applies the `heapify()` function to elements `a[n/2-1]` back through `a[0]` (which is the root of the underlying tree). The result is an array whose corresponding tree has the heap property:

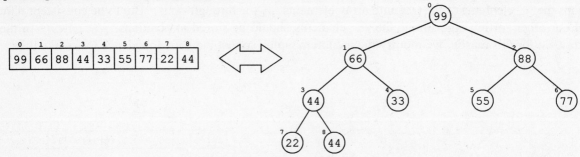

Now the main (second) `for` loop progresses through `n-1` iterations. Each iteration does two things: it swaps the root element with element `a[i]`, and then it applies the `heapify()` function to the subtree of elements `a[0:i-1]`. That subtree consists of the part of the array that is still unsorted. Before the `swap()` executes on each iteration, the subarray `a[0:i]` has the heap property, so by Corollary 12.3 `a[i]` is the largest element in that subarray. That means that the `swap()` puts element `a[i]` in its correct position.

The first seven iterations of the main `for` loop have the effect shown by the seven pictures below. The array (and its corresponding imaginary binary tree) is partitioned into two parts: the first part is the subarray `a[0:i-1]` that has the heap property, and the second part is the remaining `a[i:n-1]` whose elements are in their correct position. The second part is shaded in each of the seven pictures below. Each iteration of the main for loop decrements the size of the first part and increments the size of the second part. So when the loop has finished, the first part is empty and the second (sorted) part constitutes the entire array. This analysis verifies that the Heap Sort works:

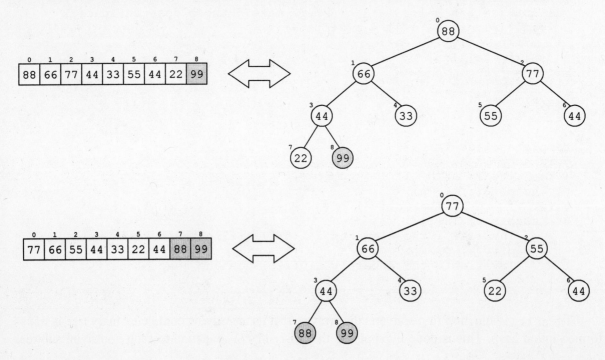

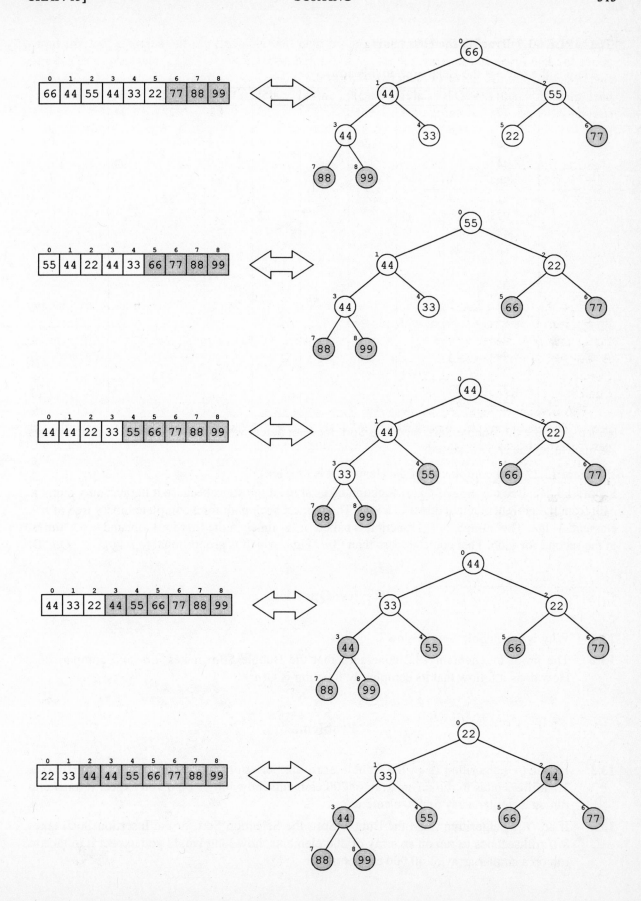

EXAMPLE 13.7 Tracing the Heap Sort

Here is the trace of the Heap Sort on this array:

a[0]	a[1]	a[2]	a[3]	a[4]	a[5]	a[6]	a[7]	a[8]
77	44	99	66	33	55	88	22	44
	66		33					
99		88				77		
44								99
88		77	44			44		
22							88	
77		55			22			
44						77		
66	44							
22					66			
55		22						
33				55				
44			33					
33			44					
44	33							
22		44						
33	22							
22	33							

Notice that, like the Bubble Sort, the Heap Sort does not detect when it is sorted. The last two swaps are made after the array is sorted.

Theorem 13.12 The complexity of the Heap Sort is $O(n \lg n)$.

Proof: Each call to the `heapify()` function takes at most $\lg n$ steps because it iterates only along a path from the current element down to a leaf. The longest such path for a complete binary tree of n elements is $\lg n$. The `heapify()` function is called `n/2` times in the first for loop, and `n-1` times in the second for loop. That comes to less than $(3n/2) \cdot \lg n$, which is proportional to $n \lg n$.   **Q.E.D.**

Review Questions

13.1   Why is the Bubble Sort so slow?

13.2   The proof to Theorem 13.2 concludes that the Bubble Sort makes $n(n–1)/2$ comparisons. How does it follow that its complexity function is $O(n^2)$?

Problems

13.3   If an $O(n^2)$ algorithm (*e.g.*, the Bubble Sort, the Selection Sort, or the Insertion Sort) takes 3.1 milliseconds to run on an array of 200 elements, how long would you expect it to take to run on a similar array of 400 elements?

13.4   If an $O(n^2)$ algorithm (*e.g.*, the Bubble Sort, the Selection Sort, or the Insertion Sort) takes 3.1 milliseconds to run on an array of 200 elements, how long would you expect it to take to run on a similar array of 40,000 elements?

13.5 If an $O(n \lg n)$ algorithm (*e.g.*, the Merge Sort, the Quick Sort, or the Heap Sort) takes 3.1 milliseconds to run on an array of 200 elements, how long would you expect it to take to run on a similar array of 40,000 elements?

13.6 The Insertion Sort runs in linear time on an array that is already sorted. How does it do on an array that is sorted in reverse order?

13.7 How does the Bubble Sort perform on
  a. an array that is already sorted?
  b. an array that is sorted in reverse order?

13.8 How does the Selection Sort perform on
  a. an array that is already sorted?
  b. an array that is sorted in reverse order?

13.9 How does the Selection Sort perform on
  a. an array that is already sorted?
  b. an array that is sorted in reverse order?

13.10 How does the Selection Sort perform on
  a. an array that is already sorted?
  b. an array that is sorted in reverse order?

13.11 How does the Selection Sort perform on
  a. an array that is already sorted?
  b. an array that is sorted in reverse order?

13.12 The Bubble Sort, the Selection Sort, and the Insertion Sort are all $O(n^2)$ algorithms. Which is the fastest, and which is the slowest among them?

13.13 The Merge Sort, the Quick Sort, and the Heap Sort are all $O(n \lg n)$ algorithms. Which is the fastest, and which is the slowest among them?

13.14 Improve the Bubble Sort by making it smart enough to stop when the array is sorted.

13.15 The Merge Sort applies the general method, known as *divide and conquer*, to sort an array. It divides the array into pieces and applies itself recursively to each piece. What other sorting algorithm(s) use this method?

13.16 The Merge Sort is *parallelizable*. That means that parts of it can be performed simultaneously, independent of each other, provided that the computer has multiple processors that can run in parallel. This works for the Merge Sort because several different parts of the array can be subdivided or merged independently of other parts. Which of the other sorting algorithms described in this chapter are parallelizable.

13.17 Trace by hand the execution of each of the six sorting algorithms on the array:

```
int a[] = { 44, 77, 55, 99, 66, 33, 22, 88, 77 }
```

Solutions

13.1 The Bubble Sort is so slow because it operates only locally. Each element moves only one position at a time. For example, the element 99 in Example 13.1 is moved by six separate calls to the `swap()` function to be put into is correct position at `a[8]`.

13.2 The jump from $n(n-1)/2$ to $O(n^2)$ is justified as follows:
  a. For large values of n (*e.g.*, $n > 1000$), $n(n-1)/2$ is nearly the same as $n^2/2$.
  b. A complexity function is used only for comparisons. For example, how much longer will it take to sort an array that is twice as large? For that analysis, proportional functions are equivalent. And since $n^2/2$ is proportional to n^2, we can drop the (1/2) factor and simplify our conclusion with $O(n^2)$.

13.3 The $O(n^2)$ algorithm should take 12.4 milliseconds (4 times as long) to run on the 400-element array.

13.4 The $O(n^2)$ algorithm should take 124 seconds (40,000 times as long) to run on the 40,000-element array. That's about 2 minutes. This answer can be computed algebraically as follows. The running time t is proportional to n^2, so there is some constant c for which $t = c \cdot n^2$. If it takes $t = 3.1$ ms to sort n = 200 elements, then $(3.1 \text{ ms}) = c \cdot (200 \text{ elts})^2$, so $c = (3.1 \text{ ms})/(200 \text{ elts})^2 = 0.0000775 \text{ ms/elt}^2$. Then, for $n = 40,000$, $t = c \cdot n^2 = (0.0000775 \text{ ms/elt}^2) \cdot (40,000 \text{ elt})^2 = 124,000 \text{ ms} = 124 \text{ s}$.

13.5 The $O(n \lg n)$ algorithm should take 1.24 seconds (400 times as long) to run on the 40,000-element array. This answer can be computed algebraically. The running time t is proportional to $n \lg n$, so there is some constant c for which $t = c \cdot n \cdot \lg n$. If it takes $t = 3.1$ ms to sort $n = 200$ elements, then $(3.1) = c \cdot (200) \lg(200)$, so $c = (3.1 \text{ms})/(200 \cdot \lg(200)) = 0.0155/\lg(200)$. Then, for $n = 40,000$, $t = c \cdot n \cdot \lg n = (0.0155/\lg(200)) \cdot (40,000 \cdot \lg(40,000)) = 620 \cdot (\lg(40,000)/\lg(200))$. Now $40,000 = 200^2$, so $\lg(40,000) = \lg(200^2) = 2 \cdot \lg 200$. Thus, $\lg(40,000)/\lg(200) = 2$, so $t = 620 \cdot 2$ ms $= 1240$ ms $= 1.24$ s.

13.6 The Insertion Sort has its worst performance on an array that is sorted in reverse order, because each new element inserted requires all of the elements on its left to be shifted one position to the right.

13.7 The Bubble Sort, as implemented in Algorithm 13.1, is *insensitive to input*. That means that it will execute the same number ($n(n-1)/2$) of comparisons regardless of the original order of the elements in the array. So it doesn't matter whether the array is already sorted or whether it is sorted in reverse order; it is still very slow.

13.8 The Selection Sort is also insensitive to input: it takes about the same amount of time to sort arrays of the same size, regardless of their initial order.

13.9 The Merge Sort is also insensitive to input: it takes about the same amount of time to sort arrays of the same size, regardless of their initial order.

13.10 The Quick Sort is quite sensitive to input. As implemented in Algorithm 13.5, the Quick Sort will degrade into an $O(n^2)$ algorithm in the special cases where the array is initially sorted in either order. That is because the pivot element will always be an extreme value within its subarray, so the partitioning splits the subarray very unevenly, thereby requiring n steps instead of $\lg n$.

13.11 The Heap Sort is a little sensitive to input, but not much. The `heapify()` function may require fewer than $\lg n$ iterations.

13.12 The Bubble Sort is slower than the Selection Sort, and the Insertion Sort (in most cases) is a little faster.

13.13 The Merge Sort is slower than the Heap Sort, and the Quick Sort (in most cases) is faster.

13.14
```
template<class T>
void sort(T* a, int n)
{ bool sorted=false;
  for (int i=1; i < n && !sorted; i++)
    for (int j=1; j <= n-i; j++)
    { sorted = true;
      if (a[j-1] > a[j])
      { swap(a[j-1], a[j]);
        sorted = false;
      }
    }
}
```

13.15 Among the six sorting algorithms presented here, only the Merge Sort and the Quick Sort apply the method of *divide and conquer*. Like the Merge Sort, the Quick Sort divides the array into pieces and then applies itself recursively to each piece.

13.16 Besides the Merge Sort, the only other sorting algorithm among the six described here that is parallelizable is the Quick Sort. The partitioning process in the quicksort() function could be performed simultaneously on several separate sections of the array.

Chapter 14

Searching

14.1 THE SEQUENTIAL SEARCH ALGORITHM

The simplest algorithm for searching a container for an element with a given value is the *Sequential Search Algorithm*. It simply iterates through the container until the item is found or the end is reached.

Algorithm 14.1 The Sequential Search

```
//  preconditions: a is an array with n elements;
//                  0 <= begin <= end <= n;
// postconditions: returns: i;
//                  begin <= i <= end;
//                  if i < end then a[i] == target.
template <class T>
int find(const T* a, int begin, int end, const T& target)
{ for (int i=begin; i<end; i++)
    if (a[i] == target) return i;
  return end;
}
```

EXAMPLE 14.1 Using the Sequential Search

This uses the `find()` function defined in Algorithm 14.1:

```
const int SIZE=12;
int a[SIZE] = { 44, 66, 77, 33, 88, 66, 99, 55, 66, 66, 44, 88 };
int target=66;
int loc=0;
for (;;)
{ loc = find(a, loc, SIZE, target);
  if (loc == SIZE) break;
  cout << target << " was found at location " << loc++ << endl;
}
```

The output from this program fragment is

```
66 was found at location 1
66 was found at location 5
66 was found at location 8
66 was found at location 9
```

Theorem 14.1 The Sequential Search Algorithm has complexity $O(n)$.

Proof: If the target is not in the container, then the algorithm will compare it with every element. If the target is in the container, then assuming that each location is equally likely, the algorithm will make $n/2$ comparisons on average. **Q.E.D.**

An algorithm that has complexity function $O(n)$ is called a *linear algorithm* and is said to run in *linear time*.

14.2 THE STANDARD C++ find() FUNCTION TEMPLATES

Standard C++ implements the Sequential Search Algorithm with a family of find() function templates for container classes. The general prototype is:

```
template <class In, class T>
In find(In begin, In end, const T& target);
```

where In is an iterator class defined within the container class.

EXAMPLE 14.2 Using the Standard find() Function for list Containers

```
list<string> presidents;
list<string>::iterator it=presidents.begin();
presidents.insert(it++, "Washington");
presidents.insert(it++, "Adams");
presidents.insert(it++, "Jefferson");
presidents.insert(it++, "Madison");
presidents.insert(it++, "Monroe");
presidents.insert(it++, "Adams");
for (;;)
{ it = find(presidents, it, presidents.end(), "Adams");
  if (it == presidents.end()) break;
  cout << "Adams was found." << endl;
}
```

The output from this program fragment is:

```
Adams was found.
Adams was found.
```

14.3 THE BINARY SEARCH ALGORITHM

The Sequential Search Algorithm is inefficient. Imagine using it to find a name in the telephone book! Fortunately, telephone books and dictionaries are sorted so that we can find things more efficiently. For example, to find "Miller" in the telephone book, most people open it somewhere near the middle. If they see the name "Parker" then they know that "Miller" must be in the first half, so they repeat the process on that half. This is the *Binary Search Algorithm*: divide the remainder in half and repeat the process on the half that could contain the target. Note that this is the same *divide-and-conquer* strategy that was used in the Merge Sort and the Quick Sort.

Algorithm 14.2 The Binary Search

```
//   preconditions: a[0] <= a[1] <= a[2] <= ... <= a[n-1];
//                   0 <= begin <= end <= n;
// postconditions: returns: i;
//                   begin <= i <= end;
//                   if i < end then a[i] == target.
template <class T>
int find(const T* a, int begin, int end, const T& target)
{ int lo=begin;
  int hi=_end-1;
  while (lo <= hi)
  { int mid = (lo + hi)/2;                        // locate the middle
    if (a[mid] == target) return mid;
    if (a[mid] > target) hi = mid - 1;   // search the lower half
    else lo = mid + 1;                   // search the upper half
  }
  return end;
}
```

EXAMPLE 14.3 Tracing the Binary Search

```
const int SIZE=12;
int target = 66;
int a[SIZE] = { 22, 33, 33, 33, 44, 55, 66, 66, 77, 88, 88, 99 };
int loc = find(a, 0, SIZE, target);
if (loc == SIZE) cout << target << " was not found\n";
else cout << target << " was found at location " << loc << endl;
```

begin	end	target	lo	hi	mid	a[mid]
0	12	66	0	11	5	55
			6		8	77
				7	6	66

The output is

```
66 was found at location 6
```

Unlike the Sequential Search, the Binary Search cannot be used to find all the occurrences of the target. Indeed, the `find()` cannot tell which occurrence it has found. The trace in Example 14.3 found the first occurrence of 66. But the call `find(a, 2, 10, target)` will find the second occurrence (`a[7]`) instead. (See Problem 14.7.)

Theorem 14.2 The Binary Search Algorithm has complexity $O(\lg n)$.

Proof: If the target is not in the array, then the algorithm will divide the array in two repeatedly until the subarray is empty. The number of times that n can be divided in two is $\lg n$. If the target is in the container, then the number of iterations will be at most $\lg n$.   **Q.E.D.**

The Binary Sort is easily expressed as a recursive algorithm:

Algorithm 14.3 The Recursive Binary Search

```
//  preconditions: a is a sorted array with n elements:
//                 a[0] <= a[1] <= a[2] <= ... <= a[n-1];
//                 0 <= begin <= end <= n;
// postconditions: returns: i;
//                 begin <= i <= end;
//                 if i < end then a[i] == target.
template <class T>
int find(const T* a, int begin, int end, const T& target)
{ if (begin > end) return -1;                  // target not found
  int mid = (begin + end)/2;                   // locate the middle
  if (a[mid] == target) return mid;
  if (a[mid] > target) return find(a, begin, mid - 1, target);
  return find(a, mid + 1, end, target);
}
```

Theorem 14.3 The Recursive Binary Search Algorithm has complexity $O(\lg n)$.

Proof: Each call makes at most one recursive call, and that recursive call is on a subarray of size at most $n/2$. Therefore, the complexity function $f(n)$ satisfies the recurrence relation:

$$f(1) = 1;$$
$$f(n) = 1 + f(n/2);$$

The function $f(n) = 1 + \lg n$ is a solution because $f(1) = 1 + \lg 1 = 1 + 0 = 1$ and $1 + f(n/2) = 1 + (1 + \lg(n/2)) = 2 + \lg(n/2) = 2 + (\lg n - \lg 2) = 2 + (\lg n - 1) = 1 + \lg n = f(n)$.   **Q.E.D.**

EXAMPLE 14.4 Tracing the Recursive Binary Search

Here is a trace of the Recursive Binary Search (Algorithm 14.3) on an array of strings:

```
string a[8]
  = {"beef", "corn", "fish", "kale", "lamb", "milk", "okra", "rice"};
int loc = find(a, 0, 8, "kale");
```

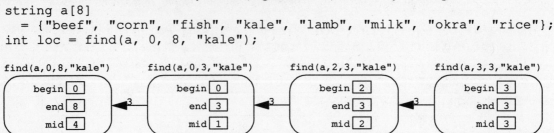

14.4 BINARY SEARCH TREES

The Binary Search algorithm uses the classic *divide-and-conquer* method to solve the problem. This method can be generalized by using a data structure that reflects the method, namely a binary tree. The main idea of the binary search is to look in the middle and then go left or right according to whether the middle is larger or smaller than what you are searching for. Applied to a binary tree, that means look in the left subtree if the root element is larger, or look in the right subtree if the root element is smaller. For this to work, every element in the left subtree must be less than (or equal to) the element in the root, and every element in the right subtree must be greater than (or equal to) the element in the root. A binary tree that has this property at every element is called a *binary search tree*.

EXAMPLE 14.5 Building a Binary Search Tree

The following sequence of pictures shows the binary search tree that results from inserting the input sequence 44, 77, 55, 22, 99, 33, 88:

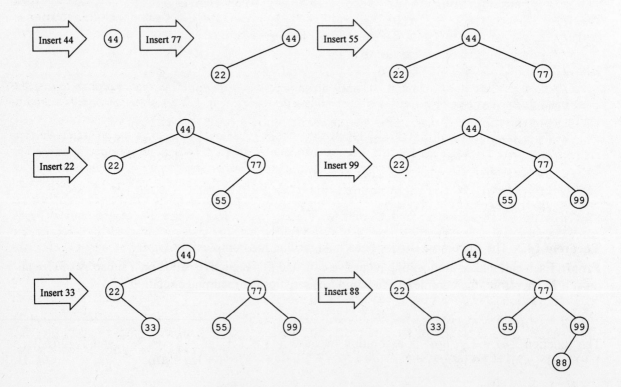

The last item, 88, was inserted with the following steps: the element at the root (44) is less than 88 so move to its right subtree; the element at that root (77) is less than 88, so move to its right subtree; the element at that root (99) is greater than 88 so move to its left subtree; that subtree is empty, so insert 88 there.

If a binary search tree is balanced, it allows for very efficient searching. Like the Binary Search, it takes $O(\lg n)$ steps to find an element in a balanced binary search tree. But without further restrictions, a binary search tree may grow to be very unbalanced. The worst case is when the elements that are being inserted are in sorted order. In that case, the tree degrades to a linked list, thereby making the search algorithm an $O(n)$ sequential search.

EXAMPLE 14.6 An Unbalanced Binary Search Tree

This is the same input data as in Example 14.5, but in a different order: 99, 22, 88, 33, 77, 55, 44. The resulting binary search tree is shown at right.

This shows that the same input in different order produces a different tree. But more importantly, it shows that it is not unlikely for the binary search tree to be linear, or nearly linear.

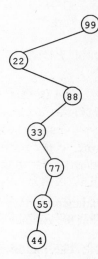

14.5 AVL TREES

The way to avoid the problem illustrated in Example 14.6 is to impose some balancing constraints on the binary search tree. An *AVL tree* is a binary search tree in which the difference between the heights of the two subtrees is no more than 1 at every element in the tree. The name comes from the two inventors of this method: G. M. Adel'son-Velskii and Y. M. Landis.

The insertion algorithm for AVL trees maintains a balance number at each node, defined to be the height of the node's right subtree minus the height of its left subtree. For the tree to remain balanced, each balance number must be 1, 0, or −1. If an insertion changes a balance number to 2 or to   −2, then the insertion algorithm performs a subtree rotation to restore the balance. The following example illustrates the algorithm.

EXAMPLE 14.7 AVL Tree Insertions

This example illustrates the various kinds of rotations required by the AVL insertion algorithm to keep the tree balanced. The data being inserted are strings holding the names of the U.S. presidents, inserted in chronological order.

The first picture shows the insertion of the seventh president, Andrew Jackson, into the tree where the first six presidents have already been inserted. The balance number for each node is shown directly beneath it. Before `Jackson` is inserted, the node containing `Adams, J.` has balance number 1, and the other 5 nodes have balance number 0. The string `Jackson` is lexicographically less than `Jefferson`, greater than `Adams, J.`, and greater than `Adams, J.Q.`, so the moves left, right, and right down the tree from the root. This leads `Jackson` to become the right child of `Adams, J.Q.`. That changes the balance number of each of the three nodes along the insertion path. The balance number for `Jefferson` decreases by 1 because the new node is to its left. The balance numbers for `Adams, J.`, and `Adams, J.Q.`, increase by 1 because the new node is to their right. The resulting changes create an imbalance (a balance number of 2) at `Adams, J.`: The node that has the illegal balance number (in this case, `Adams, J.`) is called the *pivot* for the required rotation. Since the pivot's balance number is +2, a `rotate_left` operation is performed. (A balance number of −2 would require the symmetrically opposite `rotate_right` operation.) The pivot becomes the left child of its own right child (`Adams, J.Q.`), which is moved up to take the place of the pivot. This reduces the pivot's balance number by 2 (making it 0) and it reduces the

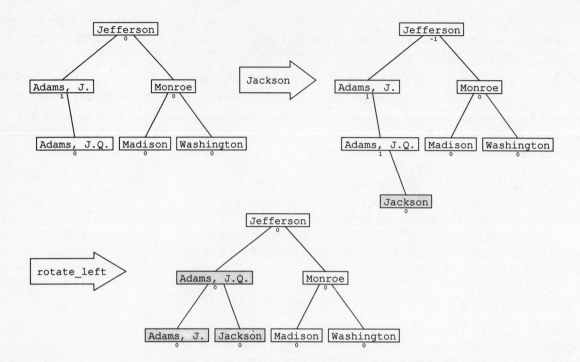

balance number of the node that replaces the pivot by 1 (making it 0 in this case). The net effect is that the balance is restored, while preserving the binary search tree property.

The picture on the next page illustrates a double rotation. The eleventh president `Polk` is inserted as the left child of `Tyler`. This causes an imbalance three levels higher, at `Monroe`, which is therefore the pivot element for the rotation. But the balance number of the pivot (2) has the opposite sign from the balance number (−1) of its child (`Van Buren`) on the insertion path. The opposite signs indicate that a double rotation is necessary to restore balance. So first, a single rotation right about the child of the pivot is performed, and then a rotation left about the pivot is performed:

Although a bit complicated, the insertion algorithm for AVL trees is very efficient, requiring the changing of only several pointers. The result is a balanced binary search tree that provides very efficient access.

14.6 HASH TABLES

The Binary Search is the prototypical method for finding things stored in a computer. Its $O(\lg n)$ speed is adequate for most tasks. The AVL tree enhances that speed with the efficiency that a binary tree provides for insertions and deletions. But these methods require the elements to be sorted according to some intrinsic ordering defined for the element type. For example, when storing strings, the lexicographic ordering is used. The evaluation of the ordering operator itself incurs some overhead. Moreover, the requirement that such an order be defined in the first place may be an imposition.

Hash tables provide an alternative to storing elements in sorted order. Instead, they use a hash function which computes the location of the element in an array. The function that computes the location is called a *hash function*, and the array where the elements are stored is called a *hash table*.

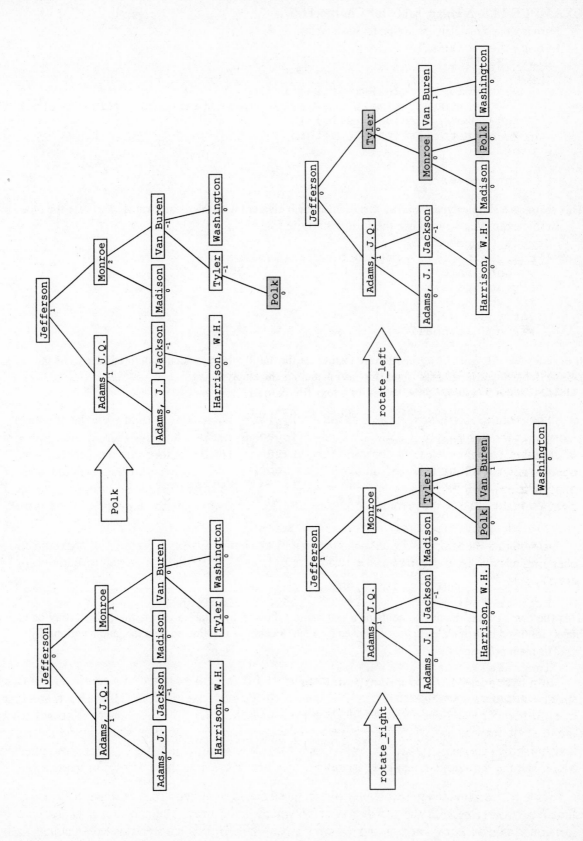

EXAMPLE 14.8 A Hash Table for Composers

Here is a class template definition for hash tables:

```cpp
template <class T>
class HashTable
{ public:
    HashTable(int size) : _size(size)
      { _v = new T[size]; for (int i=0; i<size; i++) _v[i] = T(); }
    int size() { return _size; }
    T& operator[](int k) { return _v[k]; }
  protected:
    T* _v;
    int _size;
};
```

This abstracts a simple dynamic array. It initializes each element with the default value `T()` for the type `T`.

In this example, we will use the following type for `T`:

```cpp
struct Composer
{ bool is_null() { return bool(lname.length() == 0); }
  string lname;
  string fname;
  int yob;
  int yod;
  string nationality;
};
```

It includes the `is_null()` function for testing for the "null" object, which is defined here to be the `Composer` object whose `lname` field (for "last name") is the empty string.

We use the following data, stored in a text file named `Composers.dat`:

```
Vivaldi Antonio 1678     1741       Italian
Bach    Johann Sebastian     1685    1750    German
Mozart  Wolfgang Amadeus     1756    1791    Austrian
Beethoven        Ludwig van  1770    1827    German
Berlioz Hector  1803    1869    French
Chopin  Frederic        1810    1849    Polish
Liszt   Franz   1811    1886    Hungarian
Brahms  Johannes        1833    1897    German
Dvorak  Antonin 1841    1904    Czech
Grieg   Edvard  1843    1907    Norwegian
Sibelius        Jean    1865    1957    Finnish
Stravinsky      Igor    1882    1971    Russian
Barber  Samuel  1910    1981    American
Britten Benjamin        1913    1976    English
```

This file has 14 lines. Each line contains a last name followed by a tab, a first name (which may contain a blank) followed by a tab, a birth year followed by a tab, a death year followed by a tab, and a nationality.

The main program is

```cpp
int main()
{ ifstream fin("Composers.dat");
  Composer composer;
  HashTable<Composer> table(TABLE_SIZE);
  while (get(composer, fin))
  { int k = hash(composer.lname + composer.fname);
    while (!table[k].is_null())
      k = (k+1) % TABLE_SIZE;
    table[k] = composer;
  }
  print(table);
}
```

Its output is

```
 0. Dvorak, Antonin (1841-1904), Czech
 1. Mozart, Wolfgang Amadeus (1756-1791), Austrian
 2. Vivaldi, Antonio (1678-1741), Italian
 3. Beethoven, Ludwig van (1770-1827), German
 4. Chopin, Frederic (1810-1849), Polish
 5. Bach, Johann Sebastian (1685-1750), German
 6. Grieg, Edvard (1843-1907), Norwegian
 7. Sibelius, Jean (1865-1957), Finnish
 8. Stravinsky, Igor (1882-1971), Russian
 9. Britten, Benjamin (1913-1976), English
10. Liszt, Franz (1811-1886), Hungarian
11.
12.
13.
14. Berlioz, Hector (1803-1869), French
15. Barber, Samuel (1910-1981), American
16. Brahms, Johannes (1833-1897), German
```

It has inserted each of the 14 `Composer` objects in the `table`. It uses the following `hash()` function to select a location in the `table` to insert the object:

```
int hash(string s)
{ int h=0;
  for (int i=0; i<s.length(); i++)
    h += int(s[i]);
  return h % TABLE_SIZE;
}
```

This function returns an integer that is computed from the given string `s`. The computation simply adds the characters (as integers) in the string and then computes the remainder `k % TABLE_SIZE` to ensure that `k` is in range ($0 \le k <$ `TABLE_SIZE`).

The main program uses a `while` loop to read each of the 14 records from the `Composers.dat` file and stores them in the hash `table`. For each record, it hashes the string

　　　　composer.lname + composer.fname

which is simply the concatenation of the composer's last name and first name. For example, the hash function computes the number 5 for the second record, hashing the 20-character string "`BachJohann Sebastian`". If the hashed location in the table element is already occupied by another record, then the `while` loop locates the next available position. The record is inserted at location `k` by the statement

　　　　　　`table[k] = composer;`

Finally, after all the objects have been inserted into the table, the program prints the entire table.

Here is the rest of the program:

```
#include <fstream>
#include <iomanip>
#include <iostream>
#include <sstream>                    // use <strstream> in pre-Standard C++
using namespace std;
const int BUF_SIZE=80;
const int TABLE_SIZE=17;
bool get(Composer& composer, ifstream& fin)
{ char buffer[BUF_SIZE], temp[BUF_SIZE];
  fin.getline(buffer, BUF_SIZE);
  if (fin.fail()) return false;
  istrstream ss(buffer);        // binds the string stream ss to buffer
  ss.getline(temp, BUF_SIZE, '\t');  composer.lname = temp;
  ss.getline(temp, BUF_SIZE, '\t');  composer.fname = temp;
  ss >> composer.yob >> composer.yod;
  ss.getline(temp, BUF_SIZE, '\t');  // eat tab
```

```
    ss.getline(temp, BUF_SIZE);  composer.nationality = temp;
    return true;
}
void print(Composer& composer)
{ cout << composer.lname << ", " << composer.fname << " ("
       << composer.yob << "-" << composer.yod << "), "
       << composer.nationality << "\n";
}
template <class T>
void print(HashTable<T>& t)
{ for (int k=0; k<t.size(); k++)
    { cout << setiosflags(ios::right) << setw(4) << k << ". ";
      if (!t[k].is_null()) print(t[k]);
      else cout << endl;
    }
}
```

The `get()` function reads one line at a time from the data file into the string stream (see Section 6.7 on page 118) named `ss` and then uses the `getline()` function to extract the tab-terminated fields from `ss`. It returns `true` unless the end-of-file has been detected.

EXAMPLE 14.9 Resolving Collisions

The details of how the program in Example 14.8 works can be seen by the following enhancement:

```
int main()
{ ifstream fin("Composers.dat");
  Composer composer;
  HashTable<Composer> table(TABLE_SIZE);
  int collisions=0;
  while (get(composer, fin))
  { int k = hash(composer.lname + composer.fname);
    cout << "hash(" << composer.lname + composer.fname
         << ") = " << k << endl;
    resolve_collision(table, composer, k, collisions);
    table[k] = composer;
    cout << "\t" << composer.lname << " inserted at " << k << endl;
  }
  cout << "There were " << collisions << " collisions.\n";
}
```

This relegates the collision resolution to a separate function which reports each collision:

```
template <class T>
void resolve_collision(HashTable<T>& t, Composer& c, int& k, int& n)
{ while (!t[k].is_null())
  { cout << "\tCOLLISION AT " << k << "\t";
    print(t[k]);
    k = (k+1) % TABLE_SIZE;
    ++n;
  }
}
```

Here is the output from the program running on the same input as Example 14.8:

```
hash(VivaldiAntonio) = 2
         Vivaldi inserted at 2
hash(BachJohann Sebastian) = 5
         Bach inserted at 5
hash(MozartWolfgang Amadeus) = 1
         Mozart inserted at 1
hash(BeethovenLudwig van) = 1
```

```
            COLLISION AT 1   Mozart, Wolfgang Amadeus (1756-1791), Austrian
            COLLISION AT 2   Vivaldi, Antonio (1678-1741), Italian
            Beethoven inserted at 3
   hash(BerliozHector) = 14
            Berlioz inserted at 14
   hash(ChopinFrederic) = 2
            COLLISION AT 2   Vivaldi, Antonio (1678-1741), Italian
            COLLISION AT 3   Beethoven, Ludwig van (1770-1827), German
            Chopin inserted at 4
   hash(LisztFranz) = 10
            Liszt inserted at 10
   hash(BrahmsJohannes) = 16
            Brahms inserted at 16
   hash(DvorakAntonin) = 16
            COLLISION AT 16 Brahms, Johannes (1833-1897), German
            Dvorak inserted at 0
   hash(GriegEdvard) = 4
            COLLISION AT 4   Chopin, Frederic (1810-1849), Polish
            COLLISION AT 5   Bach, Johann Sebastian (1685-1750), German
            Grieg inserted at 6
   hash(SibeliusJean) = 7
            Sibelius inserted at 7
   hash(StravinskyIgor) = 8
            Stravinsky inserted at 8
   hash(BarberSamuel) = 15
            Barber inserted at 15
   hash(BrittenBenjamin) = 2
            COLLISION AT 2   Vivaldi, Antonio (1678-1741), Italian
            COLLISION AT 3   Beethoven, Ludwig van (1770-1827), German
            COLLISION AT 4   Chopin, Frederic (1810-1849), Polish
            COLLISION AT 5   Bach, Johann Sebastian (1685-1750), German
            COLLISION AT 6   Grieg, Edvard (1843-1907), Norwegian
            COLLISION AT 7   Sibelius, Jean (1865-1957), Finnish
            COLLISION AT 8   Stravinsky, Igor (1882-1971), Russian
            Britten inserted at 9
   There were 14 collisions.
```

The first collision occurs with the insertion of the fourth record:

```
   Beethoven         Ludwig van         1770     1827     German
```

At this point in the program, the hash table looks like that shown at the top of the next page. Since the `Mozart` record is already occupying element 1, the `Beethoven` record is inserted into the next available position: element 3. This counts as 2 collisions because 2 extra table elements had to be examined before the insertion could be made.

The rest of the run reports a total of 14 collisions, 2 with the insertion of `Beethoven`, 2 with the insertion of `Chopin`, 1 with the insertion of `Dvorak`, 2 with the insertion of `Grieg`, and 7 with the insertion of `Britten`.

14.7 SEARCHING A HASH TABLE

Hash tables are valued for their fast look-up speed. Once the table has been built, any existing element can be found the same way it was inserted: hash the element's key to a number `k`, look at `table[k]`, and if it's not there follow the programmed collision resolution algorithm until the item is found or the table has been exhausted. The *key* for a record is the part of the record that is passed to

0	
1	{"Mozart", "Wolfgang Amadeus", 1756, 1791, "Austrian"}
2	{"Vivaldi", "Antonio", 1678, 1741, "Italian"}
3	
4	
5	{"Bach", "Johann Sebastian", 1685, 1750, "German"}
6	
7	
8	
9	
10	
11	
12	
13	
14	
15	
16	

the hash function. The key in Example 14.9 is the concatenated string "composer.lname + composer.fname".

EXAMPLE 14.10 Searching a Hash Table

Here is a `find()` function for the hash table created in Example 14.9:

```
template <class T>
bool find(HashTable<T>& t, Composer& c, int& k)
{ int count=0;
  while (t[k].lname != c.lname && count++ < TABLE_SIZE)
    k = (k+1) % TABLE_SIZE;
  return bool(t[k].lname == c.lname);
}
```

It follows the same steps as the `resolve_collision()` function.

EXAMPLE 14.11 Testing the `find()` Function

Here is a modification of the program in Example 14.8 that allows the user to search the hash table using a `find()` function:

```
int main()
{ ifstream fin("Composers.dat");
  Composer composer;
  HashTable<Composer> table(TABLE_SIZE);
  while (get(composer, fin))
  { int k = hash(composer.lname + composer.fname);
    while (!table[k].is_null())
      k = (k+1) % TABLE_SIZE;
    table[k] = composer;
  }
  for (;;)
  { get(composer, cin);
    int k = hash(composer.lname + composer.fname);
```

```
       cout << "hash(" << composer.lname + composer.fname
             << ") = " << k << endl;
       if (find(table, composer, k))
       { composer = table[k];
       cout << composer.fname + " " + composer.lname
             << " was born in " << composer.yob << endl;
       }
       else
          cout << composer.fname + " " + composer.lname
               << " was not found in the hash table." << endl;
       }
    }
```

It uses the following `get()` function for interactive input:

```
    void get(Composer& composer, istream& in)
    { char buf[BUF_SIZE];
      cout << "Enter composer's last name: ";
      in.getline(buf, BUF_SIZE);  composer.lname = buf;
      cout << "Enter composer's first name: ";
      in.getline(buf, BUF_SIZE);  composer.fname = buf;
    }
```

And it uses the following version of the `find()` function from Example 14.10:

```
    template <class T>
    bool find(HashTable<T>& t, Composer& c, int& k)
    { int count=0;
      while (t[k].lname != c.lname || t[k].fname != c.fname)
      { if (++count == TABLE_SIZE || t[k].is_null()) return false;
        cout << "\tNOT FOUND AT " << k << "\t";
        print(t[k]);
        k = (k + 1) % TABLE_SIZE;
      }
      return true;
    }
```

Here is the result of a test run:

```
    Enter composer's last name: Barber
    Enter composer's first name: Samuel
    hash(BarberSamuel) = 15
    Samuel Barber was born in 1910
    Enter composer's last name: Grieg
    Enter composer's first name: Edvard
    hash(GriegEdvard) = 4
            NOT FOUND AT 4  Chopin, Frederic (1810-1849), Polish
            NOT FOUND AT 5  Bach, Johann Sebastian (1685-1750), German
    Edvard Grieg was born in 1843
    Enter composer's last name: Frank
    Enter composer's first name: Cesar
    hash(FrankCesar) = 6
            NOT FOUND AT 6  Grieg, Edvard (1843-1907), Norwegian
            NOT FOUND AT 7  Sibelius, Jean (1865-1957), Finnish
            NOT FOUND AT 8  Stravinsky, Igor (1882-1971), Russian
            NOT FOUND AT 9  Britten, Benjamin (1913-1976), English
            NOT FOUND AT 10 Liszt, Franz (1811-1886), Hungarian
    Enter composer's last name: Mahler
    Enter composer's first name: Gustav
    hash(MahlerGustav) = 11
    Gustav Mahler was not found in the hash table.
```

```
Enter composer's last name: Bach
Enter composer's first name: Carl Phillipp Emanuel
hash(BachCarl Phillipp Emanuel) = 15
        NOT FOUND AT 15 Barber, Samuel (1910-1981), American
        NOT FOUND AT 16 Brahms, Johannes (1833-1897), German
        NOT FOUND AT 0  Dvorak, Antonin (1841-1904), Czech
        NOT FOUND AT 1  Mozart, Wolfgang Amadeus (1756-1791), Austrian
        NOT FOUND AT 2  Vivaldi, Antonio (1678-1741), Italian
        NOT FOUND AT 3  Beethoven, Ludwig van (1770-1827), German
        NOT FOUND AT 4  Chopin, Frederic (1810-1849), Polish
        NOT FOUND AT 5  Bach, Johann Sebastian (1685-1750), German
        NOT FOUND AT 6  Grieg, Edvard (1843-1907), Norwegian
        NOT FOUND AT 7  Sibelius, Jean (1865-1957), Finnish
        NOT FOUND AT 8  Stravinsky, Igor (1882-1971), Russian
        NOT FOUND AT 9  Britten, Benjamin (1913-1976), English
        NOT FOUND AT 10 Liszt, Franz (1811-1886), Hungarian
    Carl Phillipp Emanuel Bach was not found in the hash table.
```
The find() function has the same number of collisions as the resolve_collision() function for items that are in the table.

As Example 14.11 shows, hash tables have one significant disadvantage: searching for an item that is not in the table has $O(n)$ complexity. In other words, it degenerates into a linear search of the entire table.

14.8 COLLISION-RESOLUTION ALGORITHMS

The critical issue with hash tables is to minimize the number of collisions. The best way to do that is to ensure that the table does not become very full. As long as there are about twice as many table elements as items in the table, it will enjoy the rapid $O(1)$ search speed.

The ratio of the number n of items in the table to the number SIZE of elements in the table is called the load factor $\lambda = $ n/SIZE. As long as this ratio remains below 50%, the hash table will provide fast look-ups. If it is allowed to grow past 75% or 80%, the number of collisions will increase dramatically, causing a serious degradation of efficiency.

Another way to minimize collisions is to use an efficient collision resolution algorithm. The algorithm used in the previous examples simply followed a linear search to find the next available space to insert the new item. This is called *linear probing*. This simple method can lead to *clustering*, as the previous examples show.

EXAMPLE 14.12 Clustering of Hash Table Items
The picture at the top of the next page shows how the hash table from Example 14.8 looks after the first 10 records were inserted. This shows a serious clustering problem. Eight of the ten items (all except numbers 10 and 14) are in a single cluster. Consequently, any new item that hashes to 16 will undergo 8 collisions before it finds the empty element number 7. Any new item that hashes to 0 or to 1 will collide 7 or 6 times.

Clearly, the performance will be improved if the hash function distributes the items more evenly, spreading the gaps around to allow new items to find empty spaces more quickly. The ideal hash function distributes items uniformly, so that the load factor λ for the entire table also applies to each sub interval of the table. For example, if $\lambda = 40\%$, then every subinterval (say of SIZE/10 elements) is also 40% occupied. That of course, is a theoretical ideal which is rarely achieved in practice. But it serves to characterize the efficiency of hash functions.

0	{"Dvorak", "Antonin", 1841, 1904, "Czech"}
1	{"Mozart", "Wolfgang Amadeus", 1756, 1791, "Austrian"}
2	{"Vivaldi", "Antonio", 1678, 1741, "Italian"}
3	{"Beethoven", "Ludwin van", 1770, 1827, "German"}
4	{"Chopin", "Frederic", 1810, 1849, "Polish"}
5	{"Bach", "Johann Sebastian", 1685, 1750, "German"}
6	{"Grieg", "Edvard", 1843, 1907, "Norwegian"}
7	
8	
9	
10	{"Liszt", "Franz", 1811, 1886, "Hungarian"}
11	
12	
13	
14	{"Berlioz", "Hector", 1803, 1869, "French"}
15	
16	{"Brahms", "Johannes", 1833, 1897, "German"}

The following two theorems quantify the problem of a full hash table:

Theorem 14.4 If collisions are resolved by linear probing, then the expected number E_r of collisions when searching for a resident item in a hash table with load factor λ is

$$E_r = \frac{1}{2}\left(1 + \frac{1}{1-\lambda}\right)$$

Theorem 14.5 If collisions are resolved by linear probing, then the expected number E_a of collisions when searching for a absent item in a hash table with load factor λ is

$$E_a = \frac{1}{2}\left(1 + \frac{1}{(1-\lambda)^2}\right)$$

For example, if the table is 90% full (*i.e.*, $\lambda = 0.90$), then $E_r = 5.5$ collisions and $E_a = 50.5$ collisions! (This of course, assumes that SIZE is quite large.)

Review Questions

14.1 What are the advantages and disadvantages of using the Binary Search on an array (vector)?

14.2 What are the advantages and disadvantages of using a Binary Search tree?

14.3 What are the advantages and disadvantages of using an AVL tree?

14.4 What are the advantages and disadvantages of using a hash table?

14.5 What is *linear probing*?

14.6 What is *clustering*?

Problems

14.7   Trace the call `find(a, 2, 9, 66)` to the `find()` function implemented with the Binary Search (Algorithm 14.2) using the array given in Example 14.3.

14.8   Trace the call `find(a, 0, 7, 66)` to the `find()` function implemented with the Binary Search (Algorithm 14.2) using the array given in Example 14.3.

14.9   Trace the call `find(a, 0, 12, 20)` to the `find()` function implemented with the Binary Search (Algorithm 14.2) using the array given in Example 14.3.

14.10 Suppose that a hash table with `SIZE` 1000 contains 950 elements and linear probing is used to resolve collisions.
   a. How many collisions would you expect when searching for an item that is in the table?
   b. How many collisions would you expect when searching for an item that is not in the table?

14.11 Solve Problem 14.10 assuming that the hash table contains 990 elements.

14.12 Here are the U.S. Postal abbreviations of the first 10 states, in the order that they ratified the U.S. Constitution: DE, PA, NJ, GA, CT, MA, MD, SC, NH, VA. Show the AVL tree after the insertion of each of these strings.

Programming Problems

14.13 Append the following record to the `Composers.dat` file and then re-run Example 14.9:
   Bernstein   Leonard 1918   1990   American

14.14 Modify Example 14.9 so that it hashes only on the composer's last name. Notice how different the resulting hash table is.

14.15 The linear probing method for resolving collisions in a hash table is likely to cause clustering. A better method, called *quadratic probing*, resolves collisions by the following algorithm:
   1. Hash to a value `k`.
   2. If cell `a[k]` is occupied, try cell `a[q]` where `q = (k + 1) % TABLE_SIZE`.
   3. If that cell is occupied, try cell `a[q]` where `q = (k + 4) % TABLE_SIZE`.
   4. If that cell is occupied, try cell `a[q]` where `q = (k + 9) % TABLE_SIZE`.
   5. If that cell is occupied, try cell `a[q]` where `q = (k + 16) % TABLE_SIZE`.
   6. If that cell is occupied, try cell `a[q]` where `q = (k + 25) % TABLE_SIZE`.
   7. Continue the pattern, using the index value `q = (k + j*j) % TABLE_SIZE`, where `j` is incremented on each iteration.
   Re-run Example 14.9 using quadratic probing. Notice that this is similar to linear probing, which is the same except that it uses the new index value `q = (k + j) % TABLE_SIZE`, where `j` is incremented on each iteration.

Solutions

14.1   The only disadvantage of using the Binary Search on an array (or `vector`) is that it requires the array to be sorted. The advantage is $O(\lg n)$ search speed.

14.2   The disadvantage of a binary search tree is that it may become very unbalanced, in which case searching degenerates into an $O(n)$ algorithm. The advantage is the efficiency that a binary tree enjoys for insertions and deletions.

14.3   The advantage of an AVL tree is that it is always balanced, guaranteeing the $O(\lg n)$ speed of the Binary Search algorithm. The disadvantages the complex rotations used by the insertion and removal algorithms needed to maintain the tree's balance.

14.4   The advantages of a hash table are that it affords $O(1)$ search speed and it does not depend upon any intrinsic comparison operation for its element type. The disadvantage is that the fast search speed only applies to items that are in the table; searching for an absent item takes n probes. Another disadvantage is that the fast search speed depends upon the number of collisions incurred when the item was inserted, and that number grows rapidly when the table becomes nearly full.

14.5   Linear probing is the hashing method that resolves collisions by looking sequentially for the next unoccupied cell.

14.6   Clustering is the phenomenon that occurs in a hash table when the hash function does not distribute its values uniformly. When collisions are resolved by linear probing, the table tends to become unbalanced, with dense clusters of occupied cells and only a few runs of unoccupied cells.

14.7   Tracing the call `find(a, 2, 10, 66)`:

begin	end	target	lo	hi	mid	a[mid]
2	10	66	2	9	5	55
			6	9	7	66

The function returns 7.

14.8   Tracing the call `find(a, 0, 7, 66)`:

begin	end	target	lo	hi	mid	a[mid]
0	7	66	0	6	3	33
			4		5	55
			6		6	66

The function returns 6.

14.9   Tracing the call `find(a, 0, 12, 20)`:

begin	end	target	lo	hi	mid	a[mid]
0	12	20	0	11	5	55
				4	2	33
				1	0	22
				−1		

The function returns 12.

14.10   The load factor is $\lambda = $ n/`SIZE` $ = 950/1000 = 0.95$:

    a. By Theorem 14.4, E_r = `(1/2)(1 + 1/0.05) = 10.5 collisions`.

    b. By Theorem 14.5, $E_a = (1/2)(1 + 1/0.05^2) = 200.5$ collisions.

14.11   The load factor is $\lambda = $ n/`SIZE` $ = 990/1000 = 0.99$:

    a. By Theorem 14.4, E_r = `(1/2)(1 + 1/0.01) = 50.5 collisions`.

    b. By Theorem 14.5, $E_a = (1/2)(1 + 1/0.01^2) = 5000.5$ collisions. This number is greater than `SIZE`, so we should conclude that the correct answer is $E_a = $ `SIZE` $ = 1000$ collisions.

14.12

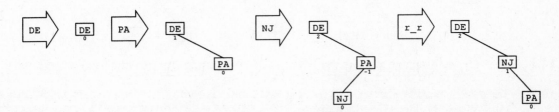

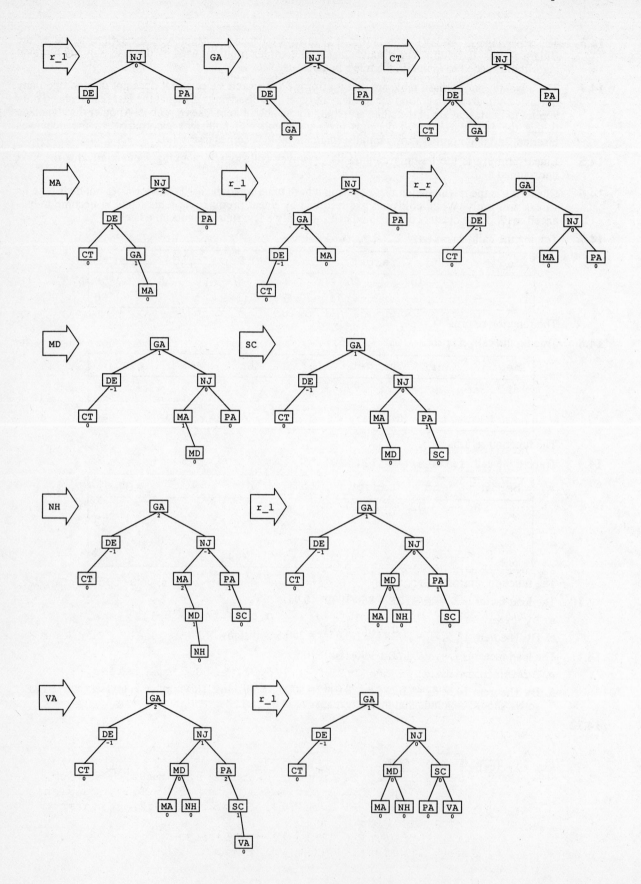

14.13 The Bernstein record hashes to 15, which then experiences 15 collisions before finally being inserted at position 11:

```
 0. Dvorak, Antonin (1841-1904), Czech
 1. Mozart, Wolfgang Amadeus (1756-1791), Austrian
 2. Vivaldi, Antonio (1678-1741), Italian
 3. Beethoven, Ludwig van (1770-1827), German
 4. Chopin, Frederic (1810-1849), Polish
 5. Bach, Johann Sebastian (1685-1750), German
 6. Grieg, Edvard (1843-1907), Norwegian
 7. Sibelius, Jean (1865-1957), Finnish
 8. Stravinsky, Igor (1882-1971), Russian
 9. Britten, Benjamin (1913-1976), English
10. Liszt, Franz (1811-1886), Hungarian
11. Bernstein, Leonard (1918-1990), American
12.
13.
14. Berlioz, Hector (1803-1869), French
15. Barber, Samuel (1910-1981), American
16. Brahms, Johannes (1833-1897), German
There were 27 collisions.
```

14.14 Here is a run of the revised program:

```
hash(Vivaldi) = 5
        Vivaldi inserted at 5
hash(Bach) = 9
        Bach inserted at 9
hash(Mozart) = 8
        Mozart inserted at 8
hash(Beethoven) = 10
        Beethoven inserted at 10
hash(Berlioz) = 13
        Berlioz inserted at 13
hash(Chopin) = 14
        Chopin inserted at 14
hash(Liszt) = 7
        Liszt inserted at 7
hash(Brahms) = 10
        COLLISION AT 10 Beethoven, Ludwig van (1770-1827), German
        Brahms inserted at 11
hash(Dvorak) = 3
        Dvorak inserted at 3
hash(Grieg) = 1
        Grieg inserted at 1
hash(Sibelius) = 16
        Sibelius inserted at 16
hash(Stravinsky) = 15
        Stravinsky inserted at 15
hash(Barber) = 12
        Barber inserted at 12
hash(Britten) = 14
        COLLISION AT 14 Chopin, Frederic (1810-1849), Polish
        COLLISION AT 15 Stravinsky, Igor (1882-1971), Russian
        COLLISION AT 16 Sibelius, Jean (1865-1957), Finnish
        Britten inserted at 0
 0. Britten, Benjamin (1913-1976), English
 1. Grieg, Edvard (1843-1907), Norwegian
 2.
```

```
 3. Dvorak, Antonin (1841-1904), Czech
 4.
 5. Vivaldi, Antonio (1678-1741), Italian
 6.
 7. Liszt, Franz (1811-1886), Hungarian
 8. Mozart, Wolfgang Amadeus (1756-1791), Austrian
 9. Bach, Johann Sebastian (1685-1750), German
10. Beethoven, Ludwig van (1770-1827), German
11. Brahms, Johannes (1833-1897), German
12. Barber, Samuel (1910-1981), American
13. Berlioz, Hector (1803-1869), French
14. Chopin, Frederic (1810-1849), Polish
15. Stravinsky, Igor (1882-1971), Russian
16. Sibelius, Jean (1865-1957), Finnish
```
There were 4 collisions.
Enter composer's last name: **Chopin**
hash(Chopin) = 14
Frederic Chopin was born in 1810
Enter composer's last name: Brahms
hash(Brahms) = 10
        NOT FOUND AT 10 Beethoven, Ludwig van (1770-1827), German
Johannes Brahms was born in 1833

14.15 Here is the revised function:

```
template <class T>
void resolve_collision(HashTable<T>& t, Composer& c, int& k,
int& n)
{ int k0=k;
  for (int j=1; !t[k].is_null(); j++, n++)
  { cout << "\tCOLLISION AT " << k << "\t";
    print(t[k]);
    k = (k0 + j*j) % TABLE_SIZE;
  }
}
```

Here is the output:

```
hash(VivaldiAntonio) = 2
        Vivaldi inserted at 2
hash(BachJohann Sebastian) = 5
        Bach inserted at 5
hash(MozartWolfgang Amadeus) = 1
        Mozart inserted at 1
hash(BeethovenLudwig van) = 1
        COLLISION AT 1  Mozart, Wolfgang Amadeus (1756-1791),
Austrian
        COLLISION AT 2  Vivaldi, Antonio (1678-1741), Italian
        COLLISION AT 5  Bach, Johann Sebastian (1685-1750), German
        Beethoven inserted at 10
hash(BerliozHector) = 14
        Berlioz inserted at 14
hash(ChopinFrederic) = 2
        COLLISION AT 2  Vivaldi, Antonio (1678-1741), Italian
        Chopin inserted at 3
hash(LisztFranz) = 10
        COLLISION AT 10 Beethoven, Ludwig van (1770-1827), German
        Liszt inserted at 11
hash(BrahmsJohannes) = 16
        Brahms inserted at 16
```

```
hash(DvorakAntonin) = 16
        COLLISION AT 16 Brahms, Johannes (1833-1897), German
        Dvorak inserted at 0
hash(GriegEdvard) = 4
        Grieg inserted at 4
hash(SibeliusJean) = 7
        Sibelius inserted at 7
hash(StravinskyIgor) = 8
        Stravinsky inserted at 8
hash(BarberSamuel) = 15
        Barber inserted at 15
hash(BrittenBenjamin) = 2
        COLLISION AT 2  Vivaldi, Antonio (1678-1741), Italian
        COLLISION AT 3  Chopin, Frederic (1810-1849), Polish
        Britten inserted at 6
   0. Dvorak, Antonin (1841-1904), Czech
   1. Mozart, Wolfgang Amadeus (1756-1791), Austrian
   2. Vivaldi, Antonio (1678-1741), Italian
   3. Chopin, Frederic (1810-1849), Polish
   4. Grieg, Edvard (1843-1907), Norwegian
   5. Bach, Johann Sebastian (1685-1750), German
   6. Britten, Benjamin (1913-1976), English
   7. Sibelius, Jean (1865-1957), Finnish
   8. Stravinsky, Igor (1882-1971), Russian
   9.
  10. Beethoven, Ludwig van (1770-1827), German
  11. Liszt, Franz (1811-1886), Hungarian
  12.
  13.
  14. Berlioz, Hector (1803-1869), French
  15. Barber, Samuel (1910-1981), American
  16. Brahms, Johannes (1833-1897), German
There were 8 collisions.
```

Appendix A

Algorithms

Appendix B

References

[Adams]

C++ An Introduction to Computing, by Joel Adams, Sanford Leestma, and Larry Nyhoff.
Prentice Hall, Englewood Cliffs, NJ (1995) 0-02-369402-5.

[Adamson]

Programming with C++, by T. A. Adamson.
Macmillan, New York, NY (1995) 0-02-300821-0.

[Aho]

Foundations of Computer Science, C Edition, by Alfred V. Aho and Jeffrey D. Ullman.
Computer Science Press, New York, NY (1995) 0-7167-8284-7.

[Ammeraal]

C++ for Programmers, by L. Ammeraal.
John Wiley & Sons, Inc, New York, NY (1991) 0-471-93011-3.

[Astrachan]

A Computer Science Tapestry, by Owen L. Astrachan.
McGraw-Hill, Inc., New York, NY (1997) 0-07-002036-1.

[Barclay]

C++: Problem Solving and Programming, by K. Barclay and B. Jordan.
Prentice Hall, Englewood Cliffs, NJ (1993) 0-13-126673-X.

[Bar-David]

Object-Oriented Design for C++, by K. Barclay and B. Jordan.
Prentice Hall, Englewood Cliffs, NJ (1993) 0-13-630260-2.

[Barton]

Scientific and Engineering C++, by John J. Barton and Lee R. Nackman.
Addison-Wesley Publishing Company, Reading, MA (1994) 0-201-53393-6.

[Benedicty]

Discrete Mathematical Structures, by Mario Benedicty and Frank R. Sledge.
Harcourt Brace Jovanovich, New York, NY (1987) 0-15-517683-8.

[Bergin]

Data Abstraction, the Object-Oriented Approach Using C++, by Joseph Bergin.
McGraw-Hill, Inc., New York, NY (1994) 0-07-911691-4.

[Berman1]

Data Structures via C++, by A. Michael Berman.
Oxford University Press, New York, NY (1997) 0-19-510843-4.

[Berman2]

Introduction to Combinatorics, by Gerald Berman and K. D. Fryer.
Academic Press, New York, NY (1972) 0-07-911691-4.

[Bronson1]

A First Book of C++, by Gary J. Bronson.
West Publishing Company, St. Paul, MN (1995) 0-12-092750-0.

[Bronson2]

Program Development and Design Using C++, by Gary J. Bronson.
PWS Publishing Company, Boston, MA (1997) 0-314-20338-9.

[Budd1]

An Introduction to Object-Oriented Programming, Second Edition, by Timothy A. Budd.
Addison-Wesley Publishing Company, Reading, MA (1994) 0-201-82419-1.

[Budd2]

Data Structures in C++ Using the Standard Template Library, by Timothy A. Budd.
Addison-Wesley Publishing Company, Reading, MA (1998) 0-201-30879-7.

[Buzzi-Ferraris]

Scientific C++, by G Buzzi-Ferraris.
Addison-Wesley Publishing Company, Reading, MA (1994) 0-201-63192-X.

[Capper]

Introducing C++ for Scientists, Engineers and Mathematicians, by D. M. Capper.
Springer-Verlag, London (1994) 3-540-19847-4.

[Cargill]

C++ Programming Style, by Tom Cargill.
Addison-Wesley Publishing Company, Reading, MA (1992) 0-201-56365-7.

[Carrano]

Data Abstraction and Problem Solving with C++, by Frank M. Carrano.
Benjamin/Cummings Publishing Company, Redwood City, CA (1993) 0-8053-1226-9.

[Carroll]

Designing and Coding Reusable C++, by Martin D. Carroll and Margaret A. Ellis.
Addison-Wesley Publishing Company, Reading, MA (1995) 0-201-51284-X.

[Christian]

Microsoft Visual C++ Run-Time Library Reference, by K. Christian.
Microsoft, Redmond, WA (1994) 1-55615-803-3.

[Cline]

C++ FAQs, by Marshall P. Cline and Greg A. Lomow.
Addison-Wesley Publishing Company, Reading, MA (1995) 0-201-58958-3.

[Cohoon]

C++ Program Design, by James P. Cohoon and Jack W. Davidson.
Richard D. Irwin, Chicago, IL (1997) 0-256-19744-X.

[Collins]

Data Structures: An Object-Oriented Approach, by William J. Collins.
Addison-Wesley Publishing Company, Reading, MA (1992) 0-201-56953-1.

[Coplien]

Advanced C++, Programming Styles and Idioms, by James O. Coplien.
Addison-Wesley Publishing Company, Reading, MA (1992) 0-201-54855-0.

[Dale]

Abstract Data Types, by Nell Dale and Henry M. Walker.
D. C. Heath and Company, Lexington, MA (1996) 0-669-35444-9.

[Decker]

Working Classes, Data Structures and Algorithms Using C++, by Rick Decker and Stuart Hirshfield
PWS Publishing Company, Boston, MA (1996) 0-534-94566-X.

[Deitel]

C++ How to Program, Second Edition, by H. M. Deitel and P. J. Deitel.
Prentice Hall, Englewood Cliffs, NJ (1998) 0-13-528910-6.

[Dorfman]

C++ by Example: Object-Oriented Analysis, Design, & Programming, by L. Dorfman.
McGraw-Hill, New York, NY (1995) 0-07-911954-9.

[Dewhurst]

Programming in C++, Second Edition, by Stephen C. Dewhurst and Kathy T. Stark.
Prentice Hall, Englewood Cliffs, NJ (1995) 0-13-182718-9.

[Drozdek]

Data Structures and Algorithms in C++, by Adam Drozdek.
PWS Publishing Company, Boston, MA (1996) 0-534-94974-6.

[Eckel]

Thinking in C++, by B. Eckel.
Prentice-Hall, Englewood Cliffs, NJ (1995) 0-13-917709-4.

[Ege]

Object-Oriented Programming with C++, by R. Ege.
AP Professional (1994) 0-12-232932-5.

[Ellis]

The Annotated C++ Reference Manual, by Margaret A. Ellis and Bjarne Stroustrup.
Addison-Wesley Publishing Company, Reading, MA (1992) 0-201-51459-1.

[Flamig]

Practical C++ Algoeirhms and Data Structures, by B. Flamig.
John Wiley & Sons, Inc, New York, NY (1993) 0-471-55863-X.

[Ford]

Data Structures with C++, by William Ford and William Topp.
Prentice-Hall, Englewood Cliffs, NJ (1996) 0-02-420971-6.

[Friedman]

Problem Solving, Abstraction, and Design Using C++, Second Edition, by Frank L. Friedman and Elliot B. Koffman.
Addison-Wesley Publishing Company, Reading, MA (1997) 0-201-30002-8.

[Gersting]

Mathematical Structures for Computer Science, Third Edition, by Judith L. Gersting.
W. H. Freeman and Company, New York, NY (1993) 0-7167-8259-6.

[Goldstine]

The Computer from Pascal to von Neumann, by Herman H. Goldstine.
Princeton University Press, Princeton, NJ (1972) 0-691-08104-2.

[Gorlen]

  Data Abstraction and Object-Oriented Programming in C++, by K. E. Gorlen, S. M. Orlow, and P. S. Plexico.
  John Wiley & Sons, Inc, New York, NY (1993) 0-471-55863-X.

[Graham]

  Learning C++, by Neill Graham.
  McGraw-Hill, Inc, New York, NY (1991) 0-07-023983-5.

[Gray]

  Programming with Class, by N. A. B. Gray.
  John Wiley & Sons, Inc, New York, NY (1994) 0-471-94350-9.

[Gurganus]

  Microsoft Visual C++ Windows Primer, by K. Gurganus and D. Alexander.
  AP Professional (1994) 0-12-308650-7.

[Hanly]

  Essential C++ for Engineers and Scientists, by Jeri R. Hanly.
  Addison-Wesley Publishing Company, Reading, MA (1997) 0-201-88495-X.

[Hansen]

  The C++ Answer Book, by Tony L. Hansen.
  Addison-Wesley Publishing Company, Reading, MA (1990) 0-201-11497-6.

[Harary]

  Graph Theory, by Frank Harary.
  Addison-Wesley Publishing Company, Reading, MA (1969).

[Hausner]

  Discrete Mathematics, by Melvin Hausner.
  Saunders College Publishing, Orlando, FL (1992) 0-03-003278-4.

[Headington]

  Data Abstraction and Structures Using C++, by Mark R. Headington and David D. Riley.
  D. C. Heath and Company, Lexington, MA (1994) 0-669-29220-6.

[Henderson]

  Object-Oriented Specification and Design with C++, by Peter Henderson.
  McGraw-Hill Book Company, London, UK (1993) 0-07-707585-4.

[Horowitz]

  Fundamentals of Data Structures in C++, by Ellis Horowitz, Sartaj Sahni, and Dinesh Mehta.
  W. H. Freeman and Company, New York, NY (1995) 0-7167-8292-8.

[Horstmann1]

  Mastering Object Oriented Design in C++, by Cay S. Horstmann.
  John Wiley & Sons, Inc, New York, NY (1994) 0-471-59484-9.

[Horstmann2]

  Computing Concepts with C++ Essentials, by Cay S. Horstmann.
  John Wiley & Sons, Inc, New York, NY (1997) 0-471-13770-7.

[Hubbard]

  Programming with C++, by John R. Hubbard.
  McGraw-Hill, New York, NY (1996) 0-07-030837-3.

[Ince]

Object-Oriented Software Engineering with C++, by D. Ince.
McGraw-Hill, New York, NY (1991) 0-07-707402-5.

[Johnsonbaugh1]

Discrete Mathematics, Third Edition, by Richard Johnsonbaugh.
Macmillan, New York, NY (1993) 0-02-360721-1.

[Johnsonbaugh2]

Object-Oriented Programming in C++, by Richard Johnsonbaugh and Martin Kalin.
Prentice Hall, Englewood Cliffs, NJ (1995) 0-02-360682-7.

[Kamin]

Programming with Class: A C++ Introduction to Computer Science, by Samuel N. Kamin and Edward M. Reingold.
McGraw-Hill, New York, NY (1996) 0-07-051833-5.

[Knuth1]

The Art of Computer Programming, Volume 1: Fundamental Algorithms, Second Edition, by Donald E. Knuth.
Addison-Wesley Publishing Company, Reading, MA (1973) 0-201-03809-9.

[Knuth2]

The Art of Computer Programming, Volume 2: Seminumerical Algorithms, Second Edition, by Donald E. Knuth.
Addison-Wesley Publishing Company, Reading, MA (1981) 0-201-03822-6.

[Knuth3]

The Art of Computer Programming, Volume 3: Sorting and Searching, by Donald E. Knuth.
Addison-Wesley Publishing Company, Reading, MA (1973) 0-201-03803-X.

[Kolman]

Discrete Mathematical Structures, Third Edition, by Bernard Kolman, R. C. Busby, and S. Ross.
Prentice Hall, Englewood Cliffs, NJ (1996) 0-13-320912-1.

[Kruglinski]

Inside Visual C++, by David J. Kruglinski.
Microsoft, Redmond, WA (1996) 1-55615-891-2.

[Ladd]

C++ Templates and Tools, by Scott Robert Ladd.
M&T Books, New York, NY (1995) 0-55851-437-6.

[Lafore]

Object-Oriented Programming in C++, Second Edition, by R. Lafore.
Waite Group Press (1994) 1-878739-73-5.

[Lambert]

Introduction to Computer Science with C++, by Kenneth A. Lambert, D. W. Nance, and T. L. Naps.
West Publishing Company, St. Paul, MN (1996) 0-314-07399-6.

[Langsam]

Data Structures Using C and C++, Second Edition, by Y. Langsam, M. Augenstein, and A. Tenenbaum.
Prentice Hall, Englewood Cliffs, NJ (1996) 0-13-036997-7.

[Leavens]

Visual C++: A Developer's Guide, by A. Leavens.
M & T (1994) 1-55851-339-6.

[Lee]

The Apprentice C++ Programmer, by Peter A. Lee and Chris Phillips.
International Thompson Computer Press, London, UK (1997) 0-534-95339-5.

[Lipschutz1]

Schaum's Outline of Discrete Mathematics, Seymour Lipschutz.
McGraw-Hill, Inc., New York, NY (1976) 0-07-037981-5.

[Lipschutz2]

Schaum's Outline of Essential Computer Mathematics, Seymour Lipschutz.
McGraw-Hill, Inc., New York, NY (1982) 0-07-037990-3.

[Lipschutz3]

Schaum's Outline of Data Structures, Seymour Lipschutz.
McGraw-Hill, Inc., New York, NY (1986) 0-07-038001-5.

[Litvin]

C++ for You++, by Maria Litvin and Gary Litvin.
Skylit Publishing, Andover, MA (1997) 0-9654853-X.

[Lippman]

The C++ Primer, Second Edition, by Stanley B. Lippman.
Addison-Wesley Publishing Company, Reading, MA (1991) 0-201-54848-8.

[Main]

Data Structures & Other Objects, by Michael Main and Walter Savitch.
Addison-Wesley Publishing Company, Reading, MA (1997) 0-8053-7470-1.

[Mercer]

Computing Fundamentals with C++, by Rick Mercer.
Franklin, Beedle & Associates Incorporated, Wilsonville, OR (1995) 0-938661-72-8.

[Meyers1]

Effective C++, by Scott Meyers.
Addison-Wesley Publishing Company, Reading, MA (1992).

[Meyers2]

More Effective C++, by Scott Meyers.
Addison-Wesley Publishing Company, Reading, MA (1992) 0-201-63371-X.

[Model]

Data Structures, Data Abstraction: A Contemporary Introduction Using C++, by M. L. Model.
Prentice Hall, Englewood Cliffs, NJ (1994) 0-13-088782-X.

[Murray1]

C++ Strategies and Tactics, by Robert B. Murray.
Addison-Wesley Publishing Company, Reading, MA (1993) 0-201-56382-7.

[Murray2]

Microsoft C++ 7: The Complete Reference, by W.H. Murray and C. Pappas.
Osborne/McGraw-Hill (1992).

[Nagler]

Learning C++, by Eric Nagler.
West Publishing Company, St. Paul, MN (1993) 0-314-02464-6.

[Nelson]

C++ Programmers Guide to the Standard Template Library, by Mark Nelson.
IDG Books Worldwide, Inc., Foster City, CA (1995) 0-56884-314-3.

[Nielsen]

Software Development with C++, by Nielsen.
AP Professional (1995) 0-12-518420-4.

[Oualline]

Practical C++ Programming, by Steve Oualline.
O'Reilly & Associates, Sebastopol, CA (1995) 1-56592-139-9.

[Parker]

Algorithms and Data Structures in C++, by A. Parker.
CRC Press (1993) 0-8493-7171-6.

[Perry]

An Introduction to Object-Oriented Design in C++, by Jo Ellen Perry and Harold D. Levin.
Addison-Wesley Publishing Company, Reading, MA (1996) 0-201-76564-0.

[Plauger1]

The Standard C Library, by P. J. Plauger.
Prentice Hall, Englewood Cliffs, NJ (1992) 0-13-131509-9.

[Plauger2]

The Draft Standard C++ Library, by P. J. Plauger.
Prentice Hall, Englewood Cliffs, NJ (1995) 0-13-117003-1.

[Pohl1]

Object-Oriented Programming Using C++, by Ira Pohl.
The Benjamin/Cummings Publishing Company, Inc, Redwood City, CA (1993) 0-8053-5384-4.

[Pohl2]

C++ for Pascal Programmers, Second Edition, by Ira Pohl.
The Benjamin/Cummings Publishing Company, Inc, Redwood City, CA (1994) 0-8053-3158-1.

[Pothering]

Introduction to Data Structures and Algorithm Analysis with C++, by G. J. Pothering and T. Naps.
West Publishing Company, St. Paul, MN (1995) 0-314-04574-0.

[Prata]

C++ Primer Plus, Third Edition, by Stephen Prata.
Waite Group Press, Corte Madera, CA (1998) 1-57169-131-6.

[Ranade & Zamir]

C++ Primer for C Programmers, by Jay Ranade and Saba Zamir.
McGraw-Hill, Inc., New York, NY (1994) 0-07-051487-9.

[Riordan]

Introduction to Combinatorial Analysis, by John Riordan.
John Wiley & Sons, Inc, New York, NY (1958).

[Rudd]

    Mastering C++, by Anthony Rudd.
    John Wiley & Sons, Inc, New York, NY (1995) 0-471-06565-X.

[Sahni]

    Data Structures, Algorithms, and Applications in C++, by Sartaj Sahni.
    ACB/McGraw-Hill, New York, NY (1998) 0-07-109219-6.

[Satir]

    C++: The Core Language, by Gregory Satir and Doug Brown.
    O'Reilly & Associates, Sebastopol, CA (1995) 0-56592-116-X.

[Savitch]

    Problem Solving with C++, by Walter Savitch.
    Addison-Wesley Publishing Company, Reading, MA (1996) 0-8053-7440-X.

[Schildt1]

    C++ from the Ground Up, by H. Schildt.
    Osborne/McGraw-Hill, New York, NY (1994) 0-07-881969-5.

[Schildt2]

    C++: The Complete reference, Third Edition, by H. Schildt.
    Osborne/McGraw-Hill, New York, NY (1995) 0-07-882123-1.

[Sedgewick]

    Algorithms in C++, by Robert Sedgewick.
    Addison-Wesley Publishing Company, Reading, MA (1992) 0-201-51059-6.

[Sengupta]

    C++ Object-Oriented Data Structures, by Saumyendra Sengupta and Carl Phillip Korobkin.
    Springer-Verlag, New York, NY (1994) 0-387-94194-0

[Sessions]

    Object-Oriented Data Structures in C++, by Roger Sessions.
    Prentice Hall, Englewood Cliffs, NJ (1992) 0-13-630104-5.

[Shammas]

    Advanced C++, by Namir Clement Shammas.
    SAMS Publishing, Carmel, IN (1992) 0-672-30158-X.

[Shiflet]

    Data Structures in C++, by Angela B. Shiflet.
    West Publishing Company, St. Paul, MN (1996) 0-314-06744-2.

[Stepanov]

    "The Standard Template Library," *Technical Report HPL-94-34*, by A. A. Stepanov and M. Lee.
    Hewlett-Packard Laboratories, April 1994.

[Stevens]

    C++ Database Development, by Al Stevens.
    MIS:Press, New York, NY (1994) 1-55828-357-9.

[Stroustrup1]

    The Design and Evolution of C++, by Bjarne Stroustrup.
    Addison-Wesley Publishing Company, Reading, MA (1994) 0-201-54330-3.

[Stroustrup2]

The C++ Programming Language, Third Edition, by Bjarne Stroustrup.
Addison-Wesley Publishing Company, Reading, MA (1997) 0-201-88954-4.

[Teale]

C++ IOStreams, by Steve Teale.
Addison-Wesley Publishing Company, Reading, MA (1993) 0-201-59641-5.

[Tucker1]

Fundamentals of Computing I, C++ Edition, by Allen B. Tucker *et al.*
McGraw-Hill, Inc., New York, NY (1995) 0-07-065506-5.

[Tucker2]

Fundamentals of Computing II, by Allen B. Tucker *et al.*
McGraw-Hill, Inc., New York, NY (1993) 0-07-065452-2.

[Wang]

C++ with Object-Oriented Programming, by Paul S. Wang.
PWS Publishing Company, Boston, MA (1994) 0-534-19644-6.

[Weiss]

Data Structures and Algorithm Analysis in C++, by Mark Allen Weiss.
Benjamin/Cummings Publishing Company, Redwood City, CA (1994) 0-8053-5443-3.

[Winston]

On to C++, by Patrick Henry Winston.
Addison-Wesley Publishing Company, Reading, MA (1994) 0-201-58043-8.

[Wirth]

Algorithms + Data Structures = Programs, by Nicklaus Wirth.
Prentice-Hall, Inc., Englewood Cliffs, NJ (1976) 0-13-022418-9.

[Zamir]

C++ Primer for Non C Programmers, by S. Zamir.
McGraw-Hill, New York, NY (1995) 0-07-072704-X.

Index